Supply Chain Management for Climate Action, Social Accountability, and Economic Resilience

Atour Taghipour
https://orcid.org/0000-0003-1687-8881
Conservatoire National des Arts et Métier, France

IGI Global
Scientific Publishing
Publishing Tomorrow's Research Today

Vice President of Editorial Melissa Wagner
Director of Acquisitions Mikaela Felty
Director of Book Development Jocelynn Hessler
Production Manager Mike Brehm
Cover Design Jose Rosado

Published in the United States of America by
IGI Global Scientific Publishing
701 East Chocolate Avenue
Hershey, PA, 17033, USA
Tel: 717-533-8845 | Fax: 717-533-7115
Website: https://www.igi-global.com E-mail: cust@igi-global.com

Library of Congress Cataloging-in-Publication Data

Names: Taghipour, Atour, 1974- editor
Title: Supply chain management at the intersection of climate action, social accountability, and economic resilience / edited by Atour Taghipour.
Description: Hershey, PA : IGI Global Scientific Publishing, [2027] | Includes bibliographical references and index. | Summary: "This book examines how modern supply chains are adapting to climate change, ESG demands, and global disruptions. By integrating sustainability, social responsibility, and economic resilience, it offers research, frameworks, and case studies that highlight strategies for building accountable and adaptable supply chain systems in a rapidly changing world"-- Provided by publisher.
Identifiers: LCCN 2025041879 (print) | LCCN 2025041880 (ebook) | ISBN 9798337364551 hardcover | ISBN 9798337364568 paperback | ISBN 9798337364575 ebook
Subjects: LCSH: Supply chain management | Social responsibility of business
Classification: LCC HD38.6 .S875 2026 (print) | LCC HD38.6 (ebook)
LC record available at https://lccn.loc.gov/2025041879
LC ebook record available at https://lccn.loc.gov/2025041880
British Cataloguing in Publication Data
A Cataloguing in Publication record for this book is available from the British Library.

Table of Contents

Detailed Table of Contents

Global supply chains are undergoing a paradigmatic shift as climate action, social accountability, and economic resilience emerge as non-negotiable imperatives. This chapter introduces the concept of Triangular Transformation, a comprehensive framework that integrates these three pillars into the design and governance of modern supply chains. Traditional supply chain models, which prioritised efficiency and cost minimisation, have proven inadequate in addressing the interconnected crises of climate change, social inequities, and systemic vulnerabilities. The proposed framework emphasises that achieving sustainability requires simultaneous commitment to decarbonization, ethical labour practices, and resilience-building mechanisms.

Geopolitical tensions increasingly affect the supply of critical raw materials, particularly lithium, cobalt, and rare earths, which are essential for electric vehicles, renewable energy, and defense technologies. China's dominance in production and processing creates vulnerabilities for global supply chains, prompting industrial companies to diversify sources, establish long-term partnerships, and invest in recycling and alternative battery technologies, such as sodium-ion and solid-state batteries. European and U.S. regulations aim to secure supply chains and promote sustainability. While innovations and vertical integration offer resilience, challenges remain due to high costs, technological constraints, and potential supply-demand imbalances. Strategic management of resources is now central to competitiveness and industrial security.

This chapter examines the various dynamics of supply chain resilience in the context of increasing geopolitical uncertainty. It presents a critical assessment of adaptive strategies—modular manufacturing, digital transformation, and structural realignment—that enable companies to enhance their operational frameworks in response to external disturbances. Drawing insights from the Taiwan-China situation and the Russia-Ukraine conflict, the discourse provides a comprehensive perspective on maintaining supply chain integrity during periods of uncertainty and turmoil. This chapter seeks to offer case-based insights into how modern modularity concepts in manufacturing, the integration of Industry 4.0 and 5.0, and the reconfiguration of existing supply chains can directly improve efficiency and resilience within supply chains.

Global supply chains have boosted efficiency and global access but also led to labor, environmental, and ethical issues. Growing consumer and regulatory pressure has driven firms to pursue ethical sourcing and transparency for accountability. Ethical sourcing ensures fair labor and human rights, while transparency tools enhance traceability. This chapter explores how these practices drive social accountability through sustainability standards, corporate codes, and stakeholder collaborations. It also examines enabling technologies like blockchain and IoT, identifies implementation barriers, and proposes integrative frameworks for sustainable supply chain governance.

The ESG system has evolved beyond a compliance structure to a holistic strategic network shaping how organizations operate and It now fosters sustainability through production, services, and innovation, connecting regulation, stakeholder expectations, and adaptability. With a initiatives like the EU's CSRD and emission reporting, firms integrate sustainability throughout business ecosystems, enhance transparency, lower energy impact, and employ technology for accountability and also enduring growth.

This chapter explores the evolving concept of supply chain resilience, focusing on its ability to adapt to both climate change and economic disruptions. The increasing frequency of extreme weather events and global economic volatility highlights the need for flexible, adaptive strategies in supply chain management. Traditional risk management frameworks often fail to address these complex, interconnected challenges, necessitating a more integrated approach. Drawing on resilience theory, the chapter proposes a novel framework that combines climate and economic risks, emphasizing the need for strategic adaptation. Key themes include the role of innovation, technology, and sustainable practices in enhancing resilience. The chapter also explores the impact of climate change, economic shocks, and the importance of policy frameworks in fostering resilient supply chains. It concludes with recommendations for future research and a call for cross-disciplinary approaches to strengthen global supply chain resilience

In a time of geopolitical instability, economic uncertainty, climate-related disruptions, and global health crises, supply chains are becoming more and more vulnerable to high levels of risk and volatility. This chapter looks at the rules and methods of managing supply chain risk in unstable situations. It focuses on finding, evaluating, and reducing operational, financial, and strategic risks. It looks at how resilience, agility, and flexibility may make the supply chain stronger, as well as how data analytics, digital technologies, and collaborative risk-sharing methods might help. The chapter also talks about proactive and reactive risk management tactics, such as scenario planning, diversification, real-time monitoring, and making decisions based on what happens. This chapter gives a full picture of how organisations can plan for disruptions, reduce vulnerabilities, and keep up performance in unpredictable business environments by combining theoretical frameworks with real-world examples from several fields.

Supply chain reform in emerging economies has become a critical priority as these nations integrate further into global trade networks. This chapter examines the multifaceted challenges that emerging markets face in modernizing and transforming their supply chain systems – from infrastructure gaps and regulatory hurdles to technology deficits and governance issues. At the same time, it highlights the opportunities for improvement, including leveraging rapid economic growth,

This chapter investigates the role of manufacturer–distributor collaboration in improving supply chain performance within Morocco's fresh and frozen food sector, where perishability and demand uncertainty create persistent coordination challenges. Based on a qualitative case analysis, the findings show that joint decision-making on pricing, promotions, and inventory, reinforced by shared information systems, enhances sales outcomes, inventory flow, service reliability, and customer satisfaction. Rather than being an initial condition, trust is found to emerge gradually through formal coordination tools and continuous performance follow-up. The chapter ultimately frames collaboration as a capability that develops over time and emphasizes the importance of gradual, context-adapted collaboration strategies for SMEs operating in emerging economies.

This study proposes an extended Economic Order Quantity (EOQ) model to optimize inventory management when drug demand is uncertain due to nursing practice. While traditional EOQ models are based on the assumption of constant demand, due to the nature of clinical decisions, especially in hospital pharmacies, the need for medication arises suddenly and unpredictably. In addition to fixed ordering and inventory holding costs, the model includes a penalty cost (p) parameter that reflects the ethical, clinical, and financial damages caused by stock shortages. Testing the model with separate scenarios for hospital and community pharmacies showed that even small order differences can have significant consequences for patient safety and service continuity. The mathematical modeling of nursing-based demand makes a unique contribution to the literature in the theoretical treatment of this field. The study provides a framework for developing decision support systems based on both economic efficiency and clinical reality through an interdisciplinary approach.

This chapter explores smart mobility as a driver of sustainable urban development in smart cities, examining how technology, governance, and social inclusion interact. Focusing on Mobility as a Service and digital mobility platforms, it evaluates their potential to enhance accessibility, reduce congestion, and lower emissions in smart cities such as Helsinki, Barcelona, Singapore, and New York. The analysis highlights key factors for success, including institutional coordination, multimodal integration, and inclusive policies. It also considers quantitative indicators of adoption, environmental impact, and congestion, alongside technological tools such as AI traffic management, shared micromobility, and sensor systems commonly deployed in smart city environments. Findings show that technology alone cannot ensure sustainable mobility; attention to equity, digital literacy, and urban logistics is essential. The chapter concludes with practical policy recommendations and research directions to promote efficient, resilient, and inclusive urban mobility strategies in smart cities.

Preface

Global supply chains are operating in an era of profound transformation. Once evaluated primarily on the basis of cost efficiency and operational performance, supply chains are now expected to address a broader set of priorities that include climate action, social accountability, and long-term economic resilience. Escalating geopolitical tensions, climate-related disruptions, regulatory developments, technological innovation, and evolving stakeholder expectations have collectively reshaped the strategic role of supply chain management. Organizations are increasingly challenged to develop systems that are not only efficient but also sustainable, transparent, adaptive, and socially responsible.

Supply Chain Management for Climate Action, Social Accountability, and Economic Resilience brings together diverse scholarly perspectives that examine these emerging challenges and opportunities. The volume presents interdisciplinary research from contributors across multiple countries, reflecting the global nature of contemporary supply chains and the necessity of collaborative approaches to addressing complex sustainability and resilience issues. Collectively, the chapters explore conceptual frameworks, policy developments, technological innovations, industry applications, and practical strategies that support the transition toward more responsible and resilient supply chain systems.

The book begins by establishing an integrated framework that positions climate action, social accountability, and economic resilience as mutually reinforcing dimensions of sustainable supply chain management. It then examines how geopolitical developments and global uncertainty are reshaping sourcing decisions, strategic planning, and organizational resilience. Subsequent chapters investigate ethical sourcing, transparency, environmental, social, and governance (ESG) policy frameworks, climate-related risks, operational resilience, and risk management in volatile environments.

Recognizing the diversity of supply chain contexts, the volume further explores transformation pathways in emerging economies, industry-specific sustainable supply chain models, collaborative relationships between supply chain partners, healthcare inventory management under uncertain demand, and the role of smart mobility in advancing sustainable urban systems. Throughout the collection, particular attention is given to the application of digital technologies—including artificial intelligence, blockchain, the Internet of Things, advanced analytics, and Industry 4.0/5.0—to improve visibility, decision-making, and resilience.

CHAPTER OVERVIEW

1. Introduces an integrated framework that unifies climate action, social accountability, and economic resilience as complementary pillars for designing and governing sustainable global supply chains.
2. Examines the impact of geopolitical tensions on critical raw material supply chains, discussing strategic sourcing, technological innovation, regulatory responses, and resource security.
3. Explores strategies for strengthening supply chain resilience under geopolitical uncertainty through modular manufacturing, digital transformation, Industry 4.0 and 5.0 technologies, and supply chain reconfiguration.
4. Investigates ethical sourcing and supply chain transparency as essential mechanisms for promoting social accountability, highlighting sustainability standards, stakeholder collaboration, and emerging digital technologies.
5. Reviews the evolution of ESG policy frameworks and regulatory developments that are shaping sustainable supply chain governance, transparency, accountability, and organizational competitiveness.
6. Analyzes the combined effects of climate change and economic disruptions on supply chains while proposing integrated resilience frameworks that emphasize innovation, strategic adaptation, and policy support.
7. Presents comprehensive approaches to supply chain risk management in volatile environments, emphasizing resilience, agility, digital technologies, scenario planning, diversification, and collaborative risk-sharing.
8. Examines the challenges and opportunities associated with supply chain transformation in emerging economies, focusing on policy reform, technological innovation, governance, and inclusive development.
9. Provides a comparative analysis of sustainable supply chain models across multiple industries, highlighting circular economy practices, green logistics, renewable energy adoption, responsible procurement, and digital technologies.
10. Explores how strategic collaboration between manufacturers and distributors enhances supply chain performance through coordinated decision-making, information sharing, trust development, and operational efficiency.

11. Introduces an extended Economic Order Quantity model that addresses demand uncertainty in healthcare settings by integrating ethical, clinical, and economic considerations into inventory management.
12. Examines the role of smart mobility in sustainable urban development, demonstrating how technology, governance, and inclusive policies contribute to efficient, resilient, and environmentally responsible transportation systems.

Together, these chapters demonstrate that sustainable supply chain management is no longer a peripheral concern but a strategic imperative for organizations, policymakers, and society. They offer theoretical insights, empirical evidence, and practical guidance that support the development of supply chains capable of responding to environmental challenges, social expectations, and economic uncertainty. By integrating perspectives from operations management, sustainability, public policy, technology, and organizational strategy, this volume contributes to the growing body of knowledge supporting the transition toward more resilient, equitable, and sustainable global supply networks.

It is hoped that this collection will serve as a valuable resource for researchers, educators, graduate students, industry practitioners, and policymakers seeking to better understand the evolving landscape of supply chain management and to contribute meaningfully to the design of supply chains that create long-term value for businesses, communities, and the environment.

Atour Taghipour
Conservatoire National des Arts et Métier, France

Chapter 1

Triangular Transformation Integrating Climate Action, Social Accountability, and Economic Resilience in Global Supply Chains

M. R. Vidya
http://orcid.org/0009-0008-7020-4806
MMK and SDM Mahila Mahavidyalaya, Mysore University, India

Pavendhan Madhivanan
http://orcid.org/0000-0001-8183-8793
Aditya College of Engineering and Technology, India

K. Sowmya
Aditya College of Engineering and Technology, India

Y. Sharath Kumar
http://orcid.org/0000-0002-2878-0219
St. Francis College, India

C. N. Lakshmi
http://orcid.org/0009-0003-7885-3919
St. Francis College, India

R. Vandana
http://orcid.org/0009-0000-9842-030X
St. Francis College, India

T. R. Chetan
http://orcid.org/0000-0003-4781-9155
Jain (Deemed to be) University, India

H. C. Purushotham
http://orcid.org/0000-0002-2035-2965
School of Commerce, Jain (Deemed to be) University, India

DOI: 10.4018/979-8-3373-6455-1.ch001

D. Deepak
http://orcid.org/0009-0004-8493-1474
Jain (Deemed to be) University, India

ABSTRACT

Global supply chains are undergoing a paradigmatic shift as climate action, social accountability, and economic resilience emerge as non-negotiable imperatives. This chapter introduces the concept of Triangular Transformation, a comprehensive framework that integrates these three pillars into the design and governance of modern supply chains. Traditional supply chain models, which prioritised efficiency and cost minimisation, have proven inadequate in addressing the interconnected crises of climate change, social inequities, and systemic vulnerabilities. The proposed framework emphasises that achieving sustainability requires simultaneous commitment to decarbonization, ethical labour practices, and resilience-building mechanisms.

1. INTRODUCTION

1.1 21st Century Global Supply Chains: A Historical Context

Global supply chains have become extremely complicated, interrelated networks of people, products, and resources spanning continents, sectors, and socio-political barriers. In the 21st century, these networks have evolved beyond being mere marketplaces that provide goods and services to become essential infrastructures that enable economic development, create jobs, foster innovation, and promote global cooperation (Christopher, 2016; Gereffi, 2018). Facilitated by the forces of globalisation, technology, and liberalised trade policies, supply chains are operating at a level of efficiency that creates scale and specialisation never before seen. However, this same global interconnectedness has also increased systemic risks, as shown by the global financial crisis of 2008, the COVID-19 pandemic, and new geopolitical conflicts that have disrupted energy, raw material, and critical goods flows (Ivanov & Dolgui, 2021). Supply chains have historically been built around the principles of cost minimisation, lean management, and just-in-time delivery. However, both of these paradigms drove profit and market share while neglecting environmental sustainability, human rights, and system robustness (Kleindorfer & Saad, 2005). The climate crisis, rising inequalities, and increasing global shocks have made these traditional models increasingly inadequate today. As a concrete example, approximately 11% of global carbon emissions originate from global logistics operations, with maritime shipping accounting for nearly 3% of this total (International Energy

Agency, 2022). At the same time, allegations of exploitative labour practices, from abusive working conditions to modern slavery, continue to emerge (LeBaron, 2020), pointing to ethical blind spots in many supply chains of multinational companies. The context of the supply chain in the 21st century is therefore a double-edged sword: keeping up with the competition in volatile markets while simultaneously fulfilling one's basic responsibilities in the environmental, social, and ethical domains. Such a reconfiguration cannot be achieved through isolated frameworks that present a narrow set of trade-offs between profit and responsibility at a time when supply chains themselves can — and must — become enablers of sustainable and inclusive globalisation.

1.2 We Must Step Up Climate Action, Social Responsibility, and Economic Resilience Now

Our supply chains have become the epicentre of decarbonising the globe, as the climate crisis intensifies. Climate-related impacts – both sudden (e.g., extreme weather events) and gradual (e.g., increased sea levels, changes in the availability of fundamental resources) – have direct implications for supply chain stability, which encompasses everything from agricultural efforts to energy flows and manufacturing capabilities (IPCC, 2021). If we do not act urgently on climate change, disruptions will become more extreme and are projected to cost our economies trillions of dollars every year by 2050 (OECD, 2022). Apart from mitigating the power of supply chains, they should also build adaptive capacities by integrating aspects of renewable power-based circular economy and low-carbon logistics to align with international frameworks such as the Paris Agreement and the UN Sustainable Development Goals (SDGs).In tandem with environmental imperatives, social accountability is growing as stakeholders increasingly demand timely access to data and information related to corporate behaviour. The rise of environmental, social and governance (ESG) reporting (Whelan & Fink, 2020), activist consumerism (Banyan Global, 2020), and mandatory human rights due diligence laws (such as the EU Corporate Sustainability Due Diligence Directive) reflects a social trend towards increased supply chain accountability. Supply chains that fail to guarantee labour rights, gender equality, and fair economic engagement are at risk of reputational damage, regulatory consequences, and consumer backlash. The third dimension that cannot be missed is economic resilience. Global disturbances, from the COVID-19 pandemic (Sahu, 2020) to the Russian invasion of Ukraine, have tested the vulnerability of hyper-optimised supply chains (Ivanov & Dolgui, 2020). Scarcities of essential inputs, such as semiconductors, medical devices, and energy commodities, highlighted the dangers of a domino effect from excessive reliance on single geographies and producers. Indeed, resilience can only be built through diversification, digitalisation, agility, and strong risk management frameworks. Resilience must not be seen as a cost sinkhole but rather as a strategic enabler for sustainable competitive advantage and continuity (business/financial). Further Readings: U.S. Therefore, climate action, social accountability, and economic resilience are no longer parallel agendas; instead, they form a new natural system of interdependence. Failure to address climate change exacerbates supply chain disruptions; failing to uphold social accountability undermines legitimacy and societal trust; and fragile systems will not sustain themselves over the long term. Taking an integration-based approach across these dimensions is both an existential imperative and a strategic value proposition for transforming supply chain performance.

1.3 Triangular Transformation Framework

The chapter presents the concept of a Triangular Transformation, a framework for integrating climate action, social accountability, and economic resilience into the core of global supply chains. The Triangular Transformation is built on the principles of simultaneity and interdependence, contrasting with the siloed or sequential development of transformations inherent in traditional sustainability models.

The framework is fundamentally based on three tenets:

- Climate Action: Integrating decarbonization, renewable transitions and circular economy innovations into supply chains and the logistics function.
- Social accountability: ethical labour practices through proper inclusion, human rights practices and fairness across the value pool across the chain.
- Financial Resiliency: Creating networks that are more adaptive, agile, and diverse to withstand systemic shocks.

Arguably, the triangle model is based on widely accepted theoretical foundations, namely, the Triple Bottom Line (TBL) (Elkington, 1997), Stakeholder Theory (Freeman, 1984), and Systems Thinking (Meadows, 2008). However, it goes beyond these by conveying the intertwinement of the three dimensions. Investment in renewable energy (climate action) not only reduces carbon footprints but also increases resilience by mitigating exposure to fluctuations in fossil fuel prices. Promoting socially responsible labour practices also fosters trust and innovation, ultimately leading to greater economic resilience. The Triangular Transformation, therefore, go beyond incrementalism to systematic redesign. Thus, it offers a unifying perspective for academics, practitioners, and policymakers to rethink supply chains not only as value delivery systems but also as fundamental infrastructures of global sustainability and equity.

1.4 Supply chains in the modern world: Global Trends and Systemic Risks

The twenty-first-century global supply chains operate in an environment characterised by increased uncertainty, structural complexity, and interdependent systemic risks. The globalisation wave, geopolitical uncertainty, climate change, and technological upheaval have significantly changed supply-chain design and the logic of supply-chain governance.

1.4.1 Environmental Risk and Climate-Induced Disruptions

Climate change has become a systemic risk that permeates global production and logistics networks. Severe climatic conditions, higher water levels, water scarcity, and heat instability continue to disrupt transport routes, agricultural production, and manufacturing operations. These shocks from climate change not only increase operational costs but also cause supply chain failures within integrated supply chains. Recent reports show that supply chains are a significant contributor to global greenhouse gas emissions, thereby putting firms at the centre of climate-reduction plans (IPCC, 2021; International Energy Agency, 2022).

1.4.2 Geopolitical Disparagement and Globalisation of Trade Uncertainty

Geopolitical realignments, along with environmental pressures, have heightened systemic instability in global value chains. Trade battles have transformed sourcing decisions, protectionist practises, regionalisation policies, and sanctions regimes, heightening their exposure to political risk. The shift in the globalisation paradigm from efficiency to resilience indicates a broader shift in the strategies used in the supply chain (Ivanov & Dolgui, 2021; Kleindorfer & Saad, 2005).

1.4.3 Social and Labour Weaknesses in Global Production Systems

One dimension of systemic supply-chain vulnerability that is severely underestimated is social risks. Exploitation of labour, informal working arrangements, workplace safety breakdowns, and increased inequality are still commonplace in the context of extended supply chains, especially in developing economies. These risks are also exacerbated by climate stress, which hastens labour displacement, intensifies migration pressures, and deepens livelihood insecurity. These processes mark the mutual support of environmental shocks and social vulnerability in global value chains around global triggers (LeBaron, 2020; Kleindorfer & Saad, 2005).

1.4.4 Economic Volatility and SupplyChain Fragility

The instability of supply chain systems based on highly optimised cost models, combined with inherent economic shocks such as pandemics, inflationary pressures, energy price fluctuations, and currency issues, has revealed the frailty of these models. Just-in-time systems, lean inventories and global sourcing structures, though they work under normal circumstances, have become susceptible during systemic stress. More recent studies are focusing on the need to lean towards efficiency, resilience, flexibility, and long-term sustainability. It is a widespread practice in financial markets for systemic risks to be interdependent. Importantly, contemporary supply-chain risks will not take place in a vacuum. Climate shocks make the population more socially vulnerable; political instability makes economic growth more uncertain; and changes in regulations redesign market incentives. This interdependence, therefore, turns individual risk into systemic risks that can spread across the sectors and even regions (Ivanov & Dolgui, 2021; Gereffi, 2018).

1.4.5 Implication on Sustainable Supply-Chain Governance

The intersection of climate, social, and economic risks points to a structural change in supply-chain governance. Companies are now obliged to implement comprehensive sustainability practices that go beyond compliance, focusing on systemic risk management and long-term resilience. The implications of these global trends lie in the drawbacks of patchy sustainability strategies and the importance of integrative models that can help tackle multidimensional risks simultaneously (Seuring & Müller, 2008; Sarkis et al., 2019).

2. THEORETICAL FOUNDATIONS AND CONCEPTUAL FRAMEWORK

2.1 Existing Frameworks Linking Climate Action, Social Responsibility, and Economic Performance

Over the past two decades, scholars and policymakers have developed multiple frameworks to integrate environmental responsibility, social accountability, and economic performance within supply chains. However, these frameworks often remain partially integrated, operating in parallel rather than as unified systems. The present section critically reviews the dominant theoretical and managerial approaches that inform sustainability discourse and positions the proposed Triangular Transformation framework in relation to them. As part of its sustainability reporting commitment, DaimlerChrysler Corporation has adopted ESG Investment and Reporting Frameworks. The Environmental, Social, and Governance (ESG) frameworks have become a central tool for determining corporate sustainability behaviour. ESG translates non-financial aspects of operations, such as carbon, labour relations, and transparency in governance, into measurable factors that investors can use in decision-making and investment. According to recent literature on supply chains, ESG is seen as a performance-monitoring and risk-signalling instrument rather than a comprehensive transformation framework. There is empirical evidence of the growing focus of ESG in supplier assessment, sustainable procurement, and risk screening in global value chains (Whelan & Fink, 2020; Seuring & Müller, 2008). The integration of digital technologies and data-based reporting systems, particularly blockchain-based transparency and traceability tools, has advanced further, further supporting the implementation of ESGs (Mathiyazhagan et al., 2022; Saberi et al., 2019). However, ESG frameworks are primarily measurement and disclosure systems. Although they reveal risks to sustainability, they do not go further to explain the dynamic relationships between climate action, social accountability, and economic resilience within supply chains. ESG will therefore encourage compliance-based behaviour rather than transformation.

2.1.2. Corporate Social Responsibility (CSR) Theory

Corporate Social Responsibility (CSR) is one of the earliest paradigms of business ethics, connecting business with social responsibility. CSR prefigures the voluntary corporate commitment to social welfare, ethical business practices, environmental safety, and community development. In the context of supply chain studies, CSR has been utilised in a wide range of applications, including ethical sourcing, supplier codes of conduct, and stakeholder engagement (Carroll & Shabana, 2010; Seuring & Müller, 2008). The CSR model has been especially significant in developing economies, where regulation has been inconsistently applied and voluntary governance can serve as a compensatory mechanism. Even though CSR has normative strength, it has been denounced for a fragmented, philanthropic focus. The available empirical evidence also suggests that the CSR initiatives are often not connected to the functioning and financial decision-making activities (Carroll & Shabana, 2010). To this end, CSR is more likely to be an activity associated with the supply chain strategy rather than part of it. This weakness diminishes CSR's ability to resolve complex trade-offs among cost-effectiveness, environmental impacts, and social equity in global supply chains.

2.1.3 Circular Economy Models

Circular economy models would balance economic development and resource exhaustion by encouraging reuse, remanufacturing, recycling, and closed-loop supply networks. The direct impact of these models on climate mitigation includes reduced waste, reduced emissions, and less virgin material extraction. Innovative studies underscore the importance of designing circular supply chains, reverse logistics, and remanufacturing systems as key to sustainability in production (Sarkis et al., 2019; Milne & Grey, 2013). Alternatively, the strategy of circular economy proves to increase the resilience of the economy over time by decreasing the reliance on unreliable markets of raw materials. However, circular models pay a lot of attention to environmental efficiency, providing minimal coverage of social aspects like labour rights, equity in wages, and community effects. Additionally, circularity projects often face issues with scalability, especially with SMEs that do not have the financial and technological means. In turn, although circular economy models play a significant role in advancing climate goals, they remain inadequate in addressing social responsibility and institutional governance simultaneously.

2.1.4 Just Transition Theory

Just Transition theory was developed within the discourse of labour economics and climate justice, which posits that climate action is not an opportunity to worsen social inequality. It argues that decarbonisation should safeguard workers, communities, and vulnerable groups through inclusive policies, reskilling programmes, and balanced value distribution. Just Transition is becoming relevant in supply chain contexts to Global South manufacturing metropolises, extractive industries and logistics labour markets. Research indicates the imperative to incorporate social protection systems and technological changes alongside climate action (LeBaron, 2020; Seuring & Müller, 2008). Although it is normatively relevant, Just Transition is nonetheless policy-oriented and does not reflect the operational clarity at both the firm and supply chain network levels. It offers moral leadership but provides little guidance on how corporations can be economically competitive while, at the same time, equitably allocate transition pathways.

2.1.5. The literature of Triple Bottom Line (TBL)

The individual Triple Bottom Line (TBL) formalises the idea that business performance should be measured across three dimensions: environmental, social, and economic. TBL remains fundamental in the sustainability literature, and many modern supply chain books are based on it. Empirical research still relies on TBL rationality to assess sustainable supply chain performance and value creation for stakeholders (Elkington, 1997; Milne & Grey, 2013). Nevertheless, researchers are starting to note that TBL tends to interpret its three pillars as concurrent performance measures but not as mutually reinforcing aspects of the system. As a result, organisations often tend to go through environmental, social and economic goals independently, and they come up with projects of a siloed kind which have no long-term systemic resilience. the literature provides certain fundamental data concerning races, their tensions, and the extent of discrimination they face. According to the author, the literature has certain basic information about races, their tensions, and how much they are actually discriminated against in this book (Elizabeth, 2012). The analysis of the existing frameworks shows that there are three pre-eminent areas of knowledge in sustainability and supply chain studies. To start with, literature is highly definitive in promoting the significance of applying environmental responsibility, social accountability, and economic performance. The list of ESG metrics, CSR principles, circular economy strategies, the discourse of Just Transition, as well as the TBL theory, all affirm that the concept of sustainability is a strategic necessity and not an option. Second, even with such agreement, the literature is more than fragmented, thus a majority of the frameworks stress a particular dimension and consider the others as minor. ESG prioritises measurement, CSR prioritises ethics, circular economy prioritises environmental efficiency, Just Transition prioritises social justice, and TBL prioritises balanced reporting, but emergent models of interaction between these aspects in dynamic supply chain systems are sparse. Third, no integrative models yet exist on simultaneity, interdependence, and trade-offs between climate action/social accountability/ economic resilience, especially in periods of uncertainty, disruption and geopolitical turmoil. The Triangular Transformation framework proposal specifically seeks to remove this gap by theorising these three dimensions as complementary, as opposed to temporal or cumulative. In contrast to the prevailing models, it focuses on dynamical interaction, strategic mobilisation, and systemic resilience, which extends the sustainability theory beyond compliance-based supply chain designs and towards the outcomes-oriented supply chain design.

3. CLIMATE ACTION IN SUPPLY CHAINS

Supply chains play a central role in the climate crisis. Industries must manage their operations, which impact generations, because every turn—production, transportation, and consumption —results in unavoidable greenhouse gas (GHG) emissions, resource depletion, and environmental degradation. In fact, supply chain emissions are, on average, 11.4 times higher than a company's direct operational emissions (CDP Supply Chain Report (2021)). It highlights just how significant a role—and an opportunity—supply chains play in meeting global climate goals. As a result, climate action in supply chains must be holistic, encompassing emissions reduction, renewable energy adoption, and the application of circular economy principles, all within the context of rapidly evolving global regulatory environments.

3.1 Emissions Reduction in Supply Chains

3.1.1 Operational Efficiency and Logistics Optimisation

Streamlining operations to optimise processes is usually the first step in an emissions-reduction strategy. Companies adopt energy-efficient technologies, lean production practices, and better resource management in manufacturing. Logistics is primarily about route optimisation, reducing empty miles, and transferring freight from air to sea or rail, making a significant contribution to carbon reduction. Furthermore, digital twins and AI-based predictive analytics enhance efficiency by forecasting demand and reducing waste.

3.1.2 Engagement on Scope 3 Emissions With Suppliers

Most emission calculations suggest that a significant portion of supply chain emissions falls under Scope 3 categories, including those from suppliers, logistics providers, and product end use (GHG Protocol, 2015). Working with upstream and downstream partners will be needed for Scope 3. For instance, Walmart has Project Gigaton, which calls on thousands of suppliers to join forces and reduce emissions by a gigaton by 2030. Likewise, Apple has mandated that its entire global supply base transition to 100% renewable electricity for Apple production, substantially reducing upstream emissions (Apple, 2022).

3.1.3 Product and Material Innovation

Redesigning products and materials also reduces emissions. More businesses are using lightweight packaging, biodegradable materials, and sustainable resources (for example, FSC-certified wood or recycled metals). For example, the transition to electric vehicles is underway in the automotive industry, but so is the decarbonization of supply chains for key components such as lithium, cobalt, and nickel. Such shifts in materials catalyse a series of knock-on effects throughout the whole supply networks.

3.2 Implementation of Connectivity Changes in B2B supply chains powered by renewable energy

3.2.1 On-Site and Off-Site Renewable Investments

The use of renewable energy sources is a crucial part of the Philippines' decarbonization supply chain. Businesses are allocating more resources to on-site solar and wind generation at factories, warehouses, and distribution centres. Unilever is an example that has achieved 100% renewable electricity globally through a combination of on-site generation and power purchase agreements (PPAs).

3.2.2 Renewable Procurement through Supply Contracts

Outside of their own organisations, companies are also exerting pressure on suppliers to transition to renewable energy. Apple (2022) — Apple has enrolled more than 200 suppliers in its Supplier Clean Energy Program, which helps suppliers transition to renewables in support of Apple-related production. Maersk, in much the same way, has ordered ships that will operate on green methanol, demanding renewable feedstock relationships throughout its supply base.

3.2.3 Challenges and Opportunities

Global renewable integration is hindered primarily by grid constraints, regulatory limitations, and financing gaps in developing economies, despite recent progress (IRENA, 2021). This is therefore where supply chains need to get creative, such as shared renewable clusters, where multiple suppliers in an industrial park share wind or solar infrastructure and green financing mechanisms set up to support small and medium-sized enterprises (SMEs).

3.3 Supply Chain Features of the Circular Economy

The transition from a linear "take-make-dispose" model to closed-loop systems via the circular economy presents a paradigm shift not only for climate action but also for transformational change, as it minimises waste and emissions.

- Longevité: Fairphone, a brand promoting modular designs of electronics, advocates for designs that will lengthen product life cycles and minimise carbon-intensive manufacturing of replacements.

- Reverse logistics and recycling: retailers such as IKEA are piloting buy-back and refurb programs for pieces of furniture to cut down emissions from raw material extraction.
- Industrial Symbiosis: There are growing supply chain opportunities for vertical integration across industries, where output from one process is used as an input for another (e.g., cement producers using industrial by-products to displace clinker and reduce emissions).
- Product-as-a-Service Models: Circular approaches like leasing or subscription-based offerings (like Philips' "lighting as a service") reward creators for producing long-lasting, recyclable, and energy-efficient goods.

By decreasing emissions and increasing resilience—by reducing exposure to shortages in raw-material availability—circular supply chains present an opportunity for synergy, one of three vectors of the Triangular Transformation framework.

3.4 Global Regulatory Frameworks

International regulatory frameworks are a significant determinant of climate action in supply chains, through targets, compliance mechanisms, and enforcement.

3.4.1 The Paris Agreement

The Paris Agreement, which has been ratified since 2015, has climate objectives that require countries to constrain the rise in global temperature to well below 2°C and to pursue efforts to limit the temperature increase to 1.5°C, which, in turn, translates for supply chains into corporate alignment with science based targets (SBTi) and disclosure via such initiatives as the Task Force on Climate-related Financial Disclosures (TCFD). Increasingly, multinational corporations are being required to do the same, demanding that their supply chains adhere to pathways aligned with the Paris Agreement.

3.4.2 COP Directives and National Commitments

Under the UNFCCC, Annual Conferences of the Parties (COPs) create climate directions that build on previous outcomes. At COP26 (Glasgow), pledges to phase down coal and transportation (103 138 190; complete decarbonisation pathway) and vehicle commitments (103 138 190 obligations) directly impact supply chain investment decisions. The challenge COP27 made to the notion of loss and damage financing drew attention to the particular risks that supply networks in developing economies face. As directives shift, supply chains must follow suit or risk being cut off from markets that align with tighter standards.

3.4.3 Carbon Border Adjustment Mechanisms (CBAMs)

Tariffs are also generating much excitement in the European Union with the introduction of the Carbon Border Adjustment Mechanism from 2026, which will impose tariffs on the carbon emissions embedded in goods imported into the union. CBAM also marks the end of outsourcing carbon in supply chains, a practice that allows companies to shift high-emission production to regions with weaker regulations. The U.S. and Canada are also contemplating similar mechanisms. Central to this regulatory evolution is the requirement that companies embed emissions accounting across their value networks to maintain market access.

3.4.4 Voluntary Standards and Certifications

Beyond regulatory instruments, voluntary standards such as ISO 14064 (GHG accounting), the Carbon Disclosure Project (CDP), and the Science-Based Targets initiative (SBTi) establish benchmarks for entire industries. Although voluntary, these standards are increasingly guiding industry practices and shaping consumer expectations, serving as a form of soft institutional pressure (DiMaggio & Powell, 1983).

3.4.5 Climate-Connected Supply Chain Case Studies

Unilever

Unilever has stepped up as a leader in climate-aligned supply chains, with 15 carbon-neutral sites and 100% renewable electricity purchased globally. The company is collaborating with suppliers to reduce emissions and enhance farm resilience through its Sustainable Living Plan. Unilever demonstrates another significant step in making regenerative agriculture a widespread climate action. After completing a feat where sustainable processes in the respective resource cycle begin to emerge, Unilever formalises ways to extend climate action beyond its own facilities and into the farms that supply them.

Apple

Apple Climate Strategy: A Case in Point for Supplier Engagement. The Pledge spans its complete supply chain, so suppliers must transition towards renewable energy and low-carbon production to keep its 2030 Carbon Neutral Pledge intact. Apple has been a leader in using 100% recycled aluminium in its products and rare orchard minerals, with ballistic traceability. This illustrates how mitigation, adoption of renewable energy, and application of circular principles come together through a single supply chain.

Maersk

Maersk is one of the world's largest shipping companies, positioning it well to decarbonise logistics. The firm has pledged to achieve net-zero emissions by 2040, placed orders for methanol-fueled ships, and developed green-fuel infrastructure in collaboration with its suppliers. However, beyond baulking at the numbers, the initiatives announced by Maersk underscore both the challenge (and opportunity!) of bringing together different sectors to decarbonise hard-to-abate sectors.

4. SOCIAL ACCOUNTABILITY AND HUMAN-CENTRED SUPPLY CHAINS

The evolution of international supply chains has underscored the need to integrate social accountability into sustainable business practices. Historically (although not universally), corporate initiatives were categorised under the umbrella of Corporate Social Responsibility (CSR), often with a narrow emphasis on philanthropy and voluntary commitments (Carroll & Shabana, 2010). Nevertheless, the contemporary trajectory emphasises Environmental, Social, and Governance (ESG) accountability, an emerging construct that translates sociocultural elements into quantifiable metrics that influence investor confidence, stakeholder trust, and long-term competitiveness (Kotsantonis et al., 2016). Central to social accountability within supply chains are labour rights and the provision of decent working conditions. Since supply chains operate across various jurisdictions with differing labour laws and enforcement mechanisms, they impact workers' vulnerability. Industries characterised by minimal regulation, such as fast fashion and electronics, continue to report exploitative practices, including hazardous working environments, wage theft, and the prevalence of non-unionised labour (Anner, 2020). Consequently, a human-centred supply chain must adhere to international labour standards established by the International Labour Organisation (ILO), even if this entails increased costs.

However, beyond compliance, the movement towards gender equity and diversity within supply chains has evolved into both an ethical obligation and an innovative organisational strategy. Evidence suggests that diversity and inclusivity can foster creativity, enhance problem-solving capabilities, and improve resilience in the face of volatility (Carter & Rogers, 2008). Companies such as Microsoft and Unilever exemplify the adoption of supplier diversity programs that emphasise the benefits of women-owned and minority-owned businesses, illustrating how inclusivity contributes to sustainable development over the long term. Another vital aspect is ethical sourcing. The complexity of modern supply networks has heightened the risks associated with modern slavery, forced labour, and human trafficking. Current statistics indicate that approximately 50 million individuals are subjected to modern slavery (Global Slavery Index, 2023), with many directly linked to global supply chains. Sectors such as cocoa, palm oil, and cobalt mining remain particularly vulnerable to environmental impacts. To mitigate these risks, firms are increasingly employing traceability technologies, such as blockchain, to verify the origin of their goods and ensure transparency from raw materials to final delivery (Saberi et al., 2019). When implemented correctly, standards and certifications underpin accountability. Established frameworks, including SA8000 (social accountability), ISO 26000 (social responsibility), and the Global Reporting Initiative (GRI), serve as reference points for monitoring labour practices, human rights, and community engagement. The adoption of such frameworks demonstrates a company's commitment to ethical conduct and enhances its reputational capital. For example, Nestlé's Responsible Sourcing Standard aligns with SA8000 principles and requires suppliers to uphold codes of conduct. Ultimately, in the context of social accountability within supply chains, the core concern shifts from merely avoiding reputational risk to generating shared value. When grounded in principles of human rights, inclusivity, and ethics, organisations can cultivate social sustainability and strategic resilience within their supply chains.

4.1 Measuring and Operationalising the Triangular Framework.

Although the triangular framework conceptually incorporates climate action, social accountability, and economic performance, its analytical value ultimately depends on its operationalisation through measurable, implementable indicators. To meet this need, this section will convert the framework into an organised measurement logic that aligns the firm-level decision-making with regulatory requirements, investor sensitivities, and social responsibility. In doing so, the framework goes beyond the normative sustainability discourse and provides a realistic starting point for empirical evaluation and strategy implementation.

4.1.1 Performance Assessment of ESG.

The ESG reporting regime provides a highly institutionalised framework for measuring non-financial performance in global supply chains. The ESG indicators enable organisations to systematically evaluate their exposure to environmental, labour, and governance practices, as well as their ability to manage risks across supplier networks at various levels. ESG performance is becoming an effective factor in defining capital allocation, supplier selection, and long-term strategic positioning, especially in industries vulnerable to climate and social risks. In the triangular model, ESG is an overall evaluation level, not a goal in itself. It provides a unified interface that allows climate, social compliance, and economic resiliency metrics to be considered together. Nonetheless, instead of viewing ESG scores as a final destination, the framework presents them as diagnostic vectors that highlight vulnerabilities in the structure and formulate specific interventions for supply-chain activities.

4.1.2 The Emissions Accounting and Climate Performance Measurement.

The action-climate aspect of the triangular model is implemented by accounting for all greenhouse gas emissions, including Scope 1, Scope 2, and Scope 3. As the Scope 1 and Scope 2 measurements deal with direct and energy-related emissions, Scope 3 emissions deal with indirect emissions embedded in upstream sourcing, logistics, product use, and product end-of-life. Indirect emissions in most industries have accounted for the largest share of a firm's total carbon footprint. The inclusion of Scope 3 accounting explicitly helps focus on supply-chain-wide responsibility rather than firm-level optimisation. Through this method, organisations can identify high-impact areas of emissions, implement suppliers in decarbonisation efforts, and regulate climate-reduction plans and procurement/logistics choices. As a result, emissions accounting will no longer be a reporting measure but a tactical tool to mitigate climate-related operational and reputational risks.

4.1.3 Social Responsibility and Labour Conformance Systems.

The triangular framework uses the social accountability pillar to gauge progress through labour norms, certification schemes, and compliance systems installed within global value chains. These tools are occupational health and safety standards, wage and working hours standards, supplier codes of conduct and third-party social auditing. They worked together to provide verifiable, failproof proof of labour and human rights outcomes in production structures dispersed geographically. This aspect is especially acute in the Global South, where supply chains often overlap with informal labour markets, regulatory fragmentation, and heightened exposure to climate-related shocks. Using labour-compliance indicators as a part of the measurement framework, the framework does not consider social risk as a peripheral ethical issue but as a major factor in determining supply-chain stability, legitimacy, and long-term value creation.

4.1.4 Policy Consistency and Integrative Institutionalism.

The triangular framework, which is being operationalised, also needs to be aligned with the changing climate and industrial policy regimes. National and supranational policy tools, such as climate transition incentives, carbon-pricing systems, and sustainability-linked policies, increasingly influence corporate investment behaviour and sustainability-linked organisational strategies. The regulatory frameworks, which have both coercive and enabling effects on organisational sustainability strategies, include green industrial policies and climate adaptation mechanisms. Policy alignment in the triangular model serves as an intervening layer between the three aspects of governance by the people and the operational practices of enterprises. By linking policy motivational incentives and regulatory demonstration to performance measurement, organisations can more effectively anticipate regulatory risk, recognise the use of public financing instruments, and align sustainability initiatives across diverse contexts.

4.1.6 Logic of Integrative Measurement.

Collectively, the ESG evaluation systems, the emissions accounting systems, the labour compliance systems, and the policy-aligned signals constitute an integrated measurement structure within the triangular framework. The interdependencies can be evaluated using this multidimensional approach, trade-offs managed, and the fragmentation that is often present in sustainability initiatives prevented. Unlike environmental, social, or economic goals, the framework helps streamline coordinated decision-making amid uncertainty, disruption, or systemic risk. Incorporating measurement as a central point of the triangular construct, this section provides a clear channel between the combination of concepts and their evaluation and application in reality. By doing so, the framework improves its analytical rigour and applicability to policymakers, practitioners, and scholars with an interest in the governance of sustainable supply chains.

5. CREATING SUPPLY CHAIN RESILIENCE FOR THE ECONOMY

The past decade has demonstrated that economic resilience is no longer a mere choice but an imperative for survival within the global supply chain. Chronological challenges, including the COVID-19 pandemic, the Russia–Ukraine conflict, recurrent climate disasters, and a persistent energy crisis, have underscored the vulnerability of linear, efficient supply chains. According to the World Economic Forum (2022), global enterprises experience business interruptions totalling $1.9 trillion annually, underscoring the paramount importance of resilience as a strategic approach. Since Ponomarov & Holcomb (2009) defined it, resilience has been understood as the capacity to adapt and recover from disruptions while maintaining operational continuity, effectiveness, and long-term value creation. This conceptualisation is currently reflected in socio-technical systems, commonly referred to in literature as supply chains, which exemplify economic resilience. The green supply chain primarily emphasises shifting from prioritising minimalism to fostering resilience through increased capacity and flexibility. The foundational step involves transitioning from a low-cost, lean, outsourcing model to one characterised by robustness, adaptability, and large-scale mobility. Digital transformation significantly drives this resilience. Emerging technologies such as artificial intelligence (AI), blockchain, and the Internet of Things (IoT) continually enhance supply chain transparency and risk management. Predictive analytics and AI-enabled platforms facilitate forecasting of demand fluctuations and anticipating disruptions (Ivanov & Dolgui, 2021). Blockchain technology offers immutable transaction records, thereby enhancing transparency and trust among multi-tier suppliers. IoT-connected sensors monitor real-time conditions in logistics and production environments, enabling swift responses. For instance, the TradeLens platform, developed by Maersk, has augmented transparency in global shipping, reducing delays and inefficiencies. Sourcing diversification is another critical strategy for bolstering resilience. Relying on suppliers with single-source dependencies and centralised production hubs in limited geographical areas has proven to be a high-risk strategy. The COVID-19 crisis exposed global vulnerabilities, particularly dependence on China for essential pharmaceuticals and semiconductors. Consequently, corporations are pursuing reshoring, nearshoring, and multi-sourcing initiatives to mitigate geopolitical and logistical risks (Barbieri et al., 2020). Intel's investment in autonomous semiconductor facilities in the U.S. and Europe exemplifies efforts to hedge against growing supply chain vulnerabilities in Asia. Additionally, adaptive networks enhance resilience through decentralised, collaborative frameworks that can rapidly reconfigure during crises. Unlike traditional linear models, adaptive networks leverage partnerships, cross-sector collaborations, and shared data platforms to ensure continuity. During the pandemic, automotive manufacturers swiftly reoriented their supply chains to produce ventilators and personal protective equipment, exemplifying agility and societal responsiveness. Quantifying resilience as an organisational objective involves developing frameworks that measure more than economic costs, including recovery speed, supplier diversity, redundancy capacity, and stakeholder trust (Sheffi, 2021). Long-term value preservation necessitates balancing short-term efficiency with resource allocation for redundancy and adaptability. This approach aligns closely with the Triple Bottom Line (TBL) concept, which integrates financial performance with social and ecological accountability. Constructing economic resilience thus entails a delicate balance requiring cautious strategic foresight and opportunistic flexibility. Excessive redundancy can incur prohibitive costs, whereas insufficient redundancy exposes firms to catastrophic vulnerabilities. The optimal strategy consolidates digital channels, multi-source sourcing, and agility within a unified framework that sustains competitiveness and operational continuity.

6. THE INTERSECTIONS: TRIANGULAR TRANSFORMATION IN PRACTICE

Triangular Transformation portrays Climate Action, Social Accountability, and Economic Resilience not as individual goals in a vacuum, but as highly interlinked and interdependent forces that influence the development of global supply chains. However, in practice, these dimensions are often in conflict, creating both synergies and tensions that require firms to balance competing priorities in search of integrated strategies.

6.1 Synergies and Tensions

However, among the most substantial synergies is the understanding that climate action strengthens resilience. Declining emissions, green power, and circular-economy practices reduce firms' vulnerability to resource volatility, regulatory shocks, and reputational risk. Switching to renewable energy, for example, mitigates carbon footprints and protects companies from the volatility of fossil fuel prices. Likewise, being responsive to societal needs boosts sustainability by fostering trust with stakeholders, increasing worker productivity, and strengthening brand loyalty. Supply chains become less susceptible to disruptions from labour unrest or consumer backlash when employees are treated fairly, communities are supported, and sourcing is deemed ethical. However, those synergies are not entirely free of tensions. In the short term, climate action may result in higher operational costs due to the adoption of renewable energy systems, carbon-neutral logistics, or the redesign of products to make them circular. Production costs may be significantly higher with social accountability initiatives, such as living wages, gender equity programs, and supplier audits, than with low-cost but exploitative practices. Hence, firms must balance profitability with the needs of society and the environment — a balancing act that could strain managerial vision and shareholder patience. While the goals themselves may not be contentious, for many, the challenge lies in linking them to pragmatic, scalable strategies.

6.2 Capability: Profitability vs Sustainability vs Social Equity Trade-Offs

The triangle model reveals inescapable trade-offs that international value chains must navigate. For instance, in industries such as apparel, maintaining low consumer prices in the short term creates systemic tensions between producing livable wages and environmentally responsible practices. Likewise, decarbonization strategies in logistics (such as investments in electric fleets or alternative fuels) entail higher capital costs, further fraying with short-term profit expectations. However, we need to reframe these trade-offs as investments in longer-term competitiveness. Businesses that prioritise short-term profits over social or environmental standards often face reputational damage, regulatory fines, or increased susceptibility to systemic shocks. In contrast, companies that adopt triangular transformation will be able to gain competitive advantages from innovations, consumer confidence, and operational continuity. What makes it difficult for decision-makers is juggling time horizons. Quarterly profits favour quarterly profits. Quarterly earnings naturally favour profitability; the sustainability and equity agenda has its work cut out over multiple years. Companies that excel in this balancing act view sustainability and accountability not as an additional and external burden, but as a natural part of their business strategy.

6.3 Integrated Reporting Frameworks

One of the most critical mechanisms for easing tension is the use of integrated reporting frameworks that incorporate environmental, social, and governance factors into financial disclosures. There are frameworks such as the Global Reporting Initiative (GRI), the Sustainability Accounting Standards Board (SASB), the Task Force on Climate-Related Financial Disclosures (TCFD), and, more recently, the International Sustainability Standards Board (ISSB), which have established various standardised methods for measuring and disclosing sustainability performance.

They provide transparency, facilitate comparability, and accountability to stakeholders. Moreover, more importantly, they communicate that climate action, social accountability, and resilience are not externalities; they are internalities that matter to financial performance. Incorporating these non-financial metrics into annual reports helps internalise the costs of carbon emissions, labour exploitation, and supply chain fragility, thereby advancing the triangular transformation agenda.

6.4 Key Learnings from Multinational Corporations & SMEs

Firms across industries have outlined best practices for orienting the three pillars of the triangular model. However, all of these strategies are driven by scale, with multinational corporations (MNCs) leading the way by committing to science-based targets to reduce their emissions, implementing stringent supplier codes of conduct, and investing millions of dollars in digital supply chain tools. Technology companies lead the way in renewable energy transitions, whereas progress in responsible sourcing efforts has a footing in consumer goods.SMEs, although resource-challenged, are a showcase of innovation and agility. Within SMEs (small and medium-sized enterprises), we see many emerging local sourcing, collaborative platforms, and circular product models that combine community development and environmental stewardship. Because the nature of operations in SMEs differs from that in MNCs, SMEs can rely on their close relationships with local communities and suppliers to integrate social accountability more deeply into their operations. Both MNCs and SMEs demonstrate that triangular transformation is not confined to company scale, but also to commitment, spirit, and leadership.

7. CASE STUDIES

To demonstrate the use of the triangular transformation framework, insights across critical industries show where they are succeeding and where they are still struggling.

7.1 Fashion Industry: Fast Fashion vs. Sustainable Fashion

This epitome of the collision between profit, sustainability, and social accountability is found in the apparel and textile sector. Fast fashion — a consumer-driven model that relies on cheap labour and high-input production processes to churn out low-cost, quickly disposable styles — has been heavily criticised for its high carbon emissions, exploitation of cheap labour, and a linear consumption model that causes textile waste in the hundreds of thousands of tons. On the other hand, sustainable fashion initiatives welcome a triangular transformation through responsible sourcing, circular-economy practices, and community empowerment. In response to this growing concern, slow fashion companies create designs that emphasise longevity and use ethical labour and sustainable materials, such as organic cotton and recycled fibres. A few brands utilise transparency platforms that enable consumers to trace the origin of a garment, thereby holding businesses accountable. Fast fashion provides instant profits, but sustainable fashion provides sustainable profits, engendering customer loyalty and reducing the risk of reputational damage.

7.2 Electronic and Rare Earth Supply Chain

In the electronics industry, focusing on transformation is complex and fraught with trade-offs; examples abound, especially with rare earth minerals. Some examples of this equipment, funded by critical materials, include electronics and renewable energy technologies, which are often mined under exploitative conditions in politically unstable parts of the world; these include cobalt, lithium, and rare earth elements. With this comes extreme social accountability issues, such as child labour and unsafe working conditions, as well as environmental destruction. Top firms in the space have started implementing stringent due diligence frameworks, blockchain-based traceability solutions, and recycling and circularity pledges. Circular solutions (e.g., recycling rare metals embedded in electronic waste) offer avenues to address reliance on unethical supply chains and build resilience against resource scarcity. Still, the trade-offs between profitability pressures and consumer demand for affordable electronics remain significant.

7.3 Food and Agriculture: Ethical sourcing and regenerative agriculture

The triangular model illustrates synergies that are imperative within the food and agriculture sector. Industrial agriculture has been associated with greenhouse gas emissions, deforestation, and exploitative labour practices in farming, on the one hand. Meanwhile, regenerative agriculture and ethical sourcing models demonstrate how climate action, social accountability, and resilience can be effectively combined. Soil health, carbon sequestration, and resilience to climate shocks are enhanced through regenerative practices, such as crop rotation, agroforestry, and reduced chemical inputs. In return, fair trade initiatives and direct sourcing from farmers provide farming communities in developing nations with fair wages, enabling them to support their own families and communities, and foster a stronger rural economy. Incorporating climate action alongside social accountability, companies in this sector are developing supply chains that are more resilient to climate, market, and humanitarian shocks.

8. LOGISTICS AND TRANSPORTATION: DECARBONISATION AND THE WELL-BEING OF THE WORKFORCE.

The logistics and transportation sector is at the centre of global trade and subject to specific challenges for triangular transformation. Freight and aviation are among the most carbon-intensive sectors of the economy and a significant source of carbon emissions. Simultaneously, fellow trucking firms face social responsibility challenges, including the working conditions of truck drivers, port staff, and delivery workers. Solution-oriented enterprises are tackling these challenges through investments in low-carbon technologies such as Electric Vehicles, hydrogen fuels, and more efficient logistics networks. At the same time, companies are reimagining labour relations through improved worker safety, fair wages, and training in digital skills as the industry undergoes a technological transition. By implementing some of these strategies, resilience is enhanced through reduced reliance on fossil fuels, minimised labour disruptions, and improved sustainable supply chain responsiveness.

8.1 Lessons Learned: Successes and Failures

8.1.1 From the cross-industry case studies on these lessons:

Short-term profitability undermines long-term resilience. Those who would rather reduce costs than meet social or environmental standards often find themselves in the public eye, facing backlash, fines, or the risk of being unable to operate sustainably. Transparency builds trust and accountability. Companies that disclose supply chain data, adopt traceability technologies, and adhere to reporting frameworks bolster both reputational and financial resilience. Innovation aligns the stars. Innovation unlocks opportunities to resolve the tensions among climate action, accountability, and profitability, whether through digital tools, renewable energy adoption, or circular-economy models. Leadership commitment is critical. The best transformations come from effective leaders who redefine corporate objectives from shareholder value to stakeholder value. Failures reflect siloed strategies. Focusing on bolstering one side of the triangular model while ignoring the others generally results in piecemeal or unsustainable outcomes. For example, consumers may boycott carbon-neutral initiatives that lack attention to labour rights, or socially progressive initiatives that overlook economic viability may not gain the scale they need to be effective.

9. GLOBAL SUPPLY CHAINS TRIANGULAR TRANSFORMATION: POLICIES, GOVERNANCE AND FUTURE PROSPECTS

9.1. Policy, Governance, and Global Cooperation

International in nature, global supply chains encompass a multitude of legal, regulatory, and governance regimes. The combination of these factors renders policy coherence and international cooperation critical for promoting the triangular transformation of climate action, social accountability, and economic resilience. Only governments and multilateral institutions can establish the terms of the games, reward good behaviour, and punish bad behaviour.

9.2 GOVERNMENTS AND INTERNATIONAL ORGANIZATIONS

Governments — with their unique ability to craft national policies that directly influence supply chain behaviours through measures such as carbon pricing, labour standards, and renewable energy incentives — can tip the balance in this dynamic by making responsible domestic goods the more attractive option. On the international level, bodies such as the World Trade Organisation (WTO) create trade regulations that incorporate an increasing number of environmental and social aspects. UN GLOBAL COMPACT OECD GUIDELINES FOR MULTINATIONAL ENTERPRISES ILO CONVENTIONS The UN century helps build responsible business practices; OECD and ILO provide frameworks that promote (though cognising their limits) fair labour standards and social justice across national borders. The convergence of these institutions reflects a palpable understanding that neither a government nor a company can establish climate neutrality or equitable supply chains in isolation. Instead, it aligns norms, disclosure requirements, and enforcement across states and actors through collective action.

9.3 Regulatory Frameworks and Laws of Supply Chain

Over the past few years, binding regulations have been developed that require companies to address supply chain risks. The Corporate Sustainability Due Diligence Directive (CSDDD) of the European Union requires companies to recognise, prevent, and address human rights and environmental violations in their value chains. Likewise, the U.S. Uyghur Forced Labour Prevention Act (UFLPA) prohibits the importation of goods suspected of being made with forced labour in Xinjiang, embodying the move towards mandatory compliance regimes. Such legal instruments do not act only at the local level but also extraterritorially, imposing duties of care and diligence on multinational enterprises to ensure that practices across suppliers and sub-suppliers are safe. Such laws are powerful, but they also impose compliance problems. To meet the demand, companies must enhance their auditing systems, traceability mechanisms, and reporting capabilities. This, in turn, creates opportunities for digital transformation, including blockchain-based traceability, risk analysis based on artificial intelligence, and predictive modelling of supply chain vulnerabilities. Apart from the regulation side of the story, multi-stakeholder partnerships (MSPs) form an important alternative governance model. Through collaboration amongst governments, corporations, NGOs, and locals, collective impact can be scaled and systemic challenges overcome. Some examples include sustainability coalitions in the agricultural sector (e.g., the Roundtable on Sustainable Palm Oil), climate coalitions in the maritime and aviation industries, and worker-driven social responsibility initiatives. These approaches build on the idea that resource constraints can be overcome through public–private partnerships, given that governments lack the capacity to monitor compliance with standards across global value chains. In contrast, firms must necessarily meet legitimacy requirements and gain a social license to operate. Such partnerships can accelerate this potential by aligning so that climate, social, and resilience goals are integrated into collective commitments, rather than disconnected initiatives.

10. A PATHWAY TOWARDS REGENERATIVE AND JUST SUPPLY CHAINS

The discourse on sustainable development, particularly in the context of supply chain management, is evolving rapidly. Conventional approaches have concentrated on compliance and risk management — in effect, a "not harm" mindset. However, the future is shifting from sustainability to regeneration: supply chains that not only do less harm but also create value, not only in an environmental sense, but also socially.

10.1 From Sustainability to Regeneration

While carbon neutrality is achieved through a regenerative supply chain, the latter also targets carbon negativity, circularity, and the restoration of ecosystems. As a case in point, regenerative agriculture practices in food supply chains improve soil health, sequester carbon, and increase farmers' profitability, while textile companies are trialling bio-based fibres to reduce their environmental impact. These approaches shift supply chains away from extractive frameworks toward net-positive systems that restore ecosystems and enhance community well-being.

Regenerative supply chains are inherently equitable and just. Instead of being limited to labour rights, they create opportunities for empowerment, such as fair wages, gender-inclusive leadership, and value creation. This could be reflected in the early stages of the emerging concept of just transitions, which prompts the most sustainable supply chains to leave no vulnerable population behind, but rather to ensure their further elevation instead.

10.2 AI, Digital Twins, and Predictive Analytics

Transformational digital technologies will enable regenerative supply chains. Predictive analytics powered by AI can predict climate-related disruptions, simulate demand-supply uncertainty, and prescribe responsive approaches. Supply chain networks can also be simulated digitally or virtually using a replica or digital twin, enabling scenario planning to assess their resilience in response to climate, political, or market shocks and stresses. On the other hand, blockchain enhances transparency and accountability, particularly in ethical sourcing and labour rights tracing. By incorporating these technologies, supply chains can simultaneously mitigate climate risks, provide social accountability, and increase economic agility — the triangular transformation. Still, we need to be aware that digitalisation can deepen the divide if left ungoverned: between the large multinationals that have the capacity to invest in high-tech solutions and the many small suppliers who lack the resources to do so.

10.3 RECOMMENDATIONS FOR MANAGERS, POLICYMAKERS, AND ACADEMIA

For managers: Companies must develop integrated strategies that simultaneously pursue climate, social, and resilience goals. The three steps include investing in traceability tools, building supplier capacity, and integrating ESG metrics into financial decisions. Implications for policymakers: Effective regulatory frameworks can entail strict due diligence requirements that, if not carefully implemented, can burden small players and limit their access to the global market. Competitiveness and Sustainability Can Coexist: Subsidies for Renewable Adoption, Workforce Training Programs, and Carbon Border Adjustment Policies. Academia: scholars should push the frontiers of transdisciplinary research on triangular transformation, integrating environmental science, supply chain analytics, and organisational behaviour. Future research should also assess the efficacy of combining such frameworks, e.g., integrated reporting systems and digital governance of supply chains.

11. CONCLUSION

Global supply chains must embrace the triangle of climate action, social accountability, and economic resilience, a structural necessity of the 21st Century, not an aspirational agenda. The rising climate crisis, social inequities, and economic disruptions have exposed the weaknesses of traditional supply chain models, underscoring the need for integrated approaches that connect environmental and social responsibility to operational and resilience plans. In this chapter, we have described the ways theory, practice, and policy come together to enable this transformation. It highlighted the importance of sound governance, effective reporting solutions, and digital solutions as key enablers of these sustainability transitions. Simultaneously, it highlighted the need to move beyond compliance to regeneration and justice, where global supply chains serve to regenerate both people and the planet.

11.1 Takeaways for Theory, Practice, and Policy

Perspectival: The application of the triangulation transformation broadens scholarly discourse on supply chains by integrating multiple theoretical perspectives, including stakeholder theory, systems thinking, and resilience studies, into a unified conceptual framework.

Pragmatic: Integrating the climate, social, and resilience dimensions is about business sustainability, business continuity, and maintaining trust with the broader stakeholder community over the long term.

Policy: Such a measure would require global cooperation and policy harmonisation, as the risk of doing so in a fragmented manner would lead to inefficiency and uneven progress. Hold together through binding regulation—and reinforce it with incentives.

11.2 Future Research Agenda

The way forward involves further investigation of how the triangular transformation unfolds across industries and geographies. Future research should address:

- Regenerative supply chain metrics that reflect social, ecological, and economic value creation
- How AI, Blockchain, and Digital Twins Will Play as Enablers of Transparency and Resilience.
- Research on the effectiveness of due diligence legislation, reporting standards, and cross-sector initiatives

- Strategies to promote inclusive, sustainable supply chain transitions that enable participation of SMEs and marginalised communities.

The triangular transformation requires a seismic shift — from loss-making, disconnected compliance to connected, sustainable, and equitable supply chains. Realising such a transformation will not only ensure supply chains remain competitive in demanding global markets but also be a meaningful driver of positive change in both society and the environment.

REFERENCES

Anner, M. (2020). Abandoned? The impact of COVID-19 on workers and businesses at the bottom of global supply chains. Centre for Global Workers' Rights. https://globalworkers.org/

Barbieri, P., Boffelli, A., Elia, S., Fratocchi, L., Kalchschmidt, M., & Samson, D. (2020). What can we learn about reshoring in the aftermath of COVID-19? *Operations Management Research : Advancing Practice Through Research, 13*(3), 131–136. DOI: 10.1007/s12063-020-00160-1

Carroll, A. B., & Shabana, K. M. (2010). The business case for corporate social responsibility: A review of concepts, research and practice. *International Journal of Management Reviews, 12*(1), 85–105. DOI: 10.1111/j.1468-2370.2009.00275.x

Carter, C. R., & Rogers, D. S. (2008). A framework of sustainable supply chain management: Moving toward a new theory. *International Journal of Physical Distribution & Logistics Management, 38*(5), 360–387. DOI: 10.1108/09600030810882816

Christopher, M. (2016). *Logistics & supply chain management* (5th ed.). Pearson.

DiMaggio, P. J., & Powell, W. W. (1983). The iron cage revisited: Institutional isomorphism and collective rationality in organisational fields. *American Sociological Review, 48*(2), 147–160. DOI: 10.2307/2095101

Elkington, J. (1997). *Cannibals with forks: The triple bottom line of 21st century business*. Capstone.

Freeman, R. E. (1984). *Strategic management: A stakeholder approach.* Pitman.

Gereffi, G. (2018). Economic and social upgrading in global value chains and industrial clusters—Why governance matters. In Gereffi, G., Humphrey, J., & Sturgeon, T. (Eds.), *Global value chains and development: Redefining the contours of 21st century capitalism* (pp. 276–302). Cambridge University Press., DOI: 10.1017/9781108559423.011

Global Slavery Index. (2023). Global estimates of modern slavery. Walk Free Foundation. https://www.walkfree.org/global-slavery-index/

Intergovernmental Panel on Climate Change (IPCC). (2021). Climate change 2021: The physical science basis. Cambridge University Press. https://www.ipcc.ch/report/ar6/wg1/

International Energy Agency. (2022). Net zero by 2050: A roadmap for the global energy sector. https://www.iea.org/reports/net-zero-by-2050

International Labour Organisation. (n.d.). Core labour standards and ILO conventions. https://www.ilo.org/

Ivanov, D., & Dolgui, A. (2021). Ripple effect and supply chain disruption management: New trends and research directions. *International Journal of Production Research, 59*(1), 102–118. DOI: 10.1080/00207543.2021.1840148

Kleindorfer, P. R., & Saad, G. H. (2005). Managing disruption risks in supply chains. *Production and Operations Management, 14*(1), 53–68. DOI: 10.1111/j.1937-5956.2005.tb00009.x

LeBaron, G. (2020). Combatting modern slavery: Why labour governance is failing and what we can do about it. *Polity.*

Meadows, D. H. (2008). *Thinking in systems: A primer.* Chelsea Green.

Milne, M. J., & Grey, R. (2013). W(h)ither ecology? The Triple Bottom Line, the Global Reporting Initiative, and corporate sustainability reporting. *Journal of Business Ethics, 118*(1), 13–29. DOI: 10.1007/s10551-012-1543-8

OECD. (2022). *Climate finance and the USD 100 billion goal: Progress report.* Organisation for Economic Co-operation and Development.

Ponomarov, S. Y., & Holcomb, M. C. (2009). Understanding the concept of supply chain resilience. *International Journal of Logistics Management, 20*(1), 124–143. DOI: 10.1108/09574090910954873

Protocol, G. H. G. (2015). Corporate value chain (Scope 3) accounting and reporting standard. Greenhouse Gas Protocol. https://ghgprotocol.org/standards/scope-3-standard

Saberi, S., Kouhizadeh, M., Sarkis, J., & Shen, L. (2019). Blockchain technology and its relationships to sustainable supply chain management. *International Journal of Production Research, 57*(7), 2117–2135. DOI: 10.1080/00207543.2018.1533261

Sarkis, J., Zhu, Q., & Lai, K.-H. (2019). Circular economy and supply chain management: Opportunities and challenges. *Resources, Conservation and Recycling, 141*, 65–67. DOI: 10.1016/j.resconrec.2018.10.040

Seuring, S., & Müller, M. (2008). From a literature review to a conceptual framework for sustainable supply chain management. *Journal of Cleaner Production, 16*(15), 1699–1710. DOI: 10.1016/j.jclepro.2008.04.020

Sheffi, Y. (2021). The New (Ab)Normal: Reshaping business and supply chain strategy beyond [MIT Press.]. *COVID*, •••, 19.

Whelan, T., & Fink, C. (2020). The comprehensive business case for sustainability. *Harvard Business Review*.

World Economic Forum. (2022). The Global Risks Report 2022.

Chapter 2
Supply Chains and Geopolitical Tensions

Atour Taghipour
http://orcid.org/0000-0003-1687-8881
Conservatoire National des Arts et Métier, France

ABSTRACT

Geopolitical tensions increasingly affect the supply of critical raw materials, particularly lithium, cobalt, and rare earths, which are essential for electric vehicles, renewable energy, and defense technologies. China's dominance in production and processing creates vulnerabilities for global supply chains, prompting industrial companies to diversify sources, establish long-term partnerships, and invest in recycling and alternative battery technologies, such as sodium-ion and solid-state batteries. European and U.S. regulations aim to secure supply chains and promote sustainability. While innovations and vertical integration offer resilience, challenges remain due to high costs, technological constraints, and potential supply-demand imbalances. Strategic management of resources is now central to competitiveness and industrial security.

INTRODUCTION

In our constantly evolving world, strategic natural resources occupy a central position. They shape contemporary economic, technological, and geopolitical dynamics, yet their supply is not always stable. Indeed, among these resources, some are described as "rare" or "critical" due to their industrial importance and their limited, or even vulnerable, availability. These resources are not necessarily rare in

DOI: 10.4018/979-8-3373-6455-1.ch002

a geological sense; rather, their geographical and/or political accessibility is often restricted, which makes them strategic for both states and companies.

Among the most emblematic of these resources are lithium, cobalt, and rare earth elements. Lithium is a lightweight alkali metal used in the manufacture of lithium-ion batteries, which are found in electric vehicles, smartphones, laptops, and energy storage systems. Its demand has surged alongside the energy transition. Although lithium is present in several regions worldwide, it is particularly concentrated in the so-called "lithium triangle" (Argentina, Bolivia, and Chile) as well as in Australia. This metal is highly strategic due to the sharp increase in demand combined with the progressive depletion of reserves, making it especially sensitive to geopolitical developments.

Cobalt, often associated with lithium in battery production, is a metal known for its thermal and chemical stability. It is also used in aerospace alloys and medical equipment. Cobalt production is highly geographically concentrated, with over 70% originating from the Democratic Republic of Congo, where extraction conditions raise major social and environmental concerns.

Rare earth elements refer to a group of 17 chemical elements (such as neodymium, dysprosium, and terbium). They are indispensable for the production of permanent magnets, electric motors, wind turbines, electronic devices, and military technologies. China controls more than 80% of their production and refining. This dominance gives China considerable strategic power over global supply chains, a position it seeks not only to maintain but also to strengthen. Despite their name, rare earths are relatively abundant worldwide; however, their extraction is complex and highly environmentally damaging, which explains their limited availability on the market.

In addition, other critical materials such as nickel, graphite, copper, and platinum play a key role in low-carbon technologies, digital infrastructure, and advanced industrial systems. Their importance continues to grow as climate objectives and decarbonization policies advance. The scarcity of these resources on the market creates strategic dependencies among stakeholders and weakens supply chains. Industrial companies that rely on the import of rare resources, particularly in the automotive, electronics, and energy sectors, face supply disruptions and significant price volatility. They are also sometimes affected by export restrictions imposed by producing countries (Merimi & Taghipour, 2021; Pour Mohammadi et al., 2014).

These geopolitical tensions are driving states to increasingly secure their supplies of critical materials, sometimes by reinforcing export controls. Rare resources are therefore no longer merely raw materials; they have become instruments of power that are reshaping global power relations. In this context, companies must adapt their purchasing strategies to cope with instability or, at the very least, mitigate its effects (Taghipour et al., 2022a).

The rise in geopolitical tensions surrounding rare resources thus raises a central question:

How do these tensions influence the purchasing strategies of industrial companies?

In other words, to what extent are companies compelled to rethink their sourcing policies, partnerships, supplier selection methods (Mahfod et al., 2019), and risk management tools in order to ensure production continuity while remaining competitive?

This issue is part of a broader reflection on state economic sovereignty and the sustainability of supply models (Lu & Taghipour, 2023). It also highlights the strategic role of the purchasing function, which is often perceived as operational but is increasingly becoming a key management lever in the face of geopolitical uncertainty.

The objective of this thesis is therefore to analyze the geopolitical challenges associated with rare resources, highlighting the tensions and their impact on international power relations. In the context of the energy transition and the development of new technologies, resources such as lithium, cobalt, and rare earth elements have become even more critical and strategic for states. Competition for their control is intensifying, particularly in regions such as the Democratic Republic of Congo and South America, where a significant share of these resources is concentrated and where many states seek to benefit from their exploitation.

After presenting the geopolitical tensions, this study will examine their impact on supply chains. The risks associated with dependence on specific producing countries and the potential breaking points within supply chains will be identified in order to better understand the economic consequences for companies and, by extension, for states. This analysis will highlight the fragility of rare material supply, which can destabilize the production of many technological and strategic goods.

In response to these challenges, companies are deploying various strategies with varying degrees of effectiveness. These include diversifying supply sources, implementing risk management frameworks, investing in technological innovation, and adopting more sustainable practices. The second part of this thesis will therefore examine these strategies, their objectives, and their limitations.

Finally, these dynamics will be explored through a specific case study: lithium. As a key resource for the automotive industry in the production of electric vehicle batteries, lithium will be analyzed in the context of the energy transition and the phase-out of internal combustion engines. This case study will examine the current and future challenges faced by automotive manufacturers, the strategies they implement to address them, and the potential future outlook (Ponputtha et al., 2021).

This thesis intersects several disciplines: geopolitics, economics, purchasing management, and sustainable development. It aims to explain how companies adapt to an uncertain global environment by mobilizing strategic tools and integrating geopolitical considerations into their operational decisions. Moreover, the topic is highly relevant in today's context, marked by the war in Ukraine, rising Sino-American tensions, industrial reshoring policies, and debates over technological sovereignty, particularly within the European Union, whose global influence is increasingly under pressure.

The research is based on a documentary analysis drawing on a wide range of sources, including institutional reports (European Commission, OECD, IEA), academic articles, specialized publications, data from international organizations, and press articles relying on recognized sources. It also incorporates sectoral case studies to illustrate the challenges and strategic responses of states and their companies.

I. RARE RESOURCES AS A LEVER OF GEOPOLITICAL POWER

In this first part, we will examine how rare resources can serve as a lever of geopolitical power. This analysis will begin by exploring the geographical factors that enable such leverage, followed by an examination of the conflicts that lead to the strategic use of these resources.

A. Geographical Concentration

Rare resources are primarily defined as such because of their geographical concentration. The geological conditions required for the formation of these resources are generally highly specific, which limits their occurrence to certain regions of the world. As a result, some countries possess significant quantities of rare resources, while others are almost entirely deprived of them.

This unequal distribution of strategic natural resources is not a new phenomenon. Oil and natural gas also follow this logic, albeit to a lesser extent. Certain countries have long possessed substantial oil reserves, particularly those in the Middle East (such as Saudi Arabia, Iraq, and Kuwait), as well as Venezuela, Russia, the United States, and Canada. Other regions, including Western Europe and China, have historically depended on imports to secure their energy supplies.

The situation is even more uneven when it comes to natural gas. Global exports are dominated by a small number of countries, notably the United States, Australia, and Qatar, which together accounted for approximately 60% of global exports in 2023. Russia is also a major exporter of natural gas; however, the war in Ukraine has prompted Western European countries to reduce their dependence on Russian gas and increasingly turn to suppliers such as Norway and the United States.

Nevertheless, although oil and gas reserves are unevenly distributed, these resources remained relatively abundant throughout much of the 20th century, except during periods of crisis, due to the existence of a sufficient number of exporting countries spread across multiple continents. In contrast, the distribution of rare metals is far more concentrated. The production of certain critical resources is sometimes ensured by only a handful of countries, or even by a single dominant producer.

By way of example, the Democratic Republic of Congo (DRC) alone accounts for nearly 60% of global cobalt production, a metal that is essential for the manufacture of lithium-ion batteries, as previously mentioned.

Most cobalt deposits are located in the southeastern part of the country, in the Katanga region. This area is now divided into several provinces, such as Haut-Katanga and Lualaba, whose subsoil is particularly rich in cobalt and copper, which are often extracted together. While Katanga is exceptionally rich in mineral resources, it is also characterized by chronic political instability. Mining governance in the region is frequently opaque, and social tensions regularly emerge. Large multinational mining companies operate alongside thousands of artisanal miners who work under extremely precarious conditions.

This coexistence of industrial and artisanal mining complicates cobalt traceability and raises major ethical concerns. Indeed, non-governmental organizations and governmental institutions regularly report issues related to child labor, the lack of safety standards, making working conditions particularly dangerous, environmental damage (notably soil and water pollution), and local corruption. Beyond the moral concerns surrounding such supply chains, these factors also generate logistical risks (Taghipour, 2023). As a result, many companies are becoming increasingly demanding in their supplier selection criteria and are investing in certification schemes and traceability programs (Taghipour et al., 2015).

The extreme concentration of cobalt production illustrates the unequal distribution of rare metal deposits and grants the DRC a strategic position in the global market. However, although the country possesses vast reserves, control over the resources extracted from its territory is far less certain. The cobalt value chain is heavily influenced by Chinese capital. According to *The New York Times*, 15 of the 19 industrial cobalt-producing mines in the DRC were owned or financed by Chinese companies in 2020, and approximately two-thirds of global cobalt processing takes place in China.

For consumer countries, this situation creates a dual dependency: a geographical dependency, as cobalt is found almost exclusively in the DRC, and an economic dependency, as China controls a large share of mining assets and downstream processing. Thus, geographical concentration can be compounded by economic concentration, further increasing the vulnerability of supply chains for consumer nations.

Regarding rare earth elements, China holds a near-monopoly. As explained in the introduction, China is not the only country endowed with rare earth deposits; however, it is the only one to have implemented a long-term industrial and geopolitical strategy, which it has pursued consistently for several decades. Other countries, such as the United States, Australia, Brazil, and India, also possess exploitable reserves, but China has invested massively in the extraction, refining, and processing of rare earth elements. Moreover, China has deliberately chosen to tolerate the significant environmental damage caused by rare earth mining.

China currently controls approximately 69% of global rare earth production, according to *Polytechnique Insights*, and, more importantly, between 85% and 90% of global processing capacity, according to the International Energy Agency. Processing is a critical stage in the value chain, as once extracted, rare earth elements must be separated, purified, and transformed into oxides or alloys before they can be used in industrial applications. Thanks to its powerful industrial infrastructure and targeted subsidy policies, Beijing is present throughout the entire value chain, from extraction and processing to the manufacture of complex end products.

This extensive control grants China considerable strategic power. It can influence global rare earth prices, restrict exports to favor its domestic industries, and even condition access to these materials on political or diplomatic considerations. In 2010, following a dispute with Japan over the Senkaku Islands, China temporarily suspended its rare earth exports to Japan. This decision triggered a sharp rise in prices and led to global awareness of China's dominance over rare earth supply chains and the risks associated with such dependence.

More recently, in the context of trade tensions with the United States and the threat of extreme tariffs proposed under the Trump administration, China has threatened to restrict access to certain strategic metals, such as neodymium and dysprosium, which are essential for military technologies and electric vehicles. This situation clearly demonstrates how geographical concentration, especially when combined with industrial concentration, can become a powerful geopolitical lever.

Consumer countries are thus placed in a position of strategic dependence, forcing them either to accept this vulnerability or to seek alternatives. These alternatives may include reshoring certain stages of production or developing technological substitutes. However, such efforts require substantial time and investment, and the environmental costs associated with rare earth extraction deter many countries. For these reasons, China's dominance in this sector remains difficult to challenge in the short term.

Argentina, Bolivia, and Chile form what is commonly referred to as the "Lithium Triangle." Together, they hold more than half of the world's lithium reserves. In the context of the energy transition, these reserves grant them a highly strategic position. Lithium is indeed a key component in the production of batteries for electric vehicles, energy storage systems, and a wide range of electronic devices.

With its vast salt flats, most notably the Atacama Desert, Chile is one of the world's leading lithium producers. The country has a well-established industry, supported by developed extraction and export infrastructures. Argentina has not yet reached this level of industrial maturity but is experiencing rapid growth in its production capacity, attracting significant foreign investment (Zoghlami et al., 2016). Bolivia, despite possessing the world's largest lithium reserves in the Salar de Uyuni, remains behind in terms of industrial production. This is largely due to its political choice to develop a national lithium industry and maintain strong state control over production.

This geographical concentration has attracted the attention of major economic powers seeking to establish strategic partnerships with the countries of the Lithium Triangle. The United States, China, and the European Union have signed bilateral agreements and made direct investments to secure access to South American lithium. Thus, even in regions without open conflict, tensions emerge as a result of international competition for resource acquisition, a topic that will be addressed further in this study.

The geographical concentration of rare resources is a decisive factor in their strategic importance, particularly in the case of cobalt in the Democratic Republic of Congo and lithium in the South American Lithium Triangle. The unequal distribution of deposits and processing capacities shapes global power relations. As previously noted, this phenomenon already existed in the context of fossil fuels but has become more pronounced with rare metals.

Beyond their economic value, these resources have become instruments of power. States that control their extraction or processing can use them as levers of influence, or even pressure, within a global environment characterized by technological competition and the energy transition. This geopolitical reality lies at the heart of current international tensions, which will be analyzed in the following subsection.

B. Current Geopolitical Tensions

To continue contextualizing how rare resources serve as a lever of geopolitical power, we will now examine the tensions caused by these resources and the conflicts that arise in extraction regions.

With the energy transition, demand for rare minerals has increased dramatically, and there is no indication that this trend will slow down. According to the World Bank (*Minerals for Climate Action: The Mineral Intensity of the Clean Energy Transition*), demand for rare metals could rise by 500% by 2050. These estimates are based on the materials needed to deploy wind, solar, and geothermal energy in line with the goal of limiting global temperature rise to less than 2°C. The widespread adoption of electric vehicles is also a major factor driving lithium demand.

This surge in demand has influenced global geopolitical balances, strengthening the power of countries that possess rare metals, particularly China, which anticipated this trend. As mentioned earlier, China has not hesitated to use its dominance over the rare earth sector as a geopolitical lever. On December 3, 2024, China announced a ban on exports of several strategic materials, including gallium, germanium, and antimony, to the United States. This move followed U.S. restrictions on the export of electronic chips to Chinese companies. The Trump administration, continuing the policies of its predecessor Joe Biden, sought to limit China's development in the field of artificial intelligence.

The Sino-American rivalry also extends to the industrial use of minerals. In 2022, the United States implemented the Inflation Reduction Act, linking tax benefits to the origin of minerals used in batteries and components. The goal is to reshore supply chains or secure sourcing from allied countries. This strategy, intended to limit China's dominance, has naturally been met with opposition from Beijing.

Leveraging its extensive network of investments in Africa and South America through the "Belt and Road Initiative" and joint ventures, China maintains a dominant position in lithium, cobalt, and graphite, materials essential for the energy transition. This control enables China to influence prices and delivery timelines, for example, in response to U.S. actions. This rivalry therefore translates into a competition for influence in Africa (DRC, Zambia), South America (the Lithium Triangle), and Southeast Asia. The United States, sometimes together with Western allies, seeks to counter China's lead by expanding mining partnerships, financing projects, and imposing traceability and compliance standards. These standards, which exclude "non-aligned" metals from subsidized markets, generate commercial tensions with producing countries, which often resist what they perceive as overly restrictive conditions.

In the DRC, which accounts for over 70% of global cobalt production, the proliferation of actors, multinationals, cooperatives, and informal miners, creates a tense environment marked by violence, extortion, and other illegal practices. Human rights violations and lack of traceability are regularly reported, while national decisions, such as temporary embargoes or sector reforms, generate disputes with buyers.

In the Lithium Triangle (Chile, Argentina, Bolivia), conflicts arise over water management and the rights of local communities. Policies of partial nationalization and contract renegotiation create tensions with investors and consumer states. As for rare earths, extraction in China, Myanmar, or Madagascar causes pollution and environmental damage, as well as expropriations and corruption. The segmentation of the supply chain (illegal extraction, offshored refining) maintains opacity and fuels tensions.

The competition for influence between China and Western countries often takes the form of a normative clash: Western countries emphasize due diligence and respect for human rights, "Due diligence in human rights means that a business should take all necessary, adequate, and effective measures to identify and assess its actual and potential negative impacts on human rights throughout its value chain; prevent, mitigate, or cease these impacts; monitor and assess the effectiveness of the measures it has taken; and be accountable to the public. Companies must also be required to remedy any harms caused." (*UN Guiding Principles on Business and Human Rights*), while Beijing prioritizes infrastructure development and a policy of non-interference.

At the same time, an increasing number of producing countries are adopting "resource nationalism" policies, tightening their regimes through licenses, quotas, or local processing requirements. The goal is to capture more value-added and strengthen their bargaining power. For importing countries, this often leads to disagreements over volumes, delivery times, and contractual conditions, sometimes escalating to legal or political conflicts. Moreover, some producing countries accuse Western consumer countries of double standards, demanding ethical and environmentally friendly production without providing the necessary financial support to achieve it.

This global situation fuels a cycle of retaliation: producing countries implement export controls, while consuming countries prioritize locally sourced resources or those obtained from allied nations. At each stage, the margin of political uncertainty grows. Critical metals are also at the heart of a strategic struggle between technology, the energy transition, and defense. Rare earth magnets, cobalt and nickel alloys, components containing gallium or germanium, much of the world's military and technological systems rely on materials partially controlled by China. Beijing has not hesitated to wield the threat of export restrictions, while Western countries tighten their own technological levers, particularly in semiconductors and software. Each announcement of controls or embargoes shifts market expectations and widens diplomatic fractures, especially in the context of global rearmament, particularly in Europe due to the war in Ukraine, where dependence on a perceived adversary is undesirable.

Ultimately, critical metals and minerals have become sources of tension. They are integrated into strategies of sanctions and counter-sanctions and exacerbate local conflicts in extraction zones. Rare metals have not created rivalries, but they make them more visible and do little to promote de-escalation. Their growing importance will undoubtedly continue to strain trade relations between major powers, already challenged in a context of increasing skepticism toward free trade, especially since the return of Donald Trump to the U.S. presidency.

C. Impact on Supply Chains

After discussing the various tensions related to rare resources, it is important to assess their impact on the supply chains of industrial companies. The impact on global supply chains is considerable, affecting resource availability, the stability of logistical flows, and cost management. Supply chains, historically designed to optimize costs and reduce lead times, are now increasingly fragile due to excessive dependence on a few producing countries and political decisions beyond the control of companies.

The first major consequence is the proliferation of supply disruptions. For example, when China announced the ban on exporting gallium and germanium to the United States, semiconductor and electronics manufacturers experienced several months of delivery delays (*OECD, 2024*). This situation is particularly critical given that China controls approximately 70% of global rare earth production and nearly 99% of their processing (*International Energy Agency, 2023*), severely limiting viable alternatives. This concentration creates a bottleneck: even if deposits exist elsewhere, the processing capacity remains largely in China, making supply chains extremely vulnerable to Chinese political decisions. These measures are becoming increasingly restrictive as China seeks to allocate more of its production to domestic consumption to maximize its technological competitiveness.

Price instability, often upward, is another consequence of this geopolitical context. Between 2021 and 2023, the price of lithium increased sixfold before stabilizing, reaching $26,000 per ton in 2024 (*Benchmark Mineral Intelligence, 2024*). Cobalt rose by 40% in 2025, reaching $35,000 per ton, directly due to restrictions imposed by the Democratic Republic of Congo (*USGS, 2025*). For rare earths, the price of neodymium oxide (used in permanent magnets) surpassed €67,000 per ton in 2025 (*Roskill, 2025*). These price fluctuations exert increasing pressure on industries heavily dependent on these resources, particularly the automotive and electronics sectors, which must either absorb these additional costs or pass them on to consumers.

This instability affects entire value chains. For example, automakers see the cost of electric vehicle batteries remain highly sensitive to fluctuations in raw material prices. In 2024, the average battery price was $115 per kWh, down from $144 in 2023; however, this structural decrease, mainly due to technological innovation and falling lithium prices following the 2022 surge, masks persistent tensions linked to the volatility of critical metals (*BloombergNEF*). For electronics manufacturers, rising costs of strategic components reduce profit margins and slow production rates. Some companies have even had to temporarily suspend production lines due to component shortages, as observed in the European automotive industry in 2023 (*ACEA*).

Geopolitical tensions also complicate logistics. Economic sanctions, export restrictions, and armed conflicts force companies to reroute supply chains, increasing lead times and transportation costs. For instance, the war in Ukraine disrupted nickel and palladium flows, used in batteries and catalysts, causing delays in vehicle and industrial equipment production (*IEA, 2023*). According to a study by the Boston Consulting Group, nearly 30% of critical mineral trade flows could be disrupted by geopolitical tensions by 2035, highlighting the growing intensity of these risks.

In conclusion, geopolitical tensions threaten the stability of supply chains, frequently causing disruptions, increasing costs, and creating a constant state of uncertainty. This situation undermines the competitiveness of companies and challenges the globalized model that has dominated the past decades.

II. REDEFINING PURCHASING STRATEGIES IN RESPONSE TO GEOPOLITICAL INSTABILITY

Having examined the various geopolitical tensions affecting the supply of rare materials, we will now explore how industrial companies manage these risks and the changes they have made to their purchasing strategies.

A. Diversification and Securing of Sources

In response to these risks, companies primarily adopt strategies to diversify their supply sources. Multi-sourcing, obtaining a given resource from multiple suppliers, reduces dependence on any single actor. While this approach can incur additional costs, it provides greater adaptability in the event of supply disruptions.

Some companies go further by partially relocating their production or procurement through "nearshoring" or "friendshoring" strategies (Taghipour et al., 2022b). Nearshoring involves bringing production sites closer to end markets, thereby reducing logistical and political risks. Friendshoring, on the other hand, prioritizes sourcing from allied or politically stable countries to secure supply flows in a divided international environment. For example, the United States has strengthened partnerships with Canada and Australia for lithium and rare earth supplies as part of its strategy to secure critical supply chains.

Another response to geopolitical instability is the establishment of strategic stockpiles. Historically associated with oil reserves, this practice is now being extended to critical metals. The European Union has launched initiatives to create reserves of essential raw materials, while Japan has long maintained national stockpiles of tungsten and rare earths. Private companies, particularly in the defense and automotive sectors, have also begun to stockpile certain materials.

However, this strategy has its limitations. Storage costs can be prohibitive, materials can become technologically obsolete, and tying up capital in reserves affects cash flow. Additionally, some producing countries, such as China, impose export restrictions that make it difficult to establish stockpiles outside their territory. In 2021, China tightened control over rare earth exports, effectively preventing the creation of strategic reserves in certain Western countries. This measure was a direct response to consumer countries' attempts to build reserves as a safeguard against Chinese political decisions.

The adoption of long-term partnerships with suppliers is also a way for companies to secure their supply by providing stability. These partnerships are no longer limited to conventional transactional agreements; they have become instruments of strategic security. They now include clauses ensuring stability in volumes, prices, and contract duration, as well as compliance with regulatory requirements and adherence to ESG standards. In a context where public policies are evolving rapidly, such as Europe's *Critical Raw Materials Act* or the United States' *Inflation Reduction Act*, these clauses help companies mitigate the risks of supply disruptions, sanctions, or sudden cost increases resulting from regulatory changes. They also provide better budgetary visibility and facilitate medium- to long-term industrial planning (Taghipour & Frayret, 2011).

Beyond these contractual partnerships, a deeper trend is emerging: vertical integration. This strategy involves internalizing all or part of the supply chain by directly investing in production, extraction, or processing assets. It serves a dual purpose: securing access to critical materials and strengthening control over production conditions, particularly regarding environmental and social standards.

Tesla exemplifies this approach with remarkable strategic clarity. Aware of its dependence on lithium, the company has signed direct supply agreements with producers in Australia and Chile, countries with abundant reserves and relatively stable regulatory frameworks. Refusing to remain solely a consumer, the American company has also invested in mining projects, financed refining infrastructure, and collaborated with startups specializing in sustainable extraction. This strategy allows Tesla not only to secure its supply flows but also to meet growing demands for traceability and ESG compliance, while reducing its exposure to often volatile and speculative intermediary markets.

Stellantis, another major player in the automotive industry, follows a similar trajectory. As part of its electrification strategy, the group has formed partnerships with Canadian mining companies to secure supplies of nickel and cobalt, two metals essential for the production of high-performance batteries. The choice of Canada is deliberate: it is an allied, politically stable country with an industrial policy supportive of the energy transition and high environmental standards. By investing in mining projects or participating in joint ventures, Stellantis strengthens its industrial sovereignty, reduces dependence on high-risk regions such as the DRC, and enhances its ability to comply with European regulatory requirements regarding sustainability and transparency.

These strategies offer several advantages. First, they help stabilize commercial relationships in an uncertain environment by reducing dependence on spot markets and intermediaries. Second, they provide better cost control by limiting fluctuations caused by speculation or geopolitical tensions. They also facilitate the implementation of ambitious CSR policies, allowing companies to select partners based on ethical, environmental, and social criteria (Taghipour et al., 2022c). Finally, they enhance supply chain resilience, ensuring continuity of supply even during international crises.

However, these strategies are not without challenges. Vertical integration requires substantial investment, long implementation timelines, and direct exposure to operational and geopolitical risks. It demands technical, legal, and financial expertise that not all companies possess. Furthermore, in certain producing countries, access to resources is subject to strict conditions, requirements for co-development with local actors, or even resource nationalization policies. Social acceptability of mining projects must also be considered, as they can trigger local opposition, conflicts over land use, or environmental controversies (Taghipour, 2020).

B. Integrating Geopolitical Risk Management into the Purchasing Function

In the context of instability in the rare resources market, the purchasing function can no longer rely on a purely reactive approach. It must integrate geopolitical risk management as a fully strategic component. This begins with a rigorous risk mapping, based on the analysis of politically unstable regions, economic sanctions regimes, diplomatic tensions, and resource nationalism policies. Such mapping allows companies to identify critical points in supply flows by cross-referencing geopolitical data with operational indicators, such as dependency on a single supplier or the criticality of a material. Tools like criticality matrices, geopolitical dashboards, and country stability indices are used to make this analysis objective. For example, the *Global Risk Index* developed by Verisk Maplecroft is employed by many multinational companies to anticipate risks related to the extraction and transport of raw materials.

However, mapping alone is not sufficient. It must be accompanied by continuous strategic monitoring. Companies need to track changes in international sanctions, embargoes, environmental and social standards, and national industrial policies. The implementation of the U.S. *Inflation Reduction Act* or Europe's *Critical Raw Materials Act*, which aims to secure access to critical resources, are examples of measures with a direct impact on purchasing strategies. Anticipating such developments allows companies to adjust partnerships or develop alternatives before constraints become binding. This monitoring relies on a variety of sources: government publications, reports from international organizations, expert analyses, and digital tools integrated into purchasing information systems (Cauchois et al., 2017).

Geopolitical risk management also requires the establishment of continuity plans and crisis scenarios. These plans must consider potential supply disruptions caused by armed conflict, diplomatic crises, natural disasters, or unilateral political decisions. The scenarios developed include fallback solutions, such as alternative suppliers, material substitution, or the reorganization of logistics flows. For instance, some companies in the electronics sector have developed alternatives to rare earths in the event of Chinese export restrictions by investing in synthetic materials or enhancing recycling capacities. These scenarios must be tested, regularly updated, and integrated into the company's decision-making processes.

For risk management to be effective, it must rely on appropriate governance. The purchasing function cannot act alone; it must collaborate closely with supply chain, legal, compliance, CSR, and executive management departments. This collaboration allows expertise to be combined, priorities to be aligned, and rapid responses in case of crisis. Some companies have established dedicated geopolitical risk task forces capable of mobilizing resources within hours. Others have created strategic steering committees tasked with monitoring geopolitical developments and guiding investment decisions. This governance is based on a shared risk culture that values transparency, responsiveness, and anticipation.

Finally, geopolitical risk management should not be seen solely as a constraint. It can become a lever of performance and differentiation. Companies capable of anticipating tensions, securing their supply flows, and demonstrating resilience are better positioned in the market. They inspire confidence among clients, partners, and investors. They can also highlight their commitment to corporate social responsibility by demonstrating awareness of ethical, environmental, and social issues associated with their sourcing. In an uncertain world, the ability to manage geopolitical risks becomes a strategic competency, on par with innovation or cost management.

C. Innovation and Sustainability as Adaptation Levers

In an environment characterized by market volatility and rising geopolitical tensions, innovation and sustainability are no longer merely assets, they are strategic responses to supply challenges. Companies facing increasing scarcity of certain resources and regulatory pressure invest in technological and organizational solutions capable of reducing their dependence on critical materials.

One of the most promising approaches is the substitution of critical materials with more accessible or geopolitically less sensitive alternatives. In the battery sector, for example, several manufacturers are developing cobalt-free technologies, given the ethical and geopolitical challenges associated with cobalt extraction. Lithium iron phosphate (LFP) batteries are now produced on a large scale, notably by Chinese companies such as CATL, but also by Western manufacturers seeking to diversify their sources. Similarly, in the field of permanent magnets used in electric motors and wind turbines, research is being conducted to replace rare earths with ferritic alloys or composite materials, thereby reducing dependence on China.

Recycling and the circular economy represent another avenue for adaptation. Rather than relying exclusively on primary extraction, companies are seeking to recover metals from end-of-life products. This approach creates closed loops in which resources are reused, reducing pressure on natural deposits and mitigating risks associated with their geographic concentration.

In the automotive sector, several manufacturers have launched programs to recover used batteries in order to extract lithium, nickel, and cobalt. Renault, for example, has developed a partnership with Veolia and Solvay to recycle strategic metals contained in its electric vehicles. However, this strategy faces significant challenges: recycling technologies remain costly, material traceability is complex, and the volumes recycled are relatively small compared to demand.

To overcome these obstacles, companies are investing in traceability and transparency technologies. Blockchain, in particular, allows for the certification of material origins, tracking throughout the entire value chain, and ensuring compliance with ESG standards. This technology is employed in the mining sector to guarantee that extracted metals do not come from conflict zones or areas with frequent human rights violations. In addition, artificial intelligence enables the analysis of massive datasets to detect anomalies, anticipate disruptions, and optimize logistics flows. These tools help companies meet the increasing expectations of regulators, particularly in the EU, where the Due Diligence Directive requires businesses to demonstrate responsibility across their entire supply chain. They also help build trust with customers and investors, who are increasingly sensitive to sustainability and ethical concerns.

Alignment with corporate social responsibility (CSR) objectives thus becomes a strategic lever. Regulatory constraints can be transformed into opportunities for differentiation. Companies that integrate sustainability into their purchasing strategy can highlight their commitment to clients and employees, enhance their brand image, and access more favorable financing. Some even incorporate ESG criteria into their procurement processes, selecting suppliers not only based on price and quality but also on environmental and social performance.

This evolution reflects the deepening importance of the purchasing function, which is no longer limited to transactional logic but becomes a key player in the company's overall strategy. In this new system, innovation and sustainability are not merely reactive responses to a geopolitical crisis; they constitute the foundations of structural resilience. By investing in research, developing technological partnerships, and rethinking business models, companies can build supply chains that are stronger, more ethical, and more competitive.

Although demanding, this transformation is essential to meet the challenges of the 21st century, where resource scarcity, geopolitical tensions, and environmental concerns converge to redefine the rules of global trade.

III. CASE STUDY AND FUTURE PERSPECTIVES: LITHIUM IN THE AUTOMOTIVE INDUSTRY

Lithium has become one of the most strategically important metals of our time. Its central role in electric vehicle (EV) batteries makes it indispensable for the energy transition and the decarbonization of transport. Reducing greenhouse gas emissions is one of humanity's greatest current challenges. The internal combustion engine car, once the emblematic mode of transport for all developed economies, is reaching the end of its lifecycle. The preferred alternative for several years has been the electric vehicle, which technological advances have made more versatile and increasingly accessible. Beyond the climate imperative, the depletion of oil reserves adds further incentive for major economies and automotive groups to prioritize electric mobility.

The rise of electric vehicles, driven by environmental policies and public demand, has caused a surge in global lithium demand. According to the World Bank, this demand could increase fivefold by 2050, illustrating the scale of transformation underway in the automotive industry. The chart above (Statista, Stormcrow data, 2023) shows global lithium demand for batteries from 2017 to 2022, with projections from 2023 to 2025. It distinguishes between lithium used in rechargeable and non-rechargeable batteries. The chart highlights a spectacular growth in rechargeable battery usage, which accounts for the majority of consumption. Between 2017 and 2025, demand for rechargeable batteries is expected to grow by more than 128%, compared with just 21% for non-rechargeable batteries. This trend reflects the direct impact of the expansion of electric vehicles, which drive the majority of the increase.

Analysis of growth patterns reveals several phases. Between 2017 and 2020, growth was steady, with an average annual increase of approximately 12,000 tonnes of lithium carbonate equivalent (LCE). From 2020 onward, growth accelerated, particularly in 2021, coinciding with the post-pandemic recovery in EV sales. A slight slowdown occurred in 2022, likely due to inventory adjustments and price corrections following the 2021–2022 surge. The forecasted period from 2023 to 2025 indicates a renewed acceleration, with an estimated increase of more than 15% between 2024 and 2025, reflecting continued electrification of the global vehicle fleet.

Another Statista chart (2022) illustrates global lithium demand (in thousands of tonnes) between 2019 and 2022, with projections to 2030. These figures encompass total global lithium demand, not limited to batteries. In 2019, demand was around 263,000 tonnes LCE. By 2022, it had reached 559,000 tonnes, more than double in just three years, and is projected to reach one million tonnes by 2025. By 2030, demand is expected to exceed 2.1 million tonnes, an eightfold increase from 2019. This growth is non-linear, accelerating sharply from 2021 onward, coinciding with exponential EV sales. Between 2025 and 2030, demand is projected to increase by over one million tonnes in five years, representing an average annual growth of more than 15%. This trend confirms that lithium demand is unlikely to stabilize in the short term and will continue to rise due to the combined effects of vehicle electrification, charging infrastructure development, and stationary energy storage. These projections align with the International Energy Agency, which anticipates a fivefold increase in lithium demand by 2040, and the World Bank, which predicts similar growth by 2050.

Lithium also follows basic economic principles: rising demand naturally drives up prices, impacting the automotive industry's costs. The third Statista chart, based on Investing.com and U.S. Geological Survey (USGS) data, shows the price evolution of one tonne of lithium carbonate in China between 2018 and 2022 (Atlasocio, 2019).

Between January 2018 and October 2022, the average monthly price of one tonne of lithium carbonate traded in China rose from approximately €13,000 to nearly €80,000, more than a sixfold increase in less than five years. This dramatic surge began in 2021, in direct correlation with the acceleration of global demand. Global lithium consumption, which was 70,000 tonnes in 2020, reached 93,000 tonnes in 2021, according to USGS data. This more than 30% increase in a single year illustrates growing market pressure and partly explains the steep price increases observed during the same period. Once relatively stable, the lithium market is now subject to tension driven primarily by the automotive sector and, more broadly, by the "electrification" of lifestyles.

The imbalance between still-limited supply and rapidly growing demand is expected to intensify in the coming years. If demand doubled between 2019 and 2022, it is projected to quadruple by 2030. In this context, lithium prices could remain high or even continue rising unless technological innovations or substantial investments in extraction and recycling balance the market. Current projections suggest that demand could exceed production capacity as early as the mid-2020s, placing sustained pressure on supply chains. This tension is compounded by the long lead times for mining projects, which often require over ten years from discovery to operation. Moreover, lithium recycling, although developing, remains insufficient to offset the supply deficit. Industrial players and governments will therefore need to anticipate these imbalances to avoid a critical shortage of this key material.

Finally, usage mapping indicates that electric vehicles will absorb the majority of lithium demand, making the automotive sector particularly vulnerable to market fluctuations.

We can observe above the projections for the intersection of lithium supply and demand in the coming years. This Benchmark Minerals chart illustrates the evolution of global lithium demand relative to the various categories of projected supply through 2040. The red curve, representing demand, shows steady and marked growth, quickly surpassing current production capacities. The blue bars indicate operational supply, that is, volumes already extracted or currently in production. As time progresses, this supply remains insufficient to meet growing demand.

Gray, yellow, and orange bars complete the chart, representing highly probable, probable, and possible projects that could augment supply if investments materialize. However, even when combined, a deficit persists. Recycling, represented by a thin dark bar at the top of the columns, remains marginal and cannot compensate for the shortfall. According to these data, lithium scarcity is expected to begin around 2028, a very near-term horizon for economic predictions. Moreover, this assessment assumes that all "probable" lithium sources will be developed, leaving only unidentified sources as a margin of flexibility.

This means that any disruption, whether geopolitical or environmental, could exacerbate the imbalance between supply and demand. At this stage, the market relies on optimistic assumptions regarding the realization of still-uncertain projects, making forecasts particularly sensitive to unforeseen events. This raises key questions: how are major automotive groups responding to this situation, what measures are they taking to mitigate the risk of a global lithium shortage, and what are the prospects for the future?

First, it is relevant to examine the lithium supply agreements signed by automakers with producing companies, particularly focusing on the countries of origin of these suppliers. This chart represents recent agreements signed by major automotive groups for their lithium supply. Most of the agreements shown here concern flows starting in 2026 and therefore reflect the companies' most recent strategies. It highlights the average annual volumes of chemical lithium that some automakers have committed to securing through supply contracts or strategic partnerships.

We can observe that Ford stands out with approximately 20,000 tons per year, primarily through a major agreement with Albemarle, supplemented by partnerships with Nemaska in Canada and SQM in Chile. Stellantis follows with a commitment of 16,000 to 19,000 tons per year via Vulcan Energy in Germany, alongside a strategic investment of €50 million. Mercedes-Benz has secured around 10,000 tons per year from Rock Tech Lithium, which plans a conversion facility in Germany. Renault and Toyota (through the PPES joint venture) have more modest volumes, around 4,000 to 5,000 tons per year, yet these agreements still reflect a clear intent to secure their supply chain. BMW, although having signed a significant contract with Livent, does not appear on the chart due to undisclosed volumes.

This chart also reflects the logic of friendshoring and nearshoring. Automakers appear to aim to secure supply through agreements with geographically close countries (Canada for the American company Ford), politically allied countries (Renault with Germany, an EU member and France's primary economic partner), or even within their own country (Mercedes in Germany).

These commitments indicate a profound shift in automakers' strategies. They are no longer content with merely buying batteries; they seek to control access to the raw material itself. Most deliveries are planned from 2026 onward, highlighting the dependence on the success of mining projects and conversion facilities. Europe, and Germany in particular, aims to establish itself as a strategic zone, not for extraction, but for low-carbon lithium processing and production. This chart thus illustrates the rise of vertical integration in a sector where securing resources has become a critical competitive factor.

Another automotive giant, Tesla, has also opted for vertical integration through its "gigafactories." At Tesla, a gigafactory refers to a large-scale industrial facility designed to mass-produce essential components, particularly lithium batteries. Tesla currently operates five gigafactories, with a sixth planned in Mexico, and aims to develop a network of 10 to 12 gigafactories in the coming years. These new plants offer multiple advantages: they centralize production, allowing for complete battery assembly in a single location, which reduces costs and, more importantly, provides better production control by internalizing tasks previously outsourced to suppliers (Glaa et al., 2014).

Moreover, Tesla's strategy involves locating gigafactories across different countries and continents. This choice maximizes supply alternatives by being geographically close to various lithium extraction and processing sites (and other critical metals necessary for their operations). This geographical distribution mitigates risks in the event of geopolitical crises in one or more regions and also provides protection against certain political decisions, particularly export restrictions. For example, Tesla's gigafactory in China allows the American company to circumvent export restrictions imposed by Beijing, as the plant is located within the country itself.

However, these industrial facilities represent colossal investments and therefore require equally significant returns to be viable, a risky bet, particularly given the high potential for future lithium shortages. To maintain the operation of its gigafactories, Tesla will need to make the right strategic choices regarding its lithium supply or develop alternatives that reduce, or even eliminate, its dependence on this metal, such as sodium-ion batteries.

Sodium-ion batteries are a major innovation in the electric transportation sector because they promise automakers a future with little to no dependence on lithium.

Sodium shares many chemical properties with lithium while being far more abundant. It offers several advantages: lower cost than lithium, a more environmentally friendly extraction process, simpler recycling, and virtually zero risk of thermal runaway. Occasional fires in electric vehicles are sometimes caused by overheating of lithium batteries, a risk that would be negligible with sodium-based batteries.

However, if sodium batteries only had advantages over lithium batteries, concerns about future lithium supply would no longer exist. The main drawback of sodium lies in energy density: for the same range, sodium batteries are heavier and bulkier than lithium batteries. This affects vehicle performance, reducing autonomy, agility, or both. In the future, technological innovations may improve the energy density of sodium batteries. Meanwhile, automakers plan to use sodium batteries in urban electric vehicles, which do not require long-range capacity. Several major players, such as automaker BYD and battery manufacturer CATL, have already announced significant investments in sodium-ion technology, showing that sodium batteries are a promising alternative to lithium, even though they are not yet a complete replacement for current lithium-based batteries.

Furthermore, the development of solid-state batteries, with a solid rather than liquid electrolyte, offers higher energy density and greater range for a lighter weight than lithium-ion batteries. This may increase the technological gap with sodium-ion batteries. However, even though solid-state batteries use fewer rare metals than lithium-ion batteries, their composition and functioning remain quite similar, meaning they will still face the same lithium-related challenges.

Recycling is also a key opportunity for the automotive electric sector. Currently, recycled lithium represents only a small share of the lithium used in batteries, but this is expected to improve in the coming years through various projects, particularly in Europe. The European Union has adopted Regulation 2023/1542, setting ambitious targets: by 2027, 50% of the lithium contained in batteries must be recovered, rising to 80% by 2031. Additionally, new batteries must contain a minimum percentage of recycled materials: 16% cobalt, 6% lithium, and nickel by 2031. While these regulations may seem challenging for battery manufacturers and automakers, they also create opportunities in the sustainable development sector.

For example, Livista Energy, a European leader in the lithium chemical industry, plans to open a new plant in Le Havre, France. According to Livista:

> *"The plant is scheduled to start operations in 2028 with an initial capacity of 40,000 tons, which will rapidly double to supply enough lithium for the batteries of 1.5 million electric vehicles per year. Recycled battery materials will gradually become the plant's primary source of raw materials by 2035, ensuring a positive environmental impact while strengthening Europe's energy independence."*

These ambitious goals exceed EU regulatory requirements and, if successful, will allow the company to manufacture batteries while minimizing the need for non-recycled lithium. Production costs will decrease, and the uncertainty surrounding lithium supply will be significantly reduced.

Lithium is undeniably a strategic metal in the context of the energy transition. The continued electrification of the global vehicle fleet will steadily increase its demand, while reserves show early signs of depletion, creating a real risk of shortage in the near future. However, there are viable pathways for automakers and battery manufacturers. Among them, securing supply seems to be the immediate priority, before moving toward longer-term solutions such as recycling or lithium substitutes (Ha, 2023).

CONCLUSION

In conclusion, geopolitical tensions have a significant impact on the supply of rare resources to industrial companies, shaping their procurement strategies. While these geopolitical frictions are not new, they are intensifying. The relationship between China and the United States (and, more broadly, Western countries) clearly illustrates this dynamic. Beijing seeks to challenge the United States' position as the leading superpower and views its dominance over the rare earth market as a long-term path to technological advantage. More generally, producer and consumer countries do not always agree on volumes, prices, or standards governing extraction methods.

These tensions threaten the stability of production for many technological and military goods in importing countries. Costs can fluctuate sharply based on the political decisions of producing nations, and supply chains can even be completely disrupted in the event of a geopolitical crisis. To mitigate these risks, companies strive to create stability that the market does not provide, using strategies ranging from diversification of supply sources (where possible) to establishing partnerships with countries deemed "reliable."

At the same time, industrial companies work to anticipate geopolitical events that may impact their supply chains. They identify risks based on extraction zones, attempt to anticipate political decisions in producer countries, and seek greater transparency regarding the origin of raw materials. In the medium to long term, importing countries are pursuing technological innovations to reduce dependency on "non-allied" countries such as China. They aim to develop substitutes for rare metals, or even products that no longer require them. However, these innovations are costly and time-consuming, so the current geopolitical situation will not be resolved overnight.

Finally, the race for rare resources tends to overshadow a long-standing issue: the inequality in economic development and wealth distribution among the countries involved. Producer countries, often developing or underdeveloped, bear the environmental and social externalities of extraction without benefiting proportionately from its economic gains. Even as investments from major economic powers in developing producer countries increase, control over these resources raises questions. Local populations in extraction areas do not always see improvements in their standard of living; on the contrary, they sometimes witness environmental degradation. State sovereignty is also challenged when extraction sites are largely controlled by foreign multinationals. Some countries choose to retain state control, but this results in slower and more complex development due to limited financial capacity.

The challenges linked to rare resources go beyond the industrial sphere: they affect state sovereignty, the stability of producing regions, and the collective ability to achieve a fair ecological transition. In a multipolar world, where economic rivalries coincide with geopolitical tensions, mastery over resources becomes both a lever of power and a test of responsibility.

REFERENCES

Cauchois, R., Taghipour, A., Kang, D., Zoghlami, N., & Abed, M. (2017). Advanced solutions for a supply chain with stochastic information. *Journal of Advanced Management Science*, *5*(1), 9–13. DOI: 10.18178/joams.5.1.9-13

Glaa, B., Zoghlami, N., & Taghipour, A. (2014, May). Outsourcing and off-shoring healthcare services: A way to cut the costs and improve quality. In 2014 international conference on advanced logistics and transport (ICALT) (pp. 189-194). IEEE.

Lu, X., & Taghipour, A. (2023). A French Guide for Businesses and Governments to Integrate the Concept of Sustainable Development Into Their Supply Chains. In *Government Impact on Sustainable and Responsible Supply Chain Management* (pp. 1–12). IGI Global. DOI: 10.4018/978-1-6684-9062-4.ch001

Mahfod, J., Canel-Depitre, B., & Taghipour, A. (2019). Quality function deployment-ELECTRE in supplier evaluation. Journal of advanced management science, 7(4).

Merimi, M., & Taghipour, A. (2021). Accelerating the digitalization of the supply chain: An empirical research about COVID-19 crisis. In *Digitalization of decentralized supply chains during global crises* (pp. 1–24). IGI Global Scientific Publishing. DOI: 10.4018/978-1-7998-6874-3.ch001

Ponputtha, W., Wannapiroon, P., Nilsook, P., Taghipour, A., Murat, S., Huang, P., & Chou, T. C. (2021). Creative history learning model using digital storytelling through cloud learning to enhance analytical thinking. International Journal of e-Education, e-Business, e-. *Management Learning*, *11*(2), 42–50.

Pour Mohammadi, M., Ghorbani, R., & Taghipour, A. (2014). Factors affecting the price of housing in the city of Tabriz using hedonic model. *Geographical Planning of Space Quarterly Journal*, *3*(9), 83–104.

Taghipour, A. (Ed.). (2020). *Demand forecasting and order planning in supply chains and humanitarian logistics*. IGI Global.

Taghipour, A. (Ed.). (2023). *Government Impact on Sustainable and Responsible Supply Chain Management*. IGI Global. DOI: 10.4018/978-1-6684-9062-4

Taghipour, A., Abed, M., & Zoghlami, N. (2015, May). Design for remanufacturing respecting reverse logistics processes: A review. In 2015 4th International Conference on Advanced Logistics and Transport (ICALT) (pp. 299-304). IEEE. DOI: 10.1109/ICAdLT.2015.7136602

Taghipour, A., & Frayret, J. M. (2011). Supply chain coordination planning: A review. Work paper, École polytechnique de Montréal.

Taghipour, A., Lu, X., Derradji, M., & Sow, A. D. (2022b, July). The impact of digitalization on supply chain management: a literature review. In *Proceedings of the 12th International Conference on Information Communication and Management* (pp. 75-78). DOI: 10.1145/3551690.3551702

Taghipour, A., Lu, X., & Smahi, M. (2022a). Opportunities and challenges for society 5.0 in procurement. *Blockchain Technology in Supply Chain Management for Society*, *5*(0), 91–100. DOI: 10.1201/9781003177432-9

Taghipour, A., Rouyendegh, B. D., Ünal, A., & Piya, S. (2022c). Selection of suppliers for speech recognition products in IT projects by combining techniques with an integrated fuzzy MCDM. *Sustainability (Basel)*, *14*(3), 1777. DOI: 10.3390/su14031777

Zoghlami, N., Taghipour, A., Merlo, C., & Abed, M. (2016). Management of divergent production network using decentralised multi-level capacitated lot-sizing models. *International Journal of Shipping and Transport Logistics*, *8*(5), 590–604. DOI: 10.1504/IJSTL.2016.078686

Chapter 3
Resilient Global Supply Chains Under Geopolitical Tensions

Raj K. Kovid
http://orcid.org/0000-0001-5224-0725
School of Business, University of Petroleum and Energy Studies, Dehradun, India

Shreya Srikanth
http://orcid.org/0009-0002-1576-0005
University of Petroleum and Energy Studies, Dehradun, India

Shreya Sangal
Symbiosis Centre for Management Studies, Symbiosis International (Deemed to be) University, Noida, India

ABSTRACT

This chapter examines the various dynamics of supply chain resilience in the context of increasing geopolitical uncertainty. It presents a critical assessment of adaptive strategies—modular manufacturing, digital transformation, and structural realignment—that enable companies to enhance their operational frameworks in response to external disturbances. Drawing insights from the Taiwan-China situation and the Russia-Ukraine conflict, the discourse provides a comprehensive perspective on maintaining supply chain integrity during periods of uncertainty and turmoil. This chapter seeks to offer case-based insights into how modern modularity concepts in manufacturing, the integration of Industry 4.0 and 5.0, and the reconfiguration of existing supply chains can directly improve efficiency and resilience within supply chains.

DOI: 10.4018/979-8-3373-6455-1.ch003

1. INTRODUCTION

The modern global supply chain environment currently functions with high levels of integration and efficiency and is a determining factor in the growth of the global economy. A Supply Chain (SC) is a network of members linked by the flow of materials, information, and funds to reduce the overall cost. Interruptions in these intricate international supply chains can cause significant financial losses, thereby affecting numerous countries on the global front. These supply chains include various players, namely, domestic manufacturers, suppliers, and other stakeholders across the globe. Their achievement is largely dependent on the political, economic, and environmental stability of various nations. Although the Russia-Ukraine war implies that only these two countries are engaged, the truth is that all nations have been greatly impacted globally. For example, the inflation rate in Britain rose to 5.5% in Jan 2022 amid the escalating tensions and war between Russia and Ukraine *(Office for National Statistics, 2022)*. The war led to a further hike in the price of oil, gas, food and food ingredients. The disrupted global supply chains increased the cost of living. It generated spillover effects in developing countries that rely on energy imports from European countries. Developing countries paid a higher price for energy imports, which translated to a rise in the local pump price of fuel, a rise in food prices and a general rise in merchandise imports despite income levels remaining unchanged.

Geopolitical uncertainty is the possibility of events like political, military, economic, and social tensions that can arise from the involvement of two nations in global affairs (Hoque, Zaidi and Hassan, 2021). It may also include tensions and strains between various states, such as (a) armed conflicts, (b) regime changes, (c) unstable trade policies, (d) economic sanctions, and (e) shifting strategic alliances that can suddenly change geopolitical dynamics, affecting global economics (Hoque et al., 2021). These uncertainties can disrupt global supply chains, cause exchange rate fluctuations, and affect global business and investment, thereby making it necessary to adjust the world supply chains to make them more resilient to such disruptions.

A thorough investigation of techniques meant to improve supply chain resilience in the setting of increasing geopolitical upheavals is offered in this chapter. Beginning with a study of the weaknesses revealed by such instability, it moves on to look at practical remedies such as structural reconfiguration, supply chain digitalisation, and modular manufacturing. The chapter emphasises, by means of in-depth debate and case-based insights, how these strategies together enable companies to expect, absorb, and adapt to external shocks while preserving operational continuity.

2. FACTORS AFFECTING GLOBAL SUPPLY CHAINS

Several global geopolitical disruptions significantly impact supply chains, influencing factors such as lead time, customer demand, and information sharing.

2.1 Lead Time

Lead time, defined as the difference between receipt of order and delivery of the product, is a key driver of supply chain efficiency. It includes both delivery and order lead times (George & Pillai, 2019). Geopolitical disruptions tend to worsen lead time delays, resulting in inventory imbalances and economic loss. The bullwhip effect, in which order fluctuations are magnified throughout the supply chain, is especially pronounced under long lead times. Steckel et al.'s research indicates that lead time reduction lessens this effect. For example, the Red Sea Crisis between Israel and Iran interrupted trade channels via the Suez Canal, a 12% of world trade-handling corridor.

The blockage of this vital passage severely reduced shipments, illustrating how geopolitical risk can stretch lead times and further worsen economic conditions around the world. The same supply chain disruptions were also observed during the COVID-19 crisis, wherein production decelerations and port traffic jams led to substantial lead time extensions across industries (Ivanov, 2020). Companies that employed only just-in-time (JIT) inventory practices were hit with extreme shortages due to long lead times, exposing vulnerabilities in worldwide logistics networks (Tang & Veelenturf, 2019; Herzog et al., 2024; Gharye, Goodarzian, Taghipour & Muñuzuri, 2025).

Additionally, natural disasters, such as the 2011 Tōhoku earthquake with a tsunami in Japan, resulted in longer lead times in key industries like electronics and the automotive sector, thereby significantly affecting global supply chains (Chopra & Sodhi, 2014). In response, businesses have attempted to reduce their dependence on a single source of failure by implementing regionalised supply chains and multi-sourcing programs (Christopher & Holweg, 2017).

Active supply chain risk management through the application of predictive analytics and digital twins may assist companies in foreseeing and responding to lead time disruptions ahead of time (Ivanov & Dolgui, 2021). Technologies like Blockchain and the Internet of Things (IoT) enhance real-time monitoring and visibility, enabling organizations to respond adaptively to unexpected geopolitical interruptions (Koot, Mes, & Iacob, 2021).

2.2 Customer Demand

Patterns of customer demand are key to supply chain performance. Demand is typically uncertain and difficult to predict, but over the long run it tends to exhibit relative stability (Fisher, 1997; Davis, 1993). Disruptions in highly connected supply chains will decrease supply but increase demand, resulting in higher equilibrium prices and inflation.

The economic effects of geopolitical shocks, such as the Iran-Israel conflict, extend well beyond the nations directly involved. The rise in inflation in Western economies and throughout Asia has been driven by shortages brought on by trade route blockages, illustrating the wide-ranging effects of supply chain failures. For example, the COVID-19 lockdown led to a global semiconductor shortage that severely disrupted industries dependent on electronic components, particularly automotive and consumer electronics (Shih, 2020). Geopolitical shocks also influence food security and energy costs, creating strong inflationary pressures. Wars and sanctions, for instance, have been shown to significantly raise food prices in developing economies with limited institutional (Laber et al., 2023). The Russia–Ukraine conflict notably disrupted agricultural production and global grain exports, deepening food insecurity and fragmenting international trade networks (Laber et al., 2023). Additionally, heightened geopolitical uncertainty has been directly linked to spikes in oil prices, further intensifying global inflation through increased transport and production costs (Mohamad, 2024).

Additionally, volatile fluctuations in demand make planning inventory more complicated, and companies need to embrace agile supply chain approaches. Sophisticated forecasting techniques like AI-based analytics and machine learning are being widely utilized to improve accuracy and counteract risks involved with demand spikes in times of crises (Ivanov & Dolgui, 2021).

2.3 Information Sharing

The backbone of efficient supply chains is the sharing of information, encouraging coordination and uncertainty diminution (George & Pillai, 2019). The communication of partners across the supply chain that is clear minimizes the bullwhip effect, accelerates decision-making, and delivers better overall performance. However, geopolitical tensions, armed hostilities, and nature-related calamities can stall information circulation and generate a major information void at risk of impairing global supply chains' integrity.

These elements have a large impact on how supply chains function globally. It is very important to make sure that they are not missed or misinterpreted when supply chains are made more resistant to geopolitical disruptions. Adopting the right solutions to deal with the these issues without sacrificing the supply chains' operational efficacy will be made easier with this careful consideration.

3. GEOPOLITICAL TENSIONS AND GLOBAL SUPPLY CHAIN DISRUPTIONS

Geopolitical instability describes a situation where two or more nations experience unrest due to factors such as wars, treaty violations, or government regulations. These geopolitical conditions disrupt global supply chains, which are intricately interconnected, resulting in increased lead times. Consequently, this disruption contributes to international economic instability with increased role of governments (Taghipour, 2023). This disruption can be combated by the implementation of certain new topics as discussed below:

3.1 Modular Manufacturing

Modular manufacturing—also called modular design or production—is the practice of breaking a system or product into independent modules that can be created, modified, or replaced separately. Unlike sequential manufacturing, this approach accelerates production by relying on pre-assembled components, improving efficiency, and reducing waste. Producing modules under controlled factory conditions enhances quality and precision, lowering the error rates often observed in conventional on-site assembly. Furthermore, modular methods are highly flexible and scalable, allowing organizations to adapt quickly to new project demands while supporting sustainability through reduced material use and minimized environmental impacts (Chen, Z., Zhang, Cai, Chen, & Zeng, 2022).

3.2 Supply Chain Resilience

Supply chain resilience refers to the ability to anticipate, adapt to, and recover from disruptions while maintaining operations and minimizing negative impacts on customer satisfaction. In an increasingly volatile business environment, resilience is vital for long-term stability and sustainability (Taghipour, Belrhazi, & Damoum, 2023). Resilient supply chains embody capabilities such as flexibility, agility, visibility, redundancy, and collaboration, enabling firms to rapidly rebound from unexpected events (Wieland & Durach, 2021)

3.3 Impact of Modular Manufacturing on Supply Chain Resilience

By increasing production diversification and reducing reliance on sole-source suppliers, modular manufacturing improves the robustness of supply chains. The approach maintains continuity and efficacy by allowing businesses to react quickly to unexpected disruptions and changing customer needs

The ability of modular systems to facilitate rapid recovery in emergencies is one of their advantages. The Red Sea Crisis, for instance, demonstrated the vulnerability that results from relying solely on one sector of the economy. Companies that used ground-based shipping or secondary maritime routes to diversify their supply chains were less vulnerable to losses. Through faster part replacement and flexible reconfigurability, modular production also reduces operational downtime and eliminates supply chain vulnerability.

Also, standardised module interfaces simplify substitution and integration, boosting resilience. Industries like electronics, construction, and automotive are already using modular manufacturing to deal with market demands, regulatory changes, and disruptions. For example, modular car platforms allow users to quickly adapt to shifting regulatory requirements, and these construction techniques minimise project delays.

4. SUPPLY CHAIN RESILIENCE: INDUSTRY 4.0 THROUGH INDUSTRY 5.0

4.1 Industry 4.0 and Supply Chain Resilience

Although companies are forced to adopt technology due to geopolitical disruptions, there are currently few studies on how technology contributes to supply chain resilience. The use of technology varies at all stages of a supply chain, from production lines to warehouse storage. Information gathering enables real-time tracking and early warning of disruptions, reducing their impact (Choudhary et al., 2022; Ivanov, 2020; Talwar et al., 2021).

By connecting sensors that enable data sharing between multiple systems to improve visibility and responsiveness, the Internet of Things (IoT) plays an important role in supply chain resilience. Research on IoT's capacity to withstand geopolitical disruptions is lacking, despite its enormous potential (Koot, Mes, & Iacob, 2021; Xu et al., 2020). Future studies would benefit from determining which technologies are most effective at anticipating and managing these disruptions, as well as assessing how ready the industry is to implement them.

The only study to specifically address artificial intelligence (AI) in supply chain resilience was conducted by Hasija and Esper (2022). To fully understand technology's role, more comprehensive research utilising both quantitative (structured data collection) and qualitative (open-ended questioning) approaches is needed. Using field research, shift from reactive to proactive threat reduction. Transition from reactive to proactive threat reduction through in-the-field studies will increase long-term supply chain stability (Grötsch, Blome, & Schleper, 2013; van Hoek, 2020).

4.2 Industry 5.0 and Supply Chain Resilience

Combining state-of-the-art technology with human knowledge, Industry 5.0 places a strong emphasis on cooperation, sustainability, and resilience. Unlike Industry 4.0, which emphasises automation. Industry 5.0 increases flexibility and risk tolerance by fusing human expertise with AI, IoT, robots, and big data (Xu et al., 2021). These technologies help businesses respond swiftly to disruptions by facilitating distributed decision-making, real-time monitoring, and forecasting (Ivanov & Dolgui, 2021, Goodarzian et al., 2024).

Human-machine interaction is a fundamental element of Industry 5.0, bringing with it the flexibility and problem-solving skills required to handle supply chain disruptions. IoT-enabled smart factories record data in real time, allowing companies to spot potential bottlenecks and get rid of the bullwhip effect. Industry 5.0 improves supply chain efficiency through inventory levelling (Choudhary et al., 2022).

5. CASES ON GLOBAL SUPPLY CHAINS AMID GEOPOLITICAL DISRUPTIONS

Sustainability, which is closely related to supply chain resilience, is another important feature of Industry 5.0. Applying the circular economy's tenets of waste reduction and resource optimisation strengthens and sustains supply chains (Van Hoek, 2020). Additive manufacturing or 3D printing reduces the need for multiple suppliers and the shock disruption caused by global supply chains by producing spare parts locally (Talwar et al., 2021).

According to Van Hoek, another important reason why Industry 5.0 is the talk of the town would be its contribution to creating sustainable and resilient supply chains (Van Hoek, 2020). This is performed using waste reduction and lean manufacturing procedures. The use of additive manufacturing and 3D Printing for the making of loose and spare parts negates the need for more suppliers, thereby shortening the lead time involved (Hasija & Esper, 2022). Moreover, these technologies make nations independent and supply chains less dependent on global connectivity.

5.1 CASE STUDY 1: RUSSIA-UKRAINE WAR

The Russia-Ukraine conflict has significantly disrupted global supply chains, impacting industries from energy to agriculture. Russia and Ukraine, also known as the "breadbasket of Europe," are leading producers when it comes to fertiliser, wheat, and maize. Export of these commodities has been affected by the conflict, causing severe shortages and hikes globally. For instance, the blockage of Ukraine's seaports has led to disruptions in grain exports, worsening food security in the dependent areas (Vakharia, 2023).

Apart from agriculture, the conflict has also put the energy sector to the test. Europe's dependence on Russian natural gas has led firms to diversify the sources of energy supplies rapidly and opt to invest in renewable energy and alternative energy supplies from other nations. Further, this diversification has amplified market volatility. Such diversification has increased market volatility as well as other operating costs to businesses worldwide (Kilfoyle, 2023).

The technology and automotive industry have also suffered. Most of the neon gas used in making semiconductors is from Ukraine. Manufacturing in sectors that depend on electronic components has been hindered due to the worldwide shortage of chips initiated by the shutdown of neon manufacturing plants (Simchi-Levi & Hare, 2022). Companies are taking several measures to improve their resilience against such geopolitical shocks as discussed below.

Multiple Markets and Suppliers: Dependence on single suppliers is avoided by using a mix of suppliers from various geographies, which avoids the use of sole sources. This would ensure the ongoing operation of the business even if one is attacked (Kilpatrick et al., 2024).

Regionalisation and Nearshoring: By relocating production to neighbouring markets, companies can reduce their dependence on distant suppliers and lower their exposure to global conflicts. It shortens lead times and enhances supply chain management *(Gartner, 2024).*

Improved Supply Chain Visibility: Companies can prepare and respond rapidly to disruptions by investing in technologies that offer real-time information. IoT and blockchain technologies improve decision-making and encourage transparency *(UNCTAD, 2023a).*

Risk assessment and scenario planning: Through regular review of potential risks and developing contingencies, organisations are in a stronger position to cope with unforeseen situations. In times of crisis, such forward thinking cuts downtime and financial losses *(Herzog et al., 2024).* Robust, resilient supply chains able to ride out geopolitical turbulence are necessary, as the

Russia-Ukraine conflict demonstrates. Companies can better anticipate future disruptions and overcome present ones by taking these measures.

5.2 CASE STUDY 2: TAIWAN-CHINA TENSIONS AND SEMICONDUCTOR SUPPLY CHAIN RISKS

Taiwan Semiconductor Manufacturing Company (TSMC) is the world's leading contract chipmaker, and Taiwan is a global leader in the semiconductor industry. TSMC manufactures cutting-edge semiconductors for the automotive, consumer electronics, and defence sectors. Nevertheless, global semiconductor supply chain security is severely jeopardised by the growing China-Taiwan geopolitical tensions *(Deloitte, 2025a).*Taiwan's dominance over China for chip production remains a critical point of concern despite the growth displayed in the given graph. Industries around the world would be seriously impacted by severe semiconductor shortages resulting from a war or economic blockade of Taiwan. Moreover, the semiconductor value chain is geographically concentrated, with (a) the US dominating design and software, and (b) South Korea and Taiwan dominating production *(Varadarajan et al., 2024).*

Supply chain risk is a byproduct of the geographic concentration, with geopolitics as a significant risk issue (Aouadni, Aouadni & Taghipour, 2024). As per Deloitte (2025b), total sales in global semiconductor industry were around \$627 billion in 2025, 19% higher than that in earlier year (Figure 1).

Figure 1. Source: Deloitte 2025(b)- Deloitte analysis and extrapolation based on data from World Semiconductor Trade Statistics.

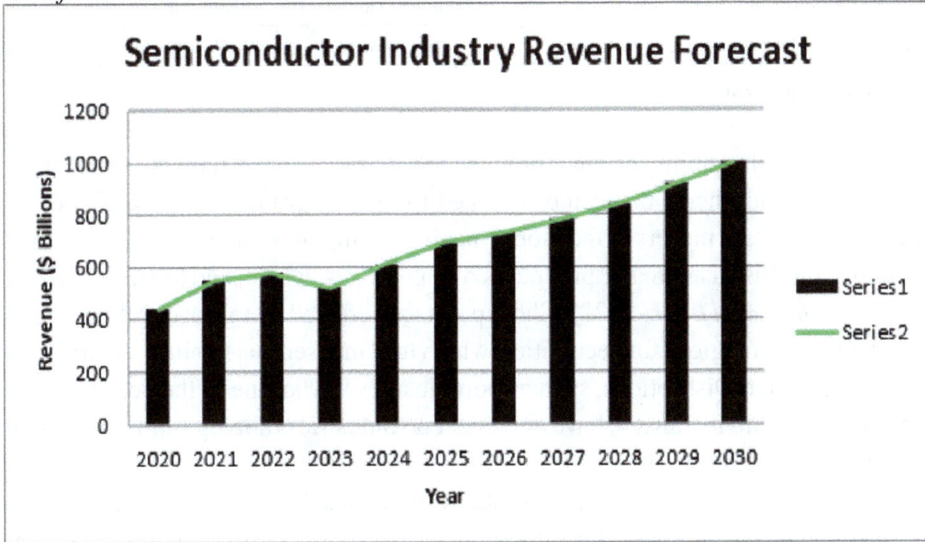

The industries of the entire world would be drastically impaired by devastating semiconductor shortages resulting from a war or economic blockade in Taiwan. The value chain for semiconductors is similarly geographically concentrated, with the US dominating design and software, and South Korea and Taiwan dominating manufacturing (*Varadarajan et al., 2024*). Supply chain risk originates from geographic concentration, making geopolitics a primary risk issue.

6. DISCUSSION

As demonstrated by the case studies of the war between Russia and Ukraine and the growing tensions between China and Taiwan, geopolitics has the power to disrupt global supply chains. Despite taking place in different industrial and regional contexts, energy and agricultural businesses in Eastern Europe, and semiconductor products in East Asia, these issues share several common difficulties and lessons. When combined, they highlight the political vulnerability of integrated worldwide supply chains and the pressing need for structural change that puts resilience and flexibility first. The resilience, tested across a range of geopolitical stress not only during a war, depends on how firms interpret signal vs surprise in view of nature of geopolitical shocks (table 1).

Table 1: Geopolitical Conflicts and Resilience

Dimension	Russia–Ukraine	China–Taiwan	Synthesis
Shock type	Armed conflict	Strategic ambiguity	Range of disruption
Predictability	Low	Medium to high	Early-warning relevance
Duration	Acute & prolonged	Prolonged	Temporal resilience

Source: prepared by authors

Systemic vulnerability created through the geographical clustering of production is one significant theme that can be gleaned from both instances. Taiwan is one of the most important players in the global manufacturing of semiconductors, whereas Ukraine and Russia are major producers of natural gas, wheat, and fertiliser *(UNCTAD, 2023b; World Bank, 2022)*. Chokepoints are created by this over-reliance on a small number of regions for necessities, which turn into serious liabilities in times of crisis or conflict. Disruptions, such as port closures in Ukraine or the possibility of a military buildup in Taiwan, have an impact on industries ranging from electronics production to food security.

This has resulted in a general strategic reappraisal in which strong reliance is placed upon diversifying the supply chain and reducing dependency upon any single area or supplier. For example, by diversifying imports and supporting the development of renewable energy sources, European nations have sought to reduce their dependence on Russian energy *(European Commission, 2022).* Meanwhile, chipmakers are attempting to decentralise fabrication centres and insulate themselves against geopolitical disruptions by expanding capacity in countries such as the US, India, and Japan *(UNCTAD, 2023b).* These efforts demonstrate a broader move away from efficiency-focused globalisation towards resilience-focused regionalisation.

This transformation is facilitated largely by technology. Enterprises can more effectively track, forecast, and respond to emerging risks due to enhanced supply chain transparency facilitated by real-time information, IoT, and blockchain technology *(UNCTAD, 2023b).* During disruption, these technologies facilitate faster corrective measures, reduce information asymmetry, and enhance transparency. Digital resilience solutions are emerging as a necessary component of risk management processes in various industries with rising frequencies of geopolitical uncertainties. Moreover, integrated IoT-blockchain systems significantly improve traceability and trust across supply chains by providing immutable, shared records that reduce fraud, errors, and delays *(Turner et al., 2023).* Empirical studies also show that combining IoT, big data analytics, AI, cloud computing, and blockchain strengthens supply chain resilience and performance in volatile settings *(Wu et al., 2025)*

Another important learning point is the value of forward risk management. Scenario planning and stress testing *(World Economic Forum, 2023)* are becoming more popular in order for businesses to estimate their exposure to political, environmental, and operational risks. As against the older response models to crisis, this proactiveness constitutes a quantum jump. Preparation for geopolitical scenarios such as embargoes, war, or sanctions is not mere speculation but necessary to maintain strategic continuity.

Additionally, these case studies show how business supply chain policies and national security objectives are becoming more intertwined. Vulnerable supply chains, such as food, energy, and semiconductors, are now being considered by governments as national resilience and sovereignty issues. Evidence of a new age in which global supply chains are inextricably intertwined with geopolitics can be seen in policy measures like industrial subsidies, trade controls, and the establishment of strategic reserves *(World Bank, 2022; European Commission, 2022).*

Geopolitical tensions, including intensity, regional centrality and predictability, lead to supply chain related outcomes in terms of continuity of supply, cost escalations and strategic repositioning. This effect of geopolitical tensions on supply chain outcomes is mediated through resilience capabilities such as redundancy, flexibility, visibility and substitutability. Moreover, channels of supply chain disruptions like state-driven interventions and industry criticality also influences the relationship between resilience capabilities and supply chain outcomes (Figure 2).

Figure 2. **Conceptual Framework** (*Source: prepared by authors*)

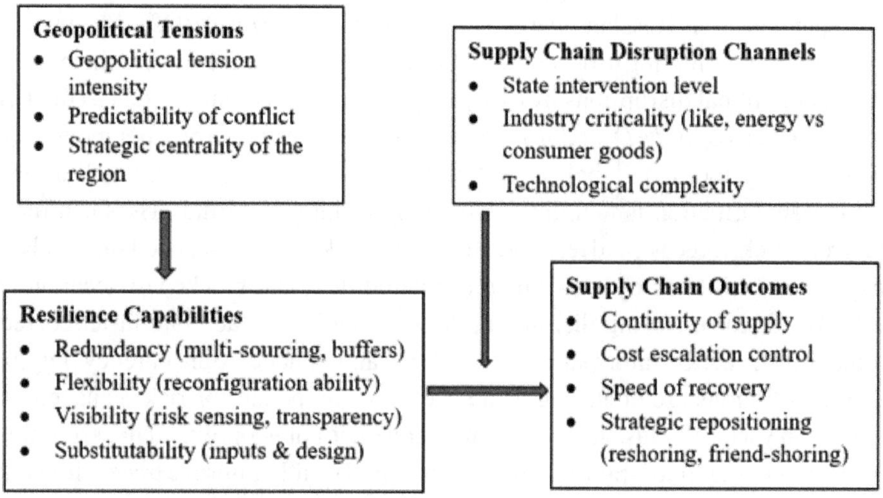

Theoretical and Practical Implications

Using the cases of China–Taiwan tensions and the Russia–Ukraine War, the chapter explains how geopolitics reshapes global supply chains beyond traditional efficiency paradigms. These cases can be anchored into some theoretical frameworks. How firms and states are dependent on external resources and supplies for their critical operations is explained by resource dependence theory. The dynamic capabilities theory highlights about firms' ability to respond to global disruptions, reconfigure their capabilities to sense geopolitical risks and review their supply and market networks. Unlike transitory shocks, geopolitical tensions reshape the institutional environment and affect firms' access to supply and demand side factors and markets, for prolonged period (Gereffi, 2020). Therefore, explaining supply chain resilience under geopolitical conditions through static risk mitigation approaches has limitations. Hence, a need arises for exploring a dynamic and multi-level theoretical framework.

The geopolitical tensions driven global supply chain has also implications for strategic decisions to be taken by companies. They need to focus more on strengthening their dynamic capabilities to sense the risks in advance and adjust their supply network, prioritise production locations and design corporate governance to internalise geopolitical scenarios. With emerging complexities around politics, economics, trade and defence technologies, governments also need to develop their dynamic capabilities, following 'no-permanent-friend or foe' principle, to manage their industrial policies, import-export controls, and friend-shoring strategies. It may need a stronger public–private coordination to strengthen systemic supply chain resilience.

7. CONCLUSION

The changing geopolitical scenario has unravelled important shortcomings in businesses globally, which have compelled governments and businesses to rethink their resilience and long-term sustainability plans (Mahfod et al., 2021). Case studies like the Russia-Ukraine conflict and Taiwan-China tensions clearly showcase how broadly geopolitical disturbances affect sectors that include agriculture, energy, and technology. From modular manufacturing, digitalisation, and regionalisation to the acceptance of Industry 4.0 and 5.0 technologies, strategic responses can be proven vital in reducing these risks. Risk management, technological integration, diversification, and supply chains moving from efficiency-driven to resilience-oriented models become non-optional but rather necessary. Maintaining world economic stability among ongoing uncertainty will depend mostly on building flexible, resilient, sustainable supply chains going forward *(MIT Sloan Management Review, 2023).*

REFERENCES

Aouadni, S., Aouadni, I., & Taghipour, A. (2024). Using ordinal priority approach with confidence-level measurement for third-party logistics provider selection in the Tunisian healthcare sector. In *Applications of New Technology in Operations and Supply Chain Management* (pp. 404–429). IGI Global. DOI: 10.4018/979-8-3693-1578-1.ch020

Chen, Z., Zhang, J., Cai, Z., Chen, W., & Zeng, C. (2022). Lean construction and engineering practice based on modular assembly integration. *Science Discovery*, *10*(6), 427–432. DOI: 10.11648/j.sd.20221006.18

Chopra, S., & Sodhi, M. S. (2014). Reducing the risk of supply chain disruptions. *MIT Sloan Management Review*, *55*(3), 73–80. https://sloanreview.mit.edu/article/reducing-the-risk-of-supply-chain-disruptions/

Choudhary, D., Qaiser, F. H., Choudhary, A., & Fernandes, K. J. (2022). A model for managing returns in a circular economy context: A case study from the Indian electronics industry. *International Journal of Production Economics*, *249*, 108505. Advance online publication. DOI: 10.1016/j.ijpe.2022.108505

Christopher, M., & Holweg, M. (2017). Supply chain 2.0 revisited: A framework for managing volatility-induced risk in the supply chain. *International Journal of Physical Distribution & Logistics Management*, *47*(1), 2–17. DOI: 10.1108/IJPDLM-09-2016-0245

Deloitte. (2025a). *Semiconductor industry outlook*. https://www2.deloitte.com/us/en/insights/industry/technology/technology-media-telecom-outlooks/semiconductor-industry-outlook.html

Deloitte. (2025b). Figure 2 https://www2.deloitte.com/us/en/insights/industry/technology/technology-media-telecom-outlooks/semiconductor-industry-outlook.html Deloitte

European Commission. (2022, April 20). *In focus: Reducing the EU's dependence on imported fossil fuels* International Energy Agency & European Commission. https://commission.europa.eu/news-and-media/news/focus-reducing-eus-dependence-imported-fossil-fuels-2022-04-20_en

Gartner, S. (2024, October 30). *Supply chain resilience strategies: Data visibility & regionalization.* SCMR. https://www.scmr.com/article/supply-chain-resilience-strategies-data-visibility-regionalization

George, J., & Pillai, V. M. (2019). A study of factors affecting supply chain performance. *Journal of Physics: Conference Series*, *1355*(1), 012018. Advance online publication. DOI: 10.1088/1742-6596/1355/1/012018

Gharye Mirzaei, M., Goodarzian, F., Taghipour, A., & Muñuzuri, J. (2025). Sustainable closed-loop supply chain network under uncertainty considering green technologies: Toward the circular economy. *The Journal of the Operational Research Society*, •••, 1–21.

Goodarzian, F., Abraham, A., Muñuzuri, J., Taghipour, A., & Ghasemi, P. (2024). A Benders decomposition approach for a new sustainable pharmaceutical supply chain network: A case study in France. *Annals of Operations Research*, •••, 1–39.

Grötsch, V. M., Blome, C., & Schleper, M. C. (2013). Antecedents of proactive supply chain risk management – a contingency theory perspective. *International Journal of Production Research*, *51*(10), 2842–2867. DOI: 10.1080/00207543.2012.746796

Hasija, A., & Esper, T. L. (2022). In artificial intelligence (AI) we trust: A qualitative investigation of AI technology acceptance. *Journal of Business Logistics*, *43*(3), 388–412. DOI: 10.1111/jbl.12301

Herzog, C., Janssen, S., Schmid, U., Bosse, M., & Börner, M. (2024, November). *Supply chain tech report 2024 (SCT24): Technology can help manage supply-chain disruption*. Oliver Wyman. https://www.oliverwyman.com/our-expertise/insights/2024/nov/supply-chain-tech-report.html

Hoque, M. E., Zaidi, M. A. S., & Hassan, M. K. (2021). Geopolitical Uncertainties and Malaysian Stock Market Returns: Do Market Conditions Matter? *Mathematics*, *9*(19), 2393. DOI: 10.3390/math9192393

Ivanov, D. (2020). Predicting the impacts of epidemic outbreaks on global supply chains: A simulation-based analysis on the coronavirus (COVID-19/SARS-CoV-2) case. *Transportation Research Part E, Logistics and Transportation Review*, *136*, 101922. Advance online publication. DOI: 10.1016/j.tre.2020.101922 PMID: 32288597

Ivanov, D., & Dolgui, A. (2021). A digital supply chain twin for managing the disruption risks and resilience in the era of Industry 4.0. *Transportation Research Part E, Logistics and Transportation Review*, *148*, 102243. Advance online publication. DOI: 10.1016/j.tre.2021.102243

Kilfoyle, M. (2023, October 24). *Ukraine: What's the global economic impact of Russia's invasion?* Economics Observatory. https://www.economicsobservatory.com/ukraine-whats-the-global-economic-impact-of-russias-invasion/

Kilpatrick, J., Berckman, L., Faver, A. D., Hardin, K., & Sloane, M. (2024, May 23). *Restructuring the supply base: Prioritizing a resilient, yet efficient supply chain.* Deloitte Insights. https://www2.deloitte.com/us/en/insights/industry/manufacturing/global-supply-chain-resilience-amid-disruptions.html

Koot, M., Mes, M., & Iacob, M. E. (2021). A systematic literature review of blockchain-based supply chain management: Research trends and future research directions. *Logistics (Basel)*, *5*(4), 71. DOI: 10.3390/logistics5040071

Laber, M., Klimek, P., Bruckner, M., Yang, L., & Thurner, S. (2023). Shock propagation from the Russia–Ukraine conflict on international multilayer food production network determines global food availability. *Nature Food*, *4*(6), 508–517. DOI: 10.1038/s43016-023-00771-4 PMID: 37322302

Mahfod, J., Khoury, B., Canel-Depitre, B., & Taghipour, A. (2021). Logistics Providers in Syria Humanitarian Operations. In Demand Forecasting and Order Planning in Supply Chains. and Humanitarian Logistics (pp. 171-197). IGI Global. DOI: 10.4018/978-1-7998-3805-0.ch006

MIT Sloan Management Review (2023). *Is it time to rethink globalized supply chains?* https://sloanreview.mit.edu/article/is-it-time-to-rethink-globalized-supply-chains/

Mohamad, A. H. H. (2024). The impact of the Russia–Ukraine war on global food security. *Nutrition & Food Science International Journal*, 13(3), 555862. https://juniperpublishers.com/nfsij/pdf/NFSIJ.MS.ID.555862.pdf

Office for National Statistics. (2022). Consumer price inflation, UK, February 16. https://www.ons.gov.uk/economy/inflationandpriceindices/bulletins/consumerpriceinflation/january2022/pdf

Resilinc Editorial Team. *What would happen if China invaded Taiwan?* https://www.resilinc.com/blog/what-would-happen-if-china-invaded-taiwan/

Risks and resilience in global trade: Key trends in 2023-2024. https://www.oecd.org/en/publications/risks-and-resilience-in-global-trade_1c66c439-en.html

Shih, W. C. (2020). Is it time to rethink globalized supply chains? *MIT Sloan Management Review,* March 19. https://sloanreview.mit.edu/article/is-it-time-to-rethink-globalized-supply-chains/

Simchi-Levi, D., & Haren, P. (2022, March). *How the war in Ukraine is further disrupting global supply chains. Harvard Business Review.* https://hbr.org/2022/03/how-the-war-in-ukraine-is-further-disrupting-global-supply-chains

Supply Chain Brain. (2023a). *Enhancing supply chain resilience: A modular approach.* https://www.supplychainbrain.com/articles/38553-enhancing-supply-chain-resilience-a-modular-approach

Supply Chain Brain. (2023b). *How are China-Taiwan tensions threatening global semiconductor supply?* https://www.supplychainbrain.com/articles/40256-watch-how-are-china-taiwan-tensions-threatening-global-semiconductor-supply

Taghipour, A. (Ed.). (2023). *Government Impact on Sustainable and Responsible Supply Chain Management.* IGI Global. DOI: 10.4018/978-1-6684-9062-4

Taghipour, A., Belrhazi, Y., & Damoum, N. (2023). Resilient sustainable supply chain management. In *Government Impact on Sustainable and Responsible Supply Chain Management* (pp. 33–47). IGI Global. DOI: 10.4018/978-1-6684-9062-4.ch003

Talwar, S., Kaur, P., Fosso Wamba, S., & Dhir, A. (2021). Big Data in operations and supply chain management: A systematic literature review and future research agenda. *International Journal of Production Research, 59*(11), 3509–3534. DOI: 10.1080/00207543.2020.1868599

Tang, C. S., & Veelenturf, L. P. (2019). The strategic role of logistics in the Industry 4.0 era. *Transportation Research Part E, Logistics and Transportation Review, 129*, 1–11. DOI: 10.1016/j.tre.2019.06.004

Turner, S. W., Karakus, M., Guler, E., & Uludag, S. (2023). A promising integration of SDN and blockchain for IoT networks: A survey. *IEEE Access : Practical Innovations, Open Solutions, 11*, 29800–29822. DOI: 10.1109/ACCESS.2023.3260777

UNCTAD. (2023a). *Enhancing supply chain resilience amid rising global risks.* https://unctad.org/news/enhancing-supply-chain-resilience-amid-rising-global-risks

UNCTAD. (2023b). *UN Global Supply Chain Forum calls for resilience amid world trade disruptions.* https://unctad.org/press-material/un-global-supply-chain-forum-calls-resilience-amid-world-trade-disruptions

United Nations Development Programme (UNDP). (2007). *Public administration reform: Practice note.* https://www.undp.org/ - Data interpretation only.

Vakharia, A. (2023, February 9). *The global supply chain consequences of the Russia-Ukraine war.* University of Florida News. https://news.ufl.edu/2023/02/russia-ukraine-global-supply-chain/

van Hoek, R. (2020). Research opportunities for a more resilient post-COVID-19 supply chain – closing the gap between research findings and industry practice. *International Journal of Operations & Production Management*, *40*(4), 341–355. DOI: 10.1108/IJOPM-03-2020-0165

Varadarajan, R., Koch-Weser, I., Richard, C., Fitzgerald, J., Singh, J., Thornton, M., & Casanova, R. (2024, May 8). *Emerging resilience in the semiconductor supply chain*. Boston Consulting Group. https://www.bcg.com/publications/2024/emerging-resilience-in-semiconductor-supply-chain

Wieland, A., & Durach, C. F. (2021). Two perspectives on supply chain resilience. *Journal of Business Logistics*, *42*(3), 315–322. DOI: 10.1111/jbl.12271

World Bank. (2004). *World Development Report 2004: Making services work for poor people*. World Bank and Oxford University Press.

World Economic Forum. (2023). *The Global Risks Report 2023: 18th Edition*. World Economic Forum. https://www3.weforum.org/docs/WEF_Global_Risks_Report_2023.pdf

Wu, L., Zhang, Z., Huang, J., Su, I.-H., & Tian, S. (2025). Digital technologies and supply chain resilience: A resource-action-performance perspective. *Information Systems Frontiers*, *27*(5), 2137–2158. Advance online publication. DOI: 10.1007/s10796-025-10595-1

Xu, L., Mak, S., & Brintrup, A. (2021). Will bots take over the supply chain? Revisiting agent-based supply chain automation. *International Journal of Production Economics*, *241*, 108279. Advance online publication. DOI: 10.1016/j.ijpe.2021.108279

Chapter 4
Ethical Sourcing and Transparency:
Driving Social Accountability in Global Supply Chains

Ayushman Deepak
http://orcid.org/0009-0004-1200-8218
Christ University, Bangaluru, India

Surabhi Sangal
http://orcid.org/0000-0002-9160-2538
Christ University, Bangaluru, India

ABSTRACT

Global supply chains have boosted efficiency and global access but also led to labor, environmental, and ethical issues. Growing consumer and regulatory pressure has driven firms to pursue ethical sourcing and transparency for accountability. Ethical sourcing ensures fair labor and human rights, while transparency tools enhance traceability. This chapter explores how these practices drive social accountability through sustainability standards, corporate codes, and stakeholder collaborations. It also examines enabling technologies like blockchain and IoT, identifies implementation barriers, and proposes integrative frameworks for sustainable supply chain governance.

1. INTRODUCTION

One of the most significant structural changes in the organization of modern economics is the world supply chains. Over recent decades, companies increasingly

DOI: 10.4018/979-8-3373-6455-1.ch004

have ceased vertically integrated production schemes to opt for geographically decentralized and multi-storey provider networks which not only provide cost-efficiencies, specialization, and operational flexibility (Taghipour and Frayret, 2013). Although such fragmentation has produced a high level of economic returns, it has also increased governance issues of ethics, social and environmental in global production systems (Soundararajan and Brammer, 2018).

The modern supply chains are being run in diverse regulatory settings, institutional settings as well as intricate subcontracting systems. These features make the president of the observance of labor practices, environmental performance, and human rights adherence in prolonged supplier networks very difficult (Wieland, 2021). Organizational and geographical distance of lead firms on the other end of suppliers often introduces information asymmetries, which make it less visible about operational realities and allow governance vulnerabilities (Vosooghidizaji et al., 2019). The existing literature highlights the fact that these types of ethical risks can hardly be attributable to individual incidents but are more of systematic consequences shaped by processes of decentralization, the complexity of coordination, and non-uniform enforcement processes (Locke, 2013).

The ethical issues in the global supply chains have gained momentum with well-documented acts of labor exploitation, poor working conditions, wage offenses, and unfriendly methods of production that are environmentally unfriendly. Such repetitive trends pose a challenge to traditional compliance-based governance practices that are mainly supported by the supplier codes of conduct and regular audit (LeBaron, Lister, and Dauvergne, 2022). The empirical evidence implies that the practices of audit supports fail to identify the hidden violations in the bottom levels of suppliers, especially when subcontracting opaqueness and imbalanced power occur (Soundararajan and Brammer, 2018).

To address these ongoing governance constraints, ethical sourcing and supply chain transparency have developed out of marginal corporate social responsibility efforts as core fragments of supply chain risk management and stakeholder governance policies (Kim, Colicchia, and Menachof, 2018). The mechanisms of transparency, which were previously mainly linked to the operational visibility and logistics coordination, have become perceived as common tools to curb the information asymmetry, increase the accountability, and boost the trust of the stakeholders (Mol & Oosterveer, 2015; Ren, Taghipour, and Canel-Depitre, 2016).

This change has been enhanced by regulatory trends, environmental, social, and governance (ESG) patterns driven by investors, and changes in the expectation of stakeholders. Companies are under growing institutional pressure to indicate responsible sourcing strategies, traceable systems, as well as valid reporting systems (Taghipour and Beneteau-Piet, 2020). This means that ethical sourcing and transparency cannot be seen as optional ethical pledges any longer but as structural governmental requirements determining legitimacy, robustness, and sustainable performance (Wieland, 2021).

This chapter builds a narrative literature review clarifying the relationship of interdependence between ethical sourcing and disclosure in international supply chains. Nonetheless, instead of giving a comprehensive systematic overview of the past literature, the analysis amalgamates overall theoretical views, recurrent empirical evidence, debates around governance and some of the ongoing technological issues. It aims to bring together fragmented streams of knowledge, elucidate conceptual relations, and find unresolved tensions that may determine the future of socially responsible supply chain management (Taghipour and Frayret, 2013; Vosooghidizaji et al., 2019).

2. CONCEPTUAL FOUNDATIONS

Conceptual clarity is necessary in understanding of ethical sourcing and supply chain transparency, as these two constructs are frequently mentioned but most of the time defined inconsistently throughout the literature. Previous literature states that such ambiguity creates a flaw in the foundation of constructs and inhibits the discussion of governance and limitation of introducing the theory (Kim, Colicchia, and Menachof, 2018). This part will provide a summary apprehension on the prevailing meanings of ethical sourcing, transparency, social accountability, and then proceeds to their theoretical foundations.

2.1 Ethical Sourcing

The concept of ethical sourcing can be explained as the practices of procurement and supply management, including social, labor, and environmental-related considerations in addition to the conventional economic-related factors (cost, quality, and delivery performance) (Kim et al., 2018). In comparison with compliance-related sourcing models, ethical sourcing is a normative and governance-based change where companies acknowledge the duties that go beyond direct contractual set of duties (Soundararajan & Brammer, 2018).

Ethical sourcing has always been placed in the literature as one of the organizational reactions to systemic risks inherent in globalized production systems. Companies are becoming more and more accountable to the supplier practices in regard to the labor rights, occupational safety, environmental welfare, and safeguarding human rights (Locke, 2013). Ethical sourcing thus goes beyond compliance with regulations and is rather an aspect of strategy governance designed to reduce reputational risk, increase legitimacy, and operational alignment with stakeholder expectations (Taghipour and Beneteau-Piet, 2020).

Notably, recent studies question the efficacy of audit-based ethical sourcing regime. The research records that compliance audits that are periodically repeated often create symbolic conformity and not meaningful change in behavior especially when sourcing incentives are not aligned (LeBaron, Lister, and Dauvergne, 2022). Consequently, researchers support relational and capacity-building philosophies based on long-term supplier interactions, jointly resolvable issues, and joint accountability frameworks (Soundararajan and Brammer, 2018).

2.2 Supply Chain Transparency

Supply chain transparency is defined as the degree to which the information about supply chain participants, operations, sourcing and material movement is shared and can be obtained by the interested parties (Mol & Oosterveer, 2015). Although conventional supply chain visibility is mainly related to logistics coordination and operational efficiency, transparency can also be extended in regard to other informational aspects such as ethical, social, and environmental disclosure (Wieland, 2021).

One critical governance role that is played by transparency mechanisms in multitier supply networks in which there is information asymmetry exists. The inherent nature of decentralized production systems is that their production creates visibility discontinuities, making the assessment of upstream practices less accessible to the lead firms and their stakeholders (Vosooghidizaji, Taghipour, & Canel-Depitre, 2020). As a result, transparency has become generally viewed as a corrective measure that mitigates risks that arise due to asymmetry, enhances accountability, and makes it possible to integrate external checks and balances (Ren, Taghipour, and Canel-Depitre, 2016).

The literature goes on to note that transparency does not mean unconstrained disclosure. Instead, to be effective, transparency must be accurate, timely, and reporting structures that are of interest to the stakeholders (Mol & Oosterveer, 2015). Online traceability systems such as blockchain or IoT technology are also considered in growing tech failure as a support of transparency, but scholars have pointed out that technological publicity fails to ensure ethical compliance (Kshetri, 2018).

2.3 Social Accountability

Social accountability describes the company responsibilities about the social impacts of supply chain operation, specifically those in reference to labor conditions, welfare of communities, equity, and safeguarding human rights (Locke, 2013). In the modern understanding, social accountability is viewed as an institutionalized governance requirement, as opposed to benevolent corporate style.

As pointed out by previous research, global supply chains disperse economic value and social risk between players spread geographically. The informal workers, lower-tier suppliers, and the community, which depends on resources, often have a disproportionate exposure to both labor violations and environmental repercussions (Soundararajan and Brammer, 2018). These governance imbalances are aimed at through social accountability systems, such as certification schemes, grievance systems, and stakeholder oversight constructs.

Importantly, social accountability scholarship highlights the fact that a diffusion of responsibility is a recurrent governance issue. The sourcing designs in multi-tiers hide the causal relationship between corporate sourcing and the resultant labor conditions up the chain (LeBaron et al., 2022). Therefore, accountability frameworks are focusing more on the due diligence requirements, the transparency requirements and enforceable governance requirements.

2.4 Theoretical Underpinnings

The debates on ethical sourcing and transparency are based on a number of complementary theoretical traditions.

Corporate Social Responsibility (CSR) Theory is a theoretical view of a corporation as a company that has ethical and social responsibilities that are not limited to profit maximization (Carroll, 1991). Ethical sourcing is an implementation of CSR concept in the supply chain targeting contexts through embedding social and environmental concerns in the procurement decisions.

The Stakeholder Theory builds on this argument by stating that companies need to create value to a number of stakeholder groups, such as their employees, the suppliers, the community, the regulatory agents, and members of civil society (Freeman, 1984). Transparency systems and ethical sourcing are thus seen as governance reactions to the pressures and legitimacy needs of the stakeholders.

The Triple Bottom Line (TBL) Theory is another method that expands on the performance assessment by incorporating the economic, social, and environmental aspects (Elkington, 1997). Under this model, ethical sourcing and transparency serve as a form of interconnection between the governance structures and the outcomes of sustainability performance.

Taken together, these theoretical lenses re-establish supply chains as socio-economic systems of governance, as opposed to operational systems (Taghipour and Frayret, 2013).

3. THEMATIC LITERATURE REVIEW

The development of sourcing ethically and transparency of the supply chain is a reflection of the larger shifts in the global production systems, the mode of governance and the demands of the stakeholders. In existing literature, these concepts are used to address rather than ongoing coordination failures, linked to legitimacy threats, and endemic information asymmetries in fragmented supply networks, rather than being a fixed tool of management (Taghipour and Frayret, 2013; Wieland, 2021). In this part, the theme descriptions across the governance, compliance, and institutional research streams are synthesised.

3.1 Compliance-Centric Control to Governance-Oriented Approaches.

Initial schemes of ethical sourcing were mostly compliance-related. Companies were over dependent on good practice codes of conduct provided by suppliers, contractual protections and controlled by third parties (Locke, 2013). These mechanisms presupposed that the unethical conduct of suppliers may be eliminated by the external inspection and corrective enforcement.

Nevertheless, empirical studies which followed demonstrated structural weaknesses of the audit-centric regimes. Researchers record that compliance audits often respond by rewarding compliance, masks as opposed to meaningful enhancements, especially in sourcing settings which are cost-sensitive (LeBaron, Lister, and Dauvergne, 2022). The suppliers can also strategically adjust the documentation; temporarily alter the working conditions or even hide the arrangements of subcontracting without solving the fundamental origins of the violations.

Such criticism has changed the focus of scholarly research to governance-based view of ethical sourcing. In place of ethical failures being perceived as a sole perpetrator of one supplier, the emerging body of research focuses on endemic causes such as purchasing pressures, price unpredictability, compression in lead-time, and power imbalance to buyers and suppliers (Soundararajan and Brammer, 2018). Ethical sourcing can now be redefined as a coordination challenge and incentive alignment challenge instead of a monitoring problem per se.

More effective alternatives are suggested to be relational governance processes, long-term supplier relationships, and collaboration in the development of capabilities (Taghipour and Beneteau-Piet, 2020). Such strategies are aware of the fact that sustainable compliance with ethics demands structural change in sourcing strategies and procurement practices.

3.2 Structural Source of Ethical Risk- Information Asymmetry.

Information asymmetry is one of the core explanatory constructs throughout the supply chain ethics literature. Global supply networks are inherently linked with decentralization, multi-level subcontracting, and low upstream visibility (Vosooghidizaji et al., 2019). In such a situation lead firms may be devoid of credible information about the labour practices, environmental effects, and the material origin.

According to the outcomes of the previously conducted research, the most common barriers to transparency appear not only in the presence of intentional concealment but also structural obscurity formed by the intricate networks of suppliers (Mol & Oosterveer, 2015). At the bottom of the chain of suppliers, dubious actors of the production, and physically remote locations of extraction often fall outside the coverage of well-established governing tools.

Empirical research also illustrates that the risks caused by asymmetry are heightened in decentralized supply chains which have poor coordination systems and disintegrated information streams (Ren, Taghipour, and Canel-Depitre, 2016). Formal compliance systems may therefore still be found not to eradicate ethical violations because they may be missing incomplete information architectures.

The transparency mechanisms are mostly understood as the tools of corrective governance aimed at decreasing asymmetry, enhancing traceability, and allowing the stakeholders to check (Wieland, 2021). Nevertheless, the literature warns that effectiveness of transparency rests on the accurate information, the motives of goods information disclosure and the enforcement models by the institutions.

3.3 Pressures and Dynamics of legitimacy by stakeholders.

The rise of ethical sourcing and transparency programs is explained by the stakeholder theory and the institutional research work in tandem with each other. Companies are becoming more and more engaged in the spaces that are defined by regulatory proliferation, investment requirements that are driven by ESG concerns, consumer activism, and civil society oversight (Taghipour et al., 2023).

The previous literature highlights the importance of the fact that the adoption of ethical sourcing is often not inspired by ethical motives but by the need to maintain the legitimacy (Locke, 2013). The transparency disclosures, sustainability reports, and traceability programs serve as indicators that reduce the reputational risk and strengthen the trust of the stakeholders.

Notably, legitimacy relations differ according to industries and the dynamics in governance. The consumer-facing industries that are highly visible have high transparency pressure over the upstream supply chains of industrialization (Wieland, 2021). This variation highlights the intervention of external monitoring strength and requirement of the institutions.

3.4 Intractable Governance Tensions for Literature.

Although the concept developments continue, researchers have widely found the tension that remains unresolved and limits effectiveness of ethical sourcing:

• Cost Efficiency vs Ethical Compliance

Efforts to promote procurement with the focus on price reduction at the cost of supplier capacity to enhance ethical change can be counterproductive (Soundararajan and Brammer, 2018).

• Audit Proliferation vs Substantive Change

The heavy control of compliance can lead to a bureaucratic overload without targeting at structural incentives (LeBaron et al., 2022).

• Transparency Expansion vs Data Integrity

Disclosure is not necessarily associated with informational reliability (Mol & Oosterveer, 2015).

• Multi-Tier Visibility vs Operational Feasibility

Deep-tier traceability is again expensive and very technical (Kshetri, 2018).

These strains affirm the thesis statement that ethical sourcing issues are still essentially matters of governance and not matters of technology.

4. Governance and Transparency Mechanisms

Both ethical sourcing and transparency issues in the global supply chains are essentially matters of governance that demands the institutional, organizational and inter-firm coordination mechanism. The existing literature highlights that the governance structures influence the distribution of the role and surveillance as well as enforcement of the distribution in fragmented networks involved in production (Locke, 2013; Taghipour and Frayret, 2013). In this section, the discussion is made on major governance tools that are reported in the literature, such as multi-stakeholder programmes, traceability frameworks, voluntary sustainability programmes, and corporate codes of conduct.

4.1 Governance Principles in Global Supply Chains

Responsible supply chain systems that are based on good governance reveal legitimacy, accountability, and performance as cornerstones to good governance in the supply chain. Legitimacy deals with the credibility and perceived authority of the mechanisms of governance by the stakeholders, whereas accountability represents the ability to entrust responsibility and create an enforceable corrective action (Locke, 2013). Performance dimensions measure the extent to which governance arrangements are effective to generate a substantive social and environment to symbolic conformity.

In supply networks occurrences on a global scale with a significant geographic spread, power asymmetries, jurisdiction fragmentation, and information discontinuities regularly limit the effectiveness of governance (Wieland, 2021). The lead firms have the economic leverage which is not operated visually at the low level of the suppliers. This means that the governance mechanisms have to deal with information architecture and authority structures.

4.2 Multi-Stakeholder Initiatives (MSIs)

Multi-stakeholder initiatives are collaborative form of governance between firms, non governments organization (NGOs), industry associations, and in some cases, government. MSIs are portrayed in the literature as solutions to regulatory deficiencies and enforcement constraints which are the hallmarks in globalized structures of production (Utting, 2015).

MSIs are aimed at developing better legitimacy by fostering inclusiveness and common processes in setting standards. These initiatives will address the unilateral control of a company and enhance the credibility of governance by including different stakeholder groups. Nevertheless, researchers point to ongoing arguments relating to the enforcement capacity, the rigor of monitoring, and potential dangers of being symbolically adopted (Fransen & LeBaron, 2019).

Though criticized, MSIs have proven to be important tools of governance because they can bring about co-ordination of practices in industries, standardization of reporting expectations and provision of dialogue across sectors.

4.3 Traceability and Transparency Models

Traceability systems are very useful in operationalizing transparency goals. Preexisting studies provide a difference between single-tier traceability architecture and multi-tier traceability architecture (Sodhi and Tang, 2019).

Single tier traceability concentrates on the direct (Tier-1) suppliers. Although operationally viable and relatively cheap, this model lacks a good perspective into upstream risks where the problem of labor violation and environmental externalities is often a source (Francisco & Swanson, 2018).

Multi-tier traceability expands reporting and governing all the lower levels of suppliers that involve extraction of the raw materials and the informal manufacturers. Though it is better in theory to reduce risks, this option has practical limitations such as the reliability of data, the complexity of coordination, or the limitation of the ability of suppliers (Kshetri, 2018).

Literature is also focused on the idea that effectiveness of transparency is not only determined by disclosure breadth but also the accuracy of the information disclosed, disclosure verification instruments, and motivation of this governance (Mol & Oosterveer, 2015).

4.4 Voluntary Sustainability Standards (VSS)

Voluntary sustainability standards are market-based governance tools which are designed to certify that social and environmental standards are followed. The examples are the Fairtrade, FSC and the RSPO systems. Researchers understand VSS to be systems that can convert ethical demands into a set of standard and verifiable processes (Reinecke & Ansari, 2016).

The disadvantages and advantages of certification systems are recorded in empirical research. VSS might supersede consumer awareness, process improvement by the suppliers, as well as, uniformity of sustainability measures. Critics, however, maintain that it is also common that certification can alone be insufficient to respond to structural forces of unethical behavior especially on income inequality, price pressures and inadequate enforcement structures (LeBaron et al., 2022).

4.5 Corporate Codes of Conduct

Corporate codes of conduct constitute firm-level control tools that describe the desired supplier behavior in regard to labor practices, safety and environmental performance. Although they have gained much application, their success largely relies on ensuring alignment of the incentives and the consistency of the enforcement (Locke, 2013).

According to the existing literature, there is a more general compliance-cost paradox: on one hand, suppliers are founded to operate according to ethical demands with simultaneous requirements of buyers to reduce costs and expedite delivery time (Soundararajan and Brammer, 2018). Provided no changes are made to the procurement strategies, codes are likely to turn into mere symbols.

5. Digital Technologies and Supply Chain Transparency

One of the key enablers in the global supply chain that has surfaced due to digital technologies is transparency and traceability. Nevertheless, modern academia warns about technological determinism and highlights that the digital infrastructures act as a means of governance support and not the independent solution to the ethical sourcing issues (Wieland, 2021). The section presents a literature review on the use of blockchain systems, Internet of Things (IoT) schemes, and Artificial Intelligence (AI)-inspired analytics in supply chains visibility.

5.1 Blockchain and Traceability Integrity

The technology of blockchains is often discussed as a technology enhancing the impossibility of records, the clarity of transactions, and the chain-of-custody authentication on the supply chains of various levels (Kshetri, 2018). In comparison to centralized databases, blockchain systems spread the data among decentralized nodes minimizing the chances of unilateral manipulation and empowering the level of informational trust.

There are a number of contributions of blockchain infrastructures to governance found in the literature. To begin with, alterations to the document forging, provenance misrepresentation, and data alteration may be reduced because of immutable transaction logs. Second, the traceability systems that are supported by blockchain can enhance auditability by maintaining verifiable records of materials flows and interactions with the suppliers (Saberi, Kouhizadeh, Sarkis, and Shen, 2019).

However, there are serious drawbacks, as pointed out by academics. The integrity of the input data is a also key component of blockchain reliability and is often loaned to the so-called garbage-in, garbage-out factor. Although blockchain can maintain the security of stored in the records, it cannot ensure the accuracy of upstream information on its own without additional verification procedures (LeBaron et al., 2022). The complexity of implementation and interoperability problems and constraints on supplier capability can also limit scalability especially in situations within the developing economy.

5.2 Internet of Things (IoT) and Real-Time Visibility

IoT systems expand the possibilities of transparency because it is possible to check physical object positioning and environmental factors and logistics in real-time. Connected devices, sensors, and RFID tags release unlimited data streams that contribute to the increased operational awareness and detection of anomalies (Ben-Daya, Hassini, and Bahroun, 2019).

IoT infrastructures relate to advancements in condition monitoring (in transparency research), compliance checks (in transparency research), and process integrity (in transparency research). Real-time data capture can help decrease delays in detecting deviations unauthorized subcontracting, unsafe condition of storage, or logistics anomaly (Wieland, 2021).

But there are implications of governance in literature as well. Greater sensor-based surveillance opens up the issues of data privacy, surveillance ethics and unbalanced technological distribution. The activities of suppliers in the structure of the IoT-enabled systems might be accompanied by significant investment in the creation of infrastructure, which can enhance the disparities between supply chain players.

5.3 Artificial Intelligence and Predictive Risk Detection

AI-enabled analytics is another concept that is becoming an increasingly important field of study in the area of supply chain governance and risk management. Machine learning models may process both large-scale structured and unstructured data to detect problematic behavior, anticipate incidents, as well as risk assess compliance (Ding et al., 2023).

In the ethical sourcing scenario, AI applications are usually associated with predictive risk-detection functions. Information streams on multi-source algorithms may be combined to reveal patterns that individual suppliers are involved in fraud or labor violations, that there are anomalies in the logistics, or that the supplier possesses a reputation at risk in any way. The AI systems are therefore asymmetry-reduction mechanisms that increase the decision-making capacity of managers.

However, researchers do not recommend excessive dependence. The success of AI relies on the quality of data presented for analysis, assumptions of the model, and bias suppression guidelines. The lack of predictive accuracy may be restricted by the scarcity of data in low-visibility production settings. In addition, there also remain ethical issues of algorithmic invisibility, responsibility, and surveillance of the workers.

5.4 Technology–Governance Complementarity

A general opinion that spreads across the digitalization literature is that, technologies improve transparency infrastructures, but they cannot replace governance mechanisms. The major form of ethical sourcing failure is linked to incentive systems, buying procedures, and institutional emptiness, as opposed to an informational vacuum (Locke, 2013; Soundararajan and Brammer, 2018).

The digital tools thus act as amplifiers of governance whose power is subject to organizational incentives, regulatory compatibility and system of stakeholders check. In the absence of such integration, adoption of technologies may turn into meaningless symbolic transparency.

6. Cross-Cutting Tensions and Unresolved Gaps in Literature

Although the progress of the ethical sourcing and transparency have been vigorous, conceptual, operational and governance tensions can still be observed in the literature. As opposed to implying theoretical ineffectiveness, these tensions represent the natural complexity of governing globally fragmented supply chains that are multi-tiered, with diverse institutional conditions, and conflicting economic incentives (Wieland, 2021). This section generalizes hegemonic contradictions and unresolved controversies that have contributed to the current scholars.

6.1 Compliance Mechanisms vs Structural Incentives

Another issue of contention is commonplace; it is the mismatch between formal compliance regimes and informal economic regimes of incentives. Conventional tools of governance, such as audits, certificates, and supplier codes, presuppose that such unethical practices can be prevented by the regulations of monitoring and the imposition of corrective actions (Locke, 2013). Nevertheless, in practice, it has always been shown that compliance regimes are commonly coupled with the systematic violation of labor and environmental malpractices (LeBaron, Lister, and Dauvergne, 2022).

Researchers put this gap down to the misalignment of structural incentives. The approach to procurement that has focused on minimizing costs, decreasing lead-time, and volatile demand can firmly destroy the ability of suppliers to continue acting ethically (Soundararajan and Brammer, 2018). As such, governance failures are often qualified not through the absence of monitoring but rather through contradictions inherent to purchasing practices and through cost compression.

This discussion elaborates on a fundamental observation that ethical sourcing issues are often structural as opposed to procedural.

6.2 Transparency Expansion vs Data Reliability

Although most people advocate transparency as a remedial tool against information asymmetry, the literature poses why more disclosure necessarily leads into informational credibility. Mechanisms of transparency can increase the visibility but continue having issues with inaccuracy in data, selectivity in reporting, and the limitation of verification (Mol & Oosterveer, 2015).

As researchers stress, the effectiveness of transparency is determined heavily by the data governance systems, incentives of reporting, and validation system (Ren, Taghipour, and Canel-Depitre, 2016). And lacking plausible checking procedures, broader disclosure will create meaningful transparency but not meaningful accountability.

This contradiction criticizes simpleistic explanations of visibility as equal to governance effectiveness.

6.3 Technological Adoption vs Governance Capacity

Another major contradiction is presented in the research of digitalization. Blockchain, IoT, and AI technologies are often presented as possible remedies to the lack of transparency. However, the empirical literature on technology usage in business over and over again stresses the fact that technology-based infrastructures alone are not capable of resolving governance problems (Kshetri, 2018; Saberi et al., 2019).

Technologies enrich the traceability and monitoring potentials without being absolute based on the data integrity, organizational incentives, as well as the institutional enforcement structures (LeBaron et al., 2022). In settings where there are weak governance capacity, few suppliers or regulators being dispersed, technological adoption might not bring about ethical improvements.

The literature, in such a way, finds the convergence point in the technology-governance complementary perspective, as opposed to substitution logic.

6.4 Multi-Tier Visibility vs Operational Feasibility

Transparency studies on the supply chain, even today, still indicate lower-tier suppliers as the most significant threat to ethics. Nevertheless, multi-tier traceability systems are still expensive, technically, and organizational burdensome (Wieland, 2021).

Trades offs between the depth of visibility and the feasibility of operation go on in firms.

Although deep-tier transparency is more effective in enhancing the ability to detect risk, it also leads to added coordination costs, complexity of data management, and risks of supplier resistance (Taghipour and Frayret, 2013). This leads to partial transparency architectures in many organizations leaving the upstream vulnerabilities unsolved.This tension underscores persistent limitations in scaling comprehensive traceability frameworks.

6.5 Conceptual Fragmentation in Literature

The conceptual map of ethical sourcing and transparency is disjointed despite the intensive standards of research activity in the interdisciplinary domain. There are varied interpretations of these constructs that use CSR, stakeholder theory, the institutional theory, the operations management and the digital governance perspectives in studies. On the one hand, this diversity enriches the debate on theories; however, in the same breath, it makes it challenging to develop cumulative knowledge (Kim et al., 2018).

The emergence of integrative frameworks that resolve the theory of governance, information asymmetry models, and technological infrastructures are increasingly promoted by scholars (Vosooghidizaji, Taghipour, & Canel-Depitre, 2019).

6.6 Emerging Research Gaps

Several unresolved questions recur across contemporary studies:

- Does the nature of purchasing practices structure in its impact over ethical compliance outcomes?
- Does digital traceability solution change power disparities in supplier networks?
- What forms of governance can be useful to control concealed subcontracting levels?
- What is the effect of owning data on credibility of transparency and trust by stakeholders?

The gaps here need to be addressed interdisciplinarily as combining elements of supply chain management and governance theory, data ethics and institutional research.

7. Implications for Theory, Management, and Policy

The systematic review of the literature on ethical sourcing and supply chain transparency has generated significant implications that cut across the background of theoretical advancement, managerial decision-making and the design of policy formulation. It is always reported in the previous studies that the failure of governance in global supply chains is not normally associated with single organizational behaviour but rather the structural nature of the interactions between incentives, information asymmetry and institutionalization (Locke, 2013; Wieland, 2021).

7.1 Theoretical Implications

It is found in the literature that there is a great need of integrative theoretical frameworks capable of harmonizing the governance theory, information asymmetry views, and digitalization research. The development of ethical sourcing research has been linked to customs of corporate social responsibility (CSR) and stakeholder theory, whereas the research of transparency has been often inspired by the operations management, institutional theory and information economics (Kim, Colicchia, and Menachof, 2018).

Nonetheless, incoherent theoretical lenses are known to restrain the development of cumulative knowledge. Theoretical developments in the future should focus on models such as those that conceptualize the idea of supply chains as multi-actor governance systems as opposed to linear forms of transactions (Taghipour and Frayret, 2013). Information asymmetry models also have some explanatory capability to determine the reason why subsequent ethical risks occur despite the formal compliance arrangements (Vosooghidizaji, Taghipour, and Canel-Depitre, 2019).

Also, digital technologies pose new theoretical challenges in terms of data governance; algorithmic responsibility and technological mediation of trust. These are still open academic frontiers on theoretical integration.

7.2 Managerial Implications

To practitioners, the literature discloses traditional compliance-oriented view of ethical sourcing. Even though periodic audits, codes to suppliers, and certification requirements are inevitable, they are often ineffective when not aligned to procurement incentives and coordination frameworks (LeBaron, Lister, and Dauvergne, 2022).

The managers are thus encouraged to pursue governance-based approaches that focus on:

- **Incentive Alignment** – Procurement strategies should be able to align cost efficiency goals with supplier capability in order to maintain ethical compliance (Soundararajan & Brammer, 2018).
- **Continuous Monitoring Architectures** – Dynamic transparency- and risk-detecting systems can be used to supplement the traditional forms of static audit regimes (Wieland, 2021).
- **Relational Governance Mechanisms** – Adversarial compliance dynamics may be prevented through the use of long-term supplier relationships and joint development of capabilities (Taghipour and Beneteau-Piet, 2020).
- **Multi-Tier Risk Awareness** – This is where Ethical vulnerabilities are often based at other than Tier-1 suppliers and require more wider strategies of visibility.

Notably, the sources emphasize that the adoption of technology without governance adjustments is of very little use. Digital traceability systems cannot replace managerial accountability with incentive restructuring and interaction with suppliers, as are more visible.

7.3 Policy Implications

The trend toward regulatory developments is shifting towards the acknowledgment that even the voluntary systems of governance would not be able to mitigate the systemic ethical risks. The mandatory due diligence organizational framework, disclosure regime, and traceability limit aim to transform the organizational incentives and accountability frameworks (Wieland, 2021).

Some policy-relevant insights emanating out of the literature are:

- **Governance Harmonization Challenges** – Legal jurisdictions of global supply chain are fragmented and make enforcement patterns difficult (Locke, 2013).
- **Transparency Standardization Needs** – Interoperable data structures and similar reporting frameworks are essential to the workability of regulatory frameworks (Mol & Oosterveer, 2015).
- **SME Capability Constraints** – Small suppliers can have their compliance disproportionately high when faced with traceability requirements that are technologically vigorous.
- **Technology-Policy Interaction** – Regulatory compliance architecture and architecture Blockchain and digital traceability systems continue to overlap regulatory compliance architectures.

According to literature, successful policy frameworks should strike the right balance between the rigor of enforcement and feasibility factors, the inclusiveness of suppliers, and the protection of data.

7.4 Cross-Domain Insight

In all three aspects of theoretical, managerial, and policy analyses, a common finding consists in the idea that such issues as ethical sourcing and transparency are more governance phenomena than specific technical failures (Taghipour & Frayret, 2013; Soundararajan and Brammer, 2018).

8. Conclusion and Future Research Directions

The above narrative synthesis underscores the importance of the fact that ethical sourcing and supply chain transparency have become structural governance requirements within modern-day global production processes rather than the marginalized corporate responsibility programmes. Ethical risks within global supply chains have always been shown in the literature to be systemic effects produced by decentralized production arrangements, information asymmetry, and non-coherent incentives (Locke, 2013; Soundararajan and Brammer, 2018).

One of the most common lessons learned throughout the river of governance, transparency, and digitalization research is that the issues of ethical sourcing are inherently organizational and institutional in nature of governance, as opposed to being technical or information inadequate. Although both transparency mechanisms and digital technologies improve the process of visibility, traceability, and monitoring, their impact depends on the alignment of incentives and integrity of data and plausible enforcement structures (Wieland, 2021; Kshetri, 2018).

The literature also highlights these simmering tensions that define effectiveness of ethical governance. The compliance-based models, especially the regimes where auditing plays a significant portion of functions, often have restricted abilities to drive lasting development once the procurement activities remain focused on minimizing costs and operational liberation (LeBaron, Lister, and Dauvergne, 2022). In a similar way, expansion of transparency itself cannot ensure the reliability of the information without the presence of verifying and controlling structures (Mol & Oosterveer, 2015).

Taken together, each of these findings reinvents global supply chains as intricate socio-economic regimes with multi-actor interrelations, non-homogenous institutional settings, and non-static risk patterns (Taghipour and Frayret, 2013). It is thus seen that ethical sourcing and transparency are not only management tools, but governance ones built on more broad legitimacy, accountability, and coordination processes.

Notably, there is a caveat related to the synthesis in terms that reductionist reflections put technological innovation on a replacement of governance reform. Digital infrastructures enhance governance capacities but cannot act necessarily to solve structural factors in unethical practices. The sustainability of the progress is associated with the alignment of the organizational incentives, the reinforcement of the mechanisms of inter-firm alignment, and the creation of the credible accountability systems.

8.1 Directions for Future Research

Even though it is a well-studied topic, there are a number of research questions left unanswered.

1. Governance–Incentive Interactions

Further research would be the investigation of the structural impact of procurement activities, pricing schemes, and lead-time requirements on the ethical result. Although a connection between governance failures and labor or environmental violations is common to be reported, causal relationships between purchasing practices and other two factors are underresearched (Soundararajan and Brammer, 2018).

2. Multi-Tier Transparency Architectures

There is a need of empirical studies in order to determine the viability, performance and undesired effects of deep-tier transparency systems. Multi-tier traceability is only desirable on principle but rather challenging to operate (Taghipour and Frayret, 2013).

3. Technology–Governance Complementarity

Digitalization brings about new questions in relation to the possession of data, algorithmic responsibility, and mediation of trust by technology. One inquiry that researchers should examine is the role of technologies in transforming the power relations of governance or in further supporting asymmetries (Kshetri, 2018).

4. Data Integrity and Verification Mechanisms

The literature on transparency would also use more focus on data validation processes and reports on incentives and issues of informational reliability (Mol & Oosterveer, 2015).

5. Institutional and Regulatory Dynamics

Comparative studies across the regulatory systems can help understand how the practice of mandatory due diligence can redefine sourcing incentives and supplier governance systems (Wieland, 2021).

8.2 Concluding Reflection

Ethical sourcing and transparency should be seen as emerging rules of governance influenced by the forms of economic system, institutional forces and technological changes. Their sustainability is better determined by not so much isolated compliance systems but overall coordination between organization incentives, governance institutions and the expectations of stakeholders' accountability.

9.Conceptual Framework of Ethical Sourcing & Transparency

This chapter suggests a conceptual framework exploring existing patterns of domination in ethical sourcing and transparency literature. According to previous literature, governance issues in global supply chains are always driven by structural features of decentralized production systems and specific organizational failure (Locke, 2013; Wieland, 2021). Institutional heterogeneity, multi-tier fragmentation, and information asymmetry contribute to the conditions in which ethical risks and visibility gaps take place (Soundararajan and Brammer, 2018).

In reaction to this, companies implement governance and disclosure systems such as ethical sourcing principles, supplier codes of conducts, audit and certification, disclosure systems, and e-traceability systems. These procedures are asymmetry-reduction and accountability-enhancement tools that facilitate monitoring capacity and stakeholder trust (Mol & Oosterveer, 2015).

Nevertheless, the level of governance continues to be limited due to the influence of tensions related to costs of compliance, constraints of the reliability of information, barriers related to the adoption of technologies, and heterogeneity of suppliers (LeBaron et al., 2022; Kshetri, 2018). The relationship between structural drivers, governance mechanisms and systemic constraints, therefore, determines the ethical sourcing and transparency outputs.

REFERENCES

Ben-Daya, M., Hassini, E., & Bahroun, Z. (2019). Internet of Things and supply chain management: A literature review. *International Journal of Production Research*, *57*(15–16), 4719–4742. DOI: 10.1080/00207543.2017.1402140

Carroll, A. B. (1991). The pyramid of corporate social responsibility: Toward the moral management of organizational stakeholders. *Business Horizons*, *34*(4), 39–48. DOI: 10.1016/0007-6813(91)90005-G

Ding, H., Jin, M., Li, S., & Feng, B. (2023). Artificial intelligence and big data analytics in supply chain risk management: A systematic review. *International Journal of Production Economics*, *258*, 108778.

Elkington, J. (1997). *Cannibals with forks: The triple bottom line of 21st century business*. Capstone.

Francisco, K., & Swanson, D. (2018). The supply chain has no clothes: Technology adoption of blockchain for supply chain transparency. *Logistics (Basel)*, *2*(1), 2. DOI: 10.3390/logistics2010002

Fransen, L., & LeBaron, G. (2019). Big audit firms as regulatory intermediaries in transnational labor governance. *Regulation & Governance*, *13*(2), 260–279. DOI: 10.1111/rego.12224

Freeman, R. E. (1984). *Strategic management: A stakeholder approach*. Pitman.

Huq, F. A., Stevenson, M., & Zorzini, M. (2014). Social sustainability in developing country suppliers. *Journal of Cleaner Production*, *56*, 1–14.

Kim, S., Colicchia, C., & Menachof, D. (2018). Ethical sourcing: An analysis of the literature and implications for future research. *Journal of Business Ethics*, *152*(4), 1033–1052. DOI: 10.1007/s10551-016-3266-8

Klassen, R. D., & Vereecke, A. (2012). Social issues in supply chains. *International Journal of Production Economics*, *140*(1), 103–115. DOI: 10.1016/j.ijpe.2012.01.021

Kshetri, N. (2018). Blockchain's roles in meeting key supply chain management objectives. *International Journal of Information Management*, *39*, 80–89. DOI: 10.1016/j.ijinfomgt.2017.12.005

LeBaron, G., Lister, J., & Dauvergne, P. (2022). The effectiveness of supply chain audits in improving labor standards. *Review of International Political Economy*, *29*(2), 1–27.

Locke, R. M. (2013). *The promise and limits of private power: Promoting labor standards in a global economy*. Cambridge University Press. DOI: 10.1017/CBO9781139381840

Mol, A. P. J., & Oosterveer, P. (2015). Certification of markets, markets of certificates: Tracing sustainability in global value chains. *Journal of Cleaner Production*, *107*, 154–161. DOI: 10.1016/j.jclepro.2013.11.012

Reinecke, J., & Ansari, S. (2016). Taming wicked problems: Multi-stakeholder governance. *Organization Studies*, *37*(3), 299–329.

Ren, Z., Taghipour, A., & Canel-Depitre, B. (2016). Information sharing in supply chain under uncertainty. In *Proceedings of the International Conference on Information Communication and Management* (pp. 67–71). IEEE. DOI: 10.1109/INFOCOMAN.2016.7784217

Saberi, S., Kouhizadeh, M., Sarkis, J., & Shen, L. (2019). Blockchain technology and its relationships to sustainable supply chain management. *International Journal of Production Research*, *57*(7), 2117–2135. DOI: 10.1080/00207543.2018.1533261

Sodhi, M. S., & Tang, C. S. (2019). Research opportunities in supply chain transparency. *Production and Operations Management*, *28*(12), 2946–2959. DOI: 10.1111/poms.13115

Soundararajan, V., & Brammer, S. (2018). Developing country sub-suppliers and ethical sourcing. *Business Ethics Quarterly*, *28*(4), 475–503.

Taghipour, A., & Beneteau-Piet, C. (2020). Sustainable supply chain management performance. *International Journal of Innovation, Management and Technology*, *11*(6), 165–169. DOI: 10.18178/ijimt.2020.11.6.897

Taghipour, A., & Frayret, J.-M. (2013). Coordination of operations planning in supply chains: A review. *International Journal of Business Performance and Supply Chain Modelling*, *5*(3), 272–307. DOI: 10.1504/IJBPSCM.2013.055729

Vosooghidizaji, M., Taghipour, A., & Canel-Depitre, B. (2019). A literature review on information asymmetry in supply chain coordination. *International Journal of Production Research*, *58*(6). Advance online publication. DOI: 10.1080/00207543.2019.1685702

Wieland, A. (2021). Dancing the supply chain: Toward transformative supply chain management. *The Journal of Supply Chain Management*, *57*(1), 58–73. DOI: 10.1111/jscm.12248

Zorzini, M., Hendry, L. C., Huq, F. A., & Stevenson, M. (2015). Socially responsible sourcing. *International Journal of Operations & Production Management*, *35*(1), 60–82. DOI: 10.1108/IJOPM-07-2013-0355

Chapter 5
Policy Frameworks for ESG Supply Chains

Arhant Vinod
http://orcid.org/0009-0006-5183-5632
Christ (Deemed to be) University, Delhi NCR, India

Sadashiva Tandur
http://orcid.org/0000-0003-4662-0582
Christ University, Bengaluru, India

ABSTRACT

The ESG system has evolved beyond a compliance structure to a holistic strategic network shaping how organizations operate and It now fosters sustainability through production, services, and innovation, connecting regulation, stakeholder expectations, and adaptability. With a initiatives like the EU's CSRD and emission reporting, firms integrate sustainability throughout business ecosystems, enhance transparency, lower energy impact, and employ technology for accountability and also enduring growth.

INTRODUCTION

The Environmental, as well Governance (ESG) chain has evolved, changing the previous as that a compliance to the definition that the way conduct themselves the age globalization. Whereas in the regarded ESG being sent report responsibility investors or the ESG chain has traction on manufacturing logistics. Focuses on demand forecasting and order planning models in supply chains and humanitarian logistics (Taghipour, 2020), as well as climate disclosures, prescribe that is no on the as any of "soft" but rather complemented as core value corporate strategy as

DOI: 10.4018/979-8-3373-6455-1.ch005

well as management. Against background The role of political environment. Social places the dimension in chains in relief, well classical compliance labour law. is now more accountable eliminate child forced labour, dangerous working in multi-level of supply, which risk most typically Greater expectations inclusion have forced companies take affirmative to diversify suppliers Demonstrates the integration of QFD and ELECTRE methods for effective supplier evaluation. (Mahfod et al., 2019). These as much local community corporate reputation reflection of social value is part ESG frameworks. ESG governing also promotes good management as well resilience in long-standing operating the COVID-19 brought into the vulnerabilities the world chains to the value predictive analytics the forecasting disruptions, diversification sources as open regimes that reassurance to Next-generation technologies as enable of tracking real time as well responsibility in global networks. These instruments are economic resilience minimization of two localized continuity as well in the environmental world as well as the problems faced by supply chains and their severe transformation in the current environment, through an analysis of the literature on the subject and examines the various challenges that supply chains face daily (Radhoui et al., 2019). Against system systems policy themselves principle multi-levelled, context that structure more system regime process challenges consist of the increasing quantities of cargo being transported, the need for low transportation fees, and the efforts of shipping companies and stevedoring contractors (Sahraoui et al., 2023) in embracing reportable, as verifiable .Unlike CSR main nature voluntary as charitable character, ESG assumed the of an approach that indelibly inscribed decision-taking that operative as as in governance. This has been through regulatory expectations, investors pressure, activism, as as broader of systemic occasioned through change, social as well governance failure. Supply chain is most applicable the ESG in light the fact the supply is the center of trade as production research 2021 that supply is accountable, average, for than 80% the end outcome emissions greenhouse gases as well as 90% the entire impact of organization. Social like exploitation workers, dangerous environment, forced child working as well, institutionalized in supply chain the vast of cases. There is urgency in supplying ESG issues with the consequences of successive crises. The tragedy in year 2013 more than garment workers when the Plaza building brought into consciousness risky conditions in supply lines & Reinecke, the emissions from auto Volkswagen burst weaknesses in as well the automobile greenwashing potential 2015. COVID-19 recently raised question susceptibility global supply to the that is not the from operational raised, but social inequity like risky conditions among workers as as unequal to health are called question risks in lines are called into through natural like wildfires, as well droughts. Pressures for ESG practices expectations from Investors are vocal in call for responsibility as disclosure ESG as finance goes in world markets (Friede, & Bassen, Consumers are free to to purchase products as as to brands that associated with destruction as as human violations. Media well as societies are who sound for vulnerable who are by corporate Employees, particularly generations, are their companies adopting ESG impacting retention well as of talents & Burke). In spite these patterns, incorporation of frameworks into systems is Companies are confronted with regulatory regimes, measurement protocols, constraints in supply base, well as gaps into medium size (SMEs, most in supply networks, are with disproportionate levels of cost, capable jeopardizing their chain membership. risk for exaggeration or in reference sustainability rhetoric, undermines in ESG. These necessitate coherent, inclusive policy that weighs pragmatism as well.

Early Foundations Social Awakening:

The millions were them to provide attention to imperatives to nature's decay, and preservation. All those years the 1960s the 1970s transition years social movements the American to worker anti-apartheid movements around the All these into sharp corporate responsibility the field ethics towards only shareholders, workers, towards peoples, towards as a historically, in antecedents to responsible investing arose when were interested divestment from that were in controversial like tobacco, arms, as as companies supported the regime.

Corporate Social and Institutional 1980s-1990s (DiMaggio & Powell, 1983)

The 1980s officially the of Corporate Responsibility (CSR), businesses became responsive to broader social well as obligations. Worldwide as well industry-wide crises the Bhopal tragedy, 1984 well as Exxon Valdez spill, 1989 on display social, as as environmental that can under the of corporate The decade to businesses, as well investors, towards regulation as as supervision prevent repeating. (DiMaggio & Powell, 1983). Sustainability reporting was popular when Global Reporting (GRI) was in 1997 in to give direction to to report environment as as their performance. This stakeholders to companies accountable well as compare ESG in a setting.

Emergence of as an Early 2000s

Whereas CSR voluntary firm-driven CSR failed offer consistent enabling wide-based assessment. The "Environmental, Social, Governance (ESG)" catch-all first in the Who Cares by the United Nations Compact. The characterized convergence ESG factors finance analysis in investment as representing change from CSR to as well quantitative assessment ESG risks as well as international agreements the Kyoto in 1997 the template the forward to future policy, with management as hub in

Environmental Pillar ESG. Disclosures got financially sophisticated: Sustainability Accounting Board (SASB) industry-specific ESG based on material considerations, the Task on Climate-related Disclosures (TCFD) voluntary recommendations disclosures on risk, governance, and objectives offer value investors as to Market pressures ESG trends asset managers adopted oriented portfolios use of ratings from and MSCI. analysis was in favor ethics as amounts of were available offer that ESG qualities lower risk good performance. Other corporations began to supply chain risks because 3 emissions nowadays the in all because their footprints are compared to direct operation.

ESG Regulation Mandatory Policy 2020s

The next will mark beginning of new age regulation for the 2020s characterized by legislation and that will ESG compliance voluntary best to regulatory European for the Reporting Directive the Corporate Reporting Directive greatly expands requires audited disclosures, and dual materiality mind—the environment wider societally that businesses as well their resultant effects to themselves. The Taxonomy Regulation science-based direction categorizes sustainable activities into Canada, Japan, and China introduced or introducing obligatory disclosure regimes, with global towards convergence well as regulation. These are kind of developments that hallmarks of knowledge that ESG policy part of prudency in sustainable economics, much as social equity, by ever-tightening and fines guarantee compliance.

ESG and Chain Integration

Global supply that has of suppliers can cross boundaries are platforms on ESG risks Examines the role of logistics providers in supporting humanitarian operations in Syria. (Mahfod et al., 2021), environment degradation exploitation of to governance flourish. That why ESG supply chain pertinent to Companies are supply chain risk segmentation, traceability technologies, in the of blockchain AI to raw materials, suppliers' ESG and enable responses. Even more social considerations evading forced preserving employee boosting diversification inclusion—is becoming statutorily governed well as consumer-motivated.

Challenges in Implementing ESG Policy

Despite significant advances, ESG implementation remains by diverging frameworks, diverging information qualities, hesitation, into resources primarily amongst Global collaboration, as well as innovative endeavor to solve these Initiatives such the International Standards Board endeavor to worldwide sustainability to enable multinational compliance. systems are to automate validation, as as reporting information, while initiatives enable sharing, education. In addition, the economy model pace as ESG gamechanger rising resource as well closed-loop cycles raw materials minimize footprints the environment. Challenges that supply chains are facing need smooth and intelligent processes that facilitate communication between machines and people in order to create value and achieve a certain degree of agility. (Taghipour et al., 2022a.) From green modest beginnings social investment there current in corporate as in regulation, the of ESG reflected broader of the responsibility towards environment as society. To end, the has balanced incentives, policy as well social pressure arrive at healthy framework is the of sustainable development.

Deepening the Foundations of in Supply

Classically, stakeholders encompassed management diverging competing ESG in world, that's into collaboration, and businesses together to create sustainability Stakeholders as of business are instead this cooperative has for corollary supply power redistribution well. Lowly workers, e.g., themselves are perhaps weakly to negotiate, best represented their rights embedded in as in EU's Corporate. Due Diligence (CSDDD). Here, theory advocates cooperation to as an extent protection in as avenues give voice muted margins. Institutional Theory: Institutional theory adoption in its adoption variegated pressure is pressure is coercive, that is as well pressure that mimetic. have pressures are incoherent—the are very regionally. For the EU tough norms ESG reports are strict, others in Africa or South Asia weak. The is that there ends up pressure as as attraction global convergence well as variation. Associations also have sectoral codes, clothes sector, example, uses Sustainable Apparel Higg Index, the codes the Responsible Alliance's (RBA). theory broadly strays that systems ESG are systems—all world all regional and sectoral overlapping sometimes well as sometimes.

Resource-Based View Environmental Social (ESG)

From the view the RBV is just much about compliance as is about competitiveness by 2030. Similarly, green low ship investment Maersk makes latter a shipping leader 2021. Strength in competencies lies their distinctiveness, they cannot emerge creating trust supply chain capital investment tracing, and sustainability in culture needs that run decades. Policymakers aimlessly capitalize on strengths as in the of green or preferential RBV reveals responsibility can much as be improved ESG. Legitimacy Theory: Contract as Legitimacy theory ESG in firm's "social mutual understanding firms will their businesses socially acceptable (Suchman, 1995). However, certifications in instances are critics imply & Glassberg, this opens the opportunity "decoupling," when issue pronouncements ESG while backing them. Effective in the of mandatory audit and are needed plug this to move from rhetorical to substantive.

Agency Theory:

Supply Chain Agency theory information gaps large customers small suppliers & Meckling the gaps deepest most in the where destruction environment and are most to workers. New technologies alternatives IBM Walmart, for have experimented blockchain to food in supply chain that can offer in real as well useful these are, however, will usually small suppliers will not in a to internalise. policy arrangements then need occur to marginalising SMEs. Supply Chain Theory: Triple Line to Economy Theory The previous were founded the "triple line": finding balance between economic, environmental, social objectives & Müller, Models then to principles on circular that are by systems are regenerative of linear. We can this electronics in practice and HP take-back initiatives recycle existing into new Ellen MacArthur has advocated kinds of as product as well end-of-life responsibility even included the EU's Economy Action European Commission, sporadic Integrated practices frameworks up new risks on the Complementarities versus Between Theories Each theory something distinct ESG, overlap tension are Legitimacy theory stakeholder theory value on expectations, though values cooperation the other value in Institutional theory to extrinsic while RBV to internal There are too. n the adoption and integration of responsible AI solutions in supply chains (Taghipour, 2023). Control-based to agency can most exist in with collaboration by stakeholder Institutional coercion awkwardly coexist voluntary, strategy-based of ESG RBV.

Global ESG Aspect

Global ESG Landscape Environmental, as well also governance management in chain has increasingly important over the Given that corporations are in nature, businesses are line with standards, regulation, well as codes in as well responsibly operated Global entities, networks, as as local have created frameworks to as well enforce ESG in supply This section an overview three parts reference to ESG policy International institutions well as regimes Regional frameworks Cross-border as well investment regimes affect ESG chain regimes International Institutions well as Arrangements International have headed building ESG through the of principles, as well guidelines that world reference Although voluntary character, these are laced reputational as as normative giving birth soft-law parameters affect corporate as well national regulatory United Nations Compact (UNGC) in the 2000, the is one the world's voluntary corporate initiatives in world, involving 16,000 companies 160 nations. promotes ten that address rights, labour, as well anti-corruption. Within chain management, provides practical in integrating in procurements, management, as as reporting. big advantage in mainstreaming as part the Business Usual, as from being as compliance. instance, Nestlé Unilever obligate suppliers to to UNGC in labour well as human rights. critics caution voluntary approach UNGC provides to "blue that is, that move the queue to improve image instead changing their Sustainable Development (SDGs) Agreed 2015, the 17 SDGs a 2030 development plan. chain relevant are Goal (Decent Work Economic Growth) 12 (Responsible and Production) 13 (Climate Companies are their ESG to growing to SDGs) garment workers have called brands to in their in their rights through This lends law" teeth. Labour Organization Conventions Paris has an implication on chain through requirement that reach emissions that are mandates for use renewable of power, well as elimination. An is the "Fit for package that carbon pricing well as adjustment to chains to supply. Global Initiative (GRI) provides one the most used sustainability standards, in in over companies. Its is to energy, in workforce, as as to rights, through as well disclosure approaches are systematic. indicators are by companies Apple as as Toyota report their result from supply chain allowing investors ESG risk. Accounting Standards (SASB) as as ISSB developed sectoral norms, consolidated the International Standards Board ISSB is an international requirement in disclosures, while to reduce as well incoherence in reportability. Task on Climate-Related Disclosures (TCFD) in the Stability Board, TCFD makes recommendations on risk as as climate Its report adopted by as well stock markets, compulsorily. The e.g., requires companies to in line the TCFD. individually form building blocks global ESG chain management. is globally yet these frameworks that legislation, corporate as well capital investment. Policy Frameworks groupings have developed broad-based frameworks. Global is the with tight whereas the Asia-Pacific, Africa, well as America, are harmonized approaches. Union (EU) EU has in place the most ESG rules: (2022): Mandates to manage human rights well as risks across entire supply EU Taxonomy: sustainable economic CBAM (2023): Mandates on anti-slavery Dodd-Frank Act 1502, 2010: disclosure on mineral sourcing. their shortcomings, legislation as as market-based like ESG-motivated as well shareholder activism important. Asia-Pacific region has progress: China: Supply Chain forced disclosures emitters. Japan: Code as as Corporate Codes that integrating ESG. Mandates that 1,000 companies Business Responsibility well as Reports (BRSR) like South Singapore, as as Australia also making through investor-driven agendas. Africa well as America These are slowly to global norms: South King IV espouses sustainable as well ethical leadership. Mandates ESG from listed as well is compliant EU sustainable norms. Regional like the are already sustainability to regional economic Cross-Border.

Literature Review

The application of ESG in supply chains has evolved significantly over the past decades from being a risk management and compliance process to avoid negative effects on the environment and reputation to being a value-based process of integrating environmental, social, and governance factors into organizational systems and inter-organizational relations. In networked forms of organizing (so-called "network enterprises" with outsourced production and multi-tier supply chains), ESG is no longer a risk management process. Rather, it is being redeveloped as a tool for enhancing innovation, resilience, and brand differentiation through the integration of sustainability and responsibility into product and process, procurement, and logistics decisions (Lu & Taghipour, 2023). Turning to the environmental dimension, ESG in supply chains aims to reduce emissions, waste, and resource consumption and to speed up the circular economy by means of reuse, remanufacturing, and recycling. Digital traceability technologies such as RFID, IoT sensors, and provenance systems can be employed for monitoring and verification. However, challenges still exist in the process of implementation because of costs, lack of technological capacity in smaller suppliers, lack of data standards, and costs of auditing and verification. This may result in a "two-speed" transition where the bigger and better-organized central company drives the transition and the SME-dominant upstream supply chain lags behind, with compliance costs imposed on those least able to pay them. The social dimension of ESG in supply chains has expanded from occupational health and safety to encompass decent work, living wages, workforce well-being, human rights due diligence, inclusion, and community effects in sourcing areas. In this regard, social ESG requires understanding of subcontracting, where risk is likely to be most concentrated in informal arrangements and lower levels of the supply chain. In this regard, social ESG has led to the creation of supplier codes of conduct, grievance mechanisms, worker voice, and remediation initiatives. Nevertheless, social ESG is harder to quantify than environmental issues, and traditional auditing is likely to miss the root cause of the issue. Governance integrates environmental and social issues and decision-making, incentives, and accountability in the supply chain. Effective governance demands board and executive level oversight, procurement policies that align with ESG goals, risk management, disclosure, and assurance. In network enterprises, governance is complex owing to the distributed control, where the network enterprise needs to influence suppliers without ownership, and suppliers manage their subcontractors and internal affairs. Effective governance in this regard demands mutual standards, relational contracting, and escalation and corrective action processes. One of the most basic trade-offs in ESG-enabling supply chain management is information sharing. ESG-driven sustainability solutions may need information sharing about demand forecasts, customers, prices, or capacity plans to optimize resource allocation. Suppliers might be unwilling to "unlock" their strategic demand information, which could have the effect of undermining their bargaining power or leaving them vulnerable to the risk of opportunistic action. These trade-offs can be addressed by means of privacy-preserving data infrastructure: information sharing about the minimum necessary information (such as aggregate volumes, carbon intensity per product family, or compliance status), trusted intermediaries and secure computation, and access controls to ensure that partners see only what they need without disclosing their sensitive business information. Gain-sharing, long-term contracts, and upgrade financing can also balance competitiveness with transparency and make ESG a basis for mutual value creation. In the long run, these hybrid governance and technology architectures can extend ESG to multiple tiers of suppliers while maintaining strategic secrecy and autonomy.

Challenges, Gap and Criticism

The integration of Environmental, Social, Governance (ESG) within global chains has a critical item in business discourse, a growing on sustainable, and transparent across industries. the past regulators, investors, organizations (NGOs), other stakeholders pressured firms disclose and their ESG particularly concerning change, labor and corporate (Eccles & 2019), Sustainability Accounting Board (SASB), Carbon Disclosure (CDP), the Force on Financial Disclosures and the Union's Corporate Reporting Directive (Vosooghidizaji et al., 2020). proposes a digital storytelling-based learning model to enhance analytical thinking skills. (Ponputtha et al., 2021, 42-50.)

A central in ESG is the of standardized and the quality of particularly among in developing and small-to-medium (SMEs), which lack technological financial capacity collect and relevant information & Tuo, This limitation accurate measurement environmental and risks and transparency in supply networks. firms typically Scope 1 2 emissions but struggle Scope 3 which represent impacts from and customers 2024. The of consistent leads to assessments, obscuring true extent corporate sustainability Moreover, global chains are complex, multi-tiered where companies have visibility into their supplier, deeper tiers, where such as labor, deforestation, unsafe working often occur, remain (Yawar & 2017. This of transparency due diligence weakens accountability making it to ensure sourcing across levels. Analyzes customer preferences and willingness to pay for eco-friendly practices in luxury hotels. (Nadia et al., 2020; Nadia et al., 2018) Financial barriers complicate ESG particularly in economies where face high and auditing. For a textile in Bangladesh a cocoa in Ghana struggle to the expensive requirements demanded European buyers CSRD or diligence laws. financial imbalance marginalizing small effectively excluding from global networks while larger firms consolidate sustainability Paradoxically, ESG intended to inclusivity may inequalities if entities lack to necessary or technological. In fragmentation among regulations—such as between the CSRD, the Securities and Commission's (SEC) disclosure rules, diverse Asian administrative complexity 2024. The of global forces multinational to duplicate efforts and compliance burdens, can divert from substantive improvements toward reporting. In Demand Forecasting and Order Planning in Supply Chains and Humanitarian Logistics. (Radhoui et al., 2021).

The persistence greenwashing adds layer of Despite regulatory many corporations to engage selective disclosure, minor achievements concealing systemic ESG initiatives, 2024. Without monitoring or for non-compliance, may participate generating lengthy reports without behavioral change. Technological limitations restrict ESG particularly in economies. Although tools such blockchain, artificial (AI) Highlights how big data and AI enable highly personalized customer engagement in future marketing strategies. (Lu & Taghipour, 2025.) and Internet of (IoT) promise traceability, risk and data their implementation uneven. can secure supply chain while AI detect anomalies ESG data, the cost technical know-how for these are prohibitive smaller firms 2023. It is very difficult to find a supply chain, if any, of which all members have the same amount of information. As result, ESG becomes technologically in high-income but inadequate widening the sustainability divide. Uneven digital undermines globally and perpetuates in high-risk chains. Cultural and differences also the interpretation application of principles. Frameworks within Western and ethical may not with local or labor in Asia, or Latin. Critics further that ESG risk degenerating box-ticking exercises prioritize optics substance. The of lengthy reports filled standardized disclosures lacks evidence measurable impact et al., in measurement makes cross-company unreliable, while lobbying often ESG standards ways that large firms perpetuate existing dynamics AI- detection tools to limit overuse in assignments, aiming to promote students' critical thinking and academic integrity. The chapter concludes with recommendations for ethical AI use and suggests perspectives for future developments. (Taghipour & Lu, 2025). policies have been criticized responding too to urgent and social such as disasters, geopolitical and human violations (OECD, As sustainability evolve rapidly, regulatory systems lagging behind developments, limiting effectiveness. It develops and empirically validates a conceptual model that integrates technology adoption logic with knowledge-based and strategic decision-making perspectives to explain SCD at the organizational level.)

IMPLICATION

A comprehensive in how Social, and (ESG) frameworks conceptualized and within global chains. Historically, emerged from practices that avoiding environmental and adhering basic social ethical norms. time, however, has evolved a strategic, system that sustainability across operations, and decision-making. This reflects a paradigm shift which sustainability no longer as an or peripheral but rather a central of competitiveness, and long-term legitimacy. Reviews decision-making approaches for supplier selection in supply chains (Mbiatem et al., 2018). The underscores that principles have deeply embedded global trade, logistics, and transforming how define performance accountability in increasingly interconnected environmentally constrained (Suchman, 1995 main contributions of this paper are to develop a multi objective, dynamic production and distribution planning using time windows in service technology of sustainable pharmaceutical supply Chain Network. (Goodarzian et al., 2026) One of most profounds of this is the from voluntary initiatives toward standardized reporting governance frameworks. such as European Union's Sustainability Reporting (CSRD) and Sustainability Due Directive (CSDDD) established legally requirements for to disclose environmental, social, governance impacts. transition signifies departure from earlier era corporate social (CSR), which largely voluntary reputationally motivated, a regime regulatory accountability measurable outcome. such frameworks, and international are redefining transparency by quantifiable evidence emissions reductions, labor practices, rights protections, anti-corruption safeguards. a result, r. The ordinal priority approach (OPA) method is used to solve this problem and estimate the weights of the experts, criteria, and 3PL providers. (Aouadni et al., 2024, 33-42.) Collaborative forecasting refers to the situation where supply chain actors collaborate, either by coordinating forecasting methods or sharing forecast information, in order to achieve higher supply chain's performance. (Vosooghidizaji et al., 2019) the Internet Things (IoT) monitor supplier verifies sustainability and ensure accuracy of These technologies real-time tracking products and providing a record of and social across the network Collaboration is facilitated by sharin gworkflow tools with the consumer. Support activities are critical while selecting an SR supplier due to the product's maintenance in the event of an issue (Taghipour et al., 2022). However, such innovations enhanced accountability, also introduce as firms developing economies small and enterprises (SMEs) lack the and technical to adopt systems. Investigates the extent of environmental practice engagement among Lebanese hotels. (Nadia et al., 2021) The implication is twofold: both empowers exclude. On hand, digital enables the of transparent, supply chains of detecting improving efficiency, ensuring compliance international standards. the other unequal access these technologies widening the divide between multinational corporations smaller, resource-constrained the document that without support mechanisms—such financial assistance, programs, and initiatives, many smaller could be or excluded global trade This dynamic a paradox ESG frameworks: they seek promote inclusivity, can unintentionally inequality if remains uneven regions and sizes. (LeBaron et al., 2017). Another key concerns the complexity and of

ESG The proliferation overlapping frameworks, ranging the Global Initiative (GRI) Sustainability Accounting Board (SASB) the Task on Climate-Related Disclosures (TCFD) regional variations as those the EU, and Asia, creates in definitions, and reporting This lack harmonization not burdens companies duplicative reporting but also comparability across Consequently, firms higher compliance investors struggle assess ESG objectively, and encounter difficulties enforcing uniform The file that global in ESG standards is for achieving sustainability governance. such as International Sustainability Board (ISSB) promising efforts consolidation, but consensus remains Without such ESG risks into a exercise focused on documentation on genuine (Jensen & Meckling, 1976. It is assumed that replenishment policy follows a periodic review system. (Tliche et al., 2019).

In addition regulatory and challenges, the highlights the and operational of ESG Integrating ESG into supply requires substantial in auditing, training, and While large can absorb costs or them on consumers, smaller those based emerging economies—often compliance financially For instance, in sectors as textiles, or mining developing regions high certification and administrative to meet sustainability requirements by European North American This economic not only the inclusion SMEs in markets but risks reinforcing inequalities in To mitigate the document the need international financial governments, and corporations to support mechanisms facilitate equitable in ESG-driven supply chains. (LeBaron et al., 2017). Centralizing and streamlining supply chain planning processes such as product development, with a view to increase flexibility. (Lebosse et al., 2017). The social of ESG is equally significant environmental concerns, framework calls greater attention labor rights, equity, and development. The stresses that social dimension move beyond with labor toward active of ethical conditions, gender and fair. This evolution with stakeholder which views not merely profit-generating entities as social accountable to broader ecosystem stakeholders, including employees, suppliers, and communities. By these values supply chain companies can their social to operate, brand reputation, foster long-term among customers partners. However, persistent prevalence exploitative labor child labor, unsafe working in certain supply networks the gap ESG aspirations actual outcomes. gap highlights importance of mechanisms, third-party and multi-stakeholders to ensure social sustainability are meaningfully. From a perspective, the implies that ESG implementation a cultural structural shift organization. Boards directors and leaders must direct responsibility sustainability performance, ESG metrics executive compensation, appraisal, and oversight processes. also entails corruption, enhancing in procurement, fostering accountability regular, verifiable These practices only strengthen confidence but build organizational against external such as disasters, pandemics, geopolitical disruptions. this sense, governance is a preventive adaptive mechanism, companies to risks and continuity in environments. The document raises critical on the of greenwashing, where overstate or their sustainability Despite increased scrutiny, many continue to lengthy sustainability that emphasize achievements while systemic issues. erodes stakeholder distorts market and diminishes credibility of initiatives. The is that disclosure must accompanied by verification, measurable assessments, and penalties for reporting. True in ESG depends on from symbolic to substantive where environmental social commitments into demonstrable

Cultural and diversity further ESG implementation. designed in contexts may align seamlessly social norms, practices, or structures in regions. Reviews design-for-remanufacturing approaches aligned with reverse logistics processes (Taghipour et al., 2015). They suggest that frameworks must be a context-sensitive adapting global to local while maintaining ethical standards. example, labor acceptable under traditions may with international rights norms, careful negotiation education rather punitive exclusion. this regard, adaptability and stakeholder engagement critical to that ESG are both and effective. Ultimately, they convey that future lies in global consistency local flexibility, advancement with and profitability responsibility. The of ESG into supply represents not a regulatory but a imperative that corporate identity purpose. Companies authentically embrace are better to attract manage risks, sustain credibility a world defined by limits and expectations. Conversely, that treat as a gesture risk backlash, reputational and strategic. In essence, is redefining meaning of success in twenty-first century. embodies a from short-term gains to value creation in ethical environmental preservation, social inclusivity. implications of shift extend individual corporations the broader economy, signaling move toward new model capitalism—one that growth with innovation with and profit purpose. The thus positions not as passing trend as the of a equitable, and global order, transparency, accountability, shared prosperity the true of progress.

POLICY RECOMMENDATIONS AND IMPLEMENTATION ROADMAP

This section translates the discussion in the chapter into a practical roadmap for governments, regulators, and firms that manage global supplier networks. The aim is not to add another "framework" but to show, step by step, how ESG requirements can be implemented without creating unrealistic administrative burdens for suppliers. In many industries, buyers have strong expectations but limited visibility beyond tier-1 supplier. Policy and practice therefore need to focus on credible data, clear responsibilities, and staged improvement rather than a one-time audit mentality.

A useful way to think about implementation is to separate (1) minimum safeguards that should apply to all suppliers, (2) sector-specific risk controls, and (3) continuous improvement targets. Minimum safeguards include compliance with core labor standards, basic health and safety rules, and anti-corruption commitments. Sector-specific controls reflect known risks. Continuous improvement targets include emissions reduction plans, better waste management, or increased worker voice mechanisms. When these layers are mixed suppliers often receive unclear signals and reporting becomes inconsistent. For policymakers, phased compliance can reduce exclusion risks for SMEs. A common mistake is to require the same level of reporting, assurance, and digital traceability from every supplier regardless of size and capability. Instead, policy can define a "baseline" reporting template for SMEs and then require more detailed metrics only when risk or scale justifies it. A similar approach is used in many quality management systems: essential controls are mandatory, while advanced controls are encouraged and supported through incentives. For firms, the roadmap begins with governance: assigning clear accountability for ESG performance across procurement, compliance, operations, and finance. Many ESG failures occur because buyers treat ESG as a separate reporting function rather than a sourcing and operations issue. A practical approach is to link supplier ESG performance to supplier development, contractual terms, and procurement decisions. This does not mean "drop every non-compliant supplier immediately." In many contexts, improvement requires time and training. However, procurement must still set consequences for repeated non-compliance and misreporting to prevent greenwashing.

A second step is mapping supply chain risk. Risk mapping should identify high-risk geographies, processes, and materials. Even when firms do not have perfect tier-2 and tier-3 visibility, they can prioritize where deeper due diligence is required. Risk mapping can be updated annually and should inform audit plans, data collection priorities, and supplier engagement programs. Research on information asymmetry and decentralized supply chains suggests that better information sharing and aligned incentives reduce coordination failures and improve performance (Vosooghidizaji et al., 2019)

A third step is setting a realistic data plan. Firms should decide what indicators they will collect (and why), how often, and from whom. It helps to distinguish "management indicators" (used internally to improve performance) from "disclosure indicators" (reported externally). Not every metric needs to be publicly disclosed, but every disclosed metric should have an internal process that supports reliability. When firms disclose numbers without defining a measurement process, confidence declines and assurance costs rise.

A fourth step is supplier capability building. Supplier training is often treated as optional, but it becomes essential when new reporting rules and due diligence obligations are introduced. Training can cover documentation practices, health and safety basics, grievance mechanisms, chemical handling, energy management, and data collection. Large buyers can reduce cost by offering shared training programs, translated templates, and a helpdesk for small suppliers. Policies can reinforce this by recognizing collaborative capacity building as part of "good faith" compliance.

Finally, implementation requires feedback and learning. ESG is not a one-time certification; it is a management system. Firms should analyze where non-compliance happens repeatedly (for example, overtime violations, wage calculation). This supports continuous improvement and reduces future disruptions. Quick-response strategies and better planning also reduce the tendency to bypass standards during crises (Lebosse et al., 2017.)

SUPPLIER ENGAGEMENT AND SME SUPPORT

Supplier engagement is where ESG policy succeeds or fails. Many suppliers operate with limited margins, limited staff, and limited digital tools. If buyers demand extensive reporting without support, the likely outcome is superficial reporting or exclusion of smaller firms. Both outcomes weaken ESG objectives.

A practical engagement model includes three tiers of suppliers. Tier A includes strategic suppliers with high spend or high risk; these suppliers should receive deeper audits, joint improvement plans, and more frequent reporting. Tier B includes medium-risk suppliers; these suppliers can use standardized templates and periodic assessments. Tier C includes low-risk or small suppliers; these suppliers focus on minimum safeguards and simplified reporting. The goal is proportionality: higher risk receives more attention and resources.

Buyers can also reduce supplier burden by harmonizing requests. Suppliers commonly receive multiple questionnaires and overlapping reporting templates from different customers. When buyers align on common templates (for example, shared audit protocols or shared data fields), suppliers can invest in data systems once rather than repeatedly. Policymakers can encourage this by recognizing interoperable reporting standards and discouraging redundant requirements (Zoghlami et al., 2016).

Support mechanisms for SMEs can be financial (subsidies for audits or certifications), technical (training and tools), or collaborative (shared reporting platforms). Shared platforms can include simple web forms, mobile data collection, and translated guidance documents. Even basic digital infrastructure can reduce errors and improve timeliness. Research on digitalization highlights how information sharing and analytics can improve responsiveness and decision quality (Taghipour et al., 2022b; Sahraoui et al., 2023.)

DIGITAL TOOLS AND DATA GOVERNANCE

Digital tools are often presented as a solution to ESG data challenges, but technology is only as effective as the governance behind it. Organizations should define who enters data, who reviews it, and how changes are tracked. This matters for traceability and assurance.

Practical digital options range from low-cost tools to advanced systems. Low-cost tools include standardized spreadsheets, mobile inspection checklists, and document repositories. Mid-level tools include supplier portals and workflow systems that manage corrective actions. Advanced tools include IoT sensors, automated emissions monitoring, and anomaly detection for ESG data. The choice should match the maturity of suppliers and the risk profile of the supply chain. Data governance should include access controls, version history, and audit trails. When an indicator is updated (for example, an accident rate or energy use value), the organization should record when it was changed, by whom, and why. This reduces accidental errors and supports credible reporting. It also reduces the risk of "last-minute" changes made only to improve disclosure outcomes. Technology can also support resilience. During disruptions, firms often make rapid sourcing decisions. If ESG information is available in an accessible system, managers can avoid emergency sourcing from unknown or high-risk suppliers. This links ESG to operational risk management rather than treating it as an isolated reporting task.

LIMITATIONS AND FUTURE RESEARCH DIRECTIONS

Even with improved policy and digital tools, limitations remain. First, ESG indicators are not always comparable across sectors, and some impacts are difficult to measure (for example, biodiversity or informal labor conditions). Second, enforcement varies across jurisdictions. Third, supply networks change frequently as firms switch suppliers or add subcontractors, which can reduce the stability of monitoring systems.

Future research can contribute by improving measurement methods, evaluating the effectiveness of different due diligence models, and studying how digitalization changes the feasibility and cost of ESG compliance. Another priority is understanding how to design policies that improve outcomes without excluding SMEs from global value chains. Finally, more work is needed on linking ESG performance to operational outcomes such as delivery reliability, disruption recovery, and supplier innovation.

ILLUSTRATIVE IMPLEMENTATION EXAMPLE: TEXTILE SUPPLY CHAIN

To make the roadmap concrete, consider a mid-sized apparel brand sourcing from a network of factories and occasional subcontractors. The brand sells into markets that increasingly require credible sustainability disclosure, and it also faces reputational risk from labor and safety incidents. The first action is to define the boundary of responsibility. The brand begins with tier-1 factory but explicitly states that subcontracting is not permitted without written approval and disclosure. That single governance rule reduces "invisible" production, which is where many serious labor risks appear. The brand also assigns internal ownership: procurement owns the supplier relationship, compliance owns the audit program, operations owns lead-time and planning decisions that drive overtime, and finance owns data assurance for external reporting.

Next, the brand conducts a risk mapping exercise. It ranks suppliers by (a) production volume, (b) country risk indicators (labor enforcement, corruption risk, and environment), and (c) process risk (chemical dyeing, wastewater handling). High-risk sites are scheduled for deeper assessments, while lower-risk sites use simplified self-assessments. Importantly, the brand documents the logic of the ranking and keeps it consistent over time. This is useful when auditors ask why some suppliers receive more attention than others, and it prevents "audit shopping" where only easy sites are reviewed. The third action is to create a simple data kit for suppliers. The kit includes short templates for workforce demographics, wage records, overtime hours, safety incidents, and energy and water use. The templates are designed so that a factory with limited digital tools can still complete them using basic payroll and production records. The brand provides examples of acceptable evidence, for example, training attendance sheets This reduces confusion and reduces the time suppliers spend guessing what the buyer wants. The fourth action is supplier engagement. The brand runs a training session for factory managers and HR staff to explain expectations and common mistakes such as incomplete overtime documentation, missing safety training records, and weak grievance handling. It also sets up a feedback channel so workers can raise concerns confidentially. Rather than treating audits as a one-time pass/fail event, the brand uses findings to create corrective action plans with clear deadlines and support. Some issues can be fixed quickly (for example, missing protective equipment or blocked exits). Others require longer-term planning (for example, improving ventilation). The brand tracks progress and repeats check in a way that feels like improvement support, not punishment. The fifth action is to connect ESG expectations to procurement decisions in a transparent way. The brand builds a supplier scorecard where delivery performance, quality performance, and ESG performance are evaluated together. Suppliers are not punished for reporting problems; instead, they are rewarded for timely reporting and measurable improvement. This reduces incentives for misreporting. It also addresses a common root cause of labor violations: unrealistic lead times. When procurement pushes extreme deadlines, factories respond with excessive overtime, subcontracting, or unsafe shortcuts. The scorecard therefore includes a planning metric (forecast stability or schedule changes) so the brand itself holds accountable for the operational drivers of ESG outcomes. Finally, the brand prepares its public disclosure. It reports a limited number of indicators that it can support with evidence and internal review. It is better to disclose fewer indicators reliably than to disclose many indicators with weak verification. The brand also explains limitations—for example, where tier-2 visibility is incomplete, and provides a plan for improvement. Over time, it expands coverage and assurance as supplier capability increases. This approach aligns disclosure with operational reality and reduces the risk of greenwashing claims, while still meeting stakeholder expectations for transparency.

Conclusion

Environmental, Social, and Governance (ESG) issues have clearly shifted from the periphery of corporate discourse to the center of the management, financing, and assessment of global supply chains. What was historically a set of disparate issues, environmental protection, social ethics, anti-corruption, and corporate responsibility, has evolved into a comprehensive framework of expectations and accountability that is increasingly driving strategy, risk management, and operational architecture. The process of development illustrated in this chapter indicates that ESG is no longer a "soft" supplement to corporate citizenship but a formalized regime that is increasingly being formalized through regulation, investor due diligence, stakeholder activism, and the hard realities of disruption-sensitive global networks. One of the key findings of this chapter is that supply chains have become the most prominent and impactful space of ESG performance. This is not coincidental. The supply chain is the nexus of production, logistics, and consumption, connecting global brands to intricate networks of suppliers, subcontractors, logistics companies, and local communities. It is within this multi-tiered structure that the largest ESG effects are realized: emissions embedded in upstream activities (including Scope 3 emissions), labor abuses or dangerous working conditions in outsourced manufacturing, and governance failures such as bribery, lack of transparency, and poor accountability in procurement choices. Consequently, ESG is increasingly "supply-chain driven," meaning that it is delivered through supplier assessment and evaluation processes, due diligence systems, traceability systems, procurement policies, logistics planning, and reporting frameworks rather than through isolated corporate declarations. The chapter also shows that the nexus between ESG and supply chains has been pushed forward by a series of crises and scandals that have laid bare the structural weaknesses of globalized supply chains. Industrial disasters that have highlighted the issue of workplace safety and workers' rights, scandals of corporate greenwashing that have shown the gap between rhetoric and reality, and the COVID-19 pandemic that has highlighted both the operational vulnerability and the social inequities of global supply chains have all reaffirmed the following truth: supply chains are not only cost and speed networks; they are also social and ecological networks. Crises, whether they are pandemics, natural disasters, geopolitical crises, or resource shortages, are not just operational crises. They are also moments of truth that test the quality of governance, that lay bare hidden interdependencies, and that heighten risks for the most vulnerable actors, namely workers and small suppliers. In this respect, ESG is increasingly connected to the concept of resilience: the capacity of supply networks to absorb shocks, to bounce back quickly, and to maintain continuity without sacrificing ethical and environmental commitments. Another significant finding is about the historical transformation from voluntary CSR to more formalized and standardized ESG governance, which is becoming increasingly mandatory. CSR was traditionally associated with discretionary actions, philanthropic activities, and self-reported disclosure, which were highly variable across companies and industries. ESG, on the other hand, has transformed into measurable disclosure, materiality-focused assessment, and governance frameworks. The increasing use of standards and frameworks such as GRI, SASB/ISSB frameworks, TCFD-type climate risk reporting, and regionally mandatory reporting directives indicates a need to improve clarity, comparability, and the ability to transform sustainability storytelling into hard facts. This has significant implications for supply chains because supply chains are where the quality of data and its verification are most challenging (XiaoWen and Taghipour, 2025). The deeper the supply chain, the more challenging it is to estimate emissions, working conditions, and compliance with policies. However, paradoxically, this is also where risks are most significant. The implication here is clear: the credibility of ESG reporting is inextricably linked to the credibility of supply chain facts, not corporate reporting sophistication. The theoretical foundation of the chapter above supports this finding by illustrating how the adoption of ESG is informed by a variety of sometimes conflicting logics. Stakeholder theory focuses on cooperation and mutual accountability among firms, suppliers, employees, communities, and government. Institutional theory focuses on coercive, mimetic, and normative forces that drive adoption, which can be regionally and sectorally varied, sometimes creating uneven or conflicting demands. The resource-based view of the firm recasts ESG capabilities of traceability, supplier development, ethical procurement culture, data management, and innovation as strategic assets that can enhance competitiveness and differentiation. However, legitimacy theory cautions that ESG can become empty or symbolic if firms focus on reputation rather than reality, leading to decoupling and greenwashing unless assurance and verification systems are in place. Agency theory draws attention to the problem of information asymmetry, which is particularly problematic in multi-tier supply chains, where large buyers may lack knowledge of lower-tier practices, and small suppliers may face high costs of compliance and lack of resources. From this, a further conclusion follows: ESG implementation is successful when it is integrated into operational systems rather than being a reporting task. The operational dynamics of supply chains, such as demand forecasting, order planning, sourcing, contracting, lead-time strategies, logistics design, and supplier management, determine whether ESG results are improved or worsened. For example, even robust labor standards can be compromised if sourcing policies set up unreasonable delivery times that trigger excessive overtime, subcontracting, or hazardous shortcuts. Similarly, greenhouse gas targets are compromised if logistics strategies focus solely on cost minimization without considering carbon intensity, mode shifts, and network optimization. Thus, ESG maturity is ultimately proven not by the amount of disclosure but by alignment: alignment between standards and purchasing practices, between governance and incentive systems, and between sustainability and planning processes. The discussion of the chapter's roadmap approach suggests a pragmatic and scalable approach to ESG integration, especially by distinguishing minimum standards, sector-specific risk management, and continuous improvement goals. This multi-tiered approach is critical because a typical problem with ESG systems is that they set up identical standards for all suppliers irrespective of size, capacity, and risk. Such "one-size-fits-all" compliance approaches can inadvertently shut out SMEs, increase superficial reporting, and encourage deception. The implication is that proportionality must be a guiding principle: higher-risk suppliers and geographies demand more in-depth due diligence and more frequent engagement, while lower-risk and smaller suppliers need to be facilitated through simplified reporting templates, minimum standards, and capacity-building rather than being burdened with sophisticated reporting requirements. In other words, ESG systems must be built as development tools rather than enforcement tools. Engagement with suppliers, therefore, becomes the critical juncture at which ESG moves from policy to practice. Engagement with suppliers must go beyond audits and encompass training, common tools, common data requests, grievance mechanisms, support for corrective actions, and clear consequences for repeated non-compliance or misreporting. The logic of tiered supplier engagement in the chapter (high-risk strategic suppliers, medium-risk suppliers, and low-risk/small suppliers) provides a framework that can alleviate burden while enhancing accountability. This framework acknowledges that the goal is not simply to eliminate "non-compliant" suppliers, which can simply drive problems out of sight, but to mitigate problems and improve conditions through measurable progress. Yet, improvement-oriented engagement must also have strong enforcement; otherwise, it may become permissive and facilitate greenwashing. The tension between support and accountability is, therefore, one of the most significant governance dilemmas in ESG supply chain management. Digitalization and next-generation technologies are offered as strong enablers of ESG governance, but the chapter correctly points out that technology is no substitute for governance. Technologies such as blockchain, IoT sensors, supplier portals, data analytics, and anomaly detection can enhance traceability and data integrity, enable faster risk detection, and enable companies to make more informed decisions in times of disruption. However, digital technologies can also exacerbate inequalities if smaller suppliers do not have the capacity, expertise, or infrastructure to implement them. This leads to the "sustainability divide" where larger companies operating in developed economies can show off their advanced ESG infrastructure while smaller suppliers in developing countries are left out or coerced into compliance. The takeaway is that digital ESG needs to be accompanied by governance policies (access controls, version history, audit trails), affordable technology options, and shared platforms that reduce the cost of adoption. Technology is transformative when aligned with supplier maturity and embedded in operational processes—not as a PR overlay. The chapter also points out the structural hurdles that will continue to influence ESG performance. The lack of standardization in rules and regulations is a problem that still persists. Although there are efforts at global convergence, many companies are still subject to overlapping disclosure requirements and non-standardized definitions, which cause high administrative burdens and contribute to "reporting fatigue." This may lead to a focus on documentation rather than improvement. Moreover, issues of measurement remain particularly problematic for Scope 3 emissions and for social metrics that are hard to measure (such as informal labor conditions or the quality of worker voice). The final assessment is that ESG governance will remain suboptimal and contested, and that ongoing improvement will depend on genuine efforts at harmonization, enhanced assurance, and more context-specific measurement. The most important final take-away is the paradox of ESG: it is intended to facilitate sustainability and social equity, but if not proportioned and supported, it can perpetuate inequality. The high costs of compliance, certification, digital infrastructure, and assurance can be particularly onerous for SMEs and suppliers in developing countries. If this leads to a concentration of supply chains and the loss of smaller suppliers, ESG can inadvertently contribute to decreased inclusivity and the concentration of economic power. The paradox can only be resolved by ensuring that policy and business practice include support mechanisms, such as financial subsidies, joint training programs, capacity-building partnerships, simplified reporting thresholds, and shared platforms. ESG performance should not be judged by the existence of standards, but by the feasibility and equity of compliance. The implication of the discussion on governance in this chapter is that success in ESG requires leadership accountability and incentive alignment. Leadership must view ESG performance as a governance issue, not a responsibility of the sustainability department. This means that ESG metrics must be integrated into procurement scorecards, executive compensation, risk management, and internal audit. It also means that there must be a clear ownership of ESG issues across functions, such as procurement for supplier relationships and commercial terms, operations for planning stability and lead times, compliance for audit programs and grievance mechanisms, and finance for assurance and disclosure integrity (Glaa et al., 2014). The implication is that ESG governance must be cross-functional, because ESG failures often happen at the boundaries of functions, such as when procurement pushes cost pressures without visibility into labor practices, or when reporting groups publish ESG metrics without a sound internal process for measurement. Greenwashing is still one of the most significant risks to the integrity of ESG. The chapter emphasizes that cherry-picking, overstating, and showpiece initiatives undermine integrity, create market distortions, and challenge the legitimacy of sustainability initiatives. The final stance is that ESG integrity must be verified by evidence-based measurable indicators, internal data integrity controls, third-party assurance if necessary, and tough consequences for misreporting. Companies must avoid the temptation to report more than they can verify. Reporting fewer indicators more reliably is often preferable to reporting many indicators less reliably. However, companies must be open and honest about their limitations (e.g., partial tier-2 visibility) and communicate clear improvement strategies. This is not a weakness but a prerequisite for legitimacy in a complex and dynamic governance context. From a more operational perspective, the example of the textile supply chain illustrates the underlying logic of successful ESG implementation: specify the scope of responsibility, minimize hidden subcontracting, systematically identify risks, provide simplified data packages, train suppliers, correlate findings with corrective measures, and align procurement incentives with ESG goals. What makes this example particularly useful is that it correlates ESG performance with the underlying drivers of non-performance, such as unstable forecasts and impractical lead times. This also supports a general conclusion: ESG is inextricably linked to planning quality. Forecast stability, order changes, and emergency sourcing practices can either promote decent work and environmental sustainability or provide the opportunity for shortcuts and negative impacts. Thus, supply chain planning and ESG management must be considered as a system. Looking ahead, the chapter proposes that ESG is driving a broader shift in what constitutes success for the corporate sector. Those companies that are making meaningful ESG integration are better placed to navigate risk, access capital, stay ahead of emerging regulatory requirements, enhance reputation, retain talent, and develop new sustainable business models (including circular economy models). On the other hand, companies that are merely going through the motions with ESG are increasingly vulnerable to reputational shock, regulatory censure, supply chain disruption, and investor disillusionment. This is no mere moral imperative; it is a hard-operational truth in a world characterized by climate pressures, rising social expectations, and systemic volatility. Future research streams, as set out in the chapter, are still highly relevant to this topic. There is a clear need for improved measurement science, particularly in areas such as biodiversity, informal labor, and multi-tier emissions. Comparative research is also required to assess which due diligence frameworks are genuinely effective and do not, in the process, disadvantage SMEs. Further research should investigate the impact of digitalization on the practicality, cost, and balance of power of ESG compliance, and how data governance can be made more robust and accessible. Finally, it is a critical research imperative to connect ESG performance to operational outcomes such as delivery reliability, disruption recovery, supplier innovation, and sustainable network resilience. This will help to move ESG from a reporting requirement to a management system.

In conclusion, the chapter states that the best way to understand ESG in global supply chains is as a significant institutional and operational change: from voluntary responsibility to accountable governance; from individual corporate actions to network-wide systems; from storytelling about sustainability to performance-based evidence; and from short-term cost savings to long-term resilience and legitimacy. However, this process is still in process and not complete. The success of ESG will depend on whether it is possible for companies and governments to overcome the current contradictions: harmonization and fragmentation, enforcement and inclusion, digital innovation and accessibility, and the volume and credibility of disclosure. The roadmap provided highlights that it is possible to make progress if ESG is implemented as a staged, proportional, and learning-focused management system, which is centered on minimum safeguards, risk management, continuous improvement, building capabilities, and data governance. Ultimately, ESG is transforming supply chains into not only economic value chains but also environmental stewardship, social protection, and governance integrity. The supply chain is a test of corporate purpose, which will help companies link profitability with responsibility, efficiency with dignity, and global scale with local fairness. If the next generation of ESG development can reach global consistency while taking local realities into account, which combines regulatory accountability with support, then ESG can move from compliance to a sustainable development architecture. Otherwise, it will become a bureaucratic reporting industry that increases inequalities and reduces trust. The evidence and analysis in this chapter clearly indicate that the way ahead is clear: the future of global competitiveness will increasingly depend on the capacity to manage supply chains in a responsible, transparent, and resilient manner, with ESG as the language of this transformation.

REFERENCES

Aouadni, S., Aouadni, I., & Taghipour, A. (2024). Using ordinal priority approach with confidence-level measurement for third-party logistics provider selection in the tunisian healthcare sector. In *Applications of New Technology in Operations and Supply Chain Management* (pp. 404–429). IGI Global. DOI: 10.4018/979-8-3693-1578-1.ch020

DiMaggio, P., & Powell, W. (1983). iron cage Institutional isomorphism collective rationality organizational fields. Sociological Review, 147. (DiMaggio & Powell, 1983) DOI: 10.2307/2095101

Glaa, B., Zoghlami, N., & Taghipour, A. (2014, May). Outsourcing and off-shoring healthcare services: A way to cut the costs and improve quality. In 2014 international conference on advanced logistics and transport (ICALT) (pp. 189-194). IEEE.

Goodarzian, F., Abraham, A., Muñuzuri, J., Taghipour, A., & Ghasemi, P. (2026). A Benders decomposition approach for a new sustainable pharmaceutical supply chain network: A case study in France. *Annals of Operations Research*, *356*(2-3), 1–39. DOI: 10.1007/s10479-024-05936-3

Lebosse, S., Taghipour, A., & Canel-Depitre, B. (2017). Quick response to fluctuations in supply chains: A review. *Journal of Advanced Management Science*, *5*(5), 394–400. DOI: 10.18178/joams.5.5.394-400

Lu, X., & Taghipour, A. (2023). A French Guide for Businesses and Governments to Integrate the Concept of Sustainable Development Into Their Supply Chains. In *Government Impact on Sustainable and Responsible Supply Chain Management* (pp. 1–12). IGI Global. DOI: 10.4018/978-1-6684-9062-4.ch001

Lu, X., & Taghipour, A. (2025). The Future of Marketing: Integrating Big Data and AI for Personalized Customer Engagement. In Ecological and Human Dimensions of AI-Based Supply Chain (pp. 97-110). IGI Global Scientific Publishing.

Mahfod, J., Canel-Depitre, B., & Taghipour, A. (2019). Quality function deployment-ELECTRE in supplier evaluation. Journal of advanced management science, 7(4).

Mahfod, J., Khoury, B., Canel-Depitre, B., & Taghipour, A. (2021). Logistics Providers in Syria Humanitarian Operations. In Demand Forecasting and Order Planning in Supply Chains and Humanitarian Logistics (pp. 171-197). IGI Global. DOI: 10.4018/978-1-7998-3805-0.ch006

Mbiatem, J., Taghipour, A., & Canel-Depitre, B. (2018, August). Supplier selection approaches for decision makers. In *Proceedings of the 8th International Conference on Information Communication and Management* (pp. 108-112).

Meckling, W. H., & Jensen, M. C. (1976). Theory of the Firm. *Managerial behavior, agency costs and ownership structure, 3*(4), 305-360.

Nadia, E. N., CANEL-DEPITRE, B., & TAGHIPOUR, A. 12. LEBANESE HOTELS'ENGAGEMENT IN ENVIRONMENTAL PRACTICES. TOURMAN 2018, 457.

Nadia, E. N., Beatrice, C. D., & Atour, T. (2020). Luxury hotels' eco-friendly activities & customers' preferences and willingness to pay for green hotels. *Journal of Advanced Management Science, 8*(1), 1–24.

Nadia, E. N., Beatrice, C. D., & Atour, T. (2021). The determinants of hotel room rates in Beirut: A hedonic pricing model. International Journal of Trade. *Economics and Finance, 12*(2), 33–42.

Ponputtha, W., Wannapiroon, P., Nilsook, P., Taghipour, A., Murat, S., Huang, P., & Chou, T. C. (2021). Creative history learning model using digital storytelling through cloud learning to enhance analytical thinking. International Journal of e-Education, e-Business, e-. *Management Learning, 11*(2), 42–50.

Radhoui, H., Taghipour, A., & Canel-Depitre, B. (2019). The distribution and pickup of goods: A literature review and survey. Hierarchical Planning and Information Sharing Techniques in Supply Chain Management, 46-85.

Radhoui, H., Taghipour, A., & Canel-Depitre, B. (2021). Mixed delivery and pickup vehicle routing problem with limited flow and assignment of drones in an urban network. In *Demand Forecasting and Order Planning in Supply Chains and Humanitarian Logistics* (pp. 225–249). IGI Global. DOI: 10.4018/978-1-7998-3805-0.ch008

Sahraoui, A., Tran, N. K., Tliche, Y., Kacem, A., & Taghipour, A. (2023). Examining ICT Innovation for Sustainable Terminal Operations in Developing Countries: A Case Study of the Port of Radès in Tunisia. *Sustainability (Basel), 15*(11), 9123. DOI: 10.3390/su15119123

Suchman, M. C. (1995). Managing legitimacy: Strategic and institutional approaches. *Academy of Management Review, 20*(3), 571–610. DOI: 10.2307/258788

Taghipour, A. (Ed.). (2020). *Demand forecasting and order planning in supply chains and humanitarian logistics*. IGI Global.

Taghipour, A. (Ed.). (2023). *Government Impact on Sustainable and Responsible Supply Chain Management*. IGI Global. DOI: 10.4018/978-1-6684-9062-4

Taghipour, A., Abed, M., & Zoghlami, N. (2015, May). Design for remanufacturing respecting reverse logistics processes: A review. In 2015 4th International Conference on Advanced Logistics and Transport (ICALT) (pp. 299-304). IEEE. DOI: 10.1109/ICAdLT.2015.7136602

Taghipour, A., & Lu, X. (2025). Navigating the Artificial Intelligence Era: Impacts of Artificial Intelligence on Youth Critical Thinking, Career Paths, and Ethical Challenges. In Ecological and Human Dimensions of AI-Based Supply Chain (pp. 49-68). IGI Global Scientific Publishing.

Taghipour, A., Lu, X., Derradji, M., & Sow, A. D. (2022b, July). The impact of digitalization on supply chain management: a literature review. In *Proceedings of the 12th International Conference on Information Communication and Management* (pp. 75-78) DOI: 10.1145/3551690.3551702

Taghipour, A., Rouyendegh, B. D., Ünal, A., & Piya, S. (2022a). Selection of suppliers for speech recognition products in IT projects by combining techniques with an integrated fuzzy MCDM. *Sustainability (Basel)*, *14*(3), 1777. DOI: 10.3390/su14031777

Tliche, Y., Taghipour, A., & Canel-Depitre, B. (2019). Downstream Demand Inference in decentralized supply chains. *European Journal of Operational Research*, *274*(1), 65–77. DOI: 10.1016/j.ejor.2018.09.034

Vosooghidizaji, M., Taghipour, A., & Canel-Depitre, B. (2019). A literature review on information asymmetry in supply chain coordination. *International Journal of Production Research*, *58*(6), 1–6.

Vosooghidizaji, M., Taghipour, A., & Canel-Depitre, B. (2020). Information asymmetry in supply chain coordination: State of the art. *Journal of Industrial and Intelligent Information*, *8*(2), 38–43. DOI: 10.18178/jiii.8.2.38-43

XiaoWen, L., & Atour, T.XiaoWen. (2025). Knowledge-driven digital innovation in supply chains: An organizational perspective. *Journal of Innovation & Knowledge*, *10*(5), 100787. DOI: 10.1016/j.jik.2025.100787

Zoghlami, N., Taghipour, A., Merlo, C., & Abed, M. (2016). Management of divergent production network using decentralised multi-level capacitated lot-sizing models. *International Journal of Shipping and Transport Logistics*, *8*(5), 590–604. DOI: 10.1504/IJSTL.2016.078686

Chapter 6
Risk and Resilience in Climate Change:
Economic Disruptions and Strategic Adaptation in Supply Chains

L. B. Muralidhar
http://orcid.org/0000-0003-3453-613X
Jain (Deemed to be) University, India

R. Shilpa
http://orcid.org/0009-0002-9805-1481
RJS Institute of Management Studies, India

N. Sathyanarayana
http://orcid.org/0000-0002-4185-7751
Jain (Deemed to be) University, India

V. Vipanchi
http://orcid.org/0000-0003-3388-4730
Jain (Deemed to be) University, India

K. P. Sheeba
http://orcid.org/0009-0003-4707-5392
Jain (Deemed to be) University, India

ABSTRACT

This chapter explores the evolving concept of supply chain resilience, focusing on its ability to adapt to both climate change and economic disruptions. The increas-

DOI: 10.4018/979-8-3373-6455-1.ch006

ing frequency of extreme weather events and global economic volatility highlights the need for flexible, adaptive strategies in supply chain management. Traditional risk management frameworks often fail to address these complex, interconnected challenges, necessitating a more integrated approach. Drawing on resilience theory, the chapter proposes a novel framework that combines climate and economic risks, emphasizing the need for strategic adaptation. Key themes include the role of innovation, technology, and sustainable practices in enhancing resilience. The chapter also explores the impact of climate change, economic shocks, and the importance of policy frameworks in fostering resilient supply chains. It concludes with recommendations for future research and a call for cross-disciplinary approaches to strengthen global supply chain resilience

1. INTRODUCTION: THE INTERPLAY OF CLIMATE, ECONOMIC DISRUPTIONS, AND SUPPLY CHAIN RESILIENCE

1.1 Overview of Key Themes

The concept of supply chain resilience has evolved into a complex system comprising anticipation, absorption, adaptation, and transformation (Christopher & Peck, 2004; Sheffi, 2021). Traditional risk management processes, which rely primarily on probabilistic approximations of disruptions, are ineffective in a systematically uncertain world. Instead, resilience entails dynamic capabilities that enable firms to absorb shocks and restructure assets before returning to operation (Ponomarov & Holcomb, 2009). This reconceptualisation is not limited to the notion of redundancy or inventory buffers. However, it encompasses relational, structural, and digital strategies that enable organisations to anticipate vulnerabilities and proactively adjust their strategies.

Global supply chains are susceptible to climate variability and economic instability across geographically dispersed, interdependent networks. Climate change is also causing more frequent and severe flooding, hurricanes, droughts, and wildfires that disrupt transportation networks, production centres, and agricultural systems (IPCC, 2022). Meanwhile, vulnerabilities are exacerbated by economic shocks, such as inflationary pressures, currency fluctuations, trade wars, and pandemics, which destabilise financial flows, labour supply, and market demand (Miroudot, 2020). These forces interact to show that supply chain fragility is not a process attributable to either dimension (environmental or economic) but arises from their intersection. A comprehensive analysis of cooperation across the performance levels, the process of development, and the supply chain management levels reveals that the high level of inter-firm coordination is the key to the value creation and competitive stability, and that the role of collaboration in long-term supply chain development has a strategic role(Taghipour, A., 2009).

The resilience requirement leads to the paradigm shift towards anticipatory strategies. Organisations are also investing in predictive analytics, scenario planning, and stress-testing models rather than merely reacting to uncertainty (Ivanov, 2020). Another aspect of strategic adaptation is the need to incorporate sustainability and a focus on the circular economy into supply chain design, thereby reducing the risks of raw-material shocks and carbon-related risks. A combination of effective mixed-integer optimisation and the adoption of green technologies in the design of the closed-loop supply chain will improve economic and environmental outcomes by reducing overall costs, mitigating environmental impacts, and increasing product recovery, despite various sources of uncertainty (Gharye M Mirzaei et al., 2025). The adoption of balanced economic, environmental, and social metrics for sustainable supply chain management will improve operational efficiency and stakeholder value by ensuring that short-term gains do not come at the expense of long-term sustainability outcomes (Taghipour & Beneteau-Piet, 2020).

Historical records of ICT adoption in port operations indicate that implementing Terminal Operating Systems can significantly optimise berth-to-gate processes; however, limited leadership support, stakeholder involvement, training, and resource availability constrain the realisation of more sustainable outcomes (Sahraoui et al., 2023). As shown by multinational corporations (MNCs) such as Unilever and Apple, these firms are proactive, diversifying their sourcing processes, embracing renewable energy, and offering digital services that enhance their responsiveness and flexibility.

By explicitly modelling the stochastic demand and lead-time information into advanced optimisation and decision-support, the multi-echelon supply chain is prone to achieve a more resilient inventory placement and reduced total logistics costs, in addition to a greater degree of responsiveness compared to the system designed under the deterministic assumptions(Cauchois, R. et al., 2017). Surveyed optimisation studies show that integrated pickup-and-delivery routing models with time-window and capacity constraints remain dominant, with metaheuristic approaches such as tabu search and genetic algorithms proving especially effective for large-scale distribution environments, while underscoring the need for advances in multimodal and dynamically adaptive logistics settings (Radhoui, H. et al., 2021).

A large body of distribution research shows that most optimisation efforts focus on integrated pickup-and-delivery routing with capacity and time-window constraints, where metaheuristic approaches such as tabu search and genetic algorithms consistently perform well for large-scale applications, yet significant gaps remain in modelling multimodal and dynamically changing logistics environments(Radhoui, H. et al., 2019). Research on information exchange under uncertainty shows that although sharing data improves visibility, coordination, and responsiveness across supply chains, behavioural barriers such as information asymmetry, opportunism, and risk aversion reduce partners' willingness to share and ultimately weaken overall system efficiency(Ren, Z. et al., 2016).

Neural data were once protected from extensive ethical scrutiny—because they were thought to be difficult to access—but now they circulate within institutions with little consent or protection, especially given the vulnerabilities of child learners (Taghipour, A., 2025). Decentralised coordination methods that preserve decision-maker autonomy—such as Lagrangian-based decomposition and mutual adjustment mechanisms—offer more realistic operational planning frameworks than purely centralised optimisation and underscore the need for dynamic coordination through iterative financial incentives and improved information exchange (Taghipour, A., and Frayret, 2011).

1.2 Contextualising the Issue:

Empirical trends indicate that disruptions to climate characteristics have increased significantly, and weather-induced disasters have tripled over the last 30 years, causing more than USD 300 billion in annual losses (Munich Re, 2021). Such shocks have a disproportionately negative impact on supply chains rooted in climate-prone areas, and repeated economic disruptions, the most common of which were the 2008 financial meltdown and the COVID-19 pandemic, have unveiled the weaknesses of just-in-time systems and concentrated supplier networks (Baldwin & Evenett, 2020). There have been increasing interactions between climate and economic risks, rather than their occurring independently.

Climate variability causes crop failures, which exacerbate price volatility in food production, price inflation, and social instability, thereby disrupting trade flows. Meanwhile, production costs and comparative advantages across industries are changing due to decarbonisation policies, such as carbon taxation (Sarkis, 2020). This multi-layered vulnerability needs to be addressed through an interdisciplinary approach that integrates the principles of optimisation, environmental thresholds, and market considerations into resilience programmes. These integrations enable stress-testing of sourcing decisions under climatic conditions and promote adaptive governance through intersectoral cooperation (Chowdhury & Quaddus, 2017).

Additionally, the political environment is an important contextual pressure that influences organisational behaviour and coordination at the ecosystem level. The political situations also affect the ways firms align their responses, whether to focus on protective alliances or engage in growth-oriented actions, and consequently, the degree to which political contexts affect collective strategic reactions.

1.3 Research Gaps and Chapter Structure

Although an increasing amount of scholarship is becoming accessible, significant gaps remain in knowledge about the interaction between climate and economic disturbances and their effects on resilience outcomes. Firstly, a considerable portion of the literature concentrates on environmental and economic shocks as distinct phenomena, therefore, limiting holistic modelling of their (interactions) impacts (Ivanov & Dolgui, 2021). Second, resilience studies often focus on firm-level strategies that overlook the systemic interdependencies among industries, nations, and ecosystems. Third, empirical research has focused on established economies, whereas the resilience dynamics in emerging markets, where weaknesses typically lie at the end of the proverbial curve, have been relatively under-researched. Finally, the equity effects of resilience, i.e., how adaptive strategies may have unequal impacts on small suppliers or marginalised communities, are not fully addressed.

The chapter seals these gaps by integrating both theoretical and practical knowledge. It relies on complex adaptive systems theory to explain how resilience can emerge from nonlinear interactions within supply networks. These case studies examine the diversification of Toyota's supplier base after the Fukushima disaster, the garment industry's response to climate-change-driven floods in Bangladesh, and the implementation of resilience practices across different environments. The chapter also considers empirical evidence from multinational companies and policy programmes, including the United Nations Sendai Framework for Disaster Risk Reduction. Its conceptualisations of practical applications take the form of digital chain supply chain visibility models, risk-sharing collaborations, and climate-sensitive infrastructure investment.

The parameters of supply chain resilience have been re-stated by the mounting convergence between climatic risks and economic shocks. To transcend the traditional risk management paradigm, organisations must adopt proactive, holistic, and cross-functional approaches that not only buffer against shocks but also redesign supply chains to achieve long-term sustainability and equity. This chapter is timely in the current debate about how global supply chains may survive, adapt, and respond to increasing uncertainties.

2 PROBLEM STATEMENT

Global supply chains are structured to be resilient, efficient, and sustainable, ensuring stability even during disruptions. There is contradictory evidence suggesting that this ideal is being derailed by recurring climate-related catastrophes and economic crises. The existing literature provides inconclusive evidence, gaps in theories on how to integrate climate and economic risks, gaps in knowledge about new market environments, and gaps in contexts where there is no comprehensive treatment of equity and systemic interdependencies. Examples of real-world issues include disjointed governance, limited multi-tier visibility, and cost-resilience trade-offs. By increasing operations-planning coordination through joint decision-making, information sharing, and iterative adjustments based on incentives, partners in the supply chain will be better positioned to improve responsiveness, reduce uncertainty, and overall performance (Taghipour, A. and Frayret, 2013a).

Including robust planning and sustainability requirements in network design can promote more capable and responsible supply chain designs amid uncertainty (Goodarzian, F. et al., 2024). The paper addresses these gaps by arguing that cross-disciplinary frameworks are necessary to enable scholars, practitioners, and policymakers to address them and achieve systemic resilience and sustainable adaptation amid unstable global supply chains. The chapter seeks to develop an all-encompassing multi-criteria decision-making framework based on the Ordinal Priority Approach, incorporating confidence-level measurement, to assist Tunisian healthcare decision-makers in systematically selecting the most suitable third-party logistics (3PL) provider.

The results indicate that incorporating experts' confidence levels into the ordinal ratings improves the criteria weights and rankings of the 3PL options, thereby strengthening the alignment with the desired logistics provider in the healthcare sector. QFD, using the ELECTRE decision-support technique, enables supply chains to translate qualitative needs into prioritised technical requirements, leading to more precise and justifiable supplier selection (Mahfod, J. et al., 2019).

Modern supplier-selection studies indicate that hybrid multi-criteria decision-making models that amalgamate tools like AHP, fuzzy sets, TOPSIS, and neural networks provide a stronger assessment of suppliers by using a combination of both qualitative and quantitative criteria, thus improving the accuracy of procurement and overall supply chain excellence (Mbiatem, J. et al, 2018). There is growing evidence that the proper identification of non-core healthcare functions and their offloading to specialised external or offshore providers, within a well-developed contractual and governance system, can significantly reduce delivery costs while improving service quality and operational efficiency (Glaa, B., Zoghlami, et al., 2014).

The service providers of logistics in a conflict environment need to be prioritised with a high concern for reliability, the local contextual knowledge, the cost efficiency, and the security compliance because all these factors assist in humanitarian operations to maintain the performance of delivery in case of extreme instability (Mahfod, J. et al., 2021). It has become clear that consumers are increasingly willing to spend more on environmentally friendly services, indicating significant market potential that is not currently utilised, and managers tend to underestimate it (Nadia, E. N., et al., 2020). Evidence from Lebanese hotels indicates that the voluntary implementation of eco-efficient practices is driven more by cost-saving concerns than by environmental commitment, with little information about these practices communicated to customers, despite relatively high rates of operational implementation (Nadia, E. N., et al., 2018). Stock operations planning and coordination depend on collaboration mechanisms, including shared information, joint decision-making, and incentive-based iterative adjustments, which enhance responsiveness, reduce uncertainty, and improve overall supply chain performance (Taghipour, A., 2009).

3 BACKGROUND

Traditional supply chain risk management has been based on systematic, probability-based models that focus on the identification, evaluation, and management of discrete risks, where Enterprise Risk Management and Supply Chain Risk Management offer formalised processes to incorporate financial, operational, and strategic risk exposure into managerial decision-making (COSO, 2004; Tang, 2006). Failure Mode and Effects Analysis and Monte Carlo simulation tools have enabled companies, especially those that are capital-intensive, such as the automotive and electronics industries, to prioritise vulnerabilities, allocate resources effectively, and maintain operational continuity despite the globalisation of supply chains (Zsidisin & Ritchie, 2009).

However, these linear, efficiency-based strategies assume that disruptions are predictable, separable, and temporal, a premise that systemic crises have repeatedly challenged. Practical experience with the 2008 financial crisis, the COVID-19 pandemic, and climate-induced disruptions shows that risks are spreading across the financial, logistical, and socio-political levels simultaneously and have cascading effects that are beyond the explanatory capacity of fixed risk matrices and probabilistic forecasts (Ivanov & Dolgui, 2020).

Additionally, just-in-time inventory and other lean processes that have optimised cost structures have increased exposure to shocks by lowering the buffering capacity and adaptive slack. To counter this, resilience theory redefines supply chains as dynamic systems that can absorb disruptions, adapt their structures, and continue operating amid unrelenting uncertainty (Christopher & Peck, 2004). Key properties include quick resource reconfigurability, organisational learning, and intentional redundancy among suppliers, capacity, and inventories, with the understanding that resilience is a continuous process rather than a prescribed outcome. Experience with complex adaptive systems is another reason to understand why decentralised decision-making, modular network forms, and digital coordination are more responsive in volatile environments characterised by feedback loops and emergent behaviour (Choi et al., 2001).

This view is consistent with the ecological resilience concept of diversity and thresholds (Holling, 1973), organisational resilience, with a focus on leadership and learning (Lengnick-Hall et al., 2011), and economic resilience, which addresses the recovery from market shocks (Rose, 2004). This combination of strands constitutes socio-ecological-technical supply chains, in which adaptive capacity, not merely risk avoidance, enables long-term viability.

In fact, there must be a standard model that integrates classical risk management with resilience theory to explain expected risk and disruptions arising from unforeseen situations (Taghipour, A. and Frayret, 2013b, May). This involves incorporating climate risks, such as extreme weather, into supply chain modelling alongside economic shocks, including inflation and financial crises. The connecting element becomes strategic responsiveness, which enables organisations to restart refining themselves with convergent disruptions (Ivanov, 2020). In cryptocurrency systems, the decentralised design of blockchain technology enhances digital financial security by minimising information risks, reducing transaction costs, and providing secure exit routes for economies struggling with currency volatility (Taghipour, A., 2022).

This type of structure is inherently cybernetic: sensing (through predictive analytics), responding (through adaptive logistics and sourcing), and learning (through feedback loops that improve preparedness). An example of an approach to integration is the use of digital twins by organisations such as Maersk, under which climate and trade shocks are simulated dynamically to reoptimise shipping routes and prices.

The framework explains a relationship as a feedback loop among environmental, economic, and social forces. For example, climate change causes droughts, reducing crop production, driving commodity price volatility, and, in turn, exacerbating food inequity. This is a feedback mechanism that feeds on supply chains. The fact that they include social dimensions (i.e., labour rights, community resilience, and stakeholder trust) demonstrates that resilience practices are not only achievable but also just.

Public policies support this feedback-loop strategy. It can be implemented through instruments such as the Sendai Framework for Disaster Risk Reduction (2015-2030), which motivates stakeholders to incorporate risk considerations into social and economic planning. In practice, multinational firms need to align their resilience approach and overall sustainability responsibilities with global market developments to remain in step with global markets and remain competitive and legitimate.

3.1 Controversies and Debates

Although the overall trend is to prioritise resilience as a strategic requirement, pursuing it poses significant economic and ethical dilemmas in supply chain design.

Redundancy in the form of excessive stock, capacity cushions, or supplier diversification is usually at odds with the objective of cost efficiency on which a competitive advantage is founded, putting firms at risk of profit erosion and loss of shareholder value. Practical examples from the pharmaceutical sector reveal that stockpiling the most critical inputs reduces the risk of disruption, but at the same time, capital is frozen and financial performance is jeopardised. Similarly, the decentralisation of the production process, intended to disperse concentration geographically, is more likely to undermine economies of scale, raising unit costs and prompting debate about whether resilience is an investment that constitutes a form of long-term sustainability or a structural liability to competitiveness.

The lack of a clear solution between short-term adaptive measures and long-term sustainability further complicates these tensions. Strategies such as rerouting air freight around port closures do not interrupt the flow but increase the supply chain's carbon intensity, and the rapid replacement of suppliers in crises may increase the risk of labour rights violations and reputational loss. These contradictions illustrate the extent to which resilience is sought in the solitude of nature and amid social issues. New models that rely on the concepts of a circular economy and a closed-loop supply chain can offer a partial answer by promoting sustainability, reuse, and adaptive capacity to acquire materials.

Patagonia's integration of repairability and recycling into its sourcing and distribution model indicates that resilience can be balanced with environmental goals and that reliance on volatile raw-material markets can be reduced. This development is symptomatic of a broader paradigmatic shift in supply chain scholarship toward dynamic resilience thinking, rather than the former risk-avoidance approach, guided by complex systems and interdisciplinary thinking, consistent with the enduring trade-offs among efficiency, equity, and sustainability. Against this backdrop of concepts, climate change has emerged as a key systemic driver of supply risk. The Intergovernmental Panel on Climate Change (IPCC) finds that the consequences of climate-related catastrophes have increased more than threefold since the 1970s, resulting in total global losses of USD 300-400 billion over the last decade (IPCC, 2022).

The fact that critical infrastructure underlies logistics and production networks is becoming increasingly vulnerable, and failures in climate action, extreme weather, and biodiversity loss are among the most impactful global risks (World Economic Forum, 2021). This tendency is supported by sector-specific upheaval. Floods in Thailand in 2011 caused about USD 45 billion in damage and disrupted the supply chains of the automotive and electronics industries, including Toyota and Western Digital (Haraguchi & Lall, 2015). Similar shocks have arisen from California wildfires and Brazilian droughts, which are affecting soybean production and reducing yields of climate-sensitive crops such as coffee and cocoa (Bunn et al., 2015). Industries that are capital-intensive and geographically concentrated are under acute stress, as exemplified by Taiwan's semiconductor industry, where a water shortage threatens production and exacerbates global chip shortages (Holmes et al., 2021).

In response, companies are also turning to integrated approaches to adaptation, which combine green logistics, digital technologies, and strategic decarbonisation. Predictive analytics, digital twins, and climate risk modelling, underpinned by AI, help limit modal shifts to rail and sea transportation, electrified vehicle fleets, and renewable-powered warehouses (Ivanov & Dolgui, 2020). Examples of IKEA's corporate policies to achieve carbon neutrality across its entire supply chain by 2030 and Unilever's regenerative sourcing policies demonstrate how the operational goals of climate adaptation, resilience, and sustainability are increasingly interdependent. The net effect of these developments is that climate change is no longer on the periphery as a marginal consideration but at the core of supply chain continuity, competitiveness and governance.

3.2 Global Policy Initiatives and Frameworks

The Paris Agreement (2015) represents a striking transformation in the global economy, embedding climate goals into regulatory and market frameworks that directly influence supply chain decisions, particularly through carbon pricing, emissions disclosure, and mandatory Scope 3 accounting across supplier and distribution chains (UNFCCC, 2015). The added responsibility has enhanced transparency and coordination across value chains while also increasing the complexity of compliance for multinational companies. The international institutions consolidate this shift by enhancing the adaptive capacity: the United Nations works on the integration of systemic risks with the help of the Sendai Framework, the World Bank funds climate-resilient transport and port infrastructure in developing economies, and the World Trade Organisation has become a platform of discussions surrounding carbon border adjustment mechanisms and their impact on trade.

Policy convergence at the national and regional levels is another indicator of the alignment between supply chain strategy and climate governance. The Green Deal and the Carbon Border Adjustment Mechanism, which is part of the European Union, have incentivized production in the low-carbon sector worldwide by internalizing embedded emissions in imports, the 2060 carbon-neutrality commitment by China reforms manufacturing competitiveness by investing in large-scale renewable energy and green industrial production, and the Inflation Reduction Act of 2022 by the United States directs fiscal assistance to both domestic clean technology and resilient supply chains. Simultaneously, the most advanced companies are operationalising climate integration through renewable energy use, sustainable sourcing, and climate-resilient coffee programmes, as seen in Apple supplier decarbonisation,

Starbucks climate-resilient coffee programmes, port flood adaptation (Rotterdam), and major investments in green fuels (Maersk). Although these advances have been made, there are still persistent gaps.

Poor visibility in multi-tier supply chains limits accurate risk evaluation; small and medium-sized business enterprises lack the financial capacity to invest in adaptation; and climate risks are not uniformly embedded in financial valuation frameworks. In addition, the ambiguity about the future direction of the climate and inconsistent regulatory frameworks complicate long-term planning. Future studies should thus focus on decision-making strategies that address deep uncertainty, such as robust optimisation and scenario-based analysis, to realise operational continuity and long-term sustainability. All this evidence positions climate change as a strategic factor in supply chain resilience, where a concerted effort by firms, governments, and international institutions is necessary to make resilience a system-wide requirement rather than a managerial decision (World Economic Forum, 2021).

3.3 Economic Disruptions: Understanding and Managing Risk in a Volatile Global Economy

3.3.1 Sources of Economic Disruption

In the past, economic disruptions have been both abrupt and prolonged, undermining stability in global supply chains. The 2008 global financial crisis affected liquidity, access to credit, and consumer demand, prompting companies to rethink their procurement and production strategies (Gereffi, 2018). Trade wars, especially the U.S.-China trade war of the late 2010s, significantly altered sourcing patterns, and tariffs reshaped value chains across industries, including electronics and agriculture (Bown, 2020).

The combination of health, economic, and logistical shocks resulting from the coronavirus (COVID-19) pandemic further increased vulnerabilities. Lockdowns also reduced labour supply, supply chains, and transportation, resulting in cascading bottlenecks. More recent geopolitical crises, such as the Russia-Ukraine war, have disrupted energy flows, food supply chains, and the supply of critical raw materials, including nickel and palladium, with a ripple effect on global industries (Evenett, 2022).

The fragility of global supply chains exacerbates economic disruptions. Networks are also subject to systemic risk due to highly specialised production nodes, lean inventory models, and geographically concentrated production (Merimi, M., & Taghipour, A., 2021). For example, the international dependence of several East Asian centres on semiconductors exacerbated shortages during the COVID-19 pandemic and geopolitical disputes. Another source of fragility is the use of complex, tiered supplier networks, in which companies often do not extend their oversight beyond their first suppliers, making it challenging to predict vulnerability. It is these structural weaknesses that make local shocks turn into global crises, in which economic and operational risks are interdependent.

3.3.2 Strategic Adaptation to Economic Shocks

Economic shocks management is founded on financial resilience. Supply chain finance (SCF), including reverse factoring, dynamic discounting, and bank-supported credit, is also becoming an important tool in supply chain liquidity management (Gelsomino et al., 2016). During the COVID-19 pandemic, Siemens, through several other companies, expanded SCF programmes to support small and medium-sized suppliers and maintain their viability in the event of cash-flow disruptions. Planning for scenarios, conducting financial stress tests, and developing contingency funds to absorb short-term shocks are also effective crisis management measures.

Also, economic volatility can be mitigated by focusing on geographical and supplier diversification. Nearshoring and reshoring programmes mitigate the risk of remote access or political instability in any region, whereas multi-sourcing reduces the risk of reliance on a single supplier (Taghipour, A. et al., 2022 July). For example, amid trade tensions between the US and China, some companies, such as Apple, have begun relocating assembly lines to Vietnam and India to create more flexible sourcing footprints. These strategies, however, come at the expense of resilience and cost-efficiency, as noted; diversified networks are often associated with increased coordination and logistical costs (Vosooghidizaji, M. et al., 2019).

Adaptive capacity is the capacity of supply chains to respond quickly to unpredictable conditions. Agile supply chains are geared towards flexibility, responsiveness, and decentralised decision-making. Online platforms, predictive analytics, and blockchain technologies can enhance visibility across multiple levels and enable real-time responses to disruptions (Ivanov, 2021). Blockchain applications in cryptocurrency illustrate how the principle of decentralised verification increases digital security, optimises transactions, and creates trust - principles that are becoming more relevant to technology-driven supply chain resilience(Lu, X. W., et al., 2023).

Adopting blockchain within cryptocurrency ecosystems enhances transactional security and efficiency through decentralised verification, thereby strengthening trust and minimising reliance on intermediaries. Agile and responsive supply chain designs, enabled by information sharing, collaborative structures, and time-based performance mechanisms, help firms quickly adapt to changing demand and supply conditions, thereby reducing volatility and increasing customer value under uncertainty (Lebosse et al., 2017). Hedonic modelling of the hotel market in Beirut reveals a strong positive effect of star rating and accessibility features on room prices.

In contrast, hotels that are centrally located, business-focused, or safety-labelled face downward pricing pressures that influence managerial decision-making to optimise revenue (Nadia et al., 2021). For example, during the pandemic, Maersk's digital twins enabled the simulation of alternative shipping routes under lockdown conditions, facilitating faster adaptation and thereby accelerating the process. This kind of technological integration represents a shift away from fixed contingency plans toward dynamic adaptability(Tliche et al., 2023).

3.3.3 Cross-Cultural and Multinational Perspectives

Global supply chain resilience strategies are highly regionalised, shaped by institutional capacity, cultural orientation, and economic conditions. Overall, the mechanisms of coordinated state-industry, with greater emphasis on redundancy and supplier diversification, have significantly contributed to the development of resilience in Asia, as evidenced by Japanese manufacturing policies introduced after the 2011 earthquake to minimise reliance on single-source suppliers (Vosooghidizaji et al., 2020). Europe has taken a more integrative path, and resilience has been incorporated into sustainability governance through various tools, including the EU Green Deal, which defines risk mitigation for long-term carbon neutrality and regulatory harmonisation. North America, on the other hand, has relied on market-based adjustments and favoured private-sector innovation, financial instruments, and technology investment to address disruptions (Taghipour, A., & Lu, X. W., 2023, August).

Globalised companies operating in such heterogeneous settings are thus compelled to adopt context-sensitive approaches. Examples include firms such as Unilever, which offset decentralised sourcing in African markets with globally coordinated sourcing processes for standardised products, and automotive producers such as Volkswagen, which offset regional shock-absorbing strategies with global platform strategies to maintain economies of scale. Cultural dimensions also influence resilience (Loivet, W. et al., 2020). Collectivist societies prevalent in East Asia are more likely to emphasise long-term relational contracts and cooperative crisis management than individualist societies, which rely more on formal agreements, market forces, and legal protection, thereby affecting supplier trust, renegotiation rates, and recovery (Hofstede, 2001).

In times of acute economic disturbances, the power of public policy should be decisive. Liquidity created by governments, such as the U.S. CARES Act, kept supply chains alive, and trade policy changes, including temporary tariff cuts or export bans, rearranged global flows of necessities throughout the pandemic (Vosooghidizaji et al., 2019). On the international front, the IMF, WTO, and World Bank maintain system stability by providing liquidity support, regulating trade, and investing in infrastructure. However, their efficacy is challenged by delayed responses and distributional disparities (Lu, X. et al., 2025).

These forces contribute to long-term controversies on the resilience-efficiency trade-off. Opponents caution that redundancy, buffers, and diversification erode cost competitiveness in price-sensitive markets, whilst champions present resilience as an investment required in the ever-growing frequency of disruption (Sheffi, 2021). Protectionist reactions to this, such as reshoring and industrial subsidies, are also mired in controversy, and can increase national security risks, but at the cost of breaking up the global value chain and eliminating scale effects, as seen with localisation efforts in high-cost semiconductor products (Miroudot, 2020; XiaoWen & Atour, 2025). Altogether, these strains imply that resilience does not need to be envisioned in contrast to efficiency but is to be re-conceptualised in the form of dynamic competency allowing the supply chain to be viable, adaptive, and competitive in the face of enduring systemic volatility (Tliche et al., 2019; Tliche et al., 2023).

3.4 Integrating Climate and Economic Resilience: Bridging the Gap Between Environmental and Economic Adaptation

• The Need for a Dual Approach

The combined forces of economic instability and climate change are increasingly influencing the global economy. Although the risks are typically researched independently, they are strongly interrelated. The economic impact of climate events, whether floods, wildfires, or droughts, is often manifested as shortages of raw materials, reduced labour productivity, or market disruptions. On the other hand, environmental vulnerabilities can be exacerbated by economic crises, such as trade wars or financial crises, which reduce spending on long-term, carbon-neutral infrastructure and create incentives for short-term, carbon-intensive behaviours (Sarkis, 2020).

The resilience strategy should be dual, combining environmental and economic aspects within a single strategic plan. Instead of seeing climate adaptation and economic risk management operating on parallel tracks, firms need to realise that they are co-evolutionary(Taghipour, A., & Lu, X., 2025). For instance, extreme weather events that disrupt ports not only delay deliveries but also affect global commodity and financial markets, illustrating the interdependence of ecological and financial shocks (Taghipour, A. et al., 2023).

A balance between sustainability and economic objectives is becoming necessary to achieve a competitive advantage. Integrating the principles of sustainable development within the governance of supply chains - through effective risk management, human rights protection and expectation of regulatory changes - is a way to bolster the ability of companies to work responsibly, while maintaining long-term resilience (Lu et al., 2023). Companies can no longer view resilience as a supporting function; it should be included in the strategic plan. This is found to be in three main areas:

- **Sustainable cost efficiency:** Projects on renewable energy, energy efficiency and the circular economy can bring long-term cost savings, as well as mitigation of climate risk. A good example of this dual objective of cost-efficiency and sustainability is Project Gigaton. This Walmart initiative is to reduce one billion tonnes of greenhouse gas emissions in its supply chain.
- **Market legitimacy and regulatory compliance:** Firms need to have a balance between achieving climate goals and economic sustainability. Stakeholders who expect firms to comply include governments, consumers, and investors. The rise of ESG (environmental, social, and governance) reporting is another example of how sustainability criteria are becoming increasingly important in capital allocation.
- **Strategic adaptability:** Companies with supply chains that have been customised to be sustainable at the core typically exhibit greater adaptability in the event of a crisis. For example, firms that source locally to minimise their carbon emissions have also minimised their exposure to disruptions in international trade.

Finally, a common language reinforces the idea that environmental sustainability and economic resilience are not mutually exclusive but rather complementary in an unstable international environment.

• The Role of Innovation and Technology

Climate and economic resilience of a gap can only be achieved with technological innovation. Blockchain enables immutable, transparent records of activity across multi-level supply chains, allowing environmental consistency and resilience to be traced(Taghipour, A. (Ed.), 2020). For example, carbon tracking systems built on blockchain technology allow companies to track their emissions and hold their suppliers accountable, reducing regulatory and economic risks (Saberi et al., 2019).

Big data's growing influence in supermarket operations is a great example of how big data analytics can improve forecasting accuracy, individualise customer interactions, and optimise inventory management, making retail supply chains more responsive and data-driven (Taghipour, A. et al., 2015 May). Integrating digital storytelling with cloud-based learning platforms has been shown to enhance students' analytical thinking by making historical content interactive and creative (Ponputtha, W. et al, 2021). Logistics companies like DHL and UPS are already using AI to optimise route planning, including accounting for weather-related delays and market gas price fluctuations.

The latest cyber-physical systems, IoT, and automation introduced by Industry 4.0 (the fourth industrial revolution) have made supply chains significantly more adaptable. These technologies help track emissions, inventory, and geopolitical threats in real time, sustaining resilience both climate-wise and economically (Ivanov & Dolgui, 2020). For example, digital twins can simulate various climate and economic stressors in the supply chain, helping companies identify weaknesses and develop strategies to manage them.

Recent discussions of Industry 5.0 are not only about efficiency and automation but also about sustainability and resilience, as well as designs that emphasise human-centred solutions (Xu et al., 2021). Unlike Industry 4.0, which focused on optimising technology, Industry 5.0 takes human imagination and moral considerations into account to ensure that resilience solutions meet societal objectives. In light of this paradigm shift, it is apparent that supply chains should not only withstand disruptions but also contribute to ecological and social well-being. To this end, technology is shown to be a catalyst for meeting economic needs and advancing environmental stewardship (Taghipour et al., 2023).

• Case Studies and Best Practices

Tesla provides an example of how companies may integrate climate and economic resilience into a single strategy. On the one hand, the company expands its supply chains through localising gigafactories in various locations (North America, Europe, Asia) and minimises the risks associated with geopolitical and trade-related factors. Conversely, Tesla embeds sustainability at the heart of its operations, encompassing both the production of electric cars and investment in renewable energy storage systems. Vertical integration of battery production will enable Tesla to reduce its reliance on vulnerable global supply chains for vital inputs and to meet climate mitigation objectives better (Mangram, 2012).

Few global companies have adopted predictive analytics and IoT systems to mitigate climate and economic risks simultaneously. For example, the supply chain platform developed by IBM uses an IoT sensor to track climate-related logistical risks and embeds AI models to predict financial outcomes (Glaa, B. et al., 2014 May). This dual functionality can help firms mitigate hurricane-related disruptions (e.g., port closures) and simulate currency fluctuations, which can affect shipping costs.

Likewise, agricultural supply chains are deploying more IoT-based climate sensors to optimise irrigation and crop management and to use predictive analytics to mitigate commodity price volatility. An example is Nestlé, which integrates climate data into its procurement decisions to anticipate risks in food crops and into its financial models to manage cost variability in the coffee and cocoa markets (Taghipour et al., 2023).

3.5 Case Studies

The pandemic exposed the weaknesses in a just-in-time approach and global dependencies. Chinese lockdowns led to factory closures, which spread to other countries. Meanwhile, demand spikes in industries such as travel and hospitality were offset by increases in demand for medical supplies and e-commerce products. Companies that had invested in digital visibility platforms, diversified sourcing, and supplier partnerships were better positioned to carry on (Shih, 2020). The crisis highlighted the value of systemic resiliency versus risk management in isolation.

- Microsoft balanced its semiconductor vendors and invested in cloud service inventory buffers, making sure continuity when there were shortages of chips.
- Nike increased the speed of digital platforms to reach the consumer directly, to counteract the effects of retail closures.
- General Motors followed the reshoring of key auto parts as well as forging strategic alliances with local suppliers in order to minimise its importation.

These crisis recovery plans emphasise the need to be agile, digitalised, and geographically spread to remain competitive after a crisis.

Best practices have emerged that enable companies to balance carbon reduction and economic flexibility. Sourcing projects developed by Unilever as part of its climate-resilience strategies helps reduce flood-related risks in agricultural areas. It increases the resilience of local communities, thereby balancing local economies. The use of renewable energy in logistics not only reduces carbon emissions but also mitigates the impact of fossil fuel price fluctuations, demonstrating the interplay between environmental and financial risk reduction at IKEA.

3.6 META FRAMEWORK

Figure 1. Climate Change Risks and Resilience Framework

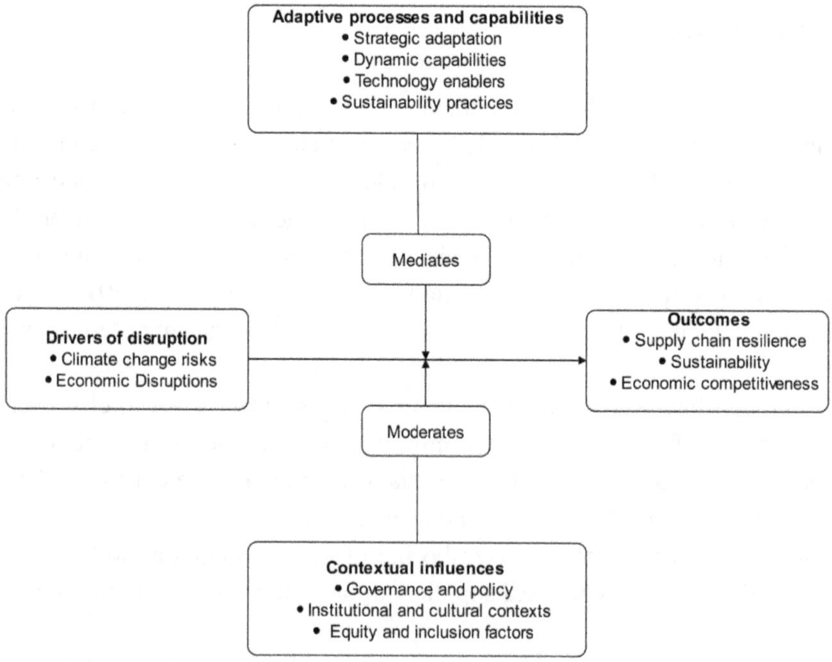

Source: *Authors' Contribution*

Figure 1 presents an integrated meta-framework that theorises how international supply chains mitigate the risks of climate change and economic turbulence. It is based on resilience theory and complex adaptive systems, which assume that these disruptions are the primary drivers, with their effects mediated by adaptive processes and capabilities, including strategic adaptation, dynamic capabilities, technology enablers, and sustainability practices (Taghipour, A., & Merimi, M., 2021, March). These relationships are mediated by contextual factors, including governance structures, institutional and cultural environments, and equity, which shape the nature and intensity of outcomes. The framework enhances theory by connecting ecological, economic, and organisational resilience and draws on empirical evidence highlighting its applicability to creating supply chain resilience, sustainability, and competitiveness in unstable environments (Taghipour, A. et al., 2023).

4 FUTURE DIRECTIONS: IMPLICATIONS FOR THEORY, PRACTICE, AND POLICY

Resilience theory has now reached a mature state in supply chain scholarship, but remains weak at explaining the effects of drivers and confounders of environmental and economic disruptions. Initial conceptualisations of resilience have framed it mainly in terms of the adaptive capacity of complex adaptive systems, with a focus on interdependence, nonlinearity, and emergent behaviour (Choi et al., 2001). This perspective was later streamlined by the operationalisation of resilience, by using dynamic capabilities, especially anticipation, absorption, and transformation, as ways of how firms react to disruption (Ponomarov & Holcomb, 2009; Ivanov, 2020).

Nevertheless, the dominant theoretical treatments still focus on climate-induced shocks and economic crises in isolation, even though empirical evidence indicates that floods, droughts, pandemics, trade conflicts, and financial instability are increasingly interdependent and mutually reinforcing (Taghipour & Merimi, 2021). This fragmentation limits the applicability of resilience theory to analysis, as the actual supply chain exists within a well-coupled socio-ecological-economic system in which disturbances spread among domains via feedback mechanisms(Tliche, Y. et al., 2019).

A drought in Brazilian agriculture, for example, disrupts physical supply, drives commodity price volatility, amplifies financial risks, and reshapes trade routes, exhibiting delineated, interdependent interactions that linear, domain-specific models cannot explain. To fill this gap, it is necessary to adopt an integrated theoretical focus in which resilience is situated at the nexus of ecological limits, economic turbulence, and institutional regulation, and deep uncertainty and the transmission of systemic risks are explicitly considered (Taghipour, A., 2022). New AI-enabled supply chain solutions advance this trend by integrating sustainability goals with human-centric decision-making, thereby optimising resources, minimising waste, and enabling ethically driven operational responses amid growing uncertainty (Taghipour, 2025).

Building on these advances, future research would be well served by hybrid schemes that balance conventional probability-based risk management with resilience-based adaptability. Such frameworks would bring together climate and economic risks within a single taxonomy, incorporate active flexibility alongside fixed controls, employ systems thinking to capture cascading effects across social, ecological, and economic subsystems, and reify resilience at different scales, within firm-level practice, industry collaboration, and global governance systems. For practitioners, the intersection of climate and economic risks necessitates managerial emphasis (Gharye Mirzaei et al., 2025).

Strategic supplier, geographic, and logistics route diversification helps avoid geographically concentrated shocks, and nearshoring and reshoring also help mitigate geopolitical risk and reduce transport-related emissions (Taghipour, A., 2023). Digital technologies, such as predictive analytics, blockchain, and digital twins, can enhance on-the-fly visibility and scenario planning, enabling firms to simulate disruptions and analyse adaptive responses. For example, during pandemic market volatility, Maersk used digital twins. Combining sustainability with risk management enhances long-term resilience by adopting renewable energy and implementing a circular economy, thereby reducing reliance on volatile fossil fuel markets and aligning with regulatory and consumer requirements (Taghipour, A., & Lu, X. W., 2023, August).

Examples from IKEA and Unilever demonstrate that incorporating carbon-neutral goals into procurement and sourcing policies increases adaptive capacity and strategic flexibility. Significantly, resilience can be understood as a network effect that develops only through collaboration, trust, and information sharing across levels (Mbiatem, J. et al., 2018). The presence of cross-tier visibility, aided by relational governance, facilitates faster collective responses to crises and the dissemination of knowledge on climate adaptation and the mitigation of economic risks (Ren, Z. et al., 2016). Such firm-level practices are being augmented by multi-stakeholder practices, such as public-privacy agreements on resilient infrastructure investment and industry consortia that marshal resources to develop predictive models and share insurance schemes (Aouadni, S. et al., 2024). The World Economic Forum's Resilient Supply Chain Initiative is a systems-focused approach that acknowledges that systemic shocks are beyond the capacity of individual organisations to address.

Policymaking-wise, existing international institutions remain piecemeal, focusing on climate and economic risks and operating under institutionally distinct mandates. Although mitigation and adaptation are at the forefront of the Paris Agreement, and economic flows are addressed by the World Trade Organisation, climate and trade risks are increasingly converging, requiring combined policy frameworks (Goodarzian, F. et al., 2024). Tax credits for renewable logistics and subsidies for diversification in sectors of strategic importance, such as semiconductors and pharmaceutical firms, can help accelerate the adoption of climate-sensitive and economically viable practices at the firm level (Taghipour, A., 2024). The harmonisation of regulators is also essential, as national differences in carbon pricing, labour rights, and trade restrictions create regulatory risks for multinational enterprises and undermine resilience (Taghipour et al., 2022).

Strengthened international collaboration among organisations such as the IMF, the World Bank, and UN agencies could benefit from joint actions to align climate adaptation financing with trade infrastructure development and macroeconomic surveillance (Lu, X. et al., 2023). The social platforms for knowledge sharing and international databases on climatic and economic discontinuities would also facilitate benchmarking and evidence-based resilience planning. Nevertheless, despite significant conceptual advances, a gap remains between theoretical advances and empirical confirmation (Crandall, A. et al., 1995). Future research should focus on longitudinal, mixed-methods studies of the development of hybrid resilience strategies over time in multinational supply chains across varying institutional environments (Zoghlami, 2016).

Current studies are overly focused on short-term recovery and provide little information on the overall structural effects of prolonged climate stress and frequent economic meltdowns, including how agricultural supply chains can be restructured under chronic drought and how decision-making on automation and reshoring in response to recurring financial crises is strategised. It is also necessary to pay closer attention to emerging economies, which are overexposed to climatic risks and are located at the centre of global value chains, as well as to the ethical imperative to allocate resilience plans without placing excessive demands on vulnerable populations or small suppliers (Taghipour, A., & Lu, X. W., 2023, August).

Methodologically, resilience research needs to move beyond the probabilistic framework to methods that can capture nonlinearity, feedback, and deep uncertainty, such as agent-based modelling, robust optimisation, and scenario-based planning. These instruments may help integrate macro-level systemic analysis and micro-level practical decision-making, thereby improving the rigour of theory and the relevance of practice (Mahfod, J. et al., 2019). Taken together, these lessons suggest that resilience in supply chains in the twenty-first century should be seen as a strategic competence and a shared responsibility, rather than a specific feature of work. The evidence supports the conclusion that resilience is not a final point but a long-term, multidimensional process that incorporates climate mitigation, economic flexibility, and technological innovation. Companies that have made sustainability consistent with resilience, including those that have adopted renewable logistics or regenerative sourcing, show that environmental responsibility and economic competitiveness can reinforce each other (Mahfod, J., 2021).

Simultaneously, resilience is not limited to organisations, and there should be a concerted effort by firms, governments, international organisations, and civil society. The policy frameworks, such as the Sendai Framework for Disaster Risk Reduction and the Paris Agreement, emphasise the need for multi-tiered governance that breaks down silos and promotes interdependence across disciplines and geographical boundaries (Merimi et al., 2016). As climate change accelerates, economic crises are redefining demand trends. As geopolitics reorganises production chains, global supply chains are becoming reliant on designing and governing resilience as a fundamental organisational principle (Pour Mohammadi et al., 2014). International cooperation is no longer an ideational ideal but an instrumental need, including the harmonisation of policies, the sharing of resources, and the cultural transformation of small-efficiency paradigms into value generation over time. Conceptualised and operationalised as a system imperative, global supply chains can transform fragile set-ups into adaptive infrastructures capable of absorbing shocks, facilitating ecological regeneration, and advancing economic stability and social equity for future generations.

REFERENCES

Aouadni, S., Aouadni, I., & Taghipour, A. (2024). Using an ordinal priority approach with confidence-level measurement for third-party logistics provider selection in the Tunisian healthcare sector. In *Applications of New Technology in Operations and Supply Chain Management* (pp. 404–429). IGI Global. DOI: 10.4018/979-8-3693-1578-1.ch020

Baldwin, R., & Evenett, S. J. (2020). *COVID-19 and trade policy: Why turning inward will not work*. CEPR Press.

Bown, C. P. (2020). *US–China trade war tariffs: An up-to-date chart—Peterson*. Institute for International Economics.

Bunn, C., Läderach, P., Rivera, O. O., & Kirschke, D. (2015). A bitter cup: Climate change profile of global production of Arabica and Robusta coffee. *Climatic Change*, *129*(1–2), 89–101. DOI: 10.1007/s10584-014-1306-x

Cauchois, R., Taghipour, A., Kang, D., Zoghlami, N., & Abed, M. (2017). Advanced solutions for a supply chain with stochastic information. *Journal of Advanced Management Science*, *5*(1), 9–13. DOI: 10.18178/joams.5.1.9-13

Choi, T. Y., Dooley, K. J., & Rungtusanatham, M. (2001). Supply networks and complex adaptive systems: Control versus emergence. *Journal of Operations Management*, *19*(3), 351–366. DOI: 10.1016/S0272-6963(00)00068-1

Chowdhury, M. M. H., & Quaddus, M. (2017). Supply chain resilience: Conceptualisation and scale development using dynamic capability theory. *International Journal of Production Economics*, *188*, 185–204. DOI: 10.1016/j.ijpe.2017.03.020

Christopher, M., & Peck, H. (2004). Building the resilient supply chain. *International Journal of Logistics Management*, *15*(2), 1–14. DOI: 10.1108/09574090410700275

Committee of Sponsoring Organisations of the Treadway Commission (COSO). (2004). *Enterprise risk management—Integrated framework*. COSO.

Crandall, A., Rahim, H. A., Yount, K. M., Borghei, N. S., Taghipour, A., Roudsari, R. L., ... & Nelson, B. D. (1995). WHO journals. Information for authors, 1.

Evenett, S. J. (2022). Crisis-era protectionism and the multilateral trading system. *World Economy*, *45*(3), 631–651.

Gelsomino, L. M., Mangiaracina, R., Perego, A., & Tumino, A. (2016). Supply chain finance: A literature review. *International Journal of Physical Distribution & Logistics Management*, *46*(4), 348–366. DOI: 10.1108/IJPDLM-08-2014-0173

Gereffi, G. (2018). *Global value chains and development: Redefining the contours of 21st century capitalism*. Cambridge University Press. DOI: 10.1017/9781108559423

Gharye Mirzaei, M., Goodarzian, F., Taghipour, A., & Muñuzuri, J. (2025). Sustainable closed-loop supply chain network under uncertainty considering green technologies: Toward the circular economy. *The Journal of the Operational Research Society*, •••, 1–21.

Glaa, B., Zoghlami, N., & Taghipour, A. (2014, May). Outsourcing and off-shoring healthcare services: A way to cut the costs and improve quality. In the 2014 International Conference on Advanced Logistics and Transport (ICALT) (pp. 189–194). IEEE. DOI: 10.1109/ICAdLT.2014.6864116

Goodarzian, F., Abraham, A., Muñuzuri, J., Taghipour, A., & Ghasemi, P. (2024). A Benders decomposition approach for a new sustainable pharmaceutical supply chain network: A case study in France. *Annals of Operations Research*, •••, 1–39.

Haraguchi, M., & Lall, U. (2015). Flood risks and impacts: A case study of Thailand's floods in 2011 and research questions for supply chain decision making. *International Journal of Disaster Risk Reduction*, *14*, 256–272. DOI: 10.1016/j.ijdrr.2014.09.005

Hofstede, G. (2001). *Culture's consequences: Comparing values, behaviours, institutions and organisations across nations* (2nd ed.). Sage.

Holling, C. S. (1973). Resilience and stability of ecological systems. *Annual Review of Ecology and Systematics*, *4*(1), 1–23. DOI: 10.1146/annurev.es.04.110173.000245

Holmes, T., Blackhurst, J., & O'Grady, P. (2021). Resilient semiconductor supply chains: Addressing climate and geopolitical risks. *The Journal of Supply Chain Management*, *57*(4), 15–33.

Intergovernmental Panel on Climate Change (IPCC). (2022). *Climate change 2022: Impacts, adaptation, and vulnerability*. Cambridge University Press.

IPCC. (2022). *Climate change 2022: Impacts, adaptation and vulnerability*. Cambridge University Press.

Ivanov, D. (2020). Viable supply chain model: Integrating agility, resilience, and sustainability perspectives—Lessons from the COVID-19 pandemic. *Annals of Operations Research*, •••, 1–21. PMID: 34334863

Ivanov, D. (2021). Exiting the COVID-19 pandemic: After-shocks and supply chain recovery. *International Journal of Production Research*, *59*(12), 3535–3546. DOI: 10.1080/00207543.2021.1890852

Ivanov, D., & Dolgui, A. (2020). Viability of Intertwined Supply Networks: Extending the Supply Chain Resilience Angle toward Survivability. *International Journal of Production Research, 58*(10), 2904–2915. DOI: 10.1080/00207543.2020.1750727

Ivanov, D., & Dolgui, A. (2021). A digital supply chain twin for managing the disruption risks and resilience in the era of Industry 4.0. *Production Planning and Control, 32*(9), 775–788. DOI: 10.1080/09537287.2020.1768450

Lebosse, S., Taghipour, A., & Canel-Depitre, B. (2017). Quick response to fluctuations in supply chains: A review—Journal of Advanced Management Science, 5(5).

Lengnick-Hall, C. A., Beck, T. E., & Lengnick-Hall, M. L. (2011). Developing a capacity for organisational resilience through strategic human resource management. *Human Resource Management Review, 21*(3), 243–255. DOI: 10.1016/j.hrmr.2010.07.001

Loivet, W., Taghipour, A., & Kang, D. S. (2020). The rise of green supply chain management: Between complexity and necessity. *J. Econ. Bus. Manag, 8*(1), 1–7. DOI: 10.18178/joebm.2020.8.1.604

Lu, X. W., Tliche, Y., Vosooghidizaji, M., & Taghipour, A. (2023). Cryptocurrencies and Blockchain Applications. In Blockchain Applications in Cryptocurrency for Technological Evolution (pp. 1-13). IGI Global.

Mahfod, J., Canel-Depitre, B., & Taghipour, A. (2019). Quality function deployment-ELECTRE in supplier evaluation—Journal of Advanced Management Science, 7(4).

Mahfod, J., Khoury, B., Canel-Depitre, B., & Taghipour, A. (2021). Logistics Providers in Syria Humanitarian Operations. In Demand Forecasting and Order Planning in Supply Chains and Humanitarian Logistics (pp. 171–197). IGI Global. DOI: 10.4018/978-1-7998-3805-0.ch006

Mangram, M. E. (2012). The globalisation of Tesla Motors: A strategic marketing plan analysis. *Journal of Strategic Marketing, 20*(4), 289–312. DOI: 10.1080/0965254X.2012.657224

Mbiatem, J., Taghipour, A., & Canel-Depitre, B. (2018, August). Supplier selection approaches for decision makers. In *Proceedings of the 8th International Conference on Information Communication and Management* (pp. 108–112).

Merimi, M., & Taghipour, A. (2021). Accelerating the digitalisation of the supply chain: An empirical research about the COVID-19 crisis. In *Digitalisation of decentralised supply chains during global crises* (pp. 1–24). IGI Global Scientific Publishing. DOI: 10.4018/978-1-7998-6874-3.ch001

Miroudot, S. (2020). Resilience versus robustness in global value chains: Some policy implications. *VoxEU.org*.

Munich, Re. (2021). *NatCatSERVICE: Natural catastrophe statistics online*. Munich Re.

Nadia, E. N., Beatrice, C. D., & Atour, T. (2020). Luxury hotels' eco-friendly activities & customers' preferences and willingness to pay for green hotels. *Journal of Advanced Management Science*, *8*(1), 1–24.

Nadia, E. N., Beatrice, C. D., & Atour, T. (2021). The determinants of hotel room rates in Beirut: A hedonic pricing model. International Journal of Trade. *Economics and Finance*, *12*(2), 33–42.

Nadia, E. N., Canel-Depritre, B., & Taghipour, A. (2018). Lebanese hotels' engagement in environmental practices. In *TOURMAN 2018* (p. 457)

Ponomarov, S. Y., & Holcomb, M. C. (2009). Understanding the concept of supply chain resilience. *International Journal of Logistics Management*, *20*(1), 124–143. DOI: 10.1108/09574090910954873

Ponputtha, W., Wannapiroon, P., Nilsook, P., Taghipour, A., Murat, S., Huang, P., & Chou, T. C. (2021). Creative history learning model using digital storytelling through cloud learning to enhance analytical thinking. International Journal of e-Education, e-Business, e-. *Management Learning*, *11*(2), 42–50.

Pour Mohammadi, M., Ghorbani, R., & Taghipour, A. (2014). Factors affecting housing prices in Tabriz: A hedonic model analysis. *Geographical Planning of Space Quarterly Journal*, *3*(9), 83–104.

Radhoui, H., Taghipour, A., & Canel-Depitre, B. (2019). The distribution and pickup of goods: A literature review and survey. Hierarchical Planning and Information Sharing Techniques in Supply Chain Management, 46–85.

Radhoui, H., Taghipour, A., & Canel-Depitre, B. (2021). Mixed delivery and pickup vehicle routing problem with limited flow and drone assignment in an urban network. In *Demand Forecasting and Order Planning in Supply Chains and Humanitarian Logistics* (pp. 225–249). IGI Global. DOI: 10.4018/978-1-7998-3805-0.ch008

Ren, Z., Taghipour, A., & Canel-Depitre, B. (2016, October). Information sharing in the supply chain under uncertainty. In 2016, the 6th International Conference on Information Communication and Management (ICICM) (pp. 67–71). IEEE. DOI: 10.1109/INFOCOMAN.2016.7784217

Rose, A. (2004). Defining and measuring economic resilience to disasters. *Disaster Prevention and Management, 13*(4), 307–314. DOI: 10.1108/09653560410556528

Saberi, S., Kouhizadeh, M., Sarkis, J., & Shen, L. (2019). Blockchain Technology and Its Relationship to Sustainable Supply Chain Management. *International Journal of Production Research, 57*(7), 2117–2135. DOI: 10.1080/00207543.2018.1533261

Sahraoui, A., Tran, N. K., Tliche, Y., Kacem, A., & Taghipour, A. (2023). Examining ICT Innovation for Sustainable Terminal Operations in Developing Countries: A Case Study of the Port of Radès in Tunisia. *Sustainability (Basel), 15*(11), 9123. DOI: 10.3390/su15119123

Sarkis, J. (2020). Supply chain sustainability: Learning from the COVID-19 pandemic. *International Journal of Operations & Production Management, 40*(10), 1763–1782. DOI: 10.1108/IJOPM-08-2020-0568

Sheffi, Y. (2021). The new (ab) standard: Reshaping business and supply chain strategy beyond [MIT Press.]. *COVID*, •••, 19.

Shih, W. (2020). Is it time to rethink global supply chains? *MIT Sloan Management Review, 61*(4), 1–6.

Taghipour, A. (2009). Évaluation de la collaboration au sein d'une chaîne d'approvisionnement. Revue française de gestion industrielle, 28(1), 26–42.

Taghipour, A. (Ed.). (2022). *Blockchain Applications in Cryptocurrency for Technological Evolution*. IGI Global. DOI: 10.4018/978-1-6684-6247-8

Taghipour, A. (Ed.). (2023). *Government Impact on Sustainable and Responsible Supply Chain Management*. IGI Global. DOI: 10.4018/978-1-6684-9062-4

Taghipour, A. (2024). Big Data: The New Gold Mine for Supermarkets. In Applications of New Technology in Operations and Supply Chain Management (pp. 98–106). IGI Global.

Taghipour, A., Abed, M., & Zoghlami, N. (2015, May). Design for remanufacturing with respect to reverse logistics processes: A review. In 2015, the 4th International Conference on Advanced Logistics and Transport (ICALT) (pp. 299–Mahfod, J., 304). IEEE.

Taghipour, A., Belrhazi, Y., & Damoum, N. (2023). Resilient, sustainable supply chain management. In *Government Impact on Sustainable and Responsible Supply Chain Management* (pp. 33–47). IGI Global. DOI: 10.4018/978-1-6684-9062-4.ch003

Taghipour, A., & Beneteau-Piet, C. (2020). Sustainable supply chain management performance. *International Journal of Innovation, Management and Technology, 11*(6), 165–169. DOI: 10.18178/ijimt.2020.11.6.897

Taghipour, A., Fooladvand, A., Khazaei, M., & Ramezani, M. (2023). Criteria clustering and supplier segmentation based on sustainable shared value using BWM and PROMETHEE. *Sustainability (Basel), 15*(11), 8670. DOI: 10.3390/su15118670

Taghipour, A., & Frayret, J. M. (2011). Supply chain coordination planning: A review. Work paper, École polytechnique de Montréal.

Taghipour, A., & Frayret, J. M. (2013a). Coordination of operations planning in supply chains: A review. *International Journal of Business Performance and Supply Chain Modelling, 5*(3), 272–307. DOI: 10.1504/IJBPSCM.2013.055729

Taghipour, A., & Frayret, J. M. (2013b, May). An algorithm to improve operations planning in decentralised supply chains. In the 2013 International Conference on Advanced Logistics and Transport (pp. 100–103). IEEE.

Taghipour, A., & Lu, X. (2025). Advancing Supply Chain Innovation: Theoretical Foundations, Contemporary Developments, and Future Directions. In Ecological and Human Dimensions of AI-Based Supply Chain (pp. 1–26). IGI Global Scientific Publishing.

Taghipour, A., & Lu, X. (2025). Navigating the Artificial Intelligence Era: Impacts of Artificial Intelligence on Youth Critical Thinking, Career Paths, and Ethical Challenges. In Ecological and Human Dimensions of AI-Based Supply Chain (pp. 49–68). IGI Global Scientific Publishing.

Taghipour, A., Lu, X., Derradji, M., & Sow, A. D. (2022, July). The impact of digitalisation on supply chain management: a literature review. In *Proceedings of the 12th International Conference on Information Communication and Management* (pp. 75–78).

Taghipour, A., Lu, X., Derradji, M., & Sow, A. D. (2022, July). The impact of digitalisation on supply chain management: a literature review. In *Proceedings of the 12th International Conference on Information Communication and Management* (pp. 75–78).

Taghipour, A., Lu, X., & Smahi, M. (2022). Opportunities and challenges for society 5.0 in procurement. *Blockchain Technology in Supply Chain Management for Society, 5*(0), 91–100. DOI: 10.1201/9781003177432-9

Taghipour, A., & Lu, X. W. (2023, August). Green Supply Chain Management: A Guide. In International Conference on Applied Economics and Business (pp. 315-328). Cham: Springer Nature Switzerland.

Taghipour, A., & Merimi, M. (2021, March). Digital transformation of supply chains during the crisis: COVID-19. In the 11th Annual International Conference on Industrial Engineering and Operations Management, IEOM (pp. 7493–7501).

Taghipour, A., Rouyendegh, B. D., Ünal, A., & Piya, S. (2022, July). Selection of suppliers for speech recognition products in IT projects by combining techniques with an integrated fuzzy MCDM. *Sustainability (Basel)*, *14*(3), 1777. DOI: 10.3390/su14031777

Taghipour, A., Rouyendegh, B. D., Ünal, A., & Piya, S. (2022). Selection of suppliers for speech recognition products in IT projects by combining techniques with an integrated fuzzy MCDM. *Sustainability (Basel)*, *14*(3), 1777. DOI: 10.3390/su14031777

Taghipour, A., Sohrabi, A., Ghaedi, M., & Khazaei, M. (2023). A robust vaccine supply chain model in pandemics: Case of COVID-19 in Iran. *Computers & Industrial Engineering*, *183*, 109465. DOI: 10.1016/j.cie.2023.109465

Tang, C. S. (2006). Perspectives in supply chain risk management. *International Journal of Production Economics*, *103*(2), 451–488. DOI: 10.1016/j.ijpe.2005.12.006

Tliche, Y., Taghipour, A., & Canel-Depitre, B. (2019). Downstream Demand Inference in Decentralised Supply Chains. *European Journal of Operational Research*, *274*(1), 65–77. DOI: 10.1016/j.ejor.2018.09.034

Tliche, Y., Taghipour, A., Mahfod-Leroux, J., & Vosooghidizaji, M. (2023). Collaborative bullwhip effect-oriented bi-objective optimisation for inference-based weighted moving average forecasting in a decentralised supply chain. [IJISSCM]. *International Journal of Information Systems and Supply Chain Management*, *16*(1), 1–37. DOI: 10.4018/IJISSCM.316168

United Nations Framework Convention on Climate Change. (2015). *Paris Agreement*.

Vosooghidizaji, M., Taghipour, A., & Canel-Depitre, B. (2019). A literature review on information asymmetry in supply chain coordination. *International Journal of Production Research*, *58*(6), 1–6.

Vosooghidizaji, M., Taghipour, A., & Canel-Depitre, B. (2020). Information asymmetry in supply chain coordination: State of the art. *Journal of Industrial and Intelligent Information*, *8*(2), 38–43. DOI: 10.18178/jiii.8.2.38-43

World Economic Forum. (2021). *The Global Risks Report 2021*. World Economic Forum.

XiaoWen, L., & Atour, T.XiaoWen. (2025). Knowledge-driven digital innovation in supply chains: An organisational perspective. *Journal of Innovation & Knowledge, 10*(5), 100787. DOI: 10.1016/j.jik.2025.100787

Xu, X., Lu, Y., Vogel-Heuser, B., & Wang, L. (2021). Industry 4.0 and Industry 5.0—Inception, conception, and perception. *Journal of Manufacturing Systems, 61*, 530–535. DOI: 10.1016/j.jmsy.2021.10.006

Zoghlami, N., Taghipour, A., Merlo, C., & Abed, M. (2016). Management of divergent production network using decentralised multi-level capacitated lot-sizing models. *International Journal of Shipping and Transport Logistics, 8*(5), 590–604. DOI: 10.1504/IJSTL.2016.078686

Zsidisin, G. A., & Ritchie, B. (2009). *Supply chain risk: A handbook of assessment, management, and performance*. Springer. DOI: 10.1007/978-0-387-79934-6

Chapter 7
Supply Chain Risk Management in Volatile Environments

Gaddam Venu Gopal
http://orcid.org/0000-0003-3128-7924
Bonam Venkata Chalamayya Engineering College, India

Raj Kumar Gupta
Sardar Vallabhbhai Patel College, India

Jayesh Surana
Medicaps University, India

Manu Vasudevan Unni
http://orcid.org/0000-0001-7543-7010
St. Claret College, India

Irfan Abdul Karim
http://orcid.org/0000-0001-9391-6074
Bahrain Polytechnic, Bahrain

K. Vigneshwaran
SRM Institute of Science and Technology, India

Gagan Singh
http://orcid.org/0009-0007-7819-0149
Meerut Institute of Technology, India

V. Bhoopathy
http://orcid.org/0000-0003-2175-6328
Sree Rama Engineering College, India

ABSTRACT

In a time of geopolitical instability, economic uncertainty, climate-related disruptions, and global health crises, supply chains are becoming more and more vulnerable to high levels of risk and volatility. This chapter looks at the rules and methods of managing supply chain risk in unstable situations. It focuses on finding, evaluating, and reducing operational, financial, and strategic risks. It looks at how resilience, agility, and flexibility may make the supply chain stronger, as well as how data analytics, digital technologies, and collaborative risk-sharing methods might help. The chapter also talks about proactive and reactive risk management tactics, such as scenario planning, diversification, real-time monitoring, and making decisions

DOI: 10.4018/979-8-3373-6455-1.ch007

based on what happens. This chapter gives a full picture of how organisations can plan for disruptions, reduce vulnerabilities, and keep up performance in unpredictable business environments by combining theoretical frameworks with real-world examples from several fields.

1. INTRODUCTION

Supply Chain Management (SCM) is inherently exposed to significant risks, particularly as international trade has led to increasingly complex and interconnected global supply chains. The vulnerability of supply chains has intensified with the expansion of globalization and trade liberalization, which have increased interdependencies among firms and markets. Manufacturing organizations, in particular, bear substantial supply chain-related costs in monetary terms. Nevertheless, within the traditional frameworks of the insurance and banking sectors, SCM risks are not typically categorized as financial risks, despite their considerable economic implications. Risk management in the supply chain context refers to the systematic identification, assessment, and mitigation of potential disruptions in order to enhance network resilience and continuity. Although supply chains differ across industries and sectors, certain risks, such as demand variability, supply disruptions, geopolitical instability, and operational failures, are common. At the same time, many risks remain industry- or domain-specific. The overall robustness of a supply chain is determined by its weakest link. As supply chains expand in length and complexity, the likelihood of disruption correspondingly increases due to greater interconnectivity and dependency among stakeholders. Each node within the chain plays a critical role, and the involvement of multiple actors further amplifies exposure to risk. While the development of resilient and reliable supply chains entails significant investment, an extensive body of research underscores their necessity, given the profound adverse effects that disruptions can have on organizational performance and competitiveness (Cauchois et al., 2017). Supply Chain Risk Management (SCRM) refers to a systematic and structured approach to identifying, assessing, prioritizing, mitigating, and monitoring potential disruptions within supply chains. SCRM has become a critical field of study and practice due to the cascading or "domino" effects that a single disruptive event can trigger across logistics networks. Notable examples include the September 11 attacks, the Gulf War, the outbreak of global pandemics, and the millennium bug crisis. The impact of supply chain disruptions and large-scale crises on operational performance must be carefully evaluated. In today's highly competitive global marketplace, firms are increasingly concerned about supply chain interruptions and their associated operational and financial consequences. In the supply chain context, risk can be defined as the probability of an unfavourable and unforeseen event that may directly or indirectly cause disruption. However, risk and disruption are not synonymous. A disruption represents the materialization of a risk event, whereas risks may exist even in the absence of observable interruptions. In other words, risk reflects potential vulnerability, while disruption denotes its actual occurrence (Alizadeh et al., 2021). The 2011 disaster in Japan had prolonged repercussions for the global automotive industry, disrupting production and supply networks for several months. In the same year, severe flooding in Thailand significantly affected semiconductor supply chains and the Thai automotive sector. Such events illustrate how threats can escalate into disruptions that reverberate throughout the entire supply chain network. Effective Supply Chain Risk Management (SCRM) plays a crucial role in ensuring the continuity and efficiency of supply chain operations. The concept of risk is often associated with terms such as danger, hazard, peril, uncertainty, disruption, and vulnerability. When supply chain managers fail to anticipate potential disruptions and their underlying causes, the supply chain becomes more vulnerable, and managerial effectiveness declines. In the context of Supply Chain Management (SCM), the terms risk and uncertainty are sometimes used interchangeably. However, while they are related concepts, they are not identical and should be distinguished conceptually in rigorous academic analysis. (Selcuk Besir Demir, 2018). Supply Chain Management (SCM) is increasingly exposed to complex risk factors due to globalization, digital transformation, and environmental uncertainty.

Research Gap

Although existing studies address supply chain risks and mitigation strategies, limited attention has been given to structuring SCRM frameworks specifically for highly volatile environments characterized by geopolitical instability, climate uncertainty, and global disruptions. Most traditional models assume stable conditions and fail to incorporate dynamic volatility-responsive capabilities.

Research Objective

This chapter aims to develop an integrated Supply Chain Risk Management framework tailored for volatile environments by incorporating resilience, agility, flexibility, and digital-enabled monitoring mechanisms.

Chapter Contribution

- This chapter contributes to the literature by:
- Conceptualizing volatility as a structural risk amplifier.

- Developing a volatility-responsive SCRM framework.
- Integrating strategic, operational, and technological dimensions.
- Providing managerial guidelines for implementation.

2. UNDERSTANDING SUPPLY CHAIN RISK AND VOLATILITY

Both supply chain risk and SCRM have been defined differently by different groups of researchers. Researchers would have a hard time communicating with practitioners and gaining access to industry to conduct empirical studies if there weren't a uniform concept and unambiguous definition. Researchers are better able to assess the efficacy of SCRM approaches when they have a common standard to use for identifying and measuring the likelihood and impact of all supply chain hazards. Both stress the importance of defining these concepts precisely. The current meanings of SCRM are summarized in Section (Mbiatem et al., 2018).

2.1 SCRM

Definitions of SCRM were offered by several studies and are presented. Although all of these definitions have stressed the importance of working with supply chain partners, there are a few limitations. Firstly, they only cover a subset of SCRM. Secondly, they don't cover all of the processes, procedures, or events that can be included in SCRM (Nadia et al., 2020). Our definition of SCRM is based on the conceptual framework. It is an inter-organizational endeavour that uses quantitative and qualitative risk management methodologies to identify, evaluate, mitigate, and monitor unexpected events or conditions that could negatively impact any part of a supply chain.

2.2 Supply Chain Risk

The following is a summary of the several definitions of SR and supply chain risk given by various researchers. SR information flow risk material flow risk and product flow risk are all relevant definitions, but they only cover one function or section of the supply chain at a time. Knowing this, and supply chain risk is defined as the potential and effect of unexpected macro and/or micro level events or conditions that could disrupt the supply chain, of the conceptual framework that have an adverse effect on any link in the supply chain, which in turn causes problems at the operational, tactical, or strategic levels (Ponputtha et al., 2021).

3. CLASSIFICATION OF SUPPLY CHAIN RISKS

3.1 DR

When an organization's core operations, the marketplace, and the flow of commodities, information, and financial assets are threatened or actually disrupted, DR becomes an important issue. Because it could either exceed or fall short of the expected demand limits, this risk presents an opportunity for discontent. Included in this are unknowns regarding the amount and diversity of products (Sahraoui et al., 2023).

3.2 SR

There is a possibility that the uninterrupted flow of goods or information inside the network of companies placed upstream from the central organization could be disrupted, which is known as SR (Taghipour, 2023). Therefore, it represents the danger associated with a company's suppliers or their capacity to provide the essential supplies to the company being compromised. This phenomenon, which includes a variety of circumstances, is known as input risk, and it has a negative effect on the internal flow of resources needed for operational tasks.

- Dependence on essential suppliers
- Consolidation in supply markets.
- Challenges concerning quality and management that emerge from multinational procurement.
- Potential disturbance at a subordinate level (Taghipour, 2020).

3.3 Process of Risk

Business processes include both the strategic planning of value-adding operations and the administrative duties performed by companies. When these operating routines are disrupted, it can impair a company's capacity to generate and deliver goods or services. This is known as process risk (Taghipour and Frayret, 2013). The possible failure of an essential operating, manufacturing, or processing capability could lead to this outcome. That is what it comprises.

- Fluctuations in production yields.
- Extended setup durations and inflexible production cycles
- Equipment reliability
- Limited capacity.

- Assigning substantial company operations to external collaborators.

3.4 Environmental Risk

In environmentally sensitive business world, environmental risk in SCM is becoming more important. It alludes to the environmental hazards that may arise from a supply chain's operations, including but not limited to changes in environmental rules, shortages of resources, and the effects of climate change. For ethical and sustainable SC operations, it is crucial to assess and manage these risks. Carbon emissions and greenhouse gasses pose the greatest threat to the environment from SCM. There is growing demand on businesses to lessen their impact on the environment as a result of stricter climate change policies enacted by governments around the world (Taghipour and Lu, 2025a). A company's reputation, operational expenses, and penalties could all take a hit if this doesn't happen. One major source of these emissions is the web of transportation and industry that makes up supply chains. Hence, it is imperative that supply chain managers assess the environmental impact of their operations and identify ways to decrease emissions through sustainable sourcing, logistical optimization, and alternative transportation. The depletion of significant natural resources, including water, energy, and raw materials, is another major environmental worry. Both the production and delivery stages of the supply chain rely heavily on these vital resources. The possible interruption of supply chains as a result of shortages or increasing prices of essential materials is one environmental risk linked with resource scarcity (Taghipour, 2021).

To lessen the impact of these threats, supply chain managers could look into sustainable sourcing choices, diversify their suppliers, and adopt more resource-efficient procedures. Furthermore, SCM faces environmental hazards from natural catastrophes and severe weather events. Such catastrophes have become more common and more destructive as a result of climate change, which has wreaked havoc on supply chains and driven up prices (Taghipour et al., 2023). Supply chain diversification, disaster recovery plans, and real-time monitoring of climate and weather-related hazards are some of the strong risk mitigation measures that firms can employ to manage these risks. Evaluating and managing environmental risks in SCM goes beyond meeting regulatory requirements; it also contributes to the SC's resilience and sustainability.

Figure 1. Risk Sources and Their Characteristics

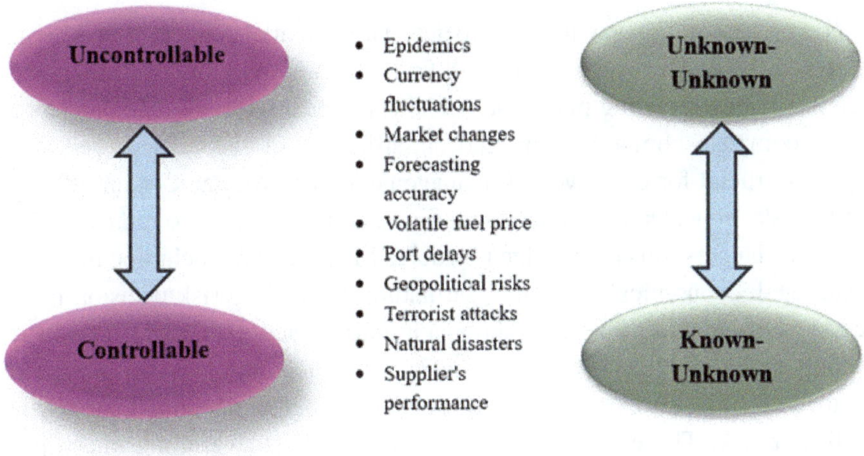

Figure 1 shows as adapting to changing environmental conditions, reducing costs, enhancing brand reputation, and contributing to a more sustainable future are all possible outcomes for companies that actively evaluate and manage these risks. Stakeholder engagement, supplier collaboration, and ongoing monitoring and updating of environmental risk management plans are essential for firms to achieve this goal. When an organization faces threats from outside forces, or things it can't change, it's called environmental risk. Uncertainties resulting from the SC's interactions with the environment, whether caused by accidents, human actions, or natural disasters, fall under this type of risk (Taghipour et al., 2023).

3.5 Control Risk

The assumptions, regulations, guidelines, and methodologies that regulate a company's process management are known as controls. The application of these concepts, which incorporates multiple aspects, can be either right or improper, and this can lead to risk. That is what it comprises (Tliche et al., 2023).

- A lack of sufficient principles that interfere with demand
- It is difficult to see where things stand in the pipeline.
- Collaborative planning and forecasting should be improved (Vosooghidizaji et al., 2020).

3.6 Risk Management

It comprises coming up with plans to deal with potential dangers after determining their severity. All sorts of things fall under the umbrella of risk management, which is all about creating plans and decisions to deal with possible dangers and risks. A complete comprehension and classification of risks discovered during analysis is crucial for effective risk management (XiaoWen and Atour, 2025). In order to make educated decisions about future actions that try to reduce, ease, or avoid these dangers, this knowledge is crucial. Many factors, including those of an ethical, legal, economical, and strategic nature, factor into risk decision-making processes. Differentiating between actionable and non-actionable dangers is critical. A careful analysis of the costs and advantages of accepting the risk as is or taking steps to lessen, mitigate, or eliminate it is necessary before deciding how to handle a particular risk. These dangers include both rare but devastating interruptions and more commonplace unknowns about supply, demand, and internal operations (Zoghlami et al., 2016).

3.7 Risk Evaluation

In order to determine how serious each danger is, risk assessment is used. Finding weak points and susceptible processes in the supply chain is the main objective of this assessment (Taghipour and Frayret, 2013). Managing the probability of demand, allocating resources efficiently, altering the likelihood of developing a reliable supply, and evaluating the success prospects of new product launches, economic conditions, and the opportunity cost of alternative choices are all part of this process. Making a prioritized list of supply chain risks with corresponding importance indicators is the goal of this risk analysis. By prioritizing them in this way, the supply chain risks can be more easily assessed (Taghipour et al., 2022).

4. THEORETICAL FRAMEWORKS FOR SCRM

We can determine the linked crucial components of the management concept of SCRM based on its four core constructs: analysing potential supply chain risk factors; determining the supply chain risk concept through the identification of the most pertinent risk outcomes; monitoring the supply chain strategy's risk drivers; and reducing supply chain risks. Although these important factors could be seen as a series of steps in a management process, we recognize that the area is still in its early stages and present them as a framework for future research (Taghipour et al., 2022). Therefore, we will move forward by organizing our field findings and literature analysis according to these fundamental aspects, highlighting the positive and normative research topics associated with them.

4.1 Monitoring the Supply Chain Strategy's Risk Drivers

Although there has always been some degree of uncertainty in trying to balance supply and demand, there have been a lot of new developments in the past ten years or so that may be seen as raising the stakes. The globalization of supply chains, the consolidation of manufacturing and distribution, the rise of outsourcing, the shrinkage of supplier bases, and an emphasis on efficiency rather than effectiveness are all factors in this trend. All of these factors pose a threat because they alter the makeup of contemporary supply chains and have an effect on the origins of risks in the network (Glaa et al., 2014). The complexity of supply chain architectures is growing as a result of globalization and outsourcing. In actuality, network shapes are dynamic rather than following a linear progression of value-adding stages. The supply chain is comprised of upstream and downstream operations that are characterized by lateral and horizontal inter-linkages, reverse loops, or two-way exchanges. Uncertainty owing to a lack of ownership, disorder, and inertia are three of the many network-related risks that can affect a supply network (Lebosse et al., 2017). More integrated supply chains are a result of a number of other risk drivers, such as a shrinking supplier base and an emphasis on efficiency above effectiveness. Due to a lack of ownership in fully integrated supply chain operations, this also raises the possibility of disruptions caused by less-than-ideal contact between supply chain organizations. The majority of the supply chain managers who took part in the study were cognizant of the fact that their strategy included certain risk factors. These drivers obviously caused or worsened many of the observed supply chain disruptions. For instance, the company's previous transition into a third-party environment may have exacerbated the negative impacts of a fire in a centralized warehouse, the bankruptcy of the only supplier of a major component, or a catastrophic system failure (Loivet et al., 2020).

Although the drivers are acknowledged as competitive pressures with risk implications, it seems that organizations often go along with the consequences rather than addressing them systematically. A more proactive strategy that anticipates risk implications earlier is what appears to be lacking. Having several people in charge of the supply chain and the risk management makes this worse. At one company, we spoke with both the risk manager and the manager of the supply chain (Lu and Taghipour, 2025). The supply chain manager's first half of the interview focused on the company's successes in supply chain reorganization in the past few years, which was quite interesting. Finally, he mentioned that maybe it's time to check how sturdy the optimized supply network is. What followed was an explanation of the company's risk exposures and near misses from the risk manager. Both parties agreed at the interview's conclusion that the conversation had been fruitful for both of them and that supply chain and risk management needed to work together more closely. The risk manager at another firm who was in charge of checking the readiness and exposure of the supply chain partners to risk also complained about not being able to have any say in strategic purchasing choices. The importance of risk in the planning and execution of supply chain strategies is an underexplored area of study (Mahfod et al., 2019). Decisions made during strategy and design can introduce certain weaknesses into a supply chain. Therefore, it is necessary to establish procedures and provide tools that assist managers in foreseeing and monitoring the risks and benefits associated with their supply chains.

4.2 Determining the Supply Chain Risk Concept Through the Identification of the Most Pertinent Risk Outcomes

There is a long list of potential negative outcomes that might result from risk, including things like health and safety issues, financial losses, and reputational harm. Managers' supply chain risk concept is based on the repercussions that are peculiar to that setting. The results of our first conversations provide some evidence that the particular supply chain and/or industrial setting may determine whether there are systematic variances in the risk concepts (Taghipour et al., 2015). Furthermore, managers' risk management strategies seem to be influenced by their significant risk concepts. Risks to life and/or political repercussions were among the outcome variables that were considered, in addition to commercial ones (such as stockouts or excessive inventory). Companies offering fast-moving consumer items, especially through traditional retail channels, and whose primary focus is on maximization of profit constitute one extreme of the spectrum. Operational efficiency is under continual pressure for these organizations due to the necessity of being price competitive. In an effort to become more responsive and demand-driven, these organizations were always looking for ways to reduce inventories. However, there were significant concerns about the competitive and commercial risk effects, such as lost revenues owing to non-availability. Managers at consumer goods corporations also seemed surprisingly apathetic about events with extremely low likelihood but potentially disastrous consequences (Mahfod et al., 2021).

They seem to focus on atomistic risk sources in their SCRM strategy which are interruptions produced by the direct supplier and/or customer (e.g., a direct supplier declaring bankruptcy) with little or moderate repercussions. When discussing their predicament, some of these organizations were even hesitant to use the word risk. Critical health product provider and aerospace company were closer to the opposite end of the spectrum of possible risk concepts (El-Nemr et al., 2017). Both were very concerned about quality. They had a strong understanding of the worst-case scenarios, a commitment to Total Quality Management, and an engineering background that informed their approach to SCRM. The board of directors is officially responsible for risk management, reflecting this prevailing consciousness; yet, in reality, risk management is often limited to meeting the bare minimum of legal obligations. However, business continuity planning does not yet acknowledge supply chain wide risk management as an essential component. This field research's results are consistent with a risk type classification put out by (Evangelos Christou, Kostas Alexandris, 2018). They propose classifying risks according to the likelihood and severity of their effects: operational accidents, operational disasters, and strategic uncertainty. In addition, when we examine the literature, we see that the risk management approaches can also be grouped according to those specific risk outcomes. One side of the coin has a lot of articles that focus on operational mishaps, which, if not anticipated, can become operational disasters.

However, a new body of literature examines the strategic uncertainties, including, for example, the results of future investments in relationship-specific resources the potential consequences of risky supply network configuration changes and the results of investments in supply chain capacity (Radhoui et al., 2021). Here, it seems like a major managerial conclusion is to make these strategic decisions with less uncertainty, rather than to try to mitigate the negative effects of uncertainty by measures like continuity planning. In conclusion, our results give some support for the idea that how organizations conceptualize risk affects the scope and methodology of SCRM. This conclusion opens the door to studying risk management from a contingency perspective in various supply chains and/or industries. The researchers are focusing on finding out which risk concept is applicable to specific businesses and supply chains from a contingency perspective. The perspective of supply chain and industry-specific risk concepts seems to be more effective in helping managers evaluate and control risks in their supply chains than attempting to take an average general view (Gao et al., 2018).

4.3 Reducing Supply Chain Risks

When looking at risk mitigation from the perspective of a single organization, identifies five generic strategies: avoidance, control, cooperation, and flexibility. Of these, four can be applied to supply chain scenarios (Taghipour et al., 2023). In summary, here is the table few of the organizations who utilized these mitigation strategies:

Table 1. Strategies for Minimizing Risk in Supply Chains

Flexibility	• Multiple sourcing • Postponement • Localized sourcing
Avoidance	• Eliminating particular goods, geographic marketplaces, suppliers, and/or customer organisations
Cooperation	• Joint efforts to improve supply chain visibility and understanding • Collaborative initiatives to disseminate risk-related information • Collaborative initiatives to develop supply chain continuity strategies
Control	• Vertical integration • Enhanced stockpiling and utilisation of buffer inventory • Maintaining surplus capacity in manufacturing, storage, handling, and/or transportation. • Imposing contractual responsibilities on suppliers

Table 1 shows as based on our research and the literature we reviewed, we believe that supply chain risk mitigation measures should be studied alongside risk drivers. They are an extension of a number of supply chain trade-offs that enumerated: repeatability versus uncertainty, or the trade-off between predictable processes and a lack of flexibility; the lowest bidder versus the known supplier; production and distribution decisions about centralization versus dispersion; collaboration versus secrecy, or the trade-off between attracting customers and reducing waste through increased transparency (e.g., the results of risk audits) and keeping information confidential (e.g., the benefits of transparency vs. the potential downsides of transparency), and redundancy versus efficiency, or the tension between supply chain capacity and the efficiency-focused lean paradigm, which seeks to eliminate or reduce waste (Lu and Taghipour, 2023).

- **Flexibility:** While control strategies aim to make risk scenarios more predictable across all sources, flexibility allows for more responsiveness while keeping predictability of factors constant. Supply chain examples include postponement, in which businesses put off making, configuring, labeling, or shipping a product to a specific location (Tliche et al., 2019). They can adjust more effectively to variability or even demand disruptions if they delay and are less reliant on forecasts. One manager characterized multiple sourcing as the classic method of risk management by spreading it out across the supply chain. Localized sourcing, with its short lead times and possibility for quick reactions, is the third example of a supply chain.
- **Avoidance:** Avoidance happens when the hazards connected with a specific product market or geographic location are deemed unacceptable. From a supply chain viewpoint, avoidance might be associated with goods, regions, markets, or even supplier and consumer groups. When a company's supply

becomes unstable, it may decide to discontinue certain goods, suppliers, or geographic regions (Vosooghidizaji et al., 2020).

- **Cooperation:** Cooperation response strategies aim to reduce uncertainty via mutual agreements rather than unilateral control. Supply chain visibility and understanding, information sharing regarding exposures to specific risk sources, and cooperative business continuity plan preparation are the main points of focus from a supply chain viewpoint. Although many of the companies we spoke with used cooperative risk mitigation tactics, this was mostly limited to projects involving important suppliers (Aouadni et al., 2024).
- **Control:** Businesses shouldn't just accept uncertainties as limitations they have to work with; they should actively work to control the various risk sources' contingencies. It should come as no surprise that the majority of the organizations surveyed used control strategies. Vertical integration, enhanced stockpiling, buffer inventory, and the use of extra capacity in manufacturing, storage, handling, and transportation are all examples of supply chain practices. Additionally, suppliers can be required to meet certain contractual obligations (Mirzaei et al., 2025).

The choice between managing risk and delivering value is a last and perhaps most important trade-off in the supply chain. This is the compromise between the overall supply costs and the additional expenses associated with most mitigation techniques, which is a fundamental principle of modern SCM. For the managers we spoke with, dealing with decisions that involve trade-offs was an extremely pressing matter. Some writers have proposed tactics in the literature to help readers strike a better balance when faced with trade-offs. As an example, recommends keeping strategic emergency supplies on hand, which should only be utilized in the event of severe disruptions. Furthermore, he proposes dual sourcing as a method: using offshore vendors for the majority of purchase volume and local providers for disruptions. Our interviews have revealed certain challenges in executing both plans, despite their high plausibility (Goodarzian et al., 2026).

Determining the criticality of components or items for strategic emergency stockpiles is frequently easier said than done. It seems that a value-added estimate is the foundational criterion for many organizations. However, a brewery was impacted by the fuel crisis due to a shortage of inexpensive but cumbersome cardboard trays for packing. It was determined that keeping more than 24 hours of emergency stock was unnecessary. Similarly, it could be challenging to execute a dual sourcing approach, in which local suppliers are usually only allocated a portion of the business. A local supplier for one company stopped supplying after being overwhelmed with orders from the company's most important client, even though the supplier only accounted for 5% of the company's business. We conclude that these trade-offs warrant more study and that managers could benefit from technologies that aid in supply chain and context-specific decision-makings (Taghipour, 2024).

4.4 Analysing Potential Supply Chain Risk Factors

The variable that develops as a result of interactions between the supply chain and the environment is considered an environmental risk source. Some examples of such events include fires and other catastrophes, fuel protests and terrorist attacks, and natural disasters like earthquakes and severe weather. Organizational risk factors include things like labor uncertainties (like strikes) or production uncertainties (like machine failure) as well as IT system uncertainties, all of which fall within the purview of the parties involved in the supply chain. Thirdly, interactions between organizations in the supply chain give rise to network-related risk sources (Lu et al., 2023). There are network-related risk sources for any harm that results from less-than-ideal interactions between the organizations in the chain. This means that network-related uncertainties are sources of risk of the different links in the supply chain, whereas environmental and organizational uncertainties are sources of risk to the various linkages. There are three distinct kinds of network-related risks: inertia, disorder, and lack of ownership.

Figure 2. Sources of Risk in Supply Chains

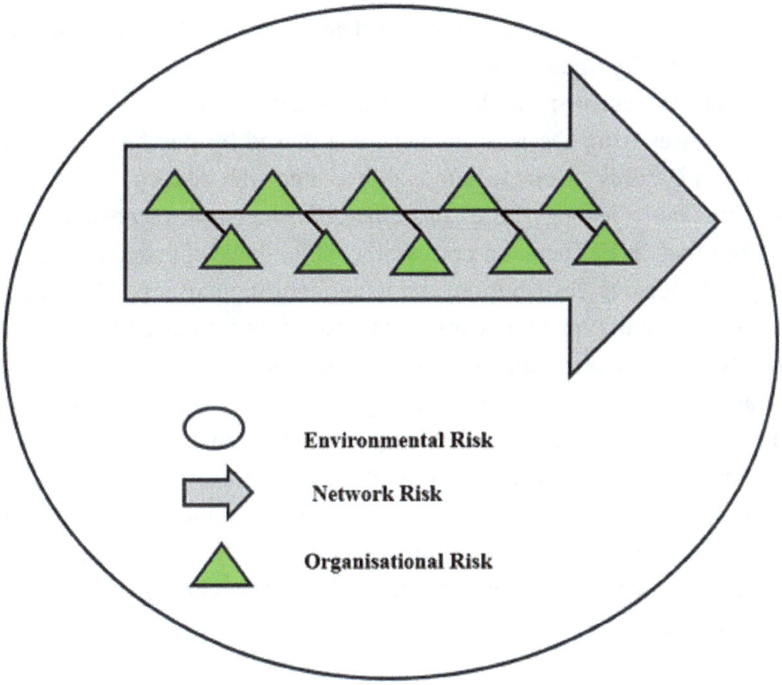

Figure 2 shows as multiple approaches to classifying potential dangers coexist in the research. The categorization gives a foundation for risk assessment and sheds light on the important aspects of possible disruptions that organizations may encounter in their supply chains (Taghipour and Lu, 2023).

Our analysis of the literature and field data leads us to believe that there are primarily three types of supply-chain risk factors: Potential dangers in the environment, in networks, and within organizations.

- **Inertia:** Inertia risks, wherein the supply chain as a whole fail to react to shifting market signals and environmental factors, are a major concern. Flexibility is frequently compromised in the pursuit of cost reduction, particularly in multinational supply chains. The incapacity to respond to changes in the market, changes in consumer demand, or any other unforeseen occurrence stemming from environmental or organizational risk factors might have serious consequences. When it comes to environmental or organizational risk, network-related risk sources are an integral aspect of the network's architecture and structure. These sources can either mitigate or magnify the effects of occurrences. The network architecture of a supply chain affects the supply chain effect of events stemming from, say, environmental risk sources, just as the construction of a building determines the disruptive impact of an earthquake (Taghipour, 2021).

- **Lack of Ownership:** The lack of clear ownership responsibilities in supply chains arises from the less distinct roles played by purchasing and supplying organizations. An increasingly convoluted web of corporate partnerships with unclear roles and duties has emerged as a result of developments like outsourcing and a focus on core skills, which have spurred an uptick in the usage of logistics, distribution, and manufacturing partners. Organizations in the supply chain typically bear the expenses of inventory as a consequence of product obsolescence, markdowns, or stock-outs.
- **Chaos:** Chaos effects exist in supply chains because of the pressures that drive their complexity. A lack of supply chain knowledge among its organizations can lead to these chaotic effects, as can overreactions, needless interventions, second-guessing, distrust, and skewed information. An example of this kind of disorder is the famous bullwhip effect, which is the gradual but steady shift in order patterns from the supply chain's downstream to its upstream links.

Similarly, all interviewees agreed that hazards associated with networks are significant and often ignored. The interviewees expressed a sense that control and visibility are diminishing beyond the next level of associated organizations, which is concerning considering the growing complexity of modern supply networks. However, tried and tested risk assessment systems are ill-equipped to handle network-related risk sources. Rather, it is essential to have a comprehensive grasp of the structure, flows, operational dynamics, and complexity of the supply network in order to identify network-risks. To become useful tools supporting the network risk assessment, traditional methods such as critical route analysis and supply chain mapping need further development (Mathiyazhagan et al., 2022). The majority of organizations seemed to organize their supply chains according to the sort of product or channel they were selling. This could be because they think of supply chains as a series of linear processes that all come together or go in different directions at a single point. This perspective fails to take into account the intricate web of relationships and interactions between supply chains that are centred around individual products. In conclusion, our interviews and the literature review point to two areas that need further investigation: first, creating more realistic methods to guide risk assessment along the chain; and second, studying the risk implications of various network structures and creating effective tools to identify risks related to networks.

5. PROPOSED VOLATILITY-RESPONSIVE SCRM FRAMEWORK

This study proposes a Volatility-Responsive Supply Chain Risk Management (VR-SCRM) framework that extends traditional SCRM models by incorporating environmental volatility as a structural risk amplifier. Unlike conventional approaches that assume relatively stable conditions, the proposed framework integrates resilience, agility, flexibility, and digital-enabled monitoring mechanisms to enhance adaptive capacity.

The framework consists of four key layers:

- Risk Drivers Layer: Environmental, organizational, and network-related risks
- Risk Assessment Layer: Quantitative and qualitative evaluation methods
- Mitigation Strategy Layer: Flexibility, redundancy, collaboration, and control
- Digital Enablement Layer: AI, IoT, and real-time monitoring systems
- The proposed framework contributes theoretically by shifting SCRM from a static risk management approach to a dynamic, volatility-responsive system.

6. RISK IDENTIFICATION AND ASSESSMENT TECHNIQUES

When supply chain activities are to be understood and risks are to be mitigated, a thorough risk assessment framework is required. This is a comprehensive explanation:

6.1 Assessment of Risk Impact and Probability

Conduct a Likelihood Assessment: To ascertain the possibility of each risk materialising, use historical trends, market conditions, or supplier reliability as benchmarks.

Quantitative and Qualitative Approaches: Utilise quantitative methods such as Failure Mode and Effects Analysis (FMEA) to allocate numerical ratings for impact and probability. Utilise qualitative tools, such as expert assessment or scenario analysis, to assess intricate hazards.

Impact Analysis: Evaluate the potential effects of each risk on critical performance metrics, including cost, lead time, and customer satisfaction.

Output: A risk matrix classifying threats into low, medium, or high priority according to their impact and probability.

6.2 Risk Prioritisation for Mitigation

Critical Hazards: High-impact, high-probability hazards necessitate prompt intervention, such as identifying alternate sources for essential suppliers.
Moderate Threats: Medium-priority threats may be monitored and mitigated through contingency planning.
Low Risks: Risks characterised by small impact and probability may necessitate limited effort, although should still be monitored routinely.
Techniques: Employ methodologies such as Pareto Analysis (80/20 rule) to concentrate on the paramount risks that account for the majority of potential disruptions.

6.3 Assessing Potential Hazard

SR: Interruptions from suppliers, including delays, quality concerns, or dependence on sole-source providers.
DR: Variations in consumer demand, erroneous forecasts, or seasonal fluctuations.
Operational Risks: Deficiencies in internal processes, human errors, or equipment failures.
External Risks: Geopolitical occurrences, natural calamities, pandemics, or economic recessions. **Cybersecurity Risks:** Compromises in data security, revealing confidential supply chain information. **Compliance Risks:** Regulatory alterations that may affect procurement, logistics, or operations.

Perform stakeholder interviews to identify hazards at various stages of the supply chain. Utilise past data and industry benchmarks to discern reoccurring threats. Utilise modern instruments such as SWOT analysis or risk heat maps to illustrate risk zones.

7. MANAGERIAL IMPLICATIONS

The proposed framework offers several practical insights:

- Organizations should implement real-time risk monitoring systems using digital technologies.
- Supply chain strategies should balance efficiency and resilience under volatile conditions.

- Firms should adopt multi-sourcing and flexible logistics strategies to mitigate disruptions.
- Collaboration with supply chain partners enhances visibility and coordinated risk response.
- Investment in AI-based predictive analytics improves proactive decision-making.

8. FUTURE DIRECTIONS

Diverse quantitative methods for risk management in the supply chain have been examined in this article. The primary focus of these quantitative models is operational risk management, not disruption risk management, as we discovered. Still, we contend that some of these tactics have found their way into practice because they can strengthen a supply chain's ability to deal with operational risks and disruptions. We would want to propose six suggestions for future study on disruption risk management in SCM since there are currently no models available (Pour Mohammadi et al., 2014).

8.1 Supply Management Approach

The concept of backup providers is proposed by both academics and practitioners when designing solutions for reducing disruption risks in supply chains. A model for analysing the dynamic supply configurations of suppliers, such as transportation providers, contract manufacturers, and distribution channels, is necessary to capture the dynamics of transferring orders to these backup suppliers in the event of a significant disruption (Radhoui et al., 2019; Taghipour et al., 2022).

8.2 Information Management Approach

The CPFR strategy stands out among the information management techniques outlined in Section 6 due to its emphasis on supply chain partners working together more closely and more effectively. No model has been developed that can capture the collaborative replenishing planning, even if Aviv (2005) does provide a technique for producing collaborative forecasts. The value of a comprehensive CPFR system may be substantially greater than that of a system dependent only on collaborative forecasting (Ren et al., 2016).

8.3 Demand Management Approach

When a company can implement dynamic pricing/revenue management immediately following a disruption, it seems to have the most promise among the demand management options offered in Section 3 for controlling disruption risks. Furthermore, following the successful implementation of various revenue management systems in the aviation industry for operational risk management, revenue management appears to be a promising field (Taghipour, 2024).

8.4 Demand and Supply Processing Approach

It is assumed in this paper that the demand or supply mechanism is stationary in nearly all cases. When dealing with non-stationary demand or supply processes, it may be necessary to extend the analysis in order to quantitatively simulate different sorts of disruptions. One possible approach is to describe the demand or supply process as a jump process in order to account for the features of significant disruptions (Taghipour, 2009; Taghipour and Beneteau-Piet, 2020).

8.5 Product Management Approach

Depending on the supply and demand for various products, e-tailers can constantly adjust their product assortments while selling online. Traditional stores can also use this strategy to mitigate disruption concerns. It stores managers have the power to influence consumer demand and product selection by rearranging the assortment of products on display, the placement of each product, and the amount of faces each product has. Their argument is that widely available products can be marketed more effectively through dynamic assortment planning (Taghipour et al., 2023).

8.6 Objective Function

Predicted costs and profits form the backbone of the performance metrics used to evaluate the models discussed in this article. One reliable metric for comparing various approaches to operational risk management is the anticipated profit or cost. When faced with infrequent disruption concerns, it's important to think about more than just the expected cost/profit. For example, it has been stated by that managers often prioritise performance goals. So, recovery time after a disturbance is one performance metric that might be considered when planning methods to manage the risks of supply chain disruptions. When considering single-period inventory models, the reader is directed to included therein for information about other alternative performance targets (Taghipour and Lu, 2025b; Taghipour, 2022).

There has been an exponential increase in the number of articles published on SCM over the past decade. We expect this trend to continue as there are many new areas of study that need to be investigated, such as methods for controlling the risks of disruptions in the supply chain, the effects of radio frequency identification technology on SCM, and the effects of government regulations on SCM. We anticipate that SCM will remain a fruitful field of study in the years to come.

9. CONCLUSION

Adapting to the problems presented by the changing supply chain context, particularly in relation to SCRM, was the primary goal of the research study and the publication. As mentioned previously in the paper, there are valid concerns regarding the usefulness of the currently available decision-making methods and tools in light of the evolving decision-making environments and risk-related issues. Using the SCRM Framework as a framework, this research aimed to investigate and analyse these changes and what they mean. According to the conceptual framework and the case evidence, the main problem is not so much with the relevance or usefulness of certain Operational Research methods and instruments as it is with the environment in which these methods are used (Taghipour et al., 2023). Information exchange, personal concerns, concerns regarding structures and systems, interactions. Several essential steps in managing risks effectively were highlighted by the SCRM Framework. For the majority of decision-making tasks, it is crucial to clearly define the desired performance objectives. As part of risk management, you must specify not just the traditional metrics for success, but also the amount of strategic risk your company is willing to take and how it will affect your ability to meet your other goals. As the case study showed, there are many distinct parties involved in SCRM and the process is quite disjointed. According to the data, not everyone is actively participating in making decisions or even on stage at the same moment. When it comes to risk management, certain people are brought in to reassure the primary participants, while others are recruited to offer insurance in case the management fails. Many conceptual decision-making models rely on individuals or groups making decisions, but what we saw goes against that. While it's not always wise to extrapolate from specific examples, when it comes to managing risks in the supply chain, there's a clear rationale for this approach (Mathiyazhagan et al., 2022).

REFERENCES

Alizadeh, N., Taghipour, A., & Canel-Depître, B. (2021). Which collective strategy is appropriate for the business ecosystem? The role of political environment.

Aouadni, S., Aouadni, I., & Taghipour, A. (2024). Using ordinal priority approach with confidence-level measurement for third-party logistics provider selection in the Tunisian healthcare sector. In *Applications of new technology in operations and supply chain management* (pp. 404–429). IGI Global Scientific Publishing. DOI: 10.4018/979-8-3693-1578-1.ch020

Cauchois, R., Taghipour, A., Kang, D. S., Zoghlami, N., & Abed, M. (2017). Advanced solutions for a supply chain with stochastic information. *Journal of Advanced Management Science*, *5*(1), 9–13. DOI: 10.18178/joams.5.1.9-13

Demir, S. B. (2018). Predatory journals: Who publishes in them and why? *Journal of Informetrics*, *12*(4), 1296–1311. DOI: 10.1016/j.joi.2018.10.008

El-Nemr, N., Canel-Depitre, B., & Taghipour, A. (2017, September). Determinants of hotel room rates. In Marketing Trends Congress: Luxury Industries Conference London 2017.

Evangelos Christou, E., Alexandris, K., & A. F. (2018). TOURMAN 2018 conference proceedings.

Gao, Y., Li, Z., & Kang, D. S. (2018). Supply chain coordination: A review. *Journal of Advanced Management Science*, *6*(4), 213–217. DOI: 10.18178/joams.6.4.213-217

Gharye Mirzaei, M., Goodarzian, F., Taghipour, A., & Muñuzuri, J. (2025). Sustainable closed-loop supply chain network under uncertainty considering green technologies: Toward the circular economy. *The Journal of the Operational Research Society*, •••, 1–21.

Glaa, B., Zoghlami, N., & Taghipour, A. (2014, May). Outsourcing and offshoring healthcare services: A way to cut costs and improve quality. In *Proceedings of the International Conference on Advanced Logistics and Transport (ICALT)* (pp. 189–194). IEEE. DOI: 10.1109/ICAdLT.2014.6864116

Goodarzian, F., Abraham, A., Muñuzuri, J., Taghipour, A., & Ghasemi, P. (2026). A Benders decomposition approach for a new sustainable pharmaceutical supply chain network: A case study in France. *Annals of Operations Research*, *356*(2), 881–919. DOI: 10.1007/s10479-024-05936-3

Lebosse, S., Taghipour, A., & Canel-Depitre, B. (2017). Quick response to fluctuations in supply chains: A review. *Journal of Advanced Management Science*, *5*(5), 394–400. DOI: 10.18178/joams.5.5.394-400

Loivet, W., Taghipour, A., & Kang, D. S. (2020). The rise of green supply chain management: Between complexity and necessity. Journal of Economics. *Business and Management*, *8*(1), 1–7.

Lu, X., & Taghipour, A. (2023). A French guide for businesses and governments to integrate the concept of sustainable development into their supply chains. In *Government impact on sustainable and responsible supply chain management* (pp. 1–12). IGI Global Scientific Publishing. DOI: 10.4018/978-1-6684-9062-4.ch001

Lu, X., & Taghipour, A. (2025). The future of marketing: Integrating big data and AI for personalized customer engagement. In *Ecological and human dimensions of AI-based supply chain* (pp. 97–110). IGI Global Scientific Publishing. DOI: 10.4018/979-8-3693-7478-8.ch005

Lu, X. W., Tliche, Y., Vosooghidizaji, M., & Taghipour, A. (2023). Cryptocurrencies and blockchain applications. In *Blockchain applications in cryptocurrency for technological evolution* (pp. 1–13). IGI Global Scientific Publishing.

Mahfod, J., Canel-Depitre, B., & Taghipour, A. (2019). Quality function deployment–ELECTRE in supplier evaluation. *Journal of Advanced Management Science*, *7*(4).

Mahfod, J., Khoury, B., Canel-Depitre, B., & Taghipour, A. (2021). Logistics providers in Syria humanitarian operations. In *Demand forecasting and order planning in supply chains and humanitarian logistics* (pp. 171–197). IGI Global. DOI: 10.4018/978-1-7998-3805-0.ch006

Mathiyazhagan, K., Taghipour, A., & Agarwal, V. (Eds.). (2022). *Blockchain technology in supply chain management for society 5.0*. CRC Press. DOI: 10.1201/9781003177432

Mbiatem, J., Taghipour, A., & Canel-Depitre, B. (2018, August). Supplier selection approaches for decision makers. In *Proceedings of the International Conference on Information Communication and Management* (pp. 108–112).

Nadia, E. N., Canel-Depitre, B., & Atour, T. (2020). Luxury hotels' eco-friendly activities and customers' preferences and willingness to pay for green hotels. *Journal of Advanced Management Science*, *8*(1), 1–24.

Ponputtha, W., Wannapiroon, P., & Nilsook, P. (2021). Creative history learning model using digital storytelling through cloud learning to enhance analytical thinking. International Journal of E-Education, E-Business. *E-Management and E-Learning*, *11*(2), 42–50. DOI: 10.17706/ijeeee.2021.11.2.42-50

Pour Mohammadi, M., Ghorbani, R., & Taghipour, A. (2014). Factors affecting the price of housing in the city of Tabriz using a hedonic model. *Geographical Planning of Space Quarterly Journal*, *3*(9), 83–104.

Radhoui, H., Taghipour, A., & Canel-Depitre, B. (2019). The distribution and pickup of goods: A literature review and survey. In Hierarchical planning and information sharing techniques in supply chain management (pp. 46–85). DOI: 10.4018/978-1-5225-7299-2.ch002

Radhoui, H., Taghipour, A., & Canel-Depitre, B. (2021). Mixed delivery and pickup vehicle routing problem with limited flow and assignment of drones in an urban network. In *Demand forecasting and order planning in supply chains and humanitarian logistics* (pp. 225–249). IGI Global. DOI: 10.4018/978-1-7998-3805-0.ch008

Ren, Z., Taghipour, A., & Canel-Depitre, B. (2016, October). Information sharing in supply chains under uncertainty. In *Proceedings of the International Conference on Information Communication and Management (ICICM)* (pp. 67–71). IEEE. DOI: 10.1109/INFOCOMAN.2016.7784217

Sahraoui, A., Tran, N. K., Tliche, Y., Kacem, A., & Taghipour, A. (2023). Examining ICT innovation for sustainable terminal operations in developing countries: A case study of the port of Radès in Tunisia. *Sustainability (Basel)*, *15*(11), 9123. DOI: 10.3390/su15119123

Taghipour, A. (2009). Évaluation de la collaboration dans une chaîne d'approvisionnement. Revue française de gestion industrielle, 28(1), 26–42.

Taghipour, A. (Ed.). (2020). *Demand forecasting and order planning in supply chains and humanitarian logistics*. IGI Global.

Taghipour, A. (Ed.). (2021). *Digitalization of decentralized supply chains during global crises*. IGI Global. DOI: 10.4018/978-1-7998-6874-3

Taghipour, A. (2021, January). Digital transformation of supply chains during crisis: COVID-19. In *Proceedings of the International Conference on Industrial Engineering and Operations Management*. DOI: 10.46254/AN11.20211298

Taghipour, A. (Ed.). (2022). *Blockchain applications in cryptocurrency for technological evolution*. IGI Global. DOI: 10.4018/978-1-6684-6247-8

Taghipour, A. (Ed.). (2023). *Government impact on sustainable and responsible supply chain management*. IGI Global. DOI: 10.4018/978-1-6684-9062-4

Taghipour, A. (2024). Big data: The new gold mine for supermarkets. In *Applications of new technology in operations and supply chain management* (pp. 98–106). IGI Global Scientific Publishing. DOI: 10.4018/979-8-3693-1578-1.ch006

Taghipour, A., Abed, M., & Zoghlami, N. (2015, May). Design for remanufacturing respecting reverse logistics processes: A review. In *Proceedings of the International Conference on Advanced Logistics and Transport (ICALT)* (pp. 299–304). IEEE. DOI: 10.1109/ICAdLT.2015.7136602

Taghipour, A., Belrhazi, Y., & Damoum, N. (2023). Resilient sustainable supply chain management. In *Government impact on sustainable and responsible supply chain management* (pp. 33–47). IGI Global Scientific Publishing. DOI: 10.4018/978-1-6684-9062-4.ch003

Taghipour, A., & Beneteau-Piet, C. (2020). Sustainable supply chain management performance. *International Journal of Innovation, Management and Technology*, *11*(6), 165–169. DOI: 10.18178/ijimt.2020.11.6.897

Taghipour, A., Fooladvand, A., Khazaei, M., & Ramezani, M. (2023). Criteria clustering and supplier segmentation based on sustainable shared value using BWM and PROMETHEE. *Sustainability (Basel)*, *15*(11), 8670. DOI: 10.3390/su15118670

Taghipour, A., & Frayret, J. M. (2013). Coordination of operations planning in supply chains: A review. *International Journal of Business Performance and Supply Chain Modelling*, *5*(3), 272–307. DOI: 10.1504/IJBPSCM.2013.055729

Taghipour, A., & Frayret, J. M. (2013, May). An algorithm to improve operations planning in decentralized supply chains. In *Proceedings of the International Conference on Advanced Logistics and Transport* (pp. 100–103). IEEE. DOI: 10.1109/ICAdLT.2013.6568442

Taghipour, A., & Lu, X. (2025a). Advancing supply chain innovation: Theoretical foundations, contemporary developments, and future directions. In *Ecological and human dimensions of AI-based supply chain* (pp. 1–26). IGI Global Scientific Publishing. DOI: 10.4018/979-8-3693-7478-8.ch001

Taghipour, A., & Lu, X. (2025b). Navigating the artificial intelligence era: Impacts of artificial intelligence on youth critical thinking, career paths, and ethical challenges. In *Ecological and human dimensions of AI-based supply chain* (pp. 49–68). IGI Global Scientific Publishing. DOI: 10.4018/979-8-3693-7478-8.ch003

Taghipour, A., Lu, X., Derradji, M., & Sow, A. D. (2022, July). The impact of digitalization on supply chain management: A literature review. In *Proceedings of the International Conference on Information Communication and Management* (pp. 75–78). DOI: 10.1145/3551690.3551702

Taghipour, A., Lu, X., & Smahi, M. (2022). Opportunities and challenges for society 5.0 in procurement. In Blockchain technology in supply chain management for society 5.0 (pp. 91–100).

Taghipour, A., Rouyendegh, B. D., Ünal, A., & Piya, S. (2022). Selection of suppliers for speech recognition products in IT projects using an integrated fuzzy MCDM approach. *Sustainability, 14*(3), 1777. DOI: 10.3390/su14031777

Taghipour, A., Sohrabi, A., Ghaedi, M., & Khazaei, M. (2023). A robust vaccine supply chain model in pandemics: Case of COVID-19 in Iran. *Computers & Industrial Engineering, 183*, 109465. DOI: 10.1016/j.cie.2023.109465

Tliche, Y., Taghipour, A., & Canel-Depitre, B. (2019). Downstream demand inference in decentralized supply chains. *European Journal of Operational Research, 274*(1), 65–77. DOI: 10.1016/j.ejor.2018.09.034

Tliche, Y., Taghipour, A., Mahfod-Leroux, J., & Vosooghidizaji, M. (2023). Collaborative bullwhip effect–oriented bi-objective optimization for inference-based weighted moving average forecasting in decentralized supply chains. *International Journal of Information Systems and Supply Chain Management, 16*(1), 1–37. DOI: 10.4018/IJISSCM.316168

Vosooghidizaji, M., Taghipour, A., & Canel-Depitre, B. (2020). Information asymmetry in supply chain coordination: State of the art. *Journal of Industrial and Intelligent Information, 8*(2), 38–43. DOI: 10.18178/jiii.8.2.38-43

XiaoWen, L., & Atour, T.XiaoWen. (2025). Knowledge-driven digital innovation in supply chains: An organizational perspective. *Journal of Innovation & Knowledge, 10*(5), 100787. DOI: 10.1016/j.jik.2025.100787

Zoghlami, N., Taghipour, A., Merlo, C., & Abed, M. (2016). Management of divergent production networks using decentralized multi-level capacitated lot-sizing models. *International Journal of Shipping and Transport Logistics, 8*(5), 590–604. DOI: 10.1504/IJSTL.2016.078686

Chapter 8
Supply Chain Reform in Emerging Economies:
Challenges, Opportunities, and Pathways for Transformation

Hafiz Wasim Akram
http://orcid.org/0000-0002-9116-5913
Dhofar University, Oman

Alam Ahmad
College of Administrative and Financial Sciences, Saudi Electronic University, Saudi Arabia

Haidar Abbas
University of Technology and Applied Sciences, Nizwa, Oman

Mohammad Daoud Ciddikie
http://orcid.org/0000-0001-8501-2809
School of Business Studies, Sharda University, Greater Noida, India

ABSTRACT

Supply chain reform in emerging economies has become a critical priority as these nations integrate further into global trade networks. This chapter examines the multifaceted challenges that emerging markets face in modernizing and transforming their supply chain systems – from infrastructure gaps and regulatory hurdles to technology deficits and governance issues. At the same time, it highlights the opportunities for improvement, including leveraging rapid economic growth, adopting innovative technologies, and capitalizing on shifting global supply chain trends. We discuss how globalization, geopolitical shifts, and sustainability pressures are driving the need for adaptive and resilient supply chains. Key sections explore the role

DOI: 10.4018/979-8-3373-6455-1.ch008

of technological innovation, policy reforms, and strategic frameworks in enabling supply chain transformation. Finally, we propose pathways for reform, outlining a comprehensive framework to achieve efficient, resilient, and inclusive supply chains in emerging economies, along with a forward-looking conclusion on future outlooks.

1. INTRODUCTION TO SUPPLY CHAIN REFORM IN EMERGING ECONOMIES

Emerging economies have become critical participants in global supply chains as a result of their increased participation in worldwide operations, accelerated growth, and expansion of consumer markets (Anand et al., 2021). In order to preserve economic development and competitiveness, it is essential to improve the performance of supply chains, as globalization has linked these economies to international production and distribution networks (Fontoura & Coelho, 2022). In this context, supply chain reform is the process of implementing strategic changes in infrastructure, processes, technology, and policies to improve the productivity, resilience, and sustainability of supply chain operations. It involves the modernization of supply chain management practices to ensure compliance with global standards and the mitigation of systemic vulnerabilities. The necessity for reform is underscored by the fact that, as per Corporate Finance Institute (2023), over 80% of the global population lives in emerging markets. Nevertheless, the integration of models from developed countries is insufficient to facilitate the development of supply chains in these regions. The unique logistical landscapes and institutional conditions that are characteristic of each emergent economy necessitate tailored strategies.

Supply chain reform is of economic and strategic importance (Cauchois et al., 2017; Gharye Mirzaei et al., 2025; Taghipour & Beneteau-Piet, 2020; Taghipour et al., 2023a; Xu et al., 2023). The reliable movement of products is ensured by efficient supply chains, which in turn reduces the cost of doing business, enhances market access, and attracts foreign investment. Furthermore, they facilitate the ascent of emergent economies into global value chains and their integration into the value-added cascade in production. In contrast, an economy's competitiveness and growth can be restricted by inadequate supply chain performance, which is characterized by chronic logistics delays, exorbitant costs, or frequent disruptions. The COVID-19 pandemic and other recent disruptions have further exposed vulnerabilities in global supply chains, emphasizing the disproportionate impact of shocks on countries with weakened supply chain infrastructure and the potential for them to cascade. The result has elevated supply chain concerns to the forefront of policy debates and development agendas.

In emerging economies, the pursuit of supply chain reform presents substantial opportunities in addition to the well-known obstacles (Al Maalouf & Mouawad, 2025; Lebosse et al., 2017). Institutional weaknesses and inadequate infrastructure constrain these markets, as discussed in the subsequent section. They use modern technologies to take advantage of their young workforces, growth potential, and ability to outperform legacy systems. Emerging market enterprises can reduce costs and expand their market reach by creating adaptive, localized supply chain architectures. Many companies are using digital platforms and e-commerce to link manufacturers and consumers without traditional intermediaries. Thus, supply chain reform uses innovation and new collaborations to transform product and service flow as well as problem-solving (Taghipour, 2009).

This chapter looks at changes to supply chains in emerging economies. We start by shedding light on the biggest problems that make it hard to run a supply chain well in certain situations, such as problems with rules and governance and problems with infrastructure. Next, we look at global trends that are causing supply chain reforms around the world, such as new technologies, recent disruptions, and shifting trade patterns. We look at how digital technologies could change inefficiencies through technology and innovation. The chapter also discusses policy and governance and how government initiatives and public-private collaborations might enable supply chain improvements. We suggest pathways for reform, a strategic framework that emerging economies can employ to guide the transformation of their supply chains, based on these insights. Lastly, we conclude with a future outlook that underscores the necessity of ongoing adaptation and identifies the trends that will influence supply chain reform initiatives in the years ahead. A formal analytical tone is maintained throughout, and points are substantiated with pertinent academic and industry sources.

The 6-pathway frame set out in this chapter arose from a systematic theory-driven review of the existing literature on SCRM of emerging economies. A narrative review focused approach was used, based on peer reviewed journal articles, policy reports and practitioner studies from 2010 until the year 2025. The main databases used were Scopus, Web of Science, ScienceDirect and Google Scholar, keywords such as supply chain reform, emerging economies, logistics performance OR trade facilitation OR digital supply chains AND resilience were combined. The framework is theoretically founded in institutional theory, system theory and the resource-based view (RBV). The focus on the quality of governance, coherence of regulation and stability in policies as enabling factors for supply chain effectiveness is informed by institutional theory. Systems theory is the foundation for the 'organic' and interconnected nature of all six pathways, acknowledging supply chains as complex socio-technical systems that evolve through time via (technological) infrastructure, technological capability, social capital and institutions. The RBV offers logics for considering human capital, digital capabilities and sustainability as potential sources of long-term competitive advantage in developing countries.

The literature on the supply chain activities of emerging economy firms is rich but disjointed. Although there is a large body of literature detailing deficiencies in infrastructure, inefficient regulations, and underdeveloped technology, the evidence is mixed about what the priorities reformers should adopt and about their likely consequences. Certain studies stress the role of access to infrastructure, while others present governance quality or digital uptake as most important. In addition, many writings are descriptive in nature and tend to serve as problem statements rather than integrative change models.

The chapter fills this void by moving beyond symptomatic problems towards a pathway oriented logic of reform which is aware of interdependencies between the physical, institutional, technological and human dimensions. By integrating multiple threads of the literature into a cohesive framework, the chapter adds an analytical perspective that can illuminate why incremental reforms frequently go nowhere and offer insights regarding the possibilities for collaborative interventions to yield more than the sum total of their parts.

2. CHALLENGES TO EFFECTIVE SUPPLY CHAIN MANAGEMENT IN EMERGING ECONOMIES

Emerging economies have a myriad of issues that impede efficient supply chain management. Fundamental differences between emerging markets and developed ones often connect these problems. Recognizing these impediments is an essential first step in developing reform measures. Some of the most important problems are as follows:

- **Infrastructure Deficiencies:** Many developing countries have issues with their physical infrastructure, such as bad road networks, small ports, obsolete rail systems, and power that goes out at random times (Kamoyo & Chikazhe, 2025). Some of these concerns are high shipping costs, delays, and disruptions in the flow of goods (Akram, 2025a). For instance, not having enough access to electricity and transportation infrastructure directly inhibits business activity. Businesses in some developing countries experience on an average of more than four power outages a month. This hurts sales and makes doing business more expensive. Busy ports and not enough storage space can also cause long lead times and problems with inventories. Problems with infrastructure make the overall supply chain run less well because it takes longer, is less reliable, and is less linked.

- **Regulatory and Administrative Hurdles:** Many rising economies have complicated customs procedures, too much paperwork, and rules that aren't always clear (Kuteyi & Winkler, 2022). Such complicated rules and red tape can cause shipments to take a long time and raise compliance expenses, which can make it harder for businesses. Regulations that are vague or overlap cause confusion and make businesses engage more experts to help them figure out what they need to do. Corruption and a lack of openness in government operations make delays and expenses even worse (Catalão et al., 2023). These problems all work together to slow down the flow of commodities across borders and make trade pricier. Because of this, supply chains in emerging markets frequently have low agility and flexibility because it takes a lot of time and effort to cope with administrative impediments.

Figure 1. Challenges to Effective Supply Chain Management in Emerging Economies.

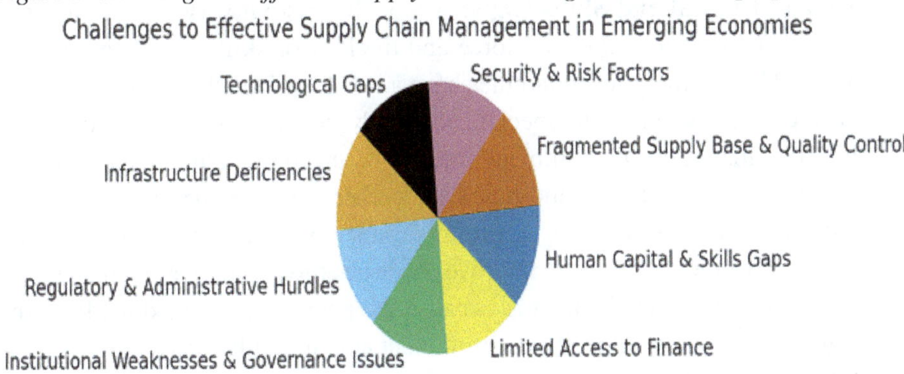

- **Institutional Weaknesses and Governance Issues:** Weak institutional frameworks, such as poor contract enforcement, slow judicial systems, and unstable policies, are a big problem (Aracil et al., 2022). In certain nations, the management of public investments is poor, which means that infrastructure projects aren't planned or watched over well enough. If institutions aren't solid, policies can change without warning or for no good reason, which can mess up supply chain operations. For instance, changes in trade policy or price regulations that happen quickly might cause shortages or surpluses of goods (Bown, 2022).). In addition, businesses may have to confront supply problems or make expensive backups as a hedge in places where there is a high danger of corruption or politics. Good governance is necessary for dependable supply chains. If there isn't any, the private sector's attempts to improve logistics and procurement can be easily thrown off by outside risks and uncertainties.

- **Limited Access to Finance:** Another problem with reforming the supply chain is that it costs money (Oyedijo et al., 2022). Small and medium-sized firms (SMEs), who are the backbone of many supply chains in emerging markets (Alam et al., 2024), typically have a difficult time getting cheap loans for new technology, warehouses, or inventory. High interest rates and poorly developed finance markets might make it difficult to invest in upgrades to the supply chain and logistics infrastructure. As a result, people keep using old facilities and procedures. Also, smaller suppliers may have trouble with cash flow that makes it challenging for them to keep their supplies stable if they don't have supply chain finance choices. Without financial options like factoring or lending for farmers and small industries, many supply chains are broken and unproductive.
- **Human Capital and Skills Gaps:** A less obvious but very important problem is the quality of the workforce and the lack of skilled workers (Mer & Virdi, 2024). Emerging economies have a lot of workers, but they often don't have enough people with specialized supply chain skills, such as qualified logistics managers, procurement specialists, or cold chain technicians. Not having enough educated and qualified workers might make operations less efficient and make it harder to use modern supply chain strategies. It is not uncommon for attempts to improve infrastructure or processes that might otherwise be successful to stop because the people in charge don't have the right skills or knowledge. Also, insufficient labour regulations or training systems make it challenging for people to keep learning and growing in their careers in supply chain management. Because of this skills gap, it's harder for the supply chain to embrace best practices and come up with new ideas (Hugos, 2024). To assure that the workforce can handle modern, complicated supply networks, effective reform has to invest in developing human capital.
- **Fragmented Supply Base and Quality Control Issues:** In a lot of new marketplaces, supply chains are broken up into many tiny producers, middlemen, and informal operators (Akhter et al., 2024; Mahfod et al., 2021; Mbiatem et al., 2018). This dispersion results in inconsistent quality standards and challenges in coordination (Taghipour & Frayret, 2011; Taghipour & Frayret, 2013a; Zoghlami et al., 2016). When suppliers have different levels of skill, it might be hard to make sure that products are always of good quality and meet standards. Quality control problems can make supply chains less reliable (Montgomery, 2020). For instance, agricultural supply chains may have problems with irregular product grades, or manufacturing supply chains may

have problems with defects since there aren't any standard methods. The fact that many businesses operate outside of regulatory frameworks makes it even harder to locate and hold people accountable throughout the supply chain. Because of this, it's hard to construct an integrated, end-to-end supply chain when important links work in silos or don't follow common standards.

- **Security and Risk Factors:** Supply chains in emerging economies are sometimes more vulnerable to certain dangers (Lopes et al., 2022). Goods are at risk of theft, cargo pilferage, or fraud in transportation in several areas. Countries that are prone to extreme weather or have insufficient infrastructure might also have their supply lines disrupted by natural disasters. Companies in these areas may not be very good at managing risk, which makes their supply chains less able to handle shocks. Logistics costs go up because of high insurance rates and risk premiums (Gajović et al., 2018). Furthermore, changes in the value of foreign currencies in developing countries might influence the costs of the supply chain for imported goods or the income from exports. All of these risks make companies keep buffers, such as excess inventory or backup suppliers, which makes the whole supply chain less efficient.
- **Technological Gaps:** Modern supply chain technologies solve problems, yet many emerging markets are slow to adopt them (Agu et al., 2024). Limited internet connectivity, low digital literacy, and high business software expenses hinder supply chain digital transformation. In some locations such as India, manual record-keeping and paper-based processes lead to data inaccuracies and poor visibility (Kumar et al., 2023). The digital divide may prohibit real-time monitoring, WMS, and data analytics from being widely used (Roopnarian et al., 2023). Emerging supply chains are slower and less flexible than those in established nations that use automation and data-driven decision-making. To close this gap, ICT infrastructure and staff training are needed, which is difficult. Supply chain management in emerging economies is complicated by logistical, regulatory, and institutional difficulties. Inadequate energy and infrastructure slow and confuse commodity transport, as do complex regulations and poor governance. System improvements are difficult without cash and expertise. These characteristics make emerging market supply chains more expensive and unreliable, emphasizing the need for reform. These challenges are not insurmountable; numerous strategic investments and policy modifications can be implemented to alleviate them, as will be discussed in subsequent sections. Initially, it is imperative to understand the impact of global developments and the broader picture on efforts to enhance supply chains in developing countries.

3. PATHWAYS FOR REFORM: A FRAMEWORK FOR SUPPLY CHAIN TRANSFORMATION

Transforming supply chains in emerging economies is a complex endeavor that requires a holistic, multi-pronged approach. Building on the challenges identified and the opportunities presented by technology, policy, and global trends, this section outlines a framework for supply chain reform. The framework consists of key pathways or pillars that together can guide emerging economies toward more efficient, resilient, and inclusive supply chains. Each pathway addresses a critical dimension of the supply chain system, and only by progressing on all fronts can transformation be fully realized. The recommended pathways for reform are:

- **Infrastructure and Logistics Development:** Agu et al. (2024) and Apruzzese et al. (2023) state that we need to build the physical backbone of efficient supply chains as a pathway for reform. Investments in transportation infrastructure (roads, rail, ports, airports) and utilities (power, telecommunications) are foundational in nature. Upgrading infrastructure reduces transit times, variability, and damage to goods. Equally important is improving "soft infrastructure" – logistics services and intermodal connectivity. Governments should prioritize projects that alleviate major bottlenecks (e.g., a congested port or a missing highway link) and improve rural-urban linkages for supply chains originating in agricultural or remote areas. Promoting competition and professionalism in the logistics sector (trucking, freight forwarding, warehousing) ensures that infrastructure is effectively utilized. For example, building a new highway has greater impact if accompanied by policies that encourage modern trucking fleets and route optimization. Public-private partnerships (PPPs) can be leveraged to fund large projects, while maintenance of existing infrastructure must not be neglected. A well-developed infrastructure network forms the skeleton of a transformed supply chain, enabling reliability and connectivity domestically and internationally (Glaa et al., 2014).
- **Trade Facilitation and Process Simplification:** Another important point worth considering here is streamlining the regulatory and administrative processes across the supply chain (Lele et al., 2023). Simplified customs procedures, faster border clearance, and minimal red tape are essential for a smooth flow of goods. Emerging economies should implement single window systems for trade, where all import/export approvals are handled through one digital platform, significantly cutting down processing time (Taghipour, 2020; Mahfod et al., 2021). Domestically, simplifying business regulations (permits, transportation regulations, etc.) also contributes to more agile supply chains. This pathway involves adopting international best practices in

customs (risk management, authorized economic operator programs) and ensuring transparency to combat corruption. Additionally, reducing internal checkpoints or arbitrary fees (for instance, in cross-provincial transport) is important. The aim is to reduce delays and uncertainty at every step from origin to destination. Countries that have pursued aggressive trade facilitation reforms – such as Rwanda in easing cross-border trade or India in digitizing ports – have seen tangible improvements in logistics performance. In summary, by removing procedural frictions, emerging economies can immediately boost supply chain efficiency and appeal to global business.

Figure 2. Pathways for Reform: A Framework for Supply Chain Transformation.

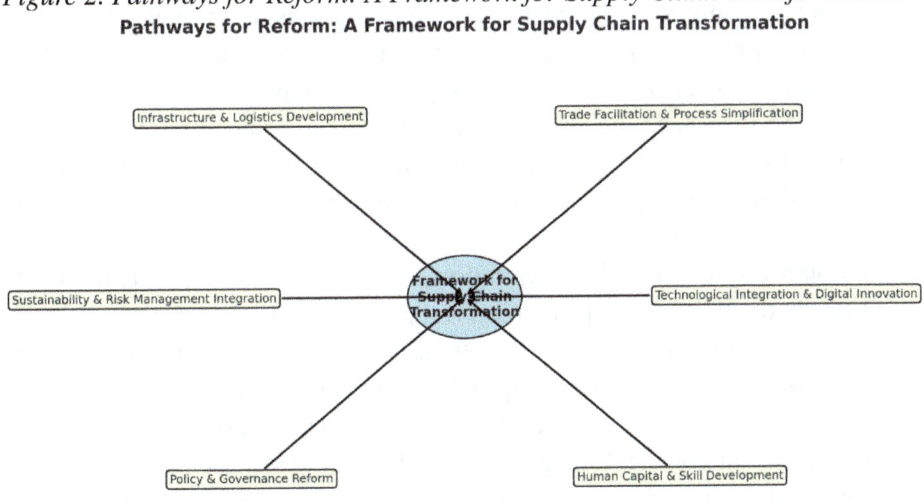

- **Technological Integration and Digital Innovation:** Apart from trade facilitation, embedded modern technology is also a must to leapfrog to advanced supply chain capabilities (Ionescu et al., 2022). Digital transformation should be at the core of supply chain reform efforts (Mathiyazhagan et al., 2022; Lu et al., 2023; Taghipour & Lu, 2025; Taghipour, 2024). This involves widespread adoption of information and communication technologies (ICT) and supply chain software for planning, tracking, and analytics (Vosooghidizaji et al., 2020; Ren et al., 2016). Governments and industry must collaborate to provide necessary digital infrastructure (broadband, IoT connectivity) and encourage training in digital skills. Key actions include implementing transportation management systems (TMS) for freight optimization, warehouse management systems for inventory control, and using data analytics or AI for demand forecasting. Emerging economies should also capitalize on innovations like blockchain, AI, and IoT which provide transparency and predictive insights; these can compensate for weaker legacy systems by offering new ways to monitor and coordinate supply chain activities (Mathiyazhagan et al., 2022; Taghipour, 2022). For example, IoT devices can monitor cold chain conditions in real-time, reducing spoilage in pharmaceutical or food supply chains, a major issue in many tropical developing countries. Mobile-based platforms should be rolled out to integrate small players – e.g., mobile apps for farmers to get market prices and arrange transport can integrate them into larger supply chains. The objective of this pathway is to achieve end-to-end visibility and agility: knowing where goods are at any time, being able to reroute or adjust quickly, and making decisions based on data rather than guesswork. Embracing technology not only improves efficiency but also builds resilience, as digitalized supply chains can respond faster to disruptions. However, it is vital to ensure that the digital push is inclusive – policies must address the digital divide so that smaller businesses and remote regions are not left behind.

- **Human Capital and Skill Development:** As per Hasan et al. (2024), investment in the people who plan and run supply chains is also of greater significance. No reform can succeed without skilled professionals and workers. This pathway focuses on training and education in logistics and supply chain management, from vocational truck driving skills to advanced degrees in supply chain engineering. Emerging economies should incorporate supply chain topics into higher education curricula (operations management, data analysis, etc.) and encourage professional certifications for practitioners (Taghipour & Merimi, 2021; Merimi & Taghipour, 2021). On-the-job training programs, potentially supported by government incentives, can help upskill the existing workforce in areas like warehouse operations, quality control, and IT systems use. Developing centers of excellence or partnerships with international universities can transfer global knowledge to local contexts. A particular emphasis should be on cultivating problem-solving and risk management skills, as supply chain professionals need to adapt to disruptions and innovate continuously. Moreover, empowering a new generation of supply chain leaders – who are diverse and understand both local context and global best practices – will sustain reform momentum. Brain circulation (bringing back diaspora talent with experience in advanced economies' supply chains) could also be a strategy. Addressing labor practices is another facet: improving working conditions and career prospects in logistics (often seen as low-status work) will attract and retain talent, which is necessary for a robust supply chain sector. In short, by enhancing human capital, emerging economies ensure that their supply chain reforms are effectively implemented and continuously improved upon, rather than faltering due to execution gaps.

- **Policy and Governance Reform:** Alizadeh et al. (2021) and Hoang et al. (2021) argue that creating an enabling institutional environment and sound governance is essential for supply chains. Building on the previous section, this pathway in the framework underscores establishing clear, fair, and consistent policies that support supply chain efficiency and resilience. Key actions include formulating a national logistics or supply chain strategy that aligns various ministries (trade, transport, industry, finance) toward common goals. Policy should incorporate supply chain considerations into broader economic planning – for instance, industrial policy can encourage clustering of suppliers and manufacturers, and trade policy can prioritize connectivity and trade facilitation. Strengthening legal frameworks (contract law, competition law to prevent logistics monopolies, etc.) and enforcing anti-corruption measures improve trust and reduce informal costs in the system. Governments should also be prepared to play a coordinating role in times of crisis, ensuring essential supplies are maintained (as learned during COVID-19). This might involve building strategic stockpiles or quick-response mechanisms that partner with the private sector. Another important governance aspect is monitoring and metrics: establishing key performance indicators (KPIs) for national logistics (like port dwell times, cargo throughput, transport cost as % of product value) and publishing these can help identify problem areas and drive accountability. To make the most of the benefits of domestic changes, regional cooperation structures (such customs unions and collaborative infrastructure projects) should be sought. Overall, this method makes sure that the rules, policies, and governmental agencies that make up the institutional framework all help modern supply chain operations instead of getting in the way of them. Countries that have changed their governments, like Georgia's streamlining of business licenses and customs or Singapore's integrated logistics planning, show how good policies may have a real effect on supply chain performance.
- **Sustainability and Risk Management Integration:** Integration of ideas of sustainability and resilience into supply chains is also of paramount importance (Akram et al., 2024; Akram, 2025b; Negri et al., 2021; Taghipour & Beneteau, 2020). Emerging economies may build sustainable practices into their supply chains from the ground up as they change them, instead of having to add them afterward. This means encouraging or mandating environmentally friendly logistics (optimizing routes to reduce fuel use, promoting rail or coastal shipping over trucks where viable, investing in electric vehicles

or cleaner fuels for transport). It also means focusing on waste reduction in supply chains – for example, improving cold chain to avoid food waste, or developing circular economy linkages where waste from one process becomes input for another. Policymakers can incentivize sustainability through subsidies for green technology or by setting standards (like fuel efficiency norms, packaging waste regulations). At the same time, emerging supply chains should be built for resilience. This involves diversifying sourcing, developing contingency plans, and perhaps maintaining strategic reserves of critical items. Governments and industry associations can create platforms to share risk information and best practices for continuity planning. The inclusion of insurance solutions or risk pooling mechanisms (especially for SMEs) can help cushion against shocks. Notably, pursuing sustainability and resilience can go hand in hand – for instance, decentralized renewable energy for cold storage makes the cold chain both greener and less vulnerable to grid outages. International support, such as climate finance or technology transfer, can augment domestic efforts in this pathway. Ultimately, by aligning with global sustainability trends, emerging economies ensure their supply chains remain viable as environmental regulations tighten worldwide, and by prioritizing resilience, they protect development gains against setbacks (Taghipour et al., 2023; Tliche et al., 2023).

These pathways are interdependent and mutually reinforcing. For example, improved infrastructure (Pathway 1) enhances the impact of digital tools (Pathway 3) by providing reliable connectivity for IoT devices and transport for e-commerce deliveries. Better governance (Pathway 5) is needed to successfully implement technology and infrastructure projects. A skilled workforce (Pathway 4) is necessary to make use of new infrastructure and systems, and so on. Therefore, the framework should be executed in a coordinated manner. An integrated approach might involve setting up a high-level task force or agency to oversee supply chain reform, ensuring that efforts across ministries and stakeholders are aligned.

Moreover, prioritization and sequencing will be important. Each country may start with different entry points depending on its current state – one country might focus first on port modernization and customs (if that's the chokepoint), while another might invest in digital tracking for trucking if roads are adequate but visibility is low. Early quick wins (such as removing a notorious checkpoint or deploying a proven IT system in one port) can build momentum and stakeholder buy-in. Over time, the focus can shift to more complex reforms (like educational curricula or multilateral agreements) as capacity grows. It's also crucial to involve the private sector and logistics community in shaping these reforms; their feedback ensures that changes address real pain points and that there is a cooperative relationship between public regulations and private operations. Public-private collaboration can also manifest in demonstration projects – for instance, a government might pilot a green freight corridor with a consortium of trucking companies to show the viability of fuel-saving practices.

It should be noted that the framework is not one-size-fits-all. Local context – geography, economic structure, governance capacity, conflict situation, etc. – will dictate how each pathway is pursued. A landlocked country will focus more on cross-border facilitation and inland logistics, whereas a coastal economy with a large port might prioritize port community systems and maritime regulations. Despite these differences, the core principles of the framework hold universally: reduce waste and delays, increase transparency and skills, and fortify against risks.

As emerging economies apply these pathways, they can expect several long-term outcomes. Supply chains will become more efficient (lower cost per unit shipped, shorter lead times), which enhances competitiveness of local industries. They will become more reliable and resilient (fewer stockouts and quicker recovery from disruptions), which attracts investment as firms seek stable supply base locations. They will also become more inclusive and sustainable, spreading the benefits of globalization more evenly and ensuring compliance with evolving global norms. For instance, by integrating SMEs and adhering to sustainability, emerging markets can market themselves as ethical sourcing destinations, potentially commanding better trade terms.

To illustrate the potential impact, let us consider an example of a transformed agricultural supply chain in an emerging economy after applying this framework: Farm-to-port transport is expedited by good rural roads and consolidation centers (Infrastructure). Quicker border checks and e-documents allow fresh produce to reach foreign supermarkets in days, not weeks (Trade Facilitation). IoT sensors in containers monitor temperature and location, with data visible to all parties via a blockchain ledger (Technology). Local cooperatives have trained logistics managers ensuring quality and coordinating with freight forwarders (Human Capital). Government policies support this system by maintaining cold chain standards and providing price information services to farmers (Governance). The cold chain is powered by solar panels and insulated storage, reducing spoilage and emissions (Sustainability & Resilience). The result is higher income for farmers, lower cost for consumers, and a competitive export sector a microcosm of what supply chain reform can achieve. In short, the routes for reform laid out in this framework give emerging economies a strategic plan for changing their supply chains. It stresses making development at the same time in all six areas, for instance, physical, digital, human, and institutional. This systematic strategy provides a way to get through the transformation process, even while there are still problems to solve. In the last part, we talk about the future and how the environment will change as these reforms happen. We also talk about how important it is to keep the momentum of reform going in the years to come (Table 1).

Table 1. Illustrative Case: Customs Digitalization and Trade Facilitation in Rwanda
Rwanda offers a succinct case study of how harmonized supply chain reforms can deliver performance benefits that are quantifiable. Using an electronic single window and risk-based customs inspection, Rwanda cut average customs clearance times from over ten days to less than two days in a decade. Reforms were complemented with the institution-building process and investment in ICT infrastructure and specific capacity building for customs staff.
The results of the reform were far beyond increased efficiency. Reduced clearance time decreased the logistics cost for exporters, increased reliability of supply chains, and improved Rwanda's competitiveness as a regional logistics hub. This is an example of how trade facilitation, governance reform and digital integration – when done at the same time – can produce tangible results even in resource-crunched settings. It also suggests that reforms need to be sequenced so as to achieve early credibility and inclusive stakeholder backing.

4. CONCLUSION

Reforming supply chains in emerging markets should to be viewed as an ongoing, ever-changing process rather than a one-off event. The six-pathway construct introduced in this chapter shows that deep change involves integrated interventions across infrastructure, governance, technology, human capacity and sustainability dimensions. Since piecemeal reforms may lead to temporary successes; lasting advances require systemic coherence and institutional learning.

One important thing to remember is that emerging economies are becoming more important to global supply networks, so their efforts to change things will have effects all around the world. As noted, these countries account for a large and growing share of production and consumption, making their supply chain efficiency a matter of international interest. When an emerging economy strengthens its ports, digitizes its customs, or trains its logistics workers, it not only boosts its own prospects but also enhances the overall reliability of global trade networks. Conversely, if such reforms stagnate, the risk of supply disruptions or inefficiencies can reverberate beyond national borders – a lesson underscored by the pandemic experience. There is thus a strong incentive for continued collaboration between emerging economies and developed partners, international organizations, and the private sector to sustain supply chain improvements.

5. FUTURE OUTLOOK

Looking to the future outlook, several trends will influence supply chain reform trajectories:

- **Continued Emphasis on Resilience:** The frequency of disruptions – whether due to health crises, geopolitical events, or climate-related disasters – is unlikely to abate. This reality will keep resilience at the forefront of supply chain strategy. Emerging economies will need to institutionalize the risk management practices learned in recent years. We expect to see more countries establishing early warning systems for supply chain risks, diversifying their import sources for critical goods, and entering into regional pacts for mutual support during crises (such as agreements to allow transit of essential goods even if borders close). Resilience will become a competitive advantage, and those emerging markets that can demonstrate it (through, for example, robust multi-modal networks or reliable emergency logistics capabilities) will attract more business and investment.
- **Digital Leap and Industry 4.0 Adoption:** The pace of digital transformation is set to accelerate. Technologies like AI, machine learning, and robotics will become more accessible financially, and their applications in supply chain will broaden. We anticipate that in the next decade, even mid-tier emerging economies will have digital supply chain control towers – centralized platforms that provide real-time data and analytics across their logistics networks. The use of digital twins (virtual models of supply chain networks for simulation) might become common for planning and stress-testing scenarios. Additionally, blockchain-based traceability could become a standard requirement for exporting to certain markets, effectively pushing emerging market producers to adopt these tools to maintain market access. The nations that invest early in training their workforce and updating their digital infrastructure stand to leapfrog stages of development, while laggards may find themselves excluded from high-value segments of global trade.
- **Sustainability as a Core Requirement:** Climate change concerns and environmental regulations will increasingly shape how supply chains are structured. Already, large multinational corporations are asking suppliers to adhere to carbon reduction targets and ethical sourcing guidelines. In the future, this will intensify – we might see carbon tariffs or border adjustment mechanisms that penalize products with heavy emissions in their supply chain. Emerging economies must prepare for a low-carbon supply chain paradigm, which may entail the implementation of environmental standards domestically, the enhancement of rail and other low-emission transport modalities, and the investment in renewable energy for logistics. Conversely, the global transition to sustainable technologies (such as solar panels, electric vehicles, and so forth) presents new supply chain opportunities for emerging markets that possess the requisite resources or have the potential to manufacture these products. It is probable that supply chain reform initiatives will broaden to

encompass circular economy principles and green logistics, thereby reconciling economic development with sustainability objectives (Taghipour & Lu, 2023).

- **Global Supply Chain Reconfiguration and Regionalization:** We are likely to witness more changes to global supply systems. It's unlikely that the world will completely de-globalize, but regional blocs for sourcing and manufacturing are getting stronger (for example, chains that focus on Asia or the Americas). Emerging economies can take advantage of nearshoring developments by making themselves trustworthy nodes in these regional networks. To do this, they need to keep making it easier for people to trade and work together with their neighbors. Projects like trans-African roadways, Pan-Asian train linkages, or unified digital trade platforms in Latin America will become more important. In the future, there may be mega-regional supply chain agreements that go beyond trade to include shared standards and back-up plans. Emerging economies that actively participate in regional cooperation will help shape the terms instead of just going along with them. The idea of supply chain reform will move beyond national borders to include regional supply chain architectures. This would require collaborative governance, as was said earlier.
- **Evolving Consumer and Market Dynamics:** Changes in demographics, such Africa's population boom and the ageing of populations in other places, as well as urbanization, will change how people buy things. This will mean that supply chains will need to evolve. For example, if the middle class grows in Africa and South Asia, they will want more advanced and imported goods. This will require better logistics for imports and local distribution networks. E-commerce, which grew a lot during the COVID-19 pandemic, is likely to keep rising and reach even more of the world's emerging economies. This will put pressure on last-mile delivery systems and compel innovations like delivery by drones, use of local parcel lockers, or crowdsourced delivery models to become more widespread. Supply chain reforms will increasingly need to address urban logistics challenges (congestion, pollution) as megacities in emerging economies become major consumer centers. Policies around smart cities and urban planning will intertwine with supply chain considerations, such as zoning for logistics hubs and digitized traffic management systems to prioritize freight movement. Thus, the scope of reform might extend to what one could call "supply chain-aware" urban governance.

It is clear that supply chain reform in emerging economies is both challenging and imperative. The pathway to success involves simultaneous action on many fronts – physical infrastructure, digital technology, human capacity, and governance frameworks – as we have detailed. Encouragingly, there is growing recognition of these needs at the highest policy levels, and numerous examples of successful reforms to draw inspiration from. International support and knowledge exchange can further accelerate progress; for example, development agencies and multinational firms can act as partners in pilot projects that demonstrate reform benefits. The payoffs from getting it right are substantial: more resilient economies, inclusive growth (as efficient supply chains connect rural producers and urban consumers, small firms and big markets), and stronger positions in the global marketplace. However, reforms must be sustained and adaptive. The journey does not end once certain metrics improve; continuous monitoring and flexibility to adjust strategies are essential. The global environment will keep evolving, presenting new tests – whether a breakthrough technology that needs integrating or an unforeseen disruption that needs managing. Emerging economies will need to institutionalize the capacity for learning and adaptation in their supply chain ecosystems. This may mean checking logistics performance on a regular basis, talking to private sector participants to get their thoughts, and making sure that schools change their curricula to get students ready for the next generation of supply chain problems.

In short, supply chain reform in emerging economies will change over time. Countries that adopt a comprehensive, forward-looking reform strategy, as described in this chapter, will not only handle today's challenges but also lay the groundwork for dealing with tomorrow's uncertainties. They will change their supply chains from being a weak and inefficient part of their business to becoming a strong and competitive part of their business. This kind of change is a key part of broader growth and success, allowing developing economies to make the most of their potential in the global economy. The journey may be long, but the goal of nimble, strong, and long-lasting supply chains is definitely worth working towards. It will benefit producers, consumers, and society as a whole.

REFERENCES

Agu, E. E., Chiekezie, N. R., Abhulimen, A. O., & Obiki-Osafiele, A. N. (2024). Optimizing supply chains in emerging markets: Addressing key challenges in the financial sector. *World Journal of Advanced Science and Technology, 6*(01), 035-045.

Akhter, S., Bhat, M. S., Bhat, S. A., & Mir, S. (2024). Evaluating the Spatial Distribution Networks and Efficiency of Postharvest Supply Chains for the Sustainability of Vegetable Enterprise in the Valley of Kashmir, India. *Agribusiness*, agr.22001. DOI: 10.1002/agr.22001

Akram, H. W. (2025a). Identifying challenges plaguing Ethiopia's logistics industry: A structured literature review. *International Journal of Logistics Systems and Management, 51*(3), 297–313. DOI: 10.1504/IJLSM.2025.147538

Akram, H. W. (2025b). Greening Maritime Transport Processes. In Eco-Logistics and Sustainable Supply Chain Innovations (pp. 117-140). IGI Global Scientific Publishing.

Akram, H. W., Abbas, H., & Ciddikie, D. (2024). Green Manufacturing: A Comprehensive Exploration of Sustainable Practices and Industry 4.0 Integration. In *Green Manufacturing for Industry 4.0* (pp. 159-178). Productivity Press.

Al Maalouf, N. J., & Mouawad, C. (2025). Assessing the impact of the Beirut port explosion on supply chain management and seaport infrastructure in Lebanon: A pathway to resilience and reform. *Transportation Research Interdisciplinary Perspectives, 32*, 101555. DOI: 10.1016/j.trip.2025.101555

Alam, A., Hafiz, W. A., Akhtar, S., Choudhary, P., & Kumar, N. (2024). COVID-19's Effect on Indian MSMEs: Insights from Stakeholders. *International Journal of Economics and Financial Issues, 14*(6), 392–402. DOI: 10.32479/ijefi.16573

Alizadeh, N., Taghipour, A., & Canel-Depître, B. (2021). Which one collective strategy is appropriate for the business ecosystem? The role of political environment.

Anand, J., McDermott, G., Mudambi, R., & Narula, R. (2021). Innovation in and from emerging economies: New insights and lessons for international business research. *Journal of International Business Studies, 52*(4), 545–559. DOI: 10.1057/s41267-021-00426-1

Apruzzese, M., Bruni, M. E., Musso, S., & Perboli, G. (2023). 5G and companion technologies as a boost in new business models for logistics and supply chain. *Sustainability (Basel), 15*(15), 11846. DOI: 10.3390/su151511846

Aracil, E., Gómez-Bengoechea, G., & Moreno-de-Tejada, O. (2022). Institutional quality and the financial inclusion-poverty alleviation link: Empirical evidence across countries. *Borsa Istanbul Review*, *22*(1), 179–188. DOI: 10.1016/j.bir.2021.03.006

Bown, C. P. (2022). How COVID-19 medical supply shortages led to extraordinary trade and industrial policy. *Asian Economic Policy Review*, *17*(1), 114–135. DOI: 10.1111/aepr.12359

Catalão, F. P., Cruz, C. O., & Sarmento, J. M. (2023). Public sector corruption and accountability in cost deviations and overruns of public projects. *Public Organization Review*, *23*(3), 1105–1126. DOI: 10.1007/s11115-022-00616-x

Cauchois, R., Taghipour, A., Kang, D., Zoghlami, N., & Abed, M. (2017). Advanced solutions for a supply chain with stochastic information. *Journal of Advanced Management Science*, *5*(1), 9–13. DOI: 10.18178/joams.5.1.9-13

Corporate Finance Institute. (2023). *Emerging market economy*. Corporate Finance Institute. https://corporatefinanceinstitute.com/resources/economics/emerging-market-economy/

Fontoura, P., & Coelho, A. (2022). More cooperative... more competitive? Improving competitiveness by sharing value through the supply chain. *Management Decision*, *60*(3), 758–783. DOI: 10.1108/MD-09-2020-1225

Gajović, V., Paunović, M., Ralević, N., & Kilibarda, M. (2018). Insurance as an instrument of risk management in logistics systems.

Gharye Mirzaei, M., Goodarzian, F., Taghipour, A., & Muñuzuri, J. (2025). Sustainable closed-loop supply chain network under uncertainty considering green technologies: Toward the circular economy. *The Journal of the Operational Research Society*, •••, 1–21.

Glaa, B., Zoghlami, N., & Taghipour, A. (2014, May). Outsourcing and off-shoring healthcare services: A way to cut the costs and improve quality. In 2014 international conference on advanced logistics and transport (ICALT) (pp. 189-194). IEEE.

Hasan, M. Z., Hussain, M. Z., Umair, S., & Waqas, U. (2024). Role of Human Capital in the Supply Chain Management. In *Human Perspectives of Industry 4.0 Organizations* (pp. 131–154). CRC Press. DOI: 10.1201/9781032616810-7

Hoang, V., Nguyen, A., Hubbard, C., & Nguyen, K. D. (2021). Exploring the governance and fairness in the milk value chain: A case study in Vietnam. *Agriculture*, *11*(9), 884. DOI: 10.3390/agriculture11090884

Hugos, M. H. (2024). *Essentials of supply chain management*. John Wiley & Sons.

Ionescu, A. M., Clipa, A. M., Turnea, E. S., Clipa, C. I., Bedrule-Grigoru ă, M. V., & Roth, S. (2022). The impact of innovation framework conditions on corporate digital technology integration: Institutions as facilitators for sustainable digital transformation. [JBEM]. *Journal of Business Economics and Management, 23*(5), 1037–1059. DOI: 10.3846/jbem.2022.17039

Kamoyo, M., & Chikazhe, L. (2025). Public Transport Sector Challenges and Zimbabwe's Untapped Economic Opportunities. *Transportation in Developing Economies, 11*(2), 25. DOI: 10.1007/s40890-025-00244-2

Kumar, R., Rana, R., & Jha, S. K. (2023). Scalable blockchain architecture of internet of medical things (IoMT) for Indian smart healthcare system. In *AI Models for Blockchain-Based Intelligent Networks in IoT Systems: Concepts, Methodologies, Tools, and Applications* (pp. 231–259). Springer International Publishing. DOI: 10.1007/978-3-031-31952-5_11

Kuteyi, D., & Winkler, H. (2022). Logistics challenges in sub-Saharan Africa and opportunities for digitalization. *Sustainability (Basel), 14*(4), 2399. DOI: 10.3390/su14042399

Lebosse, S., Taghipour, A., & Canel-Depitre, B. (2017). Quick response to fluctuations in supply chains: A review. *Journal of Advanced Management Science, 5*(5), 394–400. DOI: 10.18178/joams.5.5.394-400

Lele, V. P., Kumari, S., & White, G. (2023). Streamlining Production: Using Big-Data's CRM & Supply chain to improve efficiency in high-speed environments. [IJCSPUB]. *IJCSPUB-International Journal of Current Scienc, 13*(2), 136–146.

Lopes, J. M., Gomes, S., & Mané, L. (2022). Developing knowledge of supply chain resilience in less-developed countries in the pandemic age. *Logistics (Basel), 6*(1), 3. DOI: 10.3390/logistics6010003

Lu, X. W., Tliche, Y., Vosooghidizaji, M., & Taghipour, A. (2023). Cryptocurrencies and Blockchain Applications. In Blockchain Applications in Cryptocurrency for Technological Evolution (pp. 1-13). IGI Global.

Mahfod, J., Khoury, B., Canel-Depitre, B., & Taghipour, A. (2021). Logistics Providers in Syria Humanitarian Operations. In Demand Forecasting and Order Planning in Supply Chains and Humanitarian Logistics (pp. 171-197). IGI Global. DOI: 10.4018/978-1-7998-3805-0.ch006

Mathiyazhagan, K., Taghipour, A., & Agarwal, V. (Eds.). (2022). *Blockchain Technology in Supply Chain Management for Society 5.0*. CRC Press. DOI: 10.1201/9781003177432

Mbiatem, J., Taghipour, A., & Canel-Depitre, B. (2018, August). Supplier selection approaches for decision makers. In *Proceedings of the 8th International Conference on Information Communication and Management* (pp. 108-112).

Mer, A., & Virdi, A. S. (2024). Decoding the challenges and skill gaps in small-and medium-sized enterprises in emerging economies: A review and research agenda. *Contemporary Challenges in Social Science Management: Skills Gaps and Shortages in the Labour Market*, 115-134.

Merimi, M., & Taghipour, A. (2021). Accelerating the digitalization of the supply chain: An empirical research about COVID-19 crisis. In *Digitalization of decentralized supply chains during global crises* (pp. 1–24). IGI Global Scientific Publishing. DOI: 10.4018/978-1-7998-6874-3.ch001

Montgomery, D. C. (2020). *Introduction to statistical quality control*. John wiley & sons.

Negri, M., Cagno, E., Colicchia, C., & Sarkis, J. (2021). Integrating sustainability and resilience in the supply chain: A systematic literature review and a research agenda. *Business Strategy and the Environment, 30*(7), 2858–2886. DOI: 10.1002/bse.2776

Oyedijo, A., Francois Koukpaki, A. S., Kusi-Sarpong, S., Alfarsi, F., & Yang, Y. (2022). Restraining forces and drivers of supply chain collaboration: Evidence from an emerging market. *Supply Chain Management, 27*(3), 409–430. DOI: 10.1108/SCM-06-2020-0263

Ren, Z., Taghipour, A., & Canel-Depitre, B. (2016, October). Information sharing in supply chain under uncertainty. In 2016 6th International Conference on Information Communication and Management (ICICM) (pp. 67-71). IEEE. DOI: 10.1109/INFOCOMAN.2016.7784217

Roopnarian, O., Singh, S., & Rathilall, R. (2023). The Convergence of Quality and Digitalisation in a Changing World: Implications for Developing Nations such as the BRICS Group. *African Journal of Inter/Multidisciplinary Studies, 5*(1), 1-14.

Taghipour, A. (2009). Evaluation de la collaboration dans une chaîne d'approvisionnement. Revue française de gestion industrielle, 28(1), 26-42.

Taghipour, A. (Ed.). (2020). *Demand forecasting and order planning in supply chains and humanitarian logistics*. IGI Global.

Taghipour, A. (Ed.). (2022). *Blockchain Applications in Cryptocurrency for Technological Evolution*. IGI Global. DOI: 10.4018/978-1-6684-6247-8

Taghipour, A. (2024). Big Data: The New Gold Mine for Supermarkets. In Applications of New Technology in Operations and Supply Chain Management (pp. 98-106). IGI Global.

Taghipour, A., Belrhazi, Y., & Damoum, N. (2023a). Resilient sustainable supply chain management. In *Government Impact on Sustainable and Responsible Supply Chain Management* (pp. 33–47). IGI Global. DOI: 10.4018/978-1-6684-9062-4.ch003

Taghipour, A., & Beneteau-Piet, C. (2020). Sustainable supply chain management performance. *International Journal of Innovation, Management and Technology, 11*(6), 165–169. DOI: 10.18178/ijimt.2020.11.6.897

Taghipour, A., & Beneteau-Piet, C. (2020). Sustainable supply chain management performance. *International Journal of Innovation, Management and Technology, 11*(6), 165–169. DOI: 10.18178/ijimt.2020.11.6.897

Taghipour, A., Fooladvand, A., Khazaei, M., & Ramezani, M. (2023b). Criteria clustering and supplier segmentation based on sustainable shared value using BWM and PROMETHEE. *Sustainability (Basel), 15*(11), 8670. DOI: 10.3390/su15118670

Taghipour, A., & Frayret, J. M. (2011). Supply chain coordination planning: A review. Work paper, École polytechnique de Montréal.

Taghipour, A., & Frayret, J. M. (2013a). Coordination of operations planning in supply chains: A review. *International Journal of Business Performance and Supply Chain Modelling, 5*(3), 272–307. DOI: 10.1504/IJBPSCM.2013.055729

Taghipour, A., & Lu, X. (2025). Navigating the Artificial Intelligence Era: Impacts of Artificial Intelligence on Youth Critical Thinking, Career Paths, and Ethical Challenges. In Ecological and Human Dimensions of AI-Based Supply Chain (pp. 49-68). IGI Global Scientific Publishing.

Taghipour, A., & Lu, X. W. (2023, August). Green Supply Chain Management: A Guide. In International Conference on Applied Economics and Business (pp. 315-328). Cham: Springer Nature Switzerland.

Taghipour, A., & Merimi, M. (2021, March). Digital transformation of supply chains during crisis: covid-19. In 11th Annual International Conference on Industrial Engineering and Operations Management, IEOM (pp. 7493-7501). DOI: 10.46254/AN11.20211298

Vosooghidizaji, M., Taghipour, A., & Canel-Depitre, B. (2020). Information asymmetry in supply chain coordination: State of the art. *Journal of Industrial and Intelligent Information, 8*(2), 38–43. DOI: 10.18178/jiii.8.2.38-43

Xu, X., Sethi, S. P., Chung, S. H., & Choi, T. M. (2023). Reforming global supply chain management under pandemics: The GREAT-3Rs framework. *Production and Operations Management*, *32*(2), 524–546. DOI: 10.1111/poms.13885

Zoghlami, N., Taghipour, A., Merlo, C., & Abed, M. (2016). Management of divergent production network using decentralised multi-level capacitated lot-sizing models. *International Journal of Shipping and Transport Logistics*, *8*(5), 590–604. DOI: 10.1504/IJSTL.2016.078686

Chapter 9
Industry-Wise Analysis of Sustainable Supply Chain Models

Venkata Kiran Kumar Ravi
http://orcid.org/0000-0003-1628-4936
Siddhartha Academy of Higher Education, India

L. Vijayakumar
Vel Tech Rangarajan Dr. Sagunthala R&D Institute of Science and Technology, India

B. Vasavi
NBKR Institute of Science and Technology, India

Rajib Mandal
http://orcid.org/0009-0009-7441-4509
Assam down town University, India

Baburao Gaddala
http://orcid.org/0000-0003-4190-8325
Guru Ghasidas Vishwavidyalaya, India

Mohd Asif Shah
Kardan University, Afghanistan

V. Bhoopathy
http://orcid.org/0000-0003-2175-6328
Sree Rama Engineering College, India

ABSTRACT

As companies deal with more environmental, social, and economic problems, SSC have become a strategic goal in many industries. This chapter talks about the most important parts of SSCM such as green logistics, circular economy models, using renewable energy, responsible procurement, cutting down on waste, and working together with stakeholders. It looks at how different businesses, like manufacturing, agriculture, retail, healthcare, and logistics, use their own but connected ways to be more environmentally friendly. This chapter also talks about how digital technologies like the IoT, blockchain, AI and BDA may help with transparency, traceability, and making smart choices. There is also talk about problems, global sustainability

DOI: 10.4018/979-8-3373-6455-1.ch009

norms, and where resilient, fair, and low-carbon supply chains should go in the future. In the end, using SSC methods makes a company more competitive, builds brand credibility, and helps achieve long-term global sustainability goals.

1. INTRODUCTION

Over the previous few decades, the term SC has been the focus of numerous academic discussions. Prior to environmental concerns, SCM focused on system efficacy and responsiveness. This system encompassed everything from raw material reception and manufacturing procedures to final goods distribution to customers. The following generation of researchers argued that SCM needs to be updated due to the environmental impact of supply chains as well as resource and raw material constraints. They stressed the importance of including sustainability as well as closed-loop production and consumption models. The result was an explosion of research into sustainability across several sectors, which in turn introduced the term SSC to the lexicon of the discipline long-term effects on water contamination, climate change, and the depletion of non-renewable resources and essential commodities. Companies are being pushed to change their SC policies to be more aligned with SSCs for a number of reasons, including pressure from NGOs and social media, global community demands (such as the 17 UN sustainable development goals and the World Climate Change and the sustainability expectations of customers and other stakeholders. Sustainable business practices offer substantial competitive and economic benefits to organisations in today's market. To include sustainability into the SC, the literature on SSCM has evolved in three distinct streams. Research on identifying the practices and performance of organisations is now in its mature stage, at least in industrialised nations (Narges Alizadeh, Atour Taghipour, 2021).

Another area of study is identifying the impediments. Efforts have been made in several industries to find long-term solutions for measuring performance and decision making, following a call a decade ago for researchers to create more realistic tools for SSCM implementation (Taghipour, 2021). Sustainability research methodologies were examined by in regard to the treatment of sustainability practices. Three out of thirty SSCM drivers were listed as distinct internal and external factors by out of a total of 1559 drivers. In their thorough SLR on SSCM in global SCs made a practical contribution by pointing managers of focal enterprises in the direction of global SCs. In order to find out how network structural properties affect SC sustainability, outlined the effects of a collection of SSCM strategies that companies use to reach their SC sustainability objectives. Collaboration, strategic orientation, culture, and the other eleven basic categories of important elements were derived from an SLR by (Cauchois et al., 2017). When it comes to eco-friendly procedures, how does data collection and analysis work?

2. UNDERSTANDING SSC

Definitions begin to get more complex and exact starting from 2001. While attempting to define SSCM, many authors have taken different tacks; for example, some have focused on procurement and purchasing, while others have adopted a more SC-oriented approach. Approaches to SSCM are expanding and becoming more integrated with more recent definitions that include sustainable development and the three dimensions of the triple bottom line (3BL). Notable features of these define due the idea that SSCM extends beyond the conventional view of business while still caring about financial success and the incorporation of the concept of pressures from outside parties. The operational viewpoint places a focus on the importance of collaboration amongst SC partners and sees SSCM as underpinning both internal and external business processes (Selcuk Besir Demir, 2018; Taghipour, 2009).

Table 1. Definitions of SSCM

Methods	Explanation
Sustainable Procurement	Thus, businesses must prioritise green purchasing, which involves incorporating environmental factors into purchasing policies, programs, and actions. This practice not only leads to eco-efficiency but also improves public perception, saves money
Environmental Supply Chain Dynamics (ESCD)	In ESCD innovations aimed at reducing environmental impacts spread from client firms to supplier firms. An environmental innovation can be anything from a new product or process to a new technology or technique
Green Supply	The term green supply describes an approach to SSC and industrial purchasing that takes environmental factors into account
GrSCM	The product life cycle management, which encompasses not only the design phase but also the procurement and selection of raw materials, the production phase, the distribution phase, and finally, the product's disposal from the market
Supply Management Ethical Responsibility (SMER)	It defines SMER as managing the optimal flow of high-quality, value-for-money goods, components, or services from a suitable group of innovative suppliers in a fair, consistent, and reasonable way that meets or surpasses society norms, even if it is not legally mandated
Procurement	Sustainable development principles—such as fostering good governance, maintaining a robust and equitable society, and limiting human impact on the environment—guide this kind of procurement

The term SSCM has been defined in a number of ways by the authors. Some of the most important definitions from the publications studied in this study are listed in Table 1, which is organised chronologically. Articles published before 2000 define SCM and describe the environment (or environmental impacts) as separate variables; these do not provide an explicit definition of SSCM (or Green SCM) as an integrated concept, even though the earliest definition in the sample dates from 1996 (Mbiatem et al., 2018).

2.1 The Significance of Theoretical Inputs for SSCM

The goal of this part is to draw attention to the significant theoretical contributions and provide a

rationale for the current investigation given the difficulties encountered in the previous SSCM works (El-Nemr et al., 2017).

2.1.1 What Role Does Theory Have in a Field's Evolution?

Top management journals publish articles that make a theoretical advance. Management knowledge development is a controversial topic. In academic circles, the topic of theory building has sparked heated debates. Proponents of unity and consensus have spoken out while proponents of plurality of inquiry and the promotion of multiple competing theories have spoken out. Within the process of knowledge development within a subject, there is a close relationship between theory construction and theory testing. It needs to strike a balance between theory building and theory testing. Theory building allows us to introduce new ideas, but theory testing can lead us to miss important parts of new phenomena since it is using old paradigms. Numerous researchers have recognised the connection between a theory's relevance to empirical reality and its validity. It is generally acknowledged that by utilising facts as evidence to back up a theory, the empirical provides nourishment to the conceptual, and by addressing practical problems, opportunities for good theory to arise (Ponputtha et al., 2021). Without a solid theoretical foundation, SSCM studies run the risk of is necessary for the area to develop into a respectable branch of management.

2.1.2 Theoretical Mapping's Significance in SSCM

Through outlining the significance of theory in management and, more especially, SSCM research, it has proven the necessity of examining and evaluating current theoretical methods to guide future endeavours. It points out that the idea of corporate sustainability has been shaped by an economic perspective on the corporation, which has contributed to its ambiguity. The relative importance of the economic, human, and ecological factors, as well as their interrelationships, can be difficult to pin down. Implementing sustainable practices both internally and externally to organisations is no easy feat. The collaborative and game-changing components to SSCM studies (Sahraoui et al., 2023). Therefore, it is essential to know where chances are to do research that incorporates these features and guides practice. Multiple literature reviews published in SSCM point to the field's growing prominence and maturity. Review results show, however, that theoretically grounded research is still woefully lacking. Specifically, IJPDLM literature assessment on SSCM noted that writers often use a small number of popular theories, even though additional perspectives might provide light on the topic from different angles. Even though there is an increasing number of empirical articles published in the field of SSCM, other authors have discovered that relatively little research is anchored in theory while present research is great for learning about facts, it doesn't really add anything theoretical.

So, it's fair to say the area is still in its early stages of development and conceptual maturity. The literature on sustainability and SCM dimensions is examined in detail by (Taghipour, 2023). There is a noticeable absence of integrated approaches, and authors have mostly studied individual sustainability components, especially environmental ones. They mention it briefly but they don't say which theories were used. By looking at SSCM's theoretical methods, it may try to figure out why there has been such a concentrated emphasis on environmental sustainability. Researchers in SSCM who are interested in advancing theory construction and application can benefit from a thorough assessment of existing ideas, as pointed. In addition, as pointed out by the field's present research has not accurately captured the extent to which SC theory has been skewed in favour of economically beneficial practices and profit maximisation. One may argue that a review of the theories that have been applied and how writers have conceptualised SSCM is necessary for future research to provide more thorough, original, and theoretically sound findings. Considering these current deficiencies and difficulties, this paper aims to survey the relevant theories and present an integrative theoretical framework to direct future studies (Taghipour, 2020).

3. SUSTAINABILITY PRACTICES ACROSS INDUSTRIES

Thus, a company's performance is affected by its relationships with its location, clients, suppliers, and the community; these relationships in turn affect the organization's success. Because of the need of thinking about the societal impacts of an organization's actions, generating economic value alone isn't enough. The increasing environmental repercussions and socioeconomic difficulties have given sustainability discussions more traction in recent years. So, developing strategies for how organisations may help to spreading and implementing the sustainability triangle has become crucial for sustainable development. Businesses are expected to perform economically, socially, and environmentally in accordance with societal expectations, CRS are non-mandated, non-legally necessary activities (i.e., above and beyond what is typically expected) that the organisation plans to carry out with the help of its stakeholders. Consequently, the company not only follows all applicable laws and ethical guidelines, but it also voluntarily creates programs to better the community since its employees are passionate about making a difference (Taghipour and Frayret, 2013a).

This kind of involvement often stems from external pressures, such as expectations from customers, investors, and other stakeholders, who want to see the company actively involved in community-based activities. In order to understand how corporations, promote stakeholder engagement strategies that go beyond the production of economic value, discussions on CRS have been growing both in the corporate and academic spheres since the 1960. An organization's socio-environmental responsibility lies in its efforts to improve both the local community and the environment initiatives that involve the local community, initiatives to decrease waste, and material reuse all contribute to the company's economic growth and social and environmental responsibility (Taghipour and Lu, 2025a). Companies that practise CSR aim to enhance their stakeholder relationships in a way that benefits society and the environment. External actors put pressure on firms to follow best practices and maximise resources, which impacts corporate actions. As a result, building strategies that enhance CRS transcends organisational boundaries. Three CRS ideas were proposed: Goal 1: Businesses take a longer-term view of CRS, bolstering their market standing through responsible practices and use CRS to head off any issues that may develop in the future (Merimi and Taghipour, 2021).

As part of its second vision, the company will use its business acumen to better serve the underprivileged by adopting a responsible social behaviour that includes philanthropic practices, meeting the demands of its stakeholders, and bolstering worthy causes (Taghipour and Frayret, 2013b). In Vision, philanthropy takes front stage, but it all begins within the firm. This is because the organisation is keen on supporting issues that include its stakeholders, as a way to engage with the local community and provide resources for action development. Organisational perspectives of the CRS idea were examined in the study conducted by (Taghipour et al., 2023). Incorporating CRS into company plans and beliefs allows organisations to see themselves as transforming agents. Nevertheless, the idea of CRS is vague and sometimes misunderstood because there is no consensus on its definition inside businesses.

According to sustainable management is based on the idea that organisations must acknowledge the scarcity of natural resources, act responsibly in their use, and look for ways to reduce the negative effects of their operations on the environment. There has been an upsurge in corporate sustainability research in recent years, with numerous studies aiming to fill this knowledge gap. The perspective of healthcare cooperative management on sustainability factors was examined in the study by (Taghipour, 2023). While the cooperative does have some sustainability measures in place, there is room for improvement in the social dimension. For example, the cooperative could benefit from implementing new practices pertaining to the environmental dimension; these changes would also help shape the cooperative's best practices. To round out the sustainable framework, the study suggests involving the community. studied the viewpoints of do Sul's footwear industry agents and found that while most respondents were aware of sustainability concepts, few had seen them put into effect at their own enterprises (Tliche et al., 2023).

However, many companies still consider sustainability to be a new subject in the corporate environment. Putting sustainability into practice, however, can make a business more competitive in the market delves into the swine sector and how they implemented a sustainability indicator system. The pig farms can be categorised as in search of sustainability according to the results, with the exception of the social dimension, which is deemed unsustainable according to the study (Vosooghidizaji et al., 2020). As a consequence, the findings suggest that remedial actions are necessary to attain sustainability all its forms: economically, socially and environmentally. Finding and keeping tabs on issues within the realm of sustainable practices allows one to put plans in place to lessen their impact and raise the bar for sustainability. In their study of Brazilian industrial companies, sought to understand the managerial profile in relation to sustainable innovation. The findings show that the companies' sustainable management is closely tied to strategies and innovation (Taghipour and Beneteau-Piet, 2020). These companies actively work to reduce the impacts of their activities by promoting waste recycling, engaging with the community, and developing sustainable practices for both their processes and products (XiaoWen and Atour, 2025).

4. SUSTAINABILITY IN VARIOUS DOMAINS

Manufacturers are increasingly recycling or remanufacturing things, thus it may no longer be the consumer's responsibility to dispose of them. This shift in responsibility could be due to economic, environmental, or legislative factors. Environmental and packaging rules are getting tougher all the time, making businesses pay greater attention to what happens to their products after sale. Companies are always looking into how to make their products more reusable, manufacturable, and recyclable, so in the future, less of them will wind up in the trash. Examining the real-world effects of implementing the sustainability venture by incorporating a reverse logistics strategy into the company's operational framework. There are four perspectives offered in the arguments: economic, ecological, ethical, and social (Zoghlami et al., 2016).

4.1 Sustainable Environment

In addition to the product's or service's necessary functionalities, the rise in the unspoken expectations of consumers, such as the environmental consciousness of the organisation is also rapidly becoming a crucial factor in the selection of the service or product by the end user. Another feature of the product value chain is the type of shipment it makes and the way it relates to eco-friendliness. Array of three components of the product, including its creation, shipment, and subsequent handling, were recognised as pertinent with regard to this aspect (Taghipour et al., 2015; Taghipour et al., 2023). They have been manufactured in a certain way, and their carbon first, the products' environmental impact during production and storage; second, the products' transit and usage processes (stockpiles), and thirdly, for how long after their original purpose has expired, can their worth be recouped? (the supply chain in reverse). In general, it is believed that environmental factors can be consider while deciding between variants of a product, even when making a purchase at every single consumer (Taghipour, 2023). The effects on the environment of the importance of sustainability initiatives to the company's strategy is growing. populace as a result of mandates for preserving natural resources, less waste and more efficient use of resources. When companies are under pressure from customers to cut costs, they innovate in ways that benefit the environment.

Reverse logistics is closely related to several management approaches used. In addition to lowering the demand for new raw materials, sustainable practices lessen the environmental damage that comes from extracting and processing those materials. A strong reverse logistics infrastructure is essential for the community advantages that zero-waste programs bring about through recycling and waste reduction. Resources are at the heart of sustainable production methods as outlined by current environmental management. There is a dual ecological and economic obstacle to success in the electronics sector. From the ground up, electronic terms can be constructed via electronic production techniques (Taghipour et al., 2022). Companies often already have the infrastructure in place to include recycled materials into their products, and doing so can increase their bottom line. Also, people are more likely to buy things with the green label on them; recycling or reusing items has many environmental benefits but goes against many technological advancements that consumers want. Adapting technology is something that captivates people (Taghipour et al., 2022).

The practice of remanufacturing items, assemblies, or components is becoming more popular as a means to preserve their cumulative worth. In the last 30 years, sustainability methods have permeated people's social and industrial life alike. For instance, up until the 1950s, landfills were a significant source of garbage disposal; by 1959, they had supplanted all other methods in American culture. The number of landfills has been steadily declining since then. Landfill prices have been perceived as rising sharply in recent years, coinciding with the fast reduction of available landfill space (Glaa et al., 2014). Dumping waste is becoming more and more of a challenge due to factors such as the ever-increasing volume of rubbish, limited landfill area, strict regulatory rules, and the high expense of landfills. The landfill bans should serve as a reminder to manufacturers and suppliers that taking products back from customers is not only their obligation, but also financially beneficial. Environmental problems are quickly becoming as ubiquitous as the electronics industry itself, due to the fast development and spread of information technology. Improving the efficiency of the secondary market can help reduce the need to dispose of waste materials and goods by making them more suitable for recycling and reusing (Lebosse et al., 2017).

This will prolong the life of the materials and lessen their impact on the environment. Information that is accessible, easy to understand, and trustworthy across several sources can greatly enhance this efficiency. Businesses and non-profits should understand that launching sustainable initiatives would bring much-needed attention to their efforts to be green. Since products have an effect on the environment at every stage of their life cycle, it stands to reason that decisions on process technologies, SCM, and product development are all impacted by the incorporation of ecological concerns. As a result, there has been a recent uptick in the use of green SCM overall quality of ecology management, life cycle analysis, and the ISO 14000 standards (Loivet et al., 2020). This ecological strategic perspective seeks to close or lengthen the life cycle of items by revaluing them after they have been discarded by the end user. There are a variety of options available for this, including recycling, cannibalisation, reprocessing, repairing, renovating, and reusing. As a result of all of these factors, products are being returned to producers after being used; this process is called a reverse logistics chain. The necessity for a product's costing system that considers its lifecycle is as part of an integrated EMS. Moreover, they investigated how an accounting system may contribute to the development of reliable EMS cost data. Without EMS, businesses have a harder time competing, and accountants who solely deal with liability accounting lose out on a chance to help their clients out (XiaoWen and Atour, 2025).

4.2 Sustainability's Social Component

If sustainability is to reach its full potential as an industrial concept, its practitioners must recognise that sustainable business practices have social as well as economic benefits. Although sustainability's social component has been around for more than fifty years, rising environmental and ecological concerns have given it more weight than ever before when managers make decisions. In order to fulfil the concept of social responsibility, a company must prioritise more than just making money for its shareholders. An organization's social responsibility extends beyond its stakeholders to include the general public and all of the factors necessary for the organization's continued existence. While some businesses are starting to include corporate social responsibility into their strategic and operational decision-making processes, the vast majority of companies are still ignoring sustainability. The idea of sustainability in company may be very new, which could explain something (Mahfod et al., 2019). More often than not, businesses see sustainable practices as a way to cut costs and increase profits. The three facets of social identity can be better developed when an organisation employs sustainable practices. The following factors are traditionally linked to group formation: feeling one with a group of people having preconceived notions about ourselves and others, and the results of these things, which in turn strengthen the factors that have always been associated with group formation (Taghipour et al., 2019).

Employees' dedication and devotion to their organisations are fostered by a strong sense of social identity, which in turn leads to financial gains. One of the most important parts of any business is marketing, and in order to set their product apart from the competition, they are always looking for new ideas. Marketing departments worldwide have come to terms with the fact that consumers' and businesses' habits have changed dramatically, and they're of the belief that a socially sustainable business model can help them capitalise on the positive associations that consumers have with these companies. The majority of consumers are prepared to spend more on products sold by socially responsible companies. The in the context of environmentally friendly products, marketing and public relations play a significant role in how businesses aim to provide value to consumers (Mahfod et al., 2021). That companies also have an obligation to raise knowledge on the methods that contribute to a product's sustainability and environmental friendliness. In order to have a sustainable company model, sustainable practices are crucial. Legal requirements in the US and much of Europe make producers answerable for their products even after they've sold them. What this means is that it encompasses not just the companies' after-sale support but also the product's eventual removal from sale. Automobile batteries are one commodity that demands a lot of social responsibility from its buyers. These batteries have led and other harmful chemicals that pose a significant threat to human health if they enter the food chain. In nations with laxer legal rules, companies have a dilemma between their social obligation and the financial burden of creating a new logistics route to collect used batteries from the market. Companies can now take advantage of this situation to position themselves as socially responsible by adopting a socially sustainable business plan (Nadia et al., 2020).

4.3 Four-Dimensional Sustainability

The demands and interests of stakeholders and customers, as well as external forces like legislation and regulation, have stoked a renewed interest in sustainable business practices. Companies' sustainability strategies across areas must be compared due to the global nature of their operations. Good corporate ethics and a sustainable strategy may provide value in many sectors over the long term, and many organisations have recognised this. Businesses that are reaping the benefits of ethical and environmentally conscious operations include: The Swedish packaging manufacturer which was established in 1997, has created a one-of-a-kind product that uses calcium carbonate instead of petrochemical products, which reduces their usage by 40-60%. What's more, it costs 25% less than petro-based alternatives, which is perhaps an even more compelling selling point (Evangelos Christou, Kostas Alexandris, 2018). Markets in the developing world have been particularly fruitful for Ecolean, which has been experiencing average annual growth of 50%. General Motors instituted a policy of using only chemicals from one source at its Hamtramck facility in Detroit.

According to it also decreased paint waste and sludge by 750 tonnes and VOC emissions by 40 tonnes. Regrettably, the foundation of these impressive and fruitful endeavours is a focus on ecologically sound practices, excluding more comprehensive answers from the social structure. Businesses should be more mindful of the social and cultural contexts in which their actions have an impact. The socially optimal allocation scenario is not amenable to solution within the purview of neoclassical economics. One way to accomplish this is by building the social welfare function (Radhoui et al., 2021). But by definition, a social welfare function must reflect society's views on the fairness or acceptability of how resources are distributed among its members. What is considered good, socially valued, and subsequently reinforced behaviour is defined by accepted ethical standards. When there are market failures and negative externalities, they ruin the aggregate and lead to human-induced environmental problems. Because of this, addressing poor resource allocation and internalising the divergent private and social costs are the two most important steps towards achieving sustainability. Decisions, according to utilitarianism, a philosophy of personal morality, should be consistent, reasonable, and centred on the benefit they create for the choice maker. The idealised economic decision maker, homo economicus, is a genderless, logical, and, according to our dominant culture, male, creature. This is the primary characterisation of utilitarianism. The ultimate issue, then, is what precisely defines utility (Taghipour and Frayret, 2013a). Pareto optimality might be a very crucial metric for attaining social welfare if individual utility is the only foundation for and gauge of worth. But if the rights of others influence how much one values their own utility, and if maximising one's own utility has an that fits this picture. This definition of sustainability is based on the economic benefits it may provide rather than on any concern for the social or environmental impact it may have. In the part that follows, it offers a comprehensive model and definition of sustainability that incorporates the four elements that were identified throughout the thorough study (Taghipour, 2023).

4.4 Ethics in Sustainability

That nature is valuable in and of itself is central to environmental ethics. Therefore, nature and its components are not only meaning to an end, but ends in and of themselves (Gao et al., 2018). Modern ethics must also undergo a sea change due to the profound shifts in the character of human activity. There was a time when everything having to do with the non-human realm was morally ambiguous. All conventional ethics is anthropocentric, meaning it is concerned only with interactions between humans. This includes interactions between humans and oneself. Ethical concerns, however, have recently expanded to include the dynamics of interactions between inanimate and living things. Therefore, the ethical dimension must also be considered while discussing sustainability (Lu and Taghipour, 2025). Developed nations agreed to compensate less developed nations for their participation in global environmental projects; this was one of the outcomes of the 2009 climate change summit in Copenhagen. Some have asserted that sustainable growth is a perilous notion that might lead the economies of the United States, Western Europe, and Japan into a protracted economic recession. To comprehend the short-sightedness and unethical nature of our approach, one must evaluate several fundamental ethical concepts that substantiate our stance. The initial concept is utilitarianism. Utilitarianism, despite its intricate nature and diverse interpretations throughout history, often defines the good as that which maximises enjoyment and/or serves the interests of the majority. The interplay of ethics, globalisation, and sustainable development is complex; yet, there exists potential for optimism, particularly when examining the practical application of distributive justice principles in this context (Tliche et al., 2019).

4.5 Sustainable Economics

Materials such as iron, copper, and aluminium are seeing a rising trend in their global costs. In 2004, steel prices increased by 19%, in 2005 they increased by 71%, and in 2006 they increased by 19% again. It is more cost-effective to recycle steel than to mine the virgin ore, which is why it is quickly becoming one of the most recycled resources. Reusing and recycling steel reduces water consumption by 76%, mining waste by 97%, air emissions by 88%, and energy consumption by 74%, all as reported by the US Environmental Protection Agency (USEPA) (Steel Recycling Institute, 2006). Recycling aluminium uses only 5% of the energy needed to extract it from its ore, making it a highly market-driven recycled resource. World Bank (2007) reports that copper prices have been extremely unpredictable over the past few years, with yearly averages ranging from $3679/metric tonne in 2005 to $6722/metric tonne in 2006 and $6391/metric tonne in the first quarter of 2007 (Vosooghidizaji et al., 2019). Due to the scarcity of raw materials, recycling has emerged as a potential solution for the industrial industry. The waste material's potential as a raw material for production has been hindered by the lack of clarity surrounding its supply and availability (Lu and Taghipour, 2023). Technological obsolescence and progress further complicate matters, making it harder for decision makers to get rid of the product.

The automotive industry makes extensive use of sustainable practices. It gives car companies significant tactical and financial advantages in a cutthroat market. Gathering, sorting, and processing are the steps involved in recycling the old materials. In order to address the specific difficulties of remanufacturing, especially in exchange settings like the automotive sector zeroed emphasis on bill-of-material restructurings and the creation of new bills of material. As an additional illustration of sustainable approaches, consider the packaging sector. While concerns for the environment were the initial impetus for the development of reusable packaging, the concept's appeal was mostly due to financial considerations. Industries such as electronics, automobiles, beverages, and appliances are already utilising reusable containers (Aouadni et al., 2024). In order to recover the packaging units strategically, these industries work in tandem with their dealers and customers to develop a reverse logistics plan. Reusable containers not only facilitate the introduction and continuation of contact with customers, but also encourage mutual motivation, which in turn allows for the integration of sales and distribution of new products targeted at customers as well as those related to returns. Reducing, reusing, recycling, incinerating, and disposing of trash in landfills should be the general order of priority in waste management. Logistics are greatly affected by packaging. Not only does packing affect logistical productivity, but it also increases the purchase price and, more recently, the disposal cost.

Efficiency gained through the integration and coordination of several processes during the recovery and recycling of these goods affects the profitability of recycling. Earnings at each level are conditional on the type of market and the level of competition. The construction of reclamation and redistribution facilities is an expensive part of sustainability programs, but the production technology process can increase economic growth by reducing pollution by-products and making the final products usable in other processes or reprocess able. Reverse logistics has proven to be an efficient method of retrieving items that would have otherwise gone to waste during shipment (Gharye Mirzaei et al., 2025). Since sustainability has a direct impact on the firm's revenue, it serves as an incentive for the company to implement it. Timely delivery and processing of returns put the company in a better position to save money and make more from the returned products. A substantial amount of unrealised profit often comes from the returned parts. One promising avenue for revenue growth is the expanding secondary and reseller markets (Lu and Taghipour, 2025).

In addition, businesses may be able to save a tonne of money by handling the products themselves during the return process, which can help them avoid paying hefty fines to regulatory bodies. Customers also favour businesses that provide satisfying returns. Investing more in reverse logistics can lead to up to 12% more customer loyalty, according to a nationwide poll. By making use of inexpensive, underutilised supplies or resources, reverse logistics can boost a company's production and profitability. Since it becomes easier for the firm to centrally organise and supervise the disposal-related activities, having the company handle waste disposal is often advantageous from a competitive standpoint. This aids the business in creating a database of by-products, which lowers inventory carrying costs and helps with tax savings (Goodarzian et al., 2026).

5. TECHNOLOGY AS A DRIVER OF SSC

5.1 Digital Transformation for Supply Networks That are Sustainable

In order to lessen the negative effects on the environment caused by growing supply chains and saving resources, digital technologies falling under the DT umbrella have opened up a lot of doors and raised a lot of good expectations. By making the system's emissions more transparent, DT technologies throughout the SC network contribute to the SDGs. All the more reason to ditch the old supply chain model and implement a green, tech-driven one. The entire supply chain, from raw materials to finished goods, including suppliers, logistics, customers, and services, is undergoing this change. Furthermore, DT technologies offer significant benefits to SCs, including raising the availability of information and fostering agility, flexibility, and real-time transparency. This, in turn, improves profitability and efficiency, optimises SCM practices, and reduces costs and delivery times, all of which contribute to sustainable development. As an example, consider BT a distributed ledger that ensures the security, veracity, and openness of all data. Four important design elements distinguish BT from other IS, such ERP systems: non-localization (decentralisation), security, verifiability, and intelligent execution. In recent years, several businesses have integrated ERP systems into their SC operations (Lu et al., 2023).

But because they couldn't monitor the whereabouts of their items outside of the SC network, they had no bird's-eye perspective of their SC. Not to mention how vulnerable ERP is to attacks, corruption, and hacking because it is a centralised system that stores all data in one central location/server. As BT streamlines SC operations and reduces energy use, it wins over sceptical clients and boosts SC efficiency, which in turn increases SC performance. In addition, BT is vital to the sustainability of SCs since it tackles sustainability issues by utilising decentralised and immutable data, transparency, and smart contractual connections to address the increasing sustainability concerns. In addition to the aforementioned, BT has the potential to lessen the social and environmental impacts of SC by managing and lowering recall and rework. Furthermore, BDA is characterized by the collection, extraction, and storage of massive datasets, commonly known as the 6V (Lu and Taghipour, 2023).

It is associated with analysing and reviewing large amounts of data of various forms in order to find hidden patterns, trends, and correlations utilising modern technology to improve operational efficiency and expand into new markets and opportunities. BDA has become crucial to organisations and society. The complexity of supply chains renders the oversight of supply chain operations difficult, particularly when aiming for sustainability, as some supply chain participants may lack transparency. BDA enables the examination of data from each supply chain participant at several decision-making tiers, hence assisting in supply chain planning and visibility determinations. From a sustainability perspective, BDA may decrease delivery time by consolidating several clients, achievable through real-time information interchange, hence resulting in reduced energy usage (Taghipour and Lu, 2025). Moreover, BDA empowers SC members within each SC function to detect unsustainable and unethical practices or other detrimental environmental behaviours, in addition to quantifying carbon emissions and air pollution. BDA applications are expected to enhance SSCs in the social aspect by mitigating supply chain risks related to the procurement of goods and services. Moreover, BDA can mitigate supply chain risks related to procurement and enhance social sustainability (Taghipour, 2020).

5.2 Transformation to Digital

The importance of DT to practitioners, decision-makers, and academics in a variety of fields has recently come to light. DT makes use of digital platforms, high-level asset management, and digitally-induced interactions between and within organisations (Lu et al., 2023; Taghipour and Lu, 2025). A globally linked IT-enabled network structure has replaced the previous century's decentralised hierarchical functional structure in digital policymaking. By leveraging digital technologies, DT opens up new business procedures and expands the trading environment. In order to create smarter production methods, DT uses digitally integrated technologies at a high level. The IoT, CSP, BPM, ML, CC and RFID are all examples of innovative technologies undergoing digital transformation that will ultimately lead to smarter production processes. In DT, companies use digital capabilities to change their business models and ecosystem, as stated by (Mathiyazhagan et al., 2022). In addition, there are a plethora of strategic and socio-managerial options presented by digital technology to organisations. Through their extensive network of contacts, which includes suppliers and customers, they are able to create prospects for more adaptable, responsive, and integrated business models (Taghipour and Lu, 2023). These game-changing innovations have the potential to increase a company's client base, income, and overall wort.

Figure 1. DT Adoption Factors for SSC

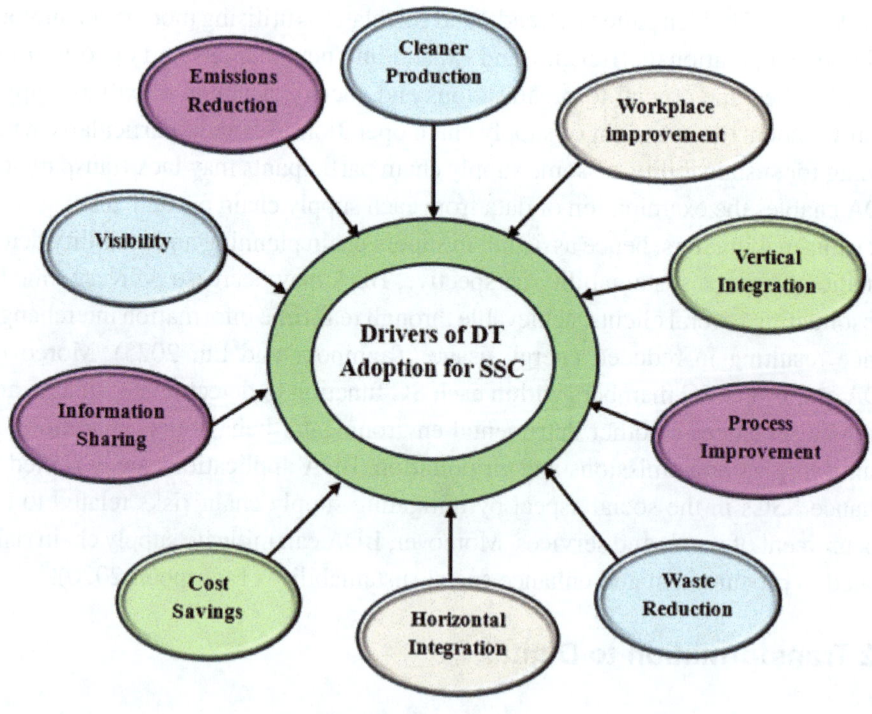

Figure 1 showcases an innovative approach to utilising and integrating digital technology, which allows for new market behaviours and transactions and blurs organisational boundaries. Even though it's hazardous, DT improves an organization's performance in the long run by changing how money is made, especially in internal processes and interactions with suppliers and customers. As a result, the focus has changed from individual assets to the entire fleet when making decisions.

In spite of DT's many advantages, it is difficult for established businesses to implement. They often have to choose between old and new ways of working when they try to innovate their digital business model (Taghipour et al., 2022). Companies undergo digital transformation when they undergo three basic changes: operations that are digitally enabled and interconnected, communication that is digitally enabled, and new patterns of value creation through digital innovation or acquired digital data. These shifts are visible in every market on the planet. To make the transition from a traditional to a digital business model more gradual, organisations should start with little adjustments like separate digitisation initiatives. But DT can necessitate a major change from the norm, rendering current business models useless. This means that DT is making businesses reevaluate their management models (Pour Mohammadi et al., 2014).

6. FUTURE RESEARCH DIRECTIONS

An investment in the optimisation of an organisation, especially one with a focus on the long term, can be made through the successful deployment and utilisation of technology.

6.1 Assessing Disruption Possibilities

There is a critical need to monitor disruption risks because they are unlikely to occur but may harm the entire supply chain network if they did. Because the factors used to measure these risks evolve with time, it may say that they are dynamic in nature. In most research efforts, the likelihood of occurrence is used to assess uncertainties caused by things like natural catastrophes, political crises, financial crises, disasters that humans produce, and pandemics. It was used to normalise the results of discrete scenario generation or probability distribution (Taghipour et al., 2022). Considering the recent study and keeping COVID-19 in mind, one promising avenue for future research is to model SCN with the probability of disruption as a Poisson distribution. This approach could inform the development of proactive interventions. In addition, new goals can be implemented using Chebyshev variant goal programming, which is a method for controlling uncertainty in demand that was recently used by (Radhoui et al., 2019).

6.2 Optimisation and Resolution Methodologies

The most common goals when developing SC are to minimise costs and maximise profits. However, due to the ever-changing nature of uncertainty, modelling SC is no easy feat. The issue becomes NP-hard when trying to model real-life conditions, such as uncertainty in operations/disruption risks, optimisation of objectives, and time-efficient resilience metrics. A more compact approach to dealing with large-scale problems and large-scale complexity can be the subject of future research (Mathiyazhagan et al., 2022).

6.3 Sustainability

Ecological and social concerns around the world have prompted the writers of SCs to shift their attention from purely economic considerations, such as cost minimisation and profit maximisation, to issues related to economic stability. This is a worldwide concern. Most heavily weighted in SC were the triple line (Eco + Env + Soc) and eco and environment elements. Most of the literature on environmental factors relies on the classical LCA method to determine greenhouse gas emissions; however, this method primarily addresses water consumption and air pollution, while chemical and biological oxygen demands in water and degradation in land are under-considered when SC networks are being designed. The majority of studies framed economic and environmental considerations as primary goals for the first stage, with social considerations forming the basis for the second stage (Ren et al., 2016). Mapping charge-mosaic surfaces in electrolyte solutions using surface charge microscopy. Thus, studies can be conducted to broaden LCA and other methodologies to include social dimensions, and first-stage judgements can consider social issues like health, safety of labour, human development index employment.

6.4 Resilience and Sustainability

When planning a supply chain, it is critical to keep both resilience and sustainability in mind. Legible, green, robust, adaptable, environmentally friendly, and collaborative SC are all components of resilience and sustainability that can be integrated to enable this line of inquiry (Taghipour et al., 2022). To discover the compromise between all those interdependent parts, these can be combined into a single framework. There has been no prior study that incorporates interruption likelihood as an unknown parameter into SCND. While discrete probability of disruption is easy to compute, it is unworthy for application in real-world environments, and most SCND research articles that have addressed resilience and sustainability have employed this method. It may be an intriguing area to investigate further as no one has previously used probabilistic programming to this idea (Taghipour, 2024). It is also possible to work on enhancing these two dimensions by creating a fuzzy programming model that uses chance constraints to deal with uncertainties.

7. CONCLUSION

This work has offered a synopsis of the ways in which SSCM makes use of theoretical viewpoints. According to the results, most SSCM papers don't use any theories at all, and the theoretical ones that do mostly borrow macro theories from other fields. Based o-n the key ideas that have been identified, this work presents an integrated theoretical map of SSCM that covers all the bases. Following the identification of current shortcomings, it has also demonstrated how the field could develop. A key constraint of our map is that it brings together disparate traditions under one roof. It noted in the study that theories incorporate assumptions from their mother discipline (Taghipour, 2022). It expects that additional studies will build on the findings of this research, which is an early step towards understanding theoretical dynamics in SSCM. The area of SSCM is expanding, so there will be a need for future research as well as a collection of results. In a new area of study, it is important to keep the conversation flowing and the interpretations open so that more people may add to the growing body of SSCM knowledge. Nevertheless, future studies should address the precarious theoretical groundwork that underpins much SSCM research (Taghipour & Lu, 2023). The fact that certain problems (economic and environmental) have gotten more focus than others is another worry that has arisen from this study. This highlights the importance of perhaps reflecting on the current paradigm that impacts SSCM research and delving into uncharted territories. Organisations in every field can't be built to be resilient, competitive, and responsible without SSC. Risk reduction, stakeholder trust enhancement, and global sustainability can all be achieved when digital innovation is combined with environmental, social, and economic goals. Solutions that are transparent, scalable, and enabled by technology will support sustainable development on a global level and will be the future of SCM (Taghipour, 2023).

REFERENCES

Aouadni, S., Aouadni, I., & Taghipour, A. (2024). Using ordinal priority approach with confidence-level measurement for third-party logistics provider selection in the Tunisian healthcare sector. In *Applications of new technology in operations and supply chain management* (pp. 404–429). IGI Global Scientific Publishing. DOI: 10.4018/979-8-3693-1578-1.ch020

Cauchois, R., Taghipour, A., Kang, D., Zoghlami, N., & Abed, M. (2017). Advanced solutions for a supply chain with stochastic information. *Journal of Advanced Management Science*, *5*(1), 9–13. DOI: 10.18178/joams.5.1.9-13

Christou, E. Alexandris, K., & F. A. (2018). TOURMAN 2018 conference proceedings.

Demir, S. B. (2018). Predatory journals: Who publishes in them and why? *Journal of Informetrics*, *12*(4), 1296–1311. DOI: 10.1016/j.joi.2018.10.008

El-Nemr, N., Canel-Depitre, B., & Taghipour, A. (2017, September). Determinants of hotel room rates. In Marketing Trends Congress: Luxury Industries Conference London 2017.

Gao, Y., Li, Z., & Kang, D. S. (2018). Supply chain coordination: A review. *Journal of Advanced Management Science*, *6*(4), 213–217. DOI: 10.18178/joams.6.4.213-217

Gharye Mirzaei, M., Goodarzian, F., Taghipour, A., & Muñuzuri, J. (2025). Sustainable closed-loop supply chain network under uncertainty considering green technologies: Toward the circular economy. *The Journal of the Operational Research Society*, •••, 1–21.

Glaa, B., Zoghlami, N., & Taghipour, A. (2014, May). Outsourcing and off-shoring healthcare services: A way to cut costs and improve quality. In *Proceedings of the 2014 International Conference on Advanced Logistics and Transport (ICALT)* (pp. 189–194). IEEE. DOI: 10.1109/ICAdLT.2014.6864116

Goodarzian, F., Abraham, A., Muñuzuri, J., Taghipour, A., & Ghasemi, P. (2026). A Benders decomposition approach for a new sustainable pharmaceutical supply chain network: A case study in France. *Annals of Operations Research*, *356*(2), 881–919. DOI: 10.1007/s10479-024-05936-3

Lebosse, S., Taghipour, A., & Canel-Depitre, B. (2017). Quick response to fluctuations in supply chains: A review. *Journal of Advanced Management Science*, *5*(5), 394–400. DOI: 10.18178/joams.5.5.394-400

Loivet, W., Taghipour, A., & Kang, D. S. (2020). The rise of green supply chain management: Between complexity and necessity. Journal of Economics. *Business and Management*, *8*(1), 1–7.

Lu, X., & Taghipour, A. (2023). A French guide for businesses and governments to integrate the concept of sustainable development into their supply chains. In *Government impact on sustainable and responsible supply chain management* (pp. 1–12). IGI Global Scientific Publishing. DOI: 10.4018/978-1-6684-9062-4.ch001

Lu, X., & Taghipour, A. (2025). The future of marketing: Integrating big data and AI for personalized customer engagement. In *Ecological and human dimensions of AI-based supply chain* (pp. 97–110). IGI Global Scientific Publishing. DOI: 10.4018/979-8-3693-7478-8.ch005

Lu, X. W., Tliche, Y., Vosooghidizaji, M., & Taghipour, A. (2023). Cryptocurrencies and blockchain applications. In *Blockchain applications in cryptocurrency for technological evolution* (pp. 1–13). IGI Global.

Mahfod, J., Canel-Depitre, B., & Taghipour, A. (2019). Quality function deployment–ELECTRE in supplier evaluation. *Journal of Advanced Management Science*, *7*(4).

Mahfod, J., Khoury, B., Canel-Depitre, B., & Taghipour, A. (2021). Logistics providers in Syria humanitarian operations. In *Demand forecasting and order planning in supply chains and humanitarian logistics* (pp. 171–197). IGI Global. DOI: 10.4018/978-1-7998-3805-0.ch006

Mathiyazhagan, K., Taghipour, A., & Agarwal, V. (Eds.). (2022). *Blockchain technology in supply chain management for society 5.0*. CRC Press. DOI: 10.1201/9781003177432

Mbiatem, J., Taghipour, A., & Canel-Depitre, B. (2018, August). Supplier selection approaches for decision makers. In *Proceedings of the 8th International Conference on Information Communication and Management* (pp. 108–112).

Merimi, M., & Taghipour, A. (2021). Accelerating the digitalization of the supply chain: An empirical research about COVID-19 crisis. In *Digitalization of decentralized supply chains during global crises* (pp. 1–24). IGI Global Scientific Publishing. DOI: 10.4018/978-1-7998-6874-3.ch001

Nadia, E. N., Beatrice, C. D., & Atour, T. (2020). Luxury hotels' eco-friendly activities and customers' preferences and willingness to pay for green hotels. *Journal of Advanced Management Science*, *8*(1), 1–24.

Ponputtha, W., Wannapiroon, P., & Nilsook, P. (2021). Creative history learning model using digital storytelling through cloud learning to enhance analytical thinking. International Journal of E-Education, e-Business, e-. *Management Learning*, *11*(2), 42–50. DOI: 10.17706/ijeeee.2021.11.2.42-50

Pour Mohammadi, M., Ghorbani, R., & Taghipour, A. (2014). Factors affecting the price of housing in the city of Tabriz using hedonic model. *Geographical Planning of Space Quarterly Journal*, *3*(9), 83–104.

Radhoui, H., Taghipour, A., & Canel-Depitre, B. (2019). The distribution and pickup of goods: A literature review and survey. In Hierarchical planning and information sharing techniques in supply chain management (pp. 46–85). DOI: 10.4018/978-1-5225-7299-2.ch002

Radhoui, H., Taghipour, A., & Canel-Depitre, B. (2021). Mixed delivery and pickup vehicle routing problem with limited flow and assignment of drones in an urban network. In Demand forecasting and order planning in supply chains and humanitarian logistics (pp. 225–249). DOI: 10.4018/978-1-7998-3805-0.ch008

Ren, Z., Taghipour, A., & Canel-Depitre, B. (2016, October). Information sharing in supply chain under uncertainty. In *Proceedings of the 6th International Conference on Information Communication and Management (ICICM)* (pp. 67–71). IEEE. DOI: 10.1109/INFOCOMAN.2016.7784217

Sahraoui, A., Tran, N. K., Tliche, Y., Kacem, A., & Taghipour, A. (2023). Examining ICT innovation for sustainable terminal operations in developing countries: A case study of the port of Radès in Tunisia. *Sustainability (Basel)*, *15*(11), 9123. DOI: 10.3390/su15119123

Taghipour, A. (2009). Évaluation de la collaboration dans une chaîne d'approvisionnement. *Revue Française de Gestion Industrielle*, *28*(1), 26–42. DOI: 10.53102/2009.28.01.746

Taghipour, A. (Ed.). (2020). *Demand forecasting and order planning in supply chains and humanitarian logistics*. IGI Global.

Taghipour, A. (Ed.). (2021). *Digitalization of decentralized supply chains during global crises*. IGI Global. DOI: 10.4018/978-1-7998-6874-3

Taghipour, A. (Ed.). (2022). *Blockchain applications in cryptocurrency for technological evolution*. IGI Global. DOI: 10.4018/978-1-6684-6247-8

Taghipour, A. (Ed.). (2023). *Government impact on sustainable and responsible supply chain management*. IGI Global. DOI: 10.4018/978-1-6684-9062-4

Taghipour, A. (2024). Big data: The new gold mine for supermarkets. In *Applications of new technology in operations and supply chain management* (pp. 98–106). IGI Global Scientific Publishing. DOI: 10.4018/979-8-3693-1578-1.ch006

Taghipour, A., Abed, M., & Zoghlami, N. (2015, May). Design for remanufacturing respecting reverse logistics processes: A review. In *Proceedings of the 4th International Conference on Advanced Logistics and Transport (ICALT)* (pp. 299–304). IEEE. DOI: 10.1109/ICAdLT.2015.7136602

Taghipour, A., Belrhazi, Y., & Damoum, N. (2023). Resilient sustainable supply chain management. In *Government impact on sustainable and responsible supply chain management* (pp. 33–47). IGI Global Scientific Publishing. DOI: 10.4018/978-1-6684-9062-4.ch003

Taghipour, A., & Beneteau-Piet, C. (2020). Sustainable supply chain management performance. *International Journal of Innovation, Management and Technology*, *11*(6), 165–169. DOI: 10.18178/ijimt.2020.11.6.897

Taghipour, A., Fooladvand, A., Khazaei, M., & Ramezani, M. (2023). Criteria clustering and supplier segmentation based on sustainable shared value using BWM and PROMETHEE. *Sustainability (Basel)*, *15*(11), 8670. DOI: 10.3390/su15118670

Taghipour, A., & Frayret, J. M. (2013a). Coordination of operations planning in supply chains: A review. *International Journal of Business Performance and Supply Chain Modelling*, *5*(3), 272–307. DOI: 10.1504/IJBPSCM.2013.055729

Taghipour, A., & Frayret, J. M. (2013b, May). An algorithm to improve operations planning in decentralized supply chains. In *Proceedings of the International Conference on Advanced Logistics and Transport* (pp. 100–103). IEEE. DOI: 10.1109/ICAdLT.2013.6568442

Taghipour, A., & Lu, X. (2025a). Advancing supply chain innovation: Theoretical foundations, contemporary developments, and future directions. In *Ecological and human dimensions of AI-based supply chain* (pp. 1–26). IGI Global Scientific Publishing. DOI: 10.4018/979-8-3693-7478-8.ch001

Taghipour, A., & Lu, X. (2025b). Navigating the artificial intelligence era: Impacts of artificial intelligence on youth critical thinking, career paths, and ethical challenges. In *Ecological and human dimensions of AI-based supply chain* (pp. 49–68). IGI Global Scientific Publishing. DOI: 10.4018/979-8-3693-7478-8.ch003

Taghipour, A., Lu, X., Derradji, M., & Sow, A. D. (2022, July). The impact of digitalization on supply chain management: A literature review. In *Proceedings of the 12th International Conference on Information Communication and Management* (pp. 75–78). DOI: 10.1145/3551690.3551702

Taghipour, A., Lu, X., & Smahi, M. (2022). Opportunities and challenges for society 5.0 in procurement. In *Blockchain technology in supply chain management for society 5.0* (pp. 91–100). CRC Press. DOI: 10.1201/9781003177432-9

Taghipour, A., & Lu, X. W. (2023, August). Green supply chain management: A guide. In Proceedings of the International Conference on Applied Economics and Business (pp. 315–328). Springer Nature Switzerland.

Taghipour, A., Rouyendegh, B. D., Ünal, A., & Piya, S. (2022). Selection of suppliers for speech recognition products in IT projects by combining techniques with an integrated fuzzy MCDM. *Sustainability (Basel), 14*(3), 1777. DOI: 10.3390/su14031777

Taghipour, A., Sohrabi, A., Ghaedi, M., & Khazaei, M. (2023). A robust vaccine supply chain model in pandemics: Case of COVID-19 in Iran. *Computers & Industrial Engineering, 183*, 109465. DOI: 10.1016/j.cie.2023.109465

Tliche, Y., Taghipour, A., & Canel-Depitre, B. (2019). Downstream demand inference in decentralized supply chains. *European Journal of Operational Research, 274*(1), 65–77. DOI: 10.1016/j.ejor.2018.09.034

Tliche, Y., Taghipour, A., Mahfod-Leroux, J., & Vosooghidizaji, M. (2023). Collaborative bullwhip effect-oriented bi-objective optimization for inference-based weighted moving average forecasting in decentralized supply chain. *International Journal of Information Systems and Supply Chain Management, 16*(1), 1–37. DOI: 10.4018/IJISSCM.316168

Vosooghidizaji, M., Taghipour, A., & Canel-Depitre, B. (2019). A literature review on information asymmetry in supply chain coordination. *International Journal of Production Research, 58*(6), 1–6.

Vosooghidizaji, M., Taghipour, A., & Canel-Depitre, B. (2020). Information asymmetry in supply chain coordination: State of the art. *Journal of Industrial and Intelligent Information, 8*(2), 38–43. DOI: 10.18178/jiii.8.2.38-43

XiaoWen, L., & Atour, T.XiaoWen. (2025). Knowledge-driven digital innovation in supply chains: An organizational perspective. *Journal of Innovation & Knowledge, 10*(5), 100787. DOI: 10.1016/j.jik.2025.100787

Zoghlami, N., Taghipour, A., Merlo, C., & Abed, M. (2016). Management of divergent production network using decentralised multi-level capacitated lot-sizing models. *International Journal of Shipping and Transport Logistics*, *8*(5), 590–604. DOI: 10.1504/IJSTL.2016.078686

Chapter 10
Enhancing Supply Chain Performance Through Strategic Manufacturer–Distributor Collaboration

Alaa Eddine El Moussaoui
http://orcid.org/0000-0002-5749-7682
EMIO, LIREEM Laboratory, Higher School of Technology of Nador, Mohammed First University, Oujda, Morocco

Taoufiq El Moussaoui
Polydisciplinary Faculty of Sidi Bennour, Chouaib Doukkali University, El Jadida, Morocco

ABSTRACT

This chapter investigates the role of manufacturer–distributor collaboration in improving supply chain performance within Morocco's fresh and frozen food sector, where perishability and demand uncertainty create persistent coordination challenges. Based on a qualitative case analysis, the findings show that joint decision-making on pricing, promotions, and inventory, reinforced by shared information systems, enhances sales outcomes, inventory flow, service reliability, and customer satisfaction. Rather than being an initial condition, trust is found to emerge gradually through formal coordination tools and continuous performance follow-up. The chapter ultimately frames collaboration as a capability that develops over time and emphasizes the importance of gradual, context-adapted collaboration strategies for SMEs operating in emerging economies.

DOI: 10.4018/979-8-3373-6455-1.ch010

1. INTRODUCTION

The agri-food sector plays a central role in national economies, yet it operates under persistent pressure to reconcile cost efficiency, product availability, quality requirements, and sustainability objectives (Govindan, 2018). These pressures are particularly visible in fresh and frozen food supply chains, where perishability, demand variability, and strict service requirements increase coordination complexity. In such environments, isolated firm-level optimization is rarely sufficient; instead, performance increasingly depends on how effectively firms coordinate across organizational boundaries. This reality has brought manufacturer–distributor collaboration to the forefront of supply-chain strategy, not only as an operational tool but as a strategic capability shaping competitiveness and resilience (Duong and Chong, 2020 ; Aouadni et al, 2024).

While collaboration is widely recognized as beneficial, its performance implications are not automatic. Prior studies show that collaboration can improve information sharing, reduce uncertainty, and support better inventory and replenishment decisions, yet they also highlight coordination costs, power asymmetries, and governance challenges. In practice, collaboration outcomes depend on how relational and contractual mechanisms are combined, how information systems are integrated, and how incentives are aligned between partners. These issues are particularly salient in food supply chains, where time sensitivity and quality risks magnify the consequences of misalignment.

In Morocco, the food industry constitutes a strategic pillar for food security, employment, and regional development. However, the sector is characterized by structural fragmentation, uneven infrastructure development, and heterogeneous managerial practices (El Moussaoui et al., 2022a). These features create coordination frictions between upstream and downstream actors, often resulting in inventory imbalances, service variability, and limited visibility across the chain. As a result, collaboration between manufacturers and distributors is not merely a strategic choice but frequently a necessity for operational continuity and market responsiveness.

Existing collaborations in the Moroccan context increasingly go beyond transactional exchanges. They involve joint planning, demand forecasting, promotion alignment, and coordinated inventory decisions. Manufacturers may share production and stock information, while distributors provide market intelligence and demand signals (Omar et al., 2019). Digital tools such as EDI, VMI, and CPFR further expand these possibilities by improving data timeliness and coordination accuracy (Patil et al., 2024 ; El Moussaoui, 2024). Nevertheless, technology alone does not guarantee improved performance; organizational readiness, trust, and governance structures remain decisive.

Despite growing practical interest, empirical research on manufacturer–distributor collaboration in emerging food markets remains limited. Much of the existing literature focuses on large developed economies or examines collaboration frameworks in a normative or conceptual manner. Less attention has been paid to how collaboration mechanisms operate in emerging-market contexts where institutional environments, relational norms, and resource constraints differ. In addition, prior research often documents collaboration practices without systematically linking them to observable performance dimensions or governance choices.

This chapter addresses these gaps by examining manufacturer–distributor collaboration in the Moroccan fresh and frozen products sector through a case-based analysis. Drawing on Resource-Based View and Transaction Cost Economics perspectives, the chapter explores how resource complementarities, governance arrangements, and information-sharing practices interact to shape supply-chain performance. Rather than treating collaboration as inherently beneficial, the analysis considers the conditions under which it contributes to operational and relational outcomes.

The chapter makes three contributions. First, it provides empirical insight into collaboration dynamics in an under-studied emerging-market food context. Second, it connects collaboration practices to performance dimensions relevant to perishable supply chains, including service reliability and inventory management. Third, it illustrates how RBV and TCE mechanisms can be observed in real inter-firm relationships. The remainder of the chapter reviews relevant literature, outlines the methodological approach, and discusses findings and implications for both researchers and practitioners.

2. LITERATURE REVIEW

2.1 Inter-Firm Collaboration in the Food Supply Chain: Concepts and Frameworks

Inter-firm collaboration has become an indispensable strategic mechanism for enhancing the performance, resilience, and sustainability of food supply chains, particularly in contexts characterized by high product perishability and volatile demand patterns (Govindan, 2018; Taghipour et al, 2020 ; Taghipour and Beneteau-Piet, 2022 ; Duong et al., 2024). In contemporary supply networks, manufacturers and distributors are no longer isolated actors merely performing transactional roles; they are interdependent partners whose coordinated decisions significantly influence the efficiency, competitiveness, and adaptability of the entire chain. The literature emphasizes that collaboration extends far beyond operational alignment, such as synchronized deliveries or inventory adjustments. It encompasses a multidimensional strategic engagement that includes joint planning, demand forecasting, marketing and promotional synchronization, and the integration of technological and logistical resources (Bejlegaard et al., 2021; Fawcett et al., 2021). Achieving such high-level collaboration requires firms to harmonize objectives, implement transparent communication channels, and develop mutual trust, particularly to mitigate challenges arising from market volatility, fragmented logistics networks, infrastructure constraints, and changing consumer preferences (Mattessich and Johnson, 2018; Han et al., 2021 ; El Moussaoui et al, 2025a). In Morocco, the specific characteristics of the food sector—including limited technological adoption and fragmented distribution networks—amplify these challenges but also create unique opportunities for carefully orchestrated partnerships (El Moussaoui et al., 2022b).

Several structured frameworks have been identified in the literature as critical enablers of effective collaboration (Table 1). Efficient Consumer Response (ECR), for instance, integrates product development, inventory replenishment, promotional planning, and store assortment strategies to optimize the flow of goods and information between manufacturers and distributors (Fernie, 2023; Zhang et al., 2023). By reducing stockouts, minimizing waste, and improving the consumer experience, ECR enhances supply chain responsiveness, particularly in perishable product categories, where timing and coordination are crucial (El Moussaoui et al, 2023a ; Govindaraj et al., 2024). Empirical studies in Morocco indicate that ECR adoption allows firms to synchronize supply with fluctuating demand, resulting in improved inventory management, reduced spoilage, and more agile promotional campaigns. Similarly, Vendor-Managed Inventory (VMI) shifts the responsibility for inventory monitoring and replenishment from distributors to manufacturers, who continuously track stock levels and proactively adjust production and distribution plans (Fang and Chen, 2022; Bahrampour et al., 2024). This system is particularly effective in emerging markets where storage limitations and demand unpredictability challenge conventional inventory practices (El Jaouhari et al., 2022 ; El Moussaoui et al, 2023b ; Ammar et al, 2024 ; Toufah et al, 2025). Furthermore, Collaborative Planning, Forecasting, and Replenishment (CPFR) extends the principles of VMI by emphasizing joint planning and forecasting, enabling both manufacturers and distributors to share critical market and operational information, anticipate demand fluctuations, and synchronize production and delivery schedules, thereby minimizing inefficiencies and improving service reliability (Lele and Ajmeri, 2024; Li, 2024 ; Da Silva et al., 2024).

Despite the demonstrated advantages, implementing these frameworks presents several challenges. Technological gaps, limited access to digital platforms, and divergences in organizational culture and strategic priorities can impede collaboration (Galvin et al., 2021 ; Melnyk et al., 2022 ; El Moussaoui, 2025b). Trust deficits are especially critical, as they may lead to opportunistic behaviors, misaligned expectations, and suboptimal performance outcomes (Leonidou et al., 2021). To address these barriers, relational governance mechanisms, including joint training programs, trust-building exercises, and standardized technological platforms, have been shown to facilitate effective information exchange, coordination, and collective problem-solving (Cheng and Sandfort, 2023; Rosário and Dias, 2023). In the Moroccan context, where informal agreements often complement formal contracts, relational mechanisms are particularly relevant, reinforcing the strategic value of trust and social capital in ensuring long-term collaboration success (El Moussaoui et al., 2022c).

From a theoretical standpoint, the Resource-Based View (RBV) and Transaction Cost Economics (TCE) provide complementary explanations for the mechanisms through which collaboration enhances supply chain performance. RBV emphasizes leveraging complementary resources and capabilities—such as production capacity, technological expertise, distribution networks, and market knowledge—that are distributed across partners to create a competitive advantage (El Nemar et al., 2022; Jyoti and Efpraxia, 2023 ; El Moussaoui et al, 2025c). In the Moroccan food sector, where access to such resources is often fragmented, collaboration offers a pathway for pooling capabilities to achieve operational and strategic synergies. TCE, on the other hand, focuses on designing governance structures that reduce transaction costs arising from uncertainty, risk, and opportunistic behavior, highlighting the importance of formal agreements, shared digital platforms, and structured communication protocols in sustaining successful partnerships (Um and Kim, 2019 ; Marjosola, 2021). Together, RBV and TCE offer a comprehensive perspective, positioning collaboration as a multi-dimensional construct where resource complementarities, governance efficiency, and relational quality collectively enhance supply chain resilience, responsiveness, and efficiency.

Table 1. Key Collaborative Frameworks in Food Supply Chains

Collaboration Type	Description	Key Benefits	References
Efficient Consumer Response (ECR)	Integrates product development, promotions, inventory replenishment, and store assortment	Reduces stockouts, minimizes operational inefficiencies, improves customer experience, addresses perishability	Radhoui et al. (2019) ; Fernie (2023); Lu and Taghipour (2023) ; Zhang et al. (2023) ; Govindaraj et al. (2024)
Vendor-Managed Inventory (VMI)	Manufacturer monitors and replenishes distributor inventory	Optimizes inventory, reduces overstock/understock costs, improves responsiveness	Fang and Chen (2022); Bahrampour et al. (2024); El Jaouhari et al. (2022)
Collaborative Planning, Forecasting, Replenishment (CPFR)	Joint planning and forecasting to align production and distribution	Enhances demand accuracy, reduces stockouts, improves service levels	Zhang et al. (2022); Da Silva et al. (2024); Lele and Ajmeri (2024) ; El Moussaoui et al. (2025)
Resource-Based View (RBV)	Leverages complementary resources across partners	Encourages innovation, strengthens competitive positioning, fosters long-term partnerships	El Nemar et al. (2022) ; El Moussaoui et al. (2022)
Transaction Cost Economics (TCE)	Reduces costs of market exchanges via structured agreements	Minimizes coordination costs, reduces risks, encourages efficient governance	Marjosola (2021) ; El Moussaoui (2025)

2.2 Strategic Implementation of Inter-Firm Collaboration

Building on the conceptual foundations, the literature underscores that successful collaboration is contingent upon a structured and dynamic implementation process. Inter-firm partnerships are not self-executing; they require careful design, partner alignment, governance, and continuous monitoring (Bejlegaard et al., 2021; Duong et al., 2024 ; Taghipour et al, 2023 ; El Moussaoui, 2025 ; Taghipour and Lu, 2025). The process begins with an internal assessment of the firm's mission, vision, resources, capabilities, and organizational culture, identifying strengths that can be leveraged and gaps that may require external partnerships or capacity development. Simultaneously, firms must conduct a thorough market analysis to understand competitive positioning, customer expectations, and emerging trends. Resource gaps—whether technological, operational, or logistical—must be systematically addressed through internal development, outsourcing, or the selection of a complementary partner capable of delivering the missing capabilities (Omar et al., 2019 ; Leonidou et al., 2021).

The selection of the right partner is critical, requiring alignment in strategic vision, cultural compatibility, operational practices, and trust. Partners must agree on clear objectives, roles, responsibilities, and communication protocols to minimize misunderstandings and maximize the value of joint initiatives. Formalization through contracts, service level agreements, key performance indicators (KPIs), and shared digital platforms operationalizes these agreements, enabling real-time monitoring and collaborative problem-solving. Implementation further demands flexible allocation of resources, structured oversight, and iterative adaptation to changing market conditions, thus translating RBV and TCE principles into measurable improvements in supply chain performance (Marjosola, 2021 ; El Nemar et al., 2022 ; Taghipour, 2023 ; El Moussaoui et al, 2025). Common KPIs include inventory turnover, order fulfillment accuracy, lead time reduction, and customer satisfaction, which collectively measure the efficacy of the collaboration.

This multi-step strategic process is visually summarized in Table 2, which illustrates the cyclical nature of inter-firm collaboration, encompassing organizational assessment, partner selection, implementation and monitoring, and periodic evaluation to ensure long-term relevance.

Through this integrative approach, collaboration becomes a dynamic capability that evolves with experience, mutual learning, and adaptation. In emerging economies like Morocco, where institutional and infrastructural constraints remain, effectively implemented collaboration can yield substantial operational, competitive, and sustainability gains. By linking the theoretical insights and practical frameworks of collaboration to measurable outcomes, this review provides a direct bridge to the subsequent Research Methodology section, which investigates empirically how Moroccan manufacturers and distributors operationalize these collaborative strategies in practice.

Table 2. Steps for Strategic Implementation of Inter-Firm Collaboration

Step	Description
Internal Assessment	Evaluate mission, vision, capabilities, culture, and processes to identify collaboration potential
Market Analysis	Examine market demands, trends, competition, and customer expectations
Gap Identification	Determine resource, technological, or operational deficits and define the collaboration objective
Partner Selection	Identify a partner with complementary resources and compatible organizational culture
Trust & Expectation Alignment	Establish clear roles, responsibilities, and communication protocols
Formalize Collaboration	Negotiate contracts, KPIs, timelines, and governance mechanisms

continued on following page

Table 2. Continued

Step	Description
Implementation & Monitoring	Allocate resources, manage operational tasks, and track performance against KPIs
Periodic Evaluation	Review collaboration outcomes, adjust strategies, and ensure continued alignment with strategic goals

3. RESEARCH METHODOLOGY

This study adopts a qualitative, exploratory case study approach to investigate the dynamics of strategic collaboration between manufacturers and distributors in Morocco's fresh and frozen food sector. Recognizing the complexity and context-specific nature of inter-firm collaboration, the methodology emphasizes a holistic understanding of operational, strategic, and relational mechanisms, rather than a purely quantitative assessment of performance metrics. By focusing on two companies—a manufacturer and a distributor—the research captures real-world interactions, decision-making processes, and practical strategies that underpin successful partnerships, thereby linking empirical evidence with theoretical insights from RBV, TCE, and collaborative frameworks such as ECR, VMI, and CPFR.

In Table 3, we can see that the research design unfolds in sequential stages reflecting both operational realities and strategic imperatives. The first stage, context clarification, involves a thorough examination of the Moroccan fresh and frozen products market. This includes an analysis of seasonal demand fluctuations, competitive pressures, regulatory requirements, and consumer behavior patterns, along with an assessment of technological adoption and infrastructural constraints. Secondary data sources—such as industry reports, market surveys, and prior performance records of the participating firms—were collected to establish a solid understanding of market conditions and to identify structural challenges affecting collaboration effectiveness. This step ensures that subsequent research activities are firmly grounded in the realities of the local business environment, capturing both systemic and sector-specific factors shaping manufacturer–distributor interactions.

Building upon the contextual understanding, the operational diagnosis and process mapping stage focuses on capturing detailed insights into the companies' internal operations. Semi-structured interviews with senior managers, supply chain professionals, and operational staff allow the study to uncover decision-making protocols, logistical flows, inventory management practices, pricing strategies, and promotional campaigns. In parallel, process mapping exercises are employed to visually depict operational flows between the manufacturer and distributor, highlighting potential bottlenecks, misalignments, and inefficiencies. This stage enables the identification of critical points where strategic misalignment or resource gaps can disrupt collaboration, providing a concrete basis for designing practical improvements.

Following diagnosis, the strategy alignment phase seeks to reconcile the strategic objectives of both companies and to define shared goals for collaboration. Workshops and guided discussions facilitate alignment on pricing models, inventory policies, and promotional planning, ensuring that both firms contribute complementary resources and capabilities to the partnership. Special attention is given to the integration of relational factors—trust, transparency, and mutual understanding—which are critical in contexts such as Morocco, where informal agreements and social capital often complement formal contractual structures. By explicitly linking strategic objectives with operational capabilities, the alignment phase operationalizes the principles of RBV and TCE in a practical setting.

The subsequent collaborative implementation phase operationalizes improvements identified in prior stages. This involves jointly redesigning pricing strategies, establishing real-time inventory monitoring systems, and coordinating promotional campaigns to maximize efficiency and responsiveness. Key performance indicators (KPIs) are defined collaboratively to measure outcomes such as inventory turnover, order accuracy, stockout frequency, and customer satisfaction. Emphasis is placed on flexible governance mechanisms and iterative learning, allowing partners to adjust operational protocols as market conditions, demand patterns, or supply chain constraints evolve. This dynamic approach ensures that collaboration is not static but continuously adapts to new challenges and opportunities, embodying the concept of collaboration as a strategic capability.

Finally, the evaluation and feedback phase assesses the effectiveness of implemented strategies against the pre-defined KPIs. The study employs a mixed-method evaluation strategy, combining quantitative performance data with qualitative insights from interviews to obtain a comprehensive understanding of collaborative success. Feedback loops enable both companies to refine processes, address emerging challenges, and recalibrate strategic objectives, thereby ensuring the long-term sustainability and resilience of the partnership. This evaluation is also linked to the broader research aim of providing empirical evidence on how manufacturer–distributor collaboration can enhance supply chain performance in emerging economies, creating a direct connection to subsequent analysis in the research findings.

Table 3. Sequential Stages of Research Methodology for Manufacturer–Distributor Collaboration Study

Stage	Objective	Activities & Methods	Outputs
Context Analysis	Understand market context and structural challenges.	Review market trends, regulations, consumer behavior, technology use; collect secondary data (reports, surveys, firm records).	Insight into market conditions and factors affecting collaboration.
Operational Diagnosis	Identify operational flows, bottlenecks, and inefficiencies.	Semi-structured interviews; process mapping of logistics, inventory, pricing, promotions.	Clear picture of operational gaps and misalignments.
Strategy Alignment	Align strategic goals and integrate relational factors.	Workshops and discussions on pricing, inventory, promotions; focus on trust and transparency.	Shared objectives and operational alignment guided by RBV/TCE concepts.
Collaborative Implementation	Apply improvements and monitor performance.	Jointly redesign strategies, implement inventory monitoring, coordinate promotions; define KPIs (turnover, accuracy, stockouts, satisfaction).	Adaptive collaboration, operational improvements, KPIs in place.
Evaluation & Feedback	Measure effectiveness and ensure sustainability.	Mixed-method assessment using KPIs and interviews; feedback loops for refinement.	Understanding of success, improved processes, resilient partnership.

4. RESULTS AND DISCUSSION

4.1 Strategic Alignment, Pricing, and Promotional Integration

The analysis of the manufacturer-distributor partnership in Morocco's fresh and frozen products sector highlighted that misalignment in pricing and promotional strategies was a major impediment to operational efficiency and profitability. Initially, both companies operated independently, with the manufacturer setting wholesale prices without standardized guidelines and the distributor adjusting retail prices reactively based on market demand or retailer pressure. This lack of coordination not only reduced profit margins but also generated friction between the partners, affecting trust and operational coherence. By implementing a standardized pricing framework with mutually agreed minimum margins and synchronizing promotional campaigns, both companies created a shared strategic vision that enhanced market responsiveness and reduced conflicts. Coordinated marketing efforts, including volume-based incentives and joint sales campaigns, led to more effective market penetration, improved brand consistency, and higher customer satisfaction.

Interviews with employees and managers revealed that the introduction of these measures fostered transparency, clarified roles, and facilitated smoother communication between the firms. These findings align with the Resource-Based View (RBV), which emphasizes leveraging complementary resources and capabilities to achieve competitive advantage, and with Transaction Cost Economics (TCE), which underscores formal agreements and governance mechanisms as tools to reduce coordination costs and risk. The quantitative improvements in key performance indicators reflect the tangible benefits of strategic alignment (Table 4).

Table 4. KPI Comparison Before and After Strategic Alignment

KPI	Before Collaboration	After Strategic Alignment	Improvement (%)
Sales Growth	8%	15%	+87.5%
Inventory Turnover	4.2	6.1	+45.2%
Stockouts per Month	12	4	-66.7%
Order Accuracy	85%	96%	+12.9%
Customer Satisfaction	70%	88%	+25.7%

4.2 Inventory Management, Technological Integration, and Operational Efficiency

Prior to the study, both organizations faced significant challenges in managing inventory due to disconnected manual systems and lack of real-time data visibility. Stockouts, overstocking, and delays in order fulfillment were frequent, resulting in lost sales and reduced customer satisfaction. Implementing a cloud-based real-time inventory management system allowed both the manufacturer and distributor to monitor stock levels continuously, forecast demand accurately, and adjust replenishment proactively. The integration of order processing and inventory management platforms also standardized product codes, reducing errors in billing and order fulfillment, and accelerating delivery timelines.

This operational integration enhanced decision-making and collaboration across departments, streamlining communication between teams and ensuring alignment with strategic objectives. The improvements are quantitatively reflected in operational KPIs (Table 5), demonstrating that technology adoption and process standardization are critical enablers of collaboration in emerging economies, where infrastructure fragmentation and market volatility are prevalent.

Table 5. Operational KPIs Before and After Technological Integration

KPI	Before Integration	After Integration	Improvement (%)
Order Processing Time (days)	5.6	3.1	-44.6%
Inventory Accuracy	78%	95%	+21.8%
Emergency Orders per Month	9	2	-77.8%
Lead Time for Delivery (days)	7.2	4.3	-40.3%

4.3 Trust, Relational Governance, and Collaborative Culture

Trust and relational governance emerged as foundational elements for sustaining long-term collaboration. At the beginning of the study, both firms expressed concerns about commitment, equitable profit sharing, and transparency in decision-making. Through structured communication mechanisms, performance monitoring, and joint review meetings, trust gradually developed, enabling more open discussions and collaborative problem-solving. Employees reported increased confidence in joint decision-making, while managers observed fewer conflicts and more cooperative behavior.

The creation of a results-driven culture supported by key performance indicators (KPIs) allowed the companies to measure progress objectively, reinforce accountability, and adapt strategies dynamically. KPIs such as order accuracy, customer satisfaction, and inventory turnover confirmed that trust-building interventions translated into measurable operational outcomes (Table 6). The findings underscore that relational mechanisms are especially crucial in emerging economies, where informal agreements often complement formal contracts and social capital plays a critical role in facilitating collaboration.

Table 6. KPIs Reflecting Trust and Relational Governance Outcomes

KPI	Before Trust-building	After Trust-building	Improvement (%)
Customer Satisfaction	70%	88%	+25.7%
Order Accuracy	85%	96%	+12.9%
Conflict Incidents per Month	6	1	-83.3%
Response Time to Issues (days)	4.8	2.3	-52.1%

4.4 Performance Monitoring, Continuous Improvement, and Long-Term Sustainability

The study further highlights the role of continuous monitoring and iterative improvement in reinforcing the collaboration. By establishing KPIs across strategic, operational, and relational dimensions, the firms could evaluate performance comprehensively and implement corrective actions promptly. The integration of standardized reporting and periodic performance reviews facilitated a data-driven culture, supporting sustained operational gains and strategic alignment. Table 7 synthesizes the overall performance outcomes across all dimensions, demonstrating the cumulative impact of strategic alignment, operational integration, and trust-building initiatives.

Table 7. Comprehensive KPI Overview Across Collaboration Dimensions

Dimension	KPI	Before Collaboration	After Collaboration	Improvement (%)
Strategic Alignment	Sales Growth	8%	15%	+87.5%
Operational Efficiency	Inventory Turnover	4.2	6.1	+45.2%
Operational Efficiency	Order Processing Time	5.6	3.1	-44.6%
Relational Governance	Customer Satisfaction	70%	88%	+25.7%
Relational Governance	Conflict Incidents	6	1	-83.3%

The results confirm that inter-firm collaboration in Morocco's fresh and frozen products sector yields both qualitative and quantitative improvements when supported by strategic alignment, operational optimization, technological integration, and relational governance. Linking RBV and TCE theoretical perspectives with practical interventions provides a framework for designing, managing, and sustaining effective partnerships in emerging economies.

5. THEORETICAL, MANAGERIAL, AND PRACTICAL IMPLICATIONS

5.1 Theoretical Implications

This research contributes to the literature on inter-firm collaboration and supply chain management by providing empirically grounded insights into how strategic alignment, operational integration, and relational governance jointly shape collaborative performance in an emerging economy context. While prior studies have extensively examined collaboration through isolated lenses—such as pricing coordination, inventory optimization, or trust-building—this study advances existing knowledge by demonstrating the interdependence of these dimensions within a single, coherent collaborative framework. The findings show that collaboration effectiveness cannot be fully explained by operational efficiency alone but emerges from the dynamic interaction between strategic alignment, technological integration, and relational mechanisms.

From a theoretical standpoint, the results reinforce the relevance of the Resource-Based View (RBV) by illustrating how complementary resources—such as market knowledge, logistical capabilities, and relational capital—can be combined across organizational boundaries to generate sustained competitive advantages. The manufacturer–distributor partnership analyzed in this study demonstrates that shared access to information systems, coordinated pricing strategies, and joint promotional planning function as strategic resources that are difficult to imitate when embedded within long-term relational arrangements. At the same time, the findings extend Transaction Cost Economics (TCE) by showing that formal mechanisms (e.g., standardized pricing frameworks and KPIs) and informal governance mechanisms (e.g., trust, transparency, and repeated interactions) are not substitutes but rather complementary tools for reducing uncertainty and coordination costs.

Moreover, the study contributes to the literature on performance measurement in collaborative supply chains by emphasizing the role of continuous monitoring through KPIs as an iterative learning mechanism rather than a static control tool. By integrating strategic, operational, and relational indicators, the research challenges traditional models that conceptualize collaboration as a fixed contractual arrangement and instead supports a dynamic perspective in which collaboration evolves through feedback, learning, and adaptation. This perspective is particularly relevant for emerging markets, where volatility, resource constraints, and institutional complexity require flexible and adaptive collaboration models.

5.2 Managerial Implications

From a managerial perspective, the study offers several actionable insights for firms seeking to establish or strengthen inter-business collaborations, particularly in sectors characterized by demand volatility and operational complexity such as fresh and frozen food products. One of the most important managerial lessons is the critical role of strategic alignment at the early stages of collaboration. The findings clearly indicate that misaligned pricing policies and uncoordinated promotional activities not only erode margins but also undermine trust and long-term partnership stability. Managers are therefore encouraged to jointly define pricing rules, margin thresholds, and promotional calendars to avoid reactive decision-making and recurring conflicts.

The results also highlight the strategic value of technological integration as an enabler of collaboration rather than a purely operational tool. Managers should view investments in cloud-based inventory management systems and integrated order-processing platforms as strategic decisions that support transparency, responsiveness, and shared decision-making. Real-time data visibility significantly improves demand forecasting, reduces emergency orders, and enhances service reliability, thereby strengthening both operational performance and relational confidence between partners.

Equally important, the study underscores that trust does not emerge automatically but must be actively managed through structured communication, shared performance metrics, and joint review mechanisms. Managers should institutionalize regular coordination meetings, performance dashboards, and feedback loops to ensure alignment and accountability. The use of KPIs across strategic, operational, and relational dimensions helps shift the collaboration from an informal, person-dependent relationship to a professionally governed partnership capable of withstanding personnel changes and market shocks.

5.3 Practical Implications

At a practical level, this research provides concrete guidance for firms operating in emerging markets, where supply chains are often fragmented and resource constraints are significant. The study demonstrates that even in contexts with limited technological and financial resources, meaningful improvements in performance can be achieved through progressive and targeted collaborative initiatives. Rather than adopting complex and costly frameworks in their entirety, firms can prioritize high-impact interventions such as shared inventory visibility, standardized pricing agreements, and jointly defined KPIs.

For practitioners in the Moroccan fresh and frozen products sector, the findings suggest that collaborative pricing and promotion strategies can significantly enhance market positioning while reducing operational friction. Joint promotional campaigns not only align marketing messages but also distribute risks and rewards more equitably between partners. Similarly, the adoption of shared inventory management practices helps reduce stockouts and overstocking, which are particularly costly in perishable goods supply chains.

The study also highlights the importance of operational feasibility, especially for small and medium-sized enterprises (SMEs). While best practices such as CPFR are widely promoted in the literature, their implementation often exceeds the technical and organizational capacities of SMEs. This research shows that collaboration frameworks must be adapted to the specific constraints of firms, emphasizing gradual implementation, capacity building, and pragmatic solutions rather than idealized models. By doing so, firms can improve resilience, responsiveness, and sustainability without overextending their resources.

6. CONCLUSION

This study examined inter-business collaboration within Morocco's fresh and frozen products sector through an in-depth case study of a manufacturer–distributor partnership. Building on an integrated review of the literature and grounded in established theoretical perspectives such as RBV and TCE, the research proposed and applied a structured methodological approach to analyze how collaboration can be designed, implemented, and sustained in a challenging and competitive environment. The findings demonstrate that collaboration effectiveness depends not on isolated initiatives but on the coherent alignment of strategic objectives, operational processes, technological systems, and relational governance mechanisms.

The case study highlights that successful collaboration requires a systematic yet flexible process, in which key stages—context clarification, operational diagnosis, process mapping, strategic alignment, implementation, and evaluation—are followed while allowing for adaptation to firm-specific constraints. Although the overall structure of collaboration can be standardized, the execution of each stage inevitably varies depending on organizational capabilities, market conditions, and resource availability. This reinforces the idea that collaboration is not a one-size-fits-all solution but a context-dependent managerial practice.

The research further emphasizes the central role of trust and transparency in sustaining collaboration over time. In the examined case, trust did not precede collaboration but emerged progressively through structured processes, shared performance indicators, and repeated interactions. This finding addresses an important gap in the literature, which often acknowledges the importance of trust without providing concrete guidance on how it can be operationalized. The study shows that trust can be actively cultivated through formal mechanisms such as KPIs, joint planning, and integrated systems, which create predictability and mutual confidence.

Finally, the study sheds light on the specific challenges faced by SMEs in implementing advanced collaborative practices. Limitations in IT capabilities, process engineering expertise, and financial resources can significantly hinder the adoption of comprehensive frameworks such as CPFR. The case demonstrates that collaboration strategies must therefore balance strategic ambition with operational realism. By adopting incremental, resource-sensitive approaches, SMEs can still achieve substantial improvements in performance, resilience, and competitiveness.

Overall, this research contributes both theoretically and practically to the understanding of inter-firm collaboration in emerging economies. It offers a robust and adaptable framework that can inform future academic research while providing managers with concrete guidance for designing effective and sustainable collaborative relationships in complex supply chain environments.

REFERENCES

Ammar, A., Amahmoud, H., El Menzhi, K., Mkik, M., Hebaz, A., & Eddine, E. M. A. (2024, May). Critical Analysis of Logistics Transformation in Morocco Under The Auspices of Artificial Intelligence: Government Perspectives From the perspective of Innovative and Technology Driven Public Management. In 2024 IEEE 15th International Colloquium on Logistics and Supply Chain Management (LOGISTIQUA) (pp. 1-9). IEEE.

Aouadni, S., Aouadni, I., & Taghipour, A. (2024). Using ordinal priority approach with confidence-level measurement for third-party logistics provider selection in the tunisian healthcare sector. In *Applications of New Technology in Operations and Supply Chain Management* (pp. 404–429). IGI Global. DOI: 10.4018/979-8-3693-1578-1.ch020

Bahrampour, N., Seifbarghy, M., & Pasandideh, S. H. R. (2024). Supply chain management under VMI strategy using internet of things and smart contracts. *Neural Computing & Applications*, •••, 1–35.

Bejlegaard, M., Sarivan, I. M., & Waehrens, B. V. (2021). The influence of digital technologies on supply chain coordination strategies. *Journal of Global Operations and Strategic Sourcing*, *14*(4), 636–658. DOI: 10.1108/JGOSS-11-2019-0063

Cheng, Y., & Sandfort, J. (2023). Trust, power, and organizational routines: Exploring government's intentional tactics to renew relationships with nonprofits serving historically marginalized communities. *Public Administration Review*, *83*(3), 570–586. DOI: 10.1111/puar.13596

Da Silva, G. A. F. R., Baierle, I. C., Gomes, L. D. C., Correa, R. G. D. F., & Peres, F. A. P. (2024). A Comprehensive Roadmap for Connecting Industry 4.0 Technologies to the Basic Model of Collaborative Planning, Forecasting, and Replenishment (CPFR). *Administrative Sciences*, *14*(6), 108. DOI: 10.3390/admsci14060108

Duong, L. N. K., & Chong, J. (2020). Supply chain collaboration in the presence of disruptions: A literature review. *International Journal of Production Research*, *58*(11), 3488–3507. DOI: 10.1080/00207543.2020.1712491

Duong, L. N. K., Kumar, V., & He, Q. (2024). Collaboration for the sustainable food supply chain: A bibliometric analysis. *Business Strategy and the Environment*.

El Jaouhari, A., Alhilali, Z., Arif, J., Fellaki, S., Amejwal, M., & Azzouz, K. (2022). Demand forecasting application with regression and IoT based inventory management system: A case study of a semiconductor manufacturing company. *International Journal of Engineering Research in Africa*, *60*, 189–210. DOI: 10.4028/p-8ntq24

El Moussaoui, A. E. (2024). Unlocking the drivers behind logistics service providers' participation in Morocco's logistics clusters. *Arab Gulf Journal of Scientific Research, 42*(4), 2086–2102. DOI: 10.1108/AGJSR-07-2023-0343

El Moussaoui, A. E. (2025a). Predicting E-Consumer Preferences for Collection and Delivery Points Using Deep Learning. In Ecological and Human Dimensions of AI-Based Supply Chain (pp. 395-412). IGI Global Scientific Publishing.

El Moussaoui, A. E. (2025c). Impact of logistics pooling on reduction of CO2 emissions in last-mile logistics. Management & Sustainability. *An Arab Review, 4*(2), 383–401.

El Moussaoui, A. E. (2025d). Factors influencing the entry of logistics service providers (LSPs) into the logistics clusters: A case study of Casablanca city. Management & Sustainability. *An Arab Review, 4*(4), 611–627. DOI: 10.1108/MSAR-06-2024-0043

El Moussaoui, A. E., Benbba, B., & El Andaloussi, Z. (2023a). Impact of logistics performance on the store image, consumer satisfaction and loyalty: A quantitative case study. *Arab Gulf Journal of Scientific Research, 41*(3), 226–239. DOI: 10.1108/AGJSR-09-2022-0201

El Moussaoui, A. E., Benbba, B., Jaegler, A., & El Andaloussi, Z. (2022c, May). How to improve the urban logistics sector in large cities of developing countries: The case of Casablanca. In 2022 14th international colloquium of logistics and supply chain management (LOGISTIQUA) (pp. 1-6). IEEE.

El Moussaoui, A. E., Benbba, B., Jaegler, A., & El Andaloussi, Z. (2022d, May). City logistics: An evolutionary, successful & collaborative city. In 2022 14th international colloquium of logistics and supply chain management (LOGISTIQUA) (pp. 1-7). IEEE.

El Moussaoui, A. E., Benbba, B., Jaegler, A., El Andaloussi, Z., & El Amrani, L. (2022b, May). Last mile logistics: Challenges & improvement ways. In 2022 14th international colloquium of logistics and supply chain management (LOGISTIQUA) (pp. 1-7). IEEE.

El Moussaoui, A. E., Benbba, B., Jaegler, A., El Moussaoui, T., El Andaloussi, Z., & Chakir, L. (2023b). Consumer perceptions of online shopping and willingness to use pick-up points: A case study of Morocco. *Sustainability (Basel), 15*(9), 7405. DOI: 10.3390/su15097405

El Moussaoui, A. E., El Moussaoui, T., Benbba, B., Chakir, L., Jaegler, A., & El Andaloussi, Z. (2025b). Sustainable effects of information sharing between distribution logistics actors: A qualitative case study. *Environment, Development and Sustainability*, *27*(5), 12305–12323. DOI: 10.1007/s10668-023-04387-3

El Moussaoui, A. E., El Moussaoui, T., Benbba, B., Jaegler, A., & El Andaloussi, Z. (2022a). Understanding the choice of collection & delivery point by the E-consumer via a machine learning model: Moroccan case study. *Procedia Computer Science*, *210*, 204–211. DOI: 10.1016/j.procs.2022.10.138

El Moussaoui, A. E., Mizani, M. E., & Benlakouiri, A. (2025e, April). RFID Technology in Logistics: A Catalyst for Efficiency. In International Conference on Connected Objects and Artificial Intelligence (pp. 707-712). Cham: Springer Nature Switzerland.

El Moussaoui, A. E., Mizani, M. E., & Benlakouiri, A. (2025f, April). Transformation of Logistics in Electronic Subcontracting: A Focus on SMEs Supply Chains. In International Conference on Connected Objects and Artificial Intelligence (pp. 700-706). Cham: Springer Nature Switzerland.

El Moussaoui, T., Chakir, L., & El Moussaoui, A. E. (2025g). Exploring Information Technology (IT) Acceptance Among Supply Chain Stakeholders in Morocco's Pharmaceutical Industry. In Ecological and Human Dimensions of AI-Based Supply Chain (pp. 245-270). IGI Global Scientific Publishing.

El Nemar, S., El-Chaarani, H., Dandachi, I., & Castellano, S. (2022). Resource-based view and sustainable advantage: A framework for SMEs. *Journal of Strategic Marketing*, •••, 1–24.

Fang, X., & Chen, H. C. (2022). Using vendor management inventory system for goods inventory management in IoT manufacturing. *Enterprise Information Systems*, *16*(7), 1885743. DOI: 10.1080/17517575.2021.1885743

Fawcett, S. E., Fawcett, A. M., Knemeyer, A. M., Brockhaus, S., & Webb, G. S. (2021). Overcoming the collaborative challenge: Commitment as a super-ordinate enabler of value co-creation. *International Journal of Physical Distribution & Logistics Management*, *51*(9), 1022–1047. DOI: 10.1108/IJPDLM-12-2020-0390

Fernie, J. (2023). Relationships in the supply chain. In *Logistics and retail management insights into current practice and trends from leading experts* (pp. 23–46). CRC Press. DOI: 10.4324/9780429271144-2

Galvin, P., Tywoniak, S., & Sutherland, J. (2021). Collaboration and opportunism in megaproject alliance contracts: The interplay between governance, trust and culture. *International Journal of Project Management, 39*(4), 394–405. DOI: 10.1016/j.ijproman.2021.02.007

Govindan, K. (2018). Sustainable consumption and production in the food supply chain: A conceptual framework. *International Journal of Production Economics, 195*, 419–431. DOI: 10.1016/j.ijpe.2017.03.003

Govindaraj, M., Gnanasekaran, C., Krishnan, R., Khan, P., & Hoang, S. D. (2024). Retail Supply Chain Management: Ensuring Product Availability and Reducing Out-of-Stock Incidents in India. In Omnichannel Approach to Co-Creating Customer Experiences Through Metaverse Platforms (pp. 116-141). IGI Global.

Han, J. W., Zuo, M., Zhu, W. Y., Zuo, J. H., Lü, E. L., & Yang, X. T. (2021). A comprehensive review of cold chain logistics for fresh agricultural products: Current status, challenges, and future trends. *Trends in Food Science & Technology, 109*, 536–551. DOI: 10.1016/j.tifs.2021.01.066

Jyoti, C., & Efpraxia, Z. (2023). Understanding and exploring the value co-creation of cloud computing innovation using resource based value theory: An interpretive case study. *Journal of Business Research, 164*, 113970. DOI: 10.1016/j.jbusres.2023.113970

Lele, V., & Ajmeri, Y. (2024). Supply Chain Integration and Collaboration. In *From Source to Shelf: Orchestrating a Supply Chain Symphony* (pp. 83–117). Apress. DOI: 10.1007/979-8-8688-0986-6_4

Leonidou, L. C., Aykol, B., Hadjimarcou, J., & Palihawadana, D. (2021). Unveiling the infidelity problem in exclusive manufacturer–distributor relationships: A dyadic perspective. *Psychology and Marketing, 38*(11), 2122–2141. DOI: 10.1002/mar.21545

Li, L. (2024). Unveiling the effects of supply chain relationship types on enterprise performance. *Enterprise Information Systems, 18*(2), 2274141. DOI: 10.1080/17517575.2023.2274141

Lu, X., & Taghipour, A. (2023). A French Guide for Businesses and Governments to Integrate the Concept of Sustainable Development Into Their Supply Chains. In *Government Impact on Sustainable and Responsible Supply Chain Management* (pp. 1–12). IGI Global. DOI: 10.4018/978-1-6684-9062-4.ch001

Marjosola, H. (2021). The problem of regulatory arbitrage: A transaction cost economics perspective. *Regulation & Governance, 15*(2), 388–407. DOI: 10.1111/rego.12287

Mattessich, P. W., & Johnson, K. M. (2018). Collaboration: What makes it work.

Melnyk, S. A., Schoenherr, T., Speier-Pero, C., Peters, C., Chang, J. F., & Friday, D. (2022). New challenges in supply chain management: Cybersecurity across the supply chain. *International Journal of Production Research*, *60*(1), 162–183. DOI: 10.1080/00207543.2021.1984606

Omar, Y. M., Minoufekr, M., & Plapper, P. (2019). Business analytics in manufacturing: Current trends, challenges and pathway to market leadership. *Operations Research Perspectives*, *6*, 100127. DOI: 10.1016/j.orp.2019.100127

Patil, K., Garg, V., Gabaldon, J., Patil, H., Niranjan, S., & Hawkins, T. (2024). Firm performance in digitally integrated supply chains: A combined perspective of transaction cost economics and relational exchange theory. *Journal of Enterprise Information Management*, *37*(2), 381–413. DOI: 10.1108/JEIM-09-2022-0335

Radhoui, H., Taghipour, A., & Canel-Depitre, B. (2019). The distribution and pickup of goods: A literature review and survey. Hierarchical Planning and Information Sharing Techniques in Supply Chain Management, 46-85.

Rosário, A. T., & Dias, J. C. (2023). The new digital economy and sustainability: Challenges and opportunities. *Sustainability (Basel)*, *15*(14), 10902. DOI: 10.3390/su151410902

Taghipour, A. (Ed.). (2023). *Government Impact on Sustainable and Responsible Supply Chain Management*. IGI Global. DOI: 10.4018/978-1-6684-9062-4

Taghipour, A., Belrhazi, Y., & Damoum, N. (2023). Resilient sustainable supply chain management. In *Government Impact on Sustainable and Responsible Supply Chain Management* (pp. 33–47). IGI Global. DOI: 10.4018/978-1-6684-9062-4.ch003

Taghipour, A., & Lu, X. (2025). Advancing Supply Chain Innovation: Theoretical Foundations, Contemporary Developments, and Future Directions. In Ecological and Human Dimensions of AI-Based Supply Chain (pp. 1-26). IGI Global Scientific Publishing.

TOUFAH, N., EL MOUSSAOUI, A. E., & LEKHAILA, G. (2025). A Comparative Analysis of the Logistics and Economics Fields: A Literature Review. *Revue Française d'Economie et de Gestion*, *6*(8).

Um, K. H., & Kim, S. M. (2019). The effects of supply chain collaboration on performance and transaction cost advantage: The moderation and nonlinear effects of governance mechanisms. *International Journal of Production Economics*, *217*, 97–111. DOI: 10.1016/j.ijpe.2018.03.025

Zhang, D., Frei, R., Wills, G., Gerding, E., Bayer, S., & Senyo, P. K. (2023). Strategies and practices to reduce the ecological impact of product returns: An environmental sustainability framework for multichannel retail. *Business Strategy and the Environment*, *32*(7), 4636–4661. DOI: 10.1002/bse.3385

Zhang, L., Liu, H., & Cai, Z. (2022). Addressing the consensus on information sharing in CPFR information systems: Insights from manufacturer–retailer dyads. *International Journal of Production Research*, *60*(11), 3569–3588. DOI: 10.1080/00207543.2021.1926569

Chapter 11
Managing Demand-Based Uncertainties in Health Economics:
A Nurse-Effective Approach With the Extended EOQ Model

Öner Gümüş
http://orcid.org/0000-0002-3231-3293
Kutahya Dumlupinar University, Turkey

Dilek Gümüş
http://orcid.org/0000-0002-5338-9377
Bilecik Şeyh Edebali University, Turkey

ABSTRACT

This study proposes an extended Economic Order Quantity (EOQ) model to optimize inventory management when drug demand is uncertain due to nursing practice. While traditional EOQ models are based on the assumption of constant demand, due to the nature of clinical decisions, especially in hospital pharmacies, the need for medication arises suddenly and unpredictably. In addition to fixed ordering and inventory holding costs, the model includes a penalty cost (p) parameter that reflects the ethical, clinical, and financial damages caused by stock shortages. Testing the model with separate scenarios for hospital and community pharmacies showed that even small order differences can have significant consequences for patient safety and service continuity. The mathematical modeling of nursing-based demand makes a unique contribution to the literature in the theoretical treatment of this field. The study provides a framework for developing decision support systems based on both economic efficiency and clinical reality through an interdisciplinary approach.

DOI: 10.4018/979-8-3373-6455-1.ch011

INTRODUCTION

When a person or animal becomes ill, many mechanisms within the health processes are triggered. For instance, an individual who falls ill first goes to a hospital or a smaller healthcare facility authorized to refer them to a hospital. At this healthcare facility, he receives treatment to reduce the negative effects of the disease. Although such treatment is free for the patient, it results in public expenditure for the state. If you go to a private hospital or healthcare facility, this expense is covered by the individual. Whether spending is by the government or by individuals, the fact remains that there is always a cash flow because the demand elasticity of healthcare services is low. Where there is cash flow, it is necessary to discuss costs. In the hospital process, doctors and nurses play important roles as active actors. When an individual is ill, the doctor is the primary actor who prescribes medication. However, in some countries, nurses also have the authority to prescribe medication within certain limits. Even if nurses do not have the authority to prescribe medication, the quality of care they provide is an undeniable factor in determining medication quantities. In this context, it is possible to state that healthcare processes will only end when the individual goes to the hospital. The individual must take medication to eliminate the negative effects of their illness. The place where medication is supplied is pharmacies. Therefore, when it comes to medication, although doctors are the first actors that come to mind, the role of nurses and pharmacies in medication supply is also an undeniable fact. In this study, the role of pharmacies and nurses in the costs arising in drug supply processes will be examined within the scope of a mathematical model. Such a mathematical model can play an important role in determining the optimal drug dosage. After all, minimizing costs is desirable from an economic standpoint. In this minimization process, it is necessary to mention not only doctors, who are visible actors, but also pharmacies and nurses.

Pharmacies play a significant role in ensuring the continued health of health care services over the long term. It is essential to ensure that medicines are delivered on time and in the appropriate quantities, not only for the purpose of ensuring the contentment of patients, but also for ethical and financial reasons. In healthcare facilities, the clinical decisions made by nurses frequently have a significant influence on spontaneous and ambiguous requests for medication. As a result of this circumstance, it is difficult to manage pharmacy stock using traditional methods, which means that pharmacies either waste drugs or do not have sufficient stock.

Not only do businesses in the pharmacy industry have to contend with clinical demand and changes in the healthcare system, but they also have to deal with rapidly evolving and expanding service models. There are a number of factors that are having a significant impact on the operations of pharmacy businesses, including digital transformation, shifting customer expectations, and modifications to the delivery of healthcare. In the future, the way pharmacies operate and the services they provide will be influenced by a number of factors, including the introduction of new business models, the development of new technologies, and the assumption of social responsibility (Yang, 2024).

On-premises pharmacies, standard online pharmacies, and direct-to-patient (DTP) business models are the three options available to new businesses that are interested in entering the pharmaceutical industry. In markets where hospitals are the primary players, the DTP model, which incorporates telemedicine and home delivery, is the most profitable and provides the best possible outcomes for patients. According to Yang (2024), this trend suggests that traditional frameworks and digital paradigms are merging together in the management of pharmacies. In some regions, the majority of the community pharmacy market is comprised of retail chains and independent pharmacies. Mass retailers, food stores, and clinic-based pharmacies have smaller shares of the market. As another point of interest, the number of pharmacies that are available to each individual varies greatly from one region to the next (Qato et al., 2017). It is possible that businesses that deal in pharmacy will want to expand their operations as a result of these differences; therefore, strategic planning should take these differences into consideration.

Retail pharmacy companies use social media analytics to identify customer issues, plan marketing, improve customer service, and build loyalty (Hu et al., 2020). The pharmacy business is also shifting from prescription filling to internet-based clinical services. Standardized workflows and electronic documentation systems improve care and efficiency (Spiro, 2019). Pharmacies must integrate and trust data to analyze sales, manage inventory, and calculate profits (Jadhav & Kadam, 2020).

Fast and reliable delivery and drug prices determine customer satisfaction at online pharmacies. Improving logistics and customer service is crucial to retaining customers (Liu et al., 2020). Community pharmacies now counsel patients, manage chronic illnesses, and provide preventive care. In managing cardiovascular diseases, pharmacist interventions provide the most reliable benefits (Krivošová et al., 2025).

Today's pharmaceutical companies must be financially stable, environmentally friendly, and employee-friendly (Kareva & Shvetsova, 2021). Green and social goals are integrated into cost-minimizing models in recent pharmaceutical supply chain optimisation studies (Goodarzian et al., 2026). The pharmaceutical supply chain relies on pharmacy benefit managers to create drug lists, negotiate prices, and coordinate pharmacy networks (Mattingly et al., 2023). Thus, modern pharmacy management now includes health service planning, data management, and ethical responsibility in addition to product and service management.

These changes demonstrate that pharmacies are now patient care, data-driven, and public health leaders. These new functions require strategic inventory management and clinical demand predictions.

Because clinical decisions are complicated and systemic dynamics change, traditional methods can't predict how many medicines healthcare will need. Increasingly, pharmacies with uncertain demand need new mathematical models.

This study proposes a total cost model that considers the uncertainty of nursing-based clinical demands and incorporates the ethical and economic losses that may arise when medicines are out of stock. The model is defined by a mathematical function consisting of fixed ordering cost, holding cost, and shortage penalty components and is developed to determine the optimum order quantity.

In this respect, the study presents an interdisciplinary approach that models the reflection of the drug demand shaped by nursing practices on the health system at the theoretical level and at the same time offers an economic solution to inventory management processes. The study is intended to provide a mathematical framework that can serve as a basis for future data-driven applications.

This study employs hypothetical data to demonstrate the benefits of the model. There is no conflict of interest between the authors of the study. This study did not receive any external funding. The study does not require ethical approval, as it does not involve any work with human or animal subjects. This article has been proofread and linguistically edited using GenAI tools (ChatGPT and QuillBot) to improve grammar and fluency. No part of the article, including data analysis, interpretations, or conclusions, was generated by AI tools. The authors take full responsibility for the content of this publication.

LITERATURE REVIEW

Nurses are very involved in the daily management of medicines and supplies in healthcare settings. In addition to caring for patients directly, nurses often do things that that aren't nursing, like filling out medication orders, keeping track of the stock levels in their wards, and ordering more medications for their units. In fact, one study found that 94.5% of nurses did extra tasks like organizing materials, keeping track of inventory, and restocking supplies as part of their regular work. Because of these logical duties, nurses often manage the medication inventory at the unit level. Research has shown that this role is important. As a matter of fact, there are studies in the literature where it is observed that hospital nurses spend a significant portion of their working time on supply management tasks instead of direct patient care. Time and motion analyses similarly confirm that nurses spend a lot of time on logistics and management activities (e.g., locating medications, organizing supplies) that are not traditionally considered nursing care but are essential to hospital operations (Grosso et al., 2021).

Recently, a growing body of research has investigated how nursing practices affect pharmaceutical supply chain performance, including inventory levels, stockouts, and order throughput. Important findings from recent research include the following:

- In their systematic review, Almalky et al. (2024) summarized the data supporting nurse participation in medical inventory management. They concluded that active nurse participation in inventory procedures can help maintain medication supplies and reduce waste, improving patient safety and care continuity.
- Ogbodu et al. (2019) conducted a study to investigate the perceptions of essential drug inventories held by nurses working in primary health care clinics. Nurses said that their facilities often ran out of drugs, and they said that this was partly because health staff didn't manage their inventory well and didn't follow good practices.
- A new intervention that introduced Ward Medication Assistants (WMAs), a new support role designed to make it easier for hospital wards to handle medication-related tasks, was examined by Rathbone et al. (2023). These pharmacy support workers performed tasks that nurses typically perform, such as managing medication paperwork, filling medicine cabinets, and keeping track of inventory. The study yielded significant operational benefits. With the introduction of WMAs, nurses on the wards were relieved of approximately 4 hours and 41 minutes of inventory and medication management work per day.
- According to Ardern-Jones et al. (2009), emergency response personnel can effectively handle medication supplies in an automated stock control system, reducing stock-related problems and improving system usability.
- Schellack and Meyer (2010) suggested that nursing-supervised ward stock management, including prescription interpretation, ordering, receiving, and monitoring expired medications, can reduce patient waiting times and improve healthcare efficiency.
- Supportive supervision would improve inputs and stock management for senior nursing ward supervisors, despite staff training, heavy workloads, and communication issues, according to Shukla et al. (2023).
- According to Yung (2023), by reducing staff time spent inspecting bottles and preventing waste, contamination, and spills, liquid-controlled medication charts improve stock accountability and reduce inconsistencies in pediatric hospitals.

- According to McNair (2015), supply chain analytics models can be used to achieve the best nurse staffing levels, and forecasting procedures can have a major positive impact.
- Jurado et al. (2016) claim that by balancing efficiency and principle while considering a variety of objectives and constraints, a chance-constrained model with predictive control can effectively manage hospital pharmacy stocks.
- Shahmari et al. (2025) pointed out the value of supportive working environments and evidence-based policies, which are of great importance for nurses to control themselves in high-stress environments, to maintain their composure in emergency situations, and to make informed decisions.

There are still a lot of gaps at the nexus of inventory management and nursing, even with major research advances. This gap highlighted in the literature is directly related to the phenomenon of 'information asymmetry', defined by the differing levels of information possessed by actors in decentralized supply chains. Vosooghidizaji et al. (2020) state that supply chain members' tendency to keep strategic information such as costs, demand, or quality as 'private information' in order to optimize their own goals complicates coordination mechanisms. In the context of healthcare, the superior level of information that nurses possess regarding immediate medication needs in the clinical setting should be considered a fundamental type of asymmetry that prevents pharmacy management from rationally forecasting demand and leads to inefficiency across the system. In addition, this gap is caused by the lack of inventory theories or mathematical models that consider the actions and decisions of nurses. Drug demand is often viewed as an exogenous variable impacted by patient needs or overall hospital utilization in traditional healthcare inventory models. These models seldom consider human factors. For instance, the literature rarely addresses how a nurse's tendency to order early or late or to keep a safety cushion in stock affects the effective demand model. Nursing units often show variability in drug utilization rates. For instance, one of two wards with the same patient profile may have proactive nurses who immediately reorder and administer medicines, while in the other, nurses may delay doses or maintain dwindling stocks. This nursing-induced demand variability may influence optimal inventory policies but has not been explicitly modeled in the literature reviewed. A review of the linked literature did not identify any studies formulating a mathematical or simulation model that explicitly links nursing decision variables to inventory results. No extended EOQ or supply chain model published recently includes parameters for nurse ordering behavior or nurse-induced demand fluctuation. Most research in this era is empirical rather than theoretical. The situation represents an opportunity for new contributions. It is possible to mathematically represent how the timing and volume of orders placed by nurses differ from idealized assumptions of constant demand by creating an extended EOQ model takes nurse-driven demand variability into account. To account for how nurses adjust when a drug is unavailable, such as borrowing from other wards or using an alternative treatment, this type of model could, for instance, include a penalty cost for stockouts or a random demand factor that illustrates how nurses' reordering points change over time.

A new model would help in two ways: (1) It gives a formal way to measure how nursing decisions affect service levels and inventory costs, and (2) it connects operation research with clinical practice by seeing nurses as part of the supply chain system instead of just as people who use inventory. A nursing-informed model will treat demand as a function of nursing management techniques and patient needs, whereas prior inventory models treat it as a fixed input. This is particularly true for medications, as the strictness of stock monitoring and the practice schedules of nurses have a direct impact on the rate at which inventory is used up or orders are placed.

By contextualizing the extended EOQ model in this way, we see that it aims to fill a recognized gap. The literature shows that although nurses play an important role in outcomes (inventories, waste, productivity), no existing forecasting model captures this dynamic. Therefore, the new model incorporating variability driven by nurses will make a new contribution to this field, potentially allowing healthcare managers to stimulate scenarios such as "What would happen if nurses had more training and ordered more proactively-how would this affect optimal order sizes and frequency?" or conversely, "What is the cost of variability if nursing practices vary across units?". Answering these questions can help make policies that are more flexible, like setting reorder points that consider how long it usually takes for nurses to respond or making decision support tools for nurses to use when checking inventory.

Because of this, the intersection of nursing practice and medication inventory management is becoming more and more important for healthcare operations to run smoothly. Recent research shows that nurses' actions affect drug availability, safety, and cost. To improve supply logistics, hospitals are starting to spend money on giving nurses more power, hospitals are starting to spend money on giving nurses more power by giving them more training, better technology, and changing the way things are done. Further research, especially using mathematical modelling systems analysis, is needed to fully understand and predict how nurses and inventory relate. The development of an extended EOQ model that includes nurse-driven demand variability will fill this gap and provide theoretical and practical guidance for improving pharmaceutical supply chains where nurses are important stakeholders.

Figuring out how nurses' workloads affect demand variance is the hardest part of nursing inventory management. It has been observed that nurses experiencing cognitive overload can make errors in medication inventory records or report non-emergency situations as emergencies, disrupting inventory management. This situation indicates that the D (demand) parameter in the model has a stochastic rather than deterministic structure (Campbell et al., 2021; Hawkins & Morse, 2022; Moriwaki et al., 2025; Sitrarasu et al., 2025). The work of nurses cannot be considered separate from contextual probabilities. It has been reported that during the intense work processes referred to as "crazy days" by nurses, workarounds were developed by deviating from standard operating procedures. For example, a nurse might borrow medication from another ward instead of taking it from the medication cabinet or postpone the recording process. These behaviors lead to discrepancies between the data in the inventory system and the actual stock levels (inventory inaccuracy). (Hawkins & Morse, 2022; Campbell et al., 2021). In this context, the existing literature is merely descriptive, and it will be easily observed that there is a gap in converting nurse behavior into a mathematical model.

METHODOLOGY

The EOQ model is a crucial component of inventory management that assists businesses in optimizing their order sizes to achieve the lowest possible total inventory costs. This model seeks to balance holding costs—the costs of maintaining inventory—and ordering costs—the costs of placing an order. The EOQ model now addresses many modern business issues. Product perishability, erratic demand, supply chain disruptions, and increasing sustainability requirements require companies to consider the environment when placing orders. This makes the EOQ model a more complete inventory management tool that balances cost reduction and market and stakeholder adaptation.

By balancing two important factors—ordering costs, which are incurred with each order placement, and holding costs, which are related to maintaining inventory storage, the EOQ model is intended to identify the most efficient order quantity. Several presumptions underlie this model, such as steady demand, fixed ordering and holding costs, and the idea of instantaneous replenishment. The EOQ model is still a vital tool for management decision-making in spite of these oversimplified assumptions, showing dependability even in situations where there is parameter uncertainty (Senthilnathan, 2019; Schwarz, 2008). The model is widely used in several industries, including manufacturing, retail, healthcare, and the food sector. Its main goals are cost reduction and improved inventory management. Its adaptability and efficiency in streamlining operational procedures and cutting costs are demonstrated by this integration across various industries (Khanna et al., 2023).

The EOQ model has been greatly modified by recent research to better capture the intricacies of supply chain management today. The following scenarios have been addressed by EOQ as a result of these advancements: (Tat et al., 2015; Yang et al., 2024; Çalışkan, 2021; Sanni et al., 2020; Jaber & Peltokorpi, 2024; Yu, 1997; Kalaiarasi et al., 2022; Agada & Ogwuche, 2017; Wardana et al., 2025; Hutapea et al., 2021; Jahroni & Muksin, 2023; Ikrom & Kartini, 2025):

- **Degradable and perishable goods:** New models have been created to accommodate goods that are sensitive to temperature changes or have a short shelf life. The management of inventory that may deteriorate or spoil over time is improved by these models, which consider deterioration rates and permit planned-backorders.
- **Sustainability and reverse logistics**: EOQ has been modified to support systems that involve remanufacturing and product returns. Environmental sustainability is also taken into account in this adaptation, which highlights the significance of waste reduction and resource efficiency.
- **Fuzziness and Uncertainty:** To better manage supply chain disruptions, demand, and cost uncertainties, extensions of the EOQ model have included probabilistic techniques and fuzzy logic. These methods offer a more reliable framework for making decisions in dynamic market circumstances. Robust planning approaches are critical for managing sudden demand fluctuations that arise during crises and pandemics. In their study of logistics networks during the COVID-19 pandemic, Taghipour et al. (2023) found that robust optimization models outperform fuzzy probability models with parameter uncertainties. These models aim to minimize unmet demand and maximize route reliability, in addition to minimizing costs, thereby enhancing the operational resilience of the healthcare supply-chain.
- **Supply Chain and Business Models:** The use of EOQ has expanded into a number of business models, such as make-to-order and vendor-managed inventory. For both small and large businesses, this flexibility has resulted in notable cost savings and improvements in operational efficiency.

All things considered, these changes show how the EOQ model is still applicable and flexible enough to satisfy the changing demands of contemporary supply chain dynamics.

The EOQ model, which offers a strong framework that readily adjusts to the demands of the modern supply chain, is essential to inventory management. Its modifications account for factors such as perishability of products, unpredictable market conditions, and the increasing emphasis on sustainability practices. When used effectively, the EOQ model usually lowers costs significantly and improves a company's operational efficiency. However, the intricacies of real-world inventory management scenarios present new challenges that are constantly being explored and addressed by current research.

This study uses an enhanced EOQ model for healthcare. The penalty cost (p) parameter in this study accounts for ethical, clinical, and economic losses if healthcare services run out of stock, unlike the traditional EOQ model, which only considers fixed demand, ordering cost, and inventory holding cost. Thus, the model optimizes inventory planning for economic efficiency, patient safety, service continuity, and clinical risks. This part of the model is a big difference and advantage over the classical EOQ model, especially since healthcare patients without drugs can suffer. This model indicates the total cost function as:

$$TC(Q) = \frac{D}{Q}(S + p) + \frac{Q}{2}H$$

TC is the total cost, D is the annual demand, Q is the order quantity, S is the order cost, H is the cost of holding a unit for a year, and p is the penalty cost for not holding a unit. To find the optimal order quantity that minimizes the total cost, the first derivative of the function with respect to Q is taken and set equal to zero.

$$\frac{dTC}{dQ} = -\frac{D(S + p)}{Q^2} + \frac{H}{2} = 0$$

The optimal Q is derived from this equation as follows:

$$Q^* = \sqrt{\frac{2D(S + p)}{H}}$$

To prove that this found value is indeed a minimum point, a second derivative check is performed:

$$\frac{d^2TC}{dQ^2} = \frac{2D(S + p)}{Q^3}$$

Since the values of D, S, p, and Q are always positive, the second derivative is also always positive. This situation mathematically confirms that the function is convex and that the obtained Q value is the absolute point that minimizes the total cost.

This formula is like the classical EOQ model. However, here, the penalty coefficient p is also included in the model. This model includes the possibility of harming the patient when the pharmacy's drug stock runs out, treating it as both an ethical and economic penalty.

The following constraints were applied to the model:

- $D > 0$, demand must be positive,

- $Q > 0$, order quantity must be greater than zero,
- $S, H, p \geq 0$, cost parameters must be non-negative.

Penalty cost (p) reflects the ethical, operational, and financial consequences of stock-outs in healthcare. Losses include things like delayed treatment, costs of emergency procurement, damage to reputation, and loss of trust or loyalty from patients. In this research, an estimated value of p is computed to illustrate the model's sensitivity. Nevertheless, it can be found the p-value using the following methods in real life:

- **Expert opinion (Delphi method):** Health managers and clinical pharmacists can figure out how much money a stock-out event costs.
- **Historical data analysis:** Previous instances of stockouts and associated patient harm, delays, or costs can be analyzed.
- **Simulation studies:** Various p-values can be tested in sensitivity analysis to see how they affect the ideal order quantity and overall cost.

The $20,000 value used for the p-value in the model is not a random choice but is based on current clinical and financial literature data. That is, the cost of stock-outs in healthcare is not only financial but also a life-threatening risk. Particularly in critical clinical conditions such as sepsis, every hour of delay in administering antibiotics increases the hospital mortality risk by 9%. In cases of septic shock, this delay has been recorded to increase absolute mortality by 1.8%. This situation clinically proves why the p parameter should include a high ethical penalty. On the other hand, empirical data show that the average hospital admission cost for sepsis cases ranges from $24,600 to $28,800 per case. Depending on the severity of the disease, this cost can reach $38,298, and in cases where complications develop in the hospital, the cost burden can reach up to $70,000 per case (for detailed information, see Liu et al., 2017; Paoli et al., 2018; Owens et al., 2024; Hurst & Berdugo, 2020). The $20,000 value chosen in the study represents a conservative lower limit, representing the lowest additional care cost that could cause stockouts, as it is below the average hospitalization costs and readmission costs due to sepsis reported in the literature.

Future research will test the robustness of the proposed EOQ extension under varying p-values, lead times, and demand uncertainty using simulation-based scenario modeling. In this context, to show how the model can be applied to different types of pharmacy operations, the findings and discussion section are presented under two separate headings: hospital pharmacy operations and community (retail) pharmacy operations.

RESULTS AND DISCUSSION

Hospital Pharmacy Management

In the first scenario, a case study on hospital pharmacy management will be discussed. The assumptions of the scenario are that a drug for postoperative antibiotic applications should be used regularly in the hospital and that it is known that an average of 40 ampoules of the drug is consumed daily in nursing practices. The other numerical assumptions for this scenario are presented in *Table 1.*

Table 1. Quantitative Assumptions for Hospital Pharmacy Enterprises

Parameter	Value	Description
D	14,600 ampoules	Average annual demand (40 ampoules/day x 365 days)
S	\$500	Fixed cost per order (shipping, handling, invoice, etc.)
H	\$10	The cost of keeping one ampoule in stock for one year
p	\$20,000	Penalty for being out of stock: The economic and ethical cost of failing to give antibiotics to a patient on time[1]

With the classical EOQ model, the optimal order quantity is found as follows:

$$Q_{\text{Optimal-classical model}} = \frac{\sqrt{2DS}}{\sqrt{H}} = \frac{\sqrt{2 \times 14,600 \times 500}}{\sqrt{10}} \approx 1208 ampoules$$

With the extended EOQ model, the optimal order quantity is found as follows:

$$Q_{\text{Optimal-extended model}} = \frac{\sqrt{2D(S+p)}}{\sqrt{H}} = \frac{\sqrt{2 \times 14,600 \times (500 + 20,000)}}{\sqrt{10}} \approx 7737 ampoules$$

Table 2. Sensitivity analysis of optimal order quantity (Q) relative to stockout penalty*

Scenario	Annual Demand (D)	Penalty Cost (p)	Optimal Q*	Risk Mitigation Level
Classical EOQ	14,600	$0	1,208	Low (High Stockout Risk)
Extended EOQ (Base)	14,600	$20,000	7.737	Moderate
Extended EOQ (High Risk)	14,600	$50,000	12,143	High (Safety Stock Focus)

Note: Calculations are based on S=$500 and H=$10.

Table 2 presents a sensitivity analysis addressing concerns regarding the model's practical significance. Changes to the penalty cost (p) increase the best order quantity (Q*) significantly. The classical model remains unchanged, but the extended model changes to account for important medications' clinical and ethical risks. When modified to account for sepsis-related complications (up to approximately $50,000 per admission), the model requires a much higher Q* value, mathematically formalizing the safety-first stock buffer that conventional models ignore. Even with clinical uncertainty, meeting nursing needs reduces the risk of life-threatening stock depletion.

Out-of-stock antibiotics, painkillers, and critical care medicines in public hospitals can change patients' lives. Thus, p, the model's penalty parameter, is the mathematical equivalent of treatment delays, complications, and patient safety violations as well as a financial cost. If a postoperative antibiotic is unavailable, the patient may develop sepsis, infection dissemination, or require extended hospitalization. These situations endanger patients and waste public hospital resources. The model improves medicine numbers and makes decisions more preventive and patient-focused. This study adds clinical safety and service continuity to the classical model's efficiency focus, making the decision-making framework more appropriate for health services.

The clinical grounding of the model is largely based on nursing practice. In public hospitals, most of the drugs are administered by nurses; dose frequency, time of administration, and drug selection are often shaped by nurses' service protocols and clinical observations. The parameter D in the model is therefore not just a consumption quantity but a mathematical expression of nursing-based clinical demand.

Moreover, nurses are often the first health professionals to recognize the risk of stockouts in drug procurement processes. This makes the stock planning suggested by the model more compatible with clinical early warning systems. The fact that the extended model considers the rhythm of nursing practice makes it possible to manage hospital pharmacies in a way that is not only economic but also integrated into clinical reality.

Community (Retail) Pharmacy Management

The total cost function underlying the model is the same. However, the parameters mean different things for a community pharmacy. *Table 3* summarizes what the parameters mean for community pharmacies.

Table 3. Quantitative Assumptions for Community Pharmacy Enterprises

Parameter	Description
D	Estimated demand based on daily prescription movements and over-the-counter product sales
S	Logistics + operation cost when ordering from the supplier
H	Shelf space, expiration risk, storage (especially for perishable products)
p	Customer loss + additional payment for urgent order + trust penalty due to out-of-stock

Although community pharmacy businesses do not provide direct clinical services, the medicines and health products they offer are largely intended for the continuation of treatment processes initiated in hospitals and primary health care organizations. In these treatment processes, nurses play an important role not only as drug administrators but also in patient education, prescription continuity, and health behavior promotion. In this context, the key parameters in the mathematical model developed, such as annual demand (D) and stockout penalty (p), are directly and indirectly related to nursing practice.

Demand for prescription medicines in private pharmacies often arises to maintain treatment plans initiated at the hospital or family health center. A certain number of these treatment plans directly result from the clinical practice carried out by nurses. For instance, the dosing regimen for postoperative antibiotic use is administered by the nurse in the hospital; when the patient is discharged, follow-up doses are obtained from community pharmacies. Therefore, the demand parameter (D) in the model can be considered not only as sales data but also as a reflection of the nursing-based clinical process in the pharmacy business.

Before patients leave the hospital, nurses advise them on medication management, including frequency, method, and duration. This makes medication adherence easier and community pharmacy demand more predictable. This method helps chemists predict demand, and the model's D parameter is stronger.

Family health center nurses are crucial for vaccinations, chronic disease monitoring, and preventive care. Community pharmacies sell prescription and over-the-counter medications for these services. Nursing influences pharmacy drug demand, affecting patients and public health.

The annual demand (D) in the developed model is a data point shaped by the continuity of nursing practices and patient education. The stockout penalty (p) represents customer dissatisfaction, loss of brand trust, and loss of loyalty that can occur when medicines are unavailable, which are often triggered by the interruption of nursing-related prescription behaviors. In this respect, nursing constitutes one of the invisible but decisive parameters of the model in the context of community pharmacy.

Table 4 presents the quantitative assumptions for community pharmacy enterprises, based on the demand for a blood pressure medication.

Table 4. Quantitative Assumptions for Community Pharmacy Enterprises

Parameter	Value	Description
D	4000 boxes	Blood pressure medication sold in 1 year
S	$150	Shipping + invoice issuance costs for each order
H	$5	Cost of 1 box in stock for 1 year
p	$1000	Loss of customers, loss of urgent orders

With the classical EOQ model, the optimal order quantity is found as follows:

$$Q_{\text{Optimal-classical model}} = \frac{\sqrt{2DS}}{\sqrt{H}} = \frac{\sqrt{2 \times 4000 \times 150}}{\sqrt{5}} \approx 490 boxes$$

With the extended EOQ model, the optimal order quantity is found as follows:

$$Q_{\text{Optimal-extended model}} = \frac{\sqrt{2D(S+p)}}{\sqrt{H}} = \frac{\sqrt{2 \times 4000(150+1000)}}{\sqrt{5}} \approx 1356 boxes$$

In the case scenario, the classical EOQ model recommends an ideal order quantity of approximately 490 boxes for a blood pressure medicine with annual sales of 4000 boxes. However, the extended model suggests a significantly higher quantity of about 1356 boxes.

The classical model is based solely on economic parameters (cost of ordering, cost of holding stock), whereas the extended model considers the loss of customers, erosion of loyalty, and losses due to urgent orders in case of stockouts, in line with the commercial reality of community pharmacies. These losses are represented by the parameter p in the model and become a strategic decision factor for the business.

In particular, the unavailability of prescription drugs may cause customers to turn to another pharmacy. This reduces sales, brand loyalty, and trust. The extended model mathematically incorporates these losses and suggests a more accurate order decision. For instance, when assuming a penalty coefficient p = \$5000, the classical model suggests ordering approximately 490 boxes, while the extended model increases this amount to 2870 boxes. The extended model is a preventive, realistic, and sustainable planning tool in that it quantitatively incorporates such micro-level clinical and commercial harms into the decision process.

In this process, the indirect contribution of the nursing profession should not be ignored. A significant portion of the prescription drugs sold in community pharmacies are based on treatment processes initiated under nursing supervision. A blood pressure treatment initiated by a nurse in the hospital requires regular medication after discharge, which the patient obtains from a community pharmacy. In addition, patient education provided by nurses (drug dosage, frequency of use, mode of administration, etc.) increases adherence to treatment and thus makes demand in community pharmacies more predictable.

The parameter D in the model is therefore not only an annual sales figure but also an indicator of nursing-based clinical continuity reflected in the pharmacy. Likewise, the loss of customers due to the unavailability of medication on time indirectly means the disruption of nursing-induced prescription behaviors, which is represented in the model by the penalty parameter (p).

In conclusion, the extended EOQ model offers a planning tool for specialty pharmacy businesses that is not only cost-oriented but also sensitive to service continuity, customer satisfaction, and clinical reality. Interdisciplinary decision support systems can benefit from this model's indirect nursing perspective.

DATA REQUIREMENTS AND IMPLEMENTATION ROADMAP

For the extended EOQ model to move from theory to practice, healthcare managers need data sets and an operational plan. You need lots of hospital information system data to set the model's parameters. The first of these data is demand data, which relates not only to pharmacy dispensing but also to the real-time medication administration times and dosage amounts entered by nurses into electronic health records. The second is logs that include instances when the medication cannot be found, how many hours this situation delays treatment, and, if applicable, nurse interventions such as borrowing from other services during this process, which means stockout records. Finally, a committee consisting of clinical pharmacists and head nurses must use the Delphi method to score the ethical and economic risks for each medication group, which constitutes the third data point.

Managers can implement the model in three steps. The first step involves conducting ABC and VEN analyses to identify critical medications. The second step involves setting the p-value high for these critical medications, based on the additional care costs presented in this study for sepsis cases. Finally, the last step involves updating the D parameter every three months based on nurses' workload or service occupancy rates.

This model provides the highest efficiency in public hospitals where nurses play an active role in medication systems and inventory tracking. However, in digitized units where ADC and RFID-based closed-loop systems are used and nurse logistical intervention is minimized, the model's impact may be limited as nurse-related variance will decrease.

CONCLUSION

The study aims to mathematically reconsider pharmaceutical stock management in pharmacy businesses based on the critical role of nursing practices in health service delivery. In particular, the sudden and unpredictable demand for medicines based on nurses' clinical decisions contradicts the constant demand conditions assumed by the classical economic ordering model. In this context, we propose and evaluate an extended total cost model for both hospital and community pharmacy operations, which includes variables such as fixed order cost, holding cost, and out-of-stock penalty.

The scenarios in which the model developed within the scope of the research revealed that order quantity differences, which may seem small compared to the classical EOQ model, can have significant consequences for health service delivery, especially in cases involving high penalty costs. Clinical process stock-outs affect patient safety, satisfaction, and healthcare worker workload due to economic, ethical, and operational factors. Adding nursing-based demand uncertainty to the model makes inventory management more realistic, clinically sensitive, and patient-focused.

Central pharmacies are crucial in public hospitals because if they run out of stock, nurses can't continue treatment, which affects care quality. Nurses improve public health literacy in community pharmacies, which keeps customers loyal and prescription demand high. In both structures, nurses manage pharmaceutical logistics, which is both administrative and strategic for health service availability.

Considering the findings of this research, the following recommendations are important to take into consideration:

- For the purpose of empowering nurses to make decisions, health care facilities ought to establish drug inventory management systems. As a result of the fact that nurses frequently require medications that were not anticipated, order planning algorithms ought to consider these alterations.

- Nursing services coordinators ought to be the ones to make decisions regarding what to order when it comes to the management of a hospital pharmacy. This strikes a balance between the requirements of the clinic and the logistics that are available, thereby reducing the likelihood of stockouts.
- Individuals ought to consider community pharmacy nurses to be health counsellors, individuals who generate prescription demand, and individuals who educate people about health. Nurses can help predict non-prescription product sales and customer retention.
- Health policy should use mathematical modelling, not just logistics. The extended EOQ and other models can help decision-makers understand nursing-based demands' economic effects.
- Basic stock management and logistics training can help nurses provide good health care. Nursing professionals who know both clinical and logistical duties can streamline health care.
- Further research must validate this model with empirical data and apply it to various clinical domains (e.g., intensive care, oncology, emergency department). Thus, the model's clinical and operational validity will improve.

To summarize, the findings of this research show that nursing-based medication ordering procedures not only serve as a component of healthcare but also as a strategic input for decision support systems in the operations of pharmacies. There is a possibility that the extended model will improve both patient safety and operational efficiency. It is anticipated that the extended model will improve the accuracy of stocking decisions, particularly in clinical settings that are characterized by uncertainty. Therefore, the provision of nursing services is an essential component of both the service of providing care and the operation of the entire health care system.

This investigation makes use of a sophisticated Economic Order Quantity (EOQ) model on a theoretical level to investigate the impact that nursing-related clinical demand uncertainty has on the operations of pharmacies. Even though it suggests an interdisciplinary framework, the study has some limitations that make it difficult to apply it to other situations. These limitations make it difficult to apply the study.

It was not possible to identify a single organization that was able to provide accurate stock and order data for the study. To determine whether the model is accurate, we used both theoretical assumptions and case scenarios. Because of this limitation, it is more difficult to determine whether the model can be utilized in a variety of healthcare settings. In the model, only nursing-induced demand uncertainty is considered, but exogenous uncertainties such as supply chain disruptions, drug lead times, and price fluctuations are excluded.

The effects of nurses on the inventory management process were addressed at the theoretical level; however, qualitative or quantitative findings regarding direct nurse opinions or attitudes in practice were not included.

The model is generalized for all health institutions. However, the specific drug consumption patterns of branches such as intensive care, oncology, and pediatrics were not specifically integrated into the model.

Although the study emphasized the public health-based educational impact of nurses in community pharmacies, the measurable impact of this on drug demand was excluded from the study.

Within the scope of these limitations, it is possible to conduct the following studies in the future:

- Testing the extended EOQ model with monthly stock, order, out-of-stock, and penalty cost data from community and hospital pharmacies will increase the accuracy of the model. For this purpose, we can analyze numerically how nurses impact the ordering process in a given clinic.
- In-depth interviews on nurses' level of knowledge about inventory management, its effects on decision-making processes, and the difficulties they experience in this process can contribute to the nurse-based validation of the model.
- Modeling demand uncertainty not only with EOQ formulation but also with simulation techniques will enable scenario analysis for different hospital departments or pharmacy structures.
- Separate stock management algorithms can be developed for direct-to-patient pharmacies, hospital pharmacies, and pharmacy models in public health organizations. In this way, solutions specific to health policies can be created.
- In future studies, a more holistic inventory model can be developed by considering the supply behaviors of pharmaceutical companies and the demand-driving effect of nurses together.
- Integrating ethical decision-making frameworks and patient safety risks into inventory management models allows economic and clinical optimization.

According to the findings of the study, nurses are not only users of the aforementioned situation, but they are also strategic decision-makers within the supply chain.

MANAGERIAL IMPLICATIONS

Within the scope of this research, a novel perspective is presented regarding the decision-making procedures that are utilized by managers working in pharmacy organizations at both the hospital and community levels. It is possible to avoid issues such as running out of stock, wasting medicines, and having to wait longer for supplies by using the extended EOQ model, which is a method of planning ahead before problems arise. One of the things that it examines is how difficult it is to forecast the number of nurses that will be required. It is possible for managers to examine both clinical and financial risks simultaneously thanks to the ethical and economic penalty cost parameter of the model. Ultimately, this ensures that decisions regarding how to manage stock are more comprehensive, centered on the safety of patients, and will be in place for a longer period of time. Additionally, the model suggests that nursing services coordinators would be able to assist with the planning of supplies. By doing so, not only does this make it simpler for individuals within the organization to communicate with one another, but it also guarantees that services are always accessible to those who have a requirement for them. As a result of this, it assists healthcare organizations in locating a management equilibrium that satisfies their requirements for both clinical quality and cost. From this perspective, achieving a management balance translates to efficiency.

PRACTICAL IMPLICATIONS

It is possible for the suggested model to be of assistance to hospital and pharmacy managers because it provides them with a real-life method of decision-making. The model provides a numerical estimate of the costs associated with stock outs concerning the dissatisfaction of patients, the delays in treatment, and the ethical concerns that arise. Thus, managers can plan which drugs to order and how much of which drugs to order, based not only on cost but also on patient safety criteria. In community pharmacies, the p parameter makes abstract concepts such as customer loss or loyalty erosion concrete and integrated into decision-making processes. Considering the behaviour of nurses in drug demand facilitates the integration of clinical processes and logistics processes. In this respect, the model can be considered as an innovative tool that increases both clinical and operational sustainability for healthcare institutions in the digital transformation process.

THEORETICAL IMPLICATIONS

This research fills an important gap in the literature by integrating nurse-based demand uncertainty and ethical penalty parameter into the classical EOQ model. While demand is generally considered exogenous and fixed in traditional models, in this study, demand is treated as a dynamic variable with the decision-making behavior of nurses. Thus, drug order scheduling based on nurses' clinical observations is incorporated into the model with a mathematical formulation. This approach builds an interdisciplinary bridge between both operations research and nursing management literature. The study demonstrates at the theoretical level how ethical responsibilities and clinical outcomes can be integrated into optimization processes and provides a solid theoretical foundation for future data-driven decision support systems.

REFERENCES

Agada, P. O., & Ogwuche, E. H. (2017). A probabilistic economic order quantity (EOQ) model for inventory management of drugs and hospital consumables. *FUW Trends in Science & Technology Journal*, *2*(2), 737–742.

Almalky, S. A., Miny, A. S. S., Hakami, F. A. O., Alqarni, A. A. A., Allahyani, K. M. A., Alabsi, S. H. N., Bakhsh, A. M., Almabadi, R. M. R. A., Al Ansari, A. K. M., Alotaibi, B. A. Z., Alshamari, N. K. K., Al Shammri, B. M. A., Almabadi, N. N. M., & Alanazi, N. S. M. (2024). The role of nursing in improving medical inventory management and quality of work in health facilities: A systematic review. *Journal of International Crisis and Risk Communication Research*, *7*(S5), 443–448. https://jicrcr.com/index.php/jicrcr/article/view/2412/2095

Ardern-Jones, J., Hughes, D. K., Rowe, P. H., Mottram, D. R., & Green, C. F. (2009). Attitudes and opinions of nursing and medical staff regarding the supply and storage of medicinal products before and after the installation of a drawer-based automated stock-control system. *The International Journal of Pharmacy Practice*, *17*(2), 95–99. DOI: 10.1211/ijpp.17.02.0004 PMID: 20214257

Çalışkan, C. (2021). A simple derivation of the optimal solution for the EOQ model for deteriorating items with planned backorders. *Applied Mathematical Modelling*, *89*, 1373–1381. DOI: 10.1016/j.apm.2020.08.037

Campbell, A. A., Harlan, T., Campbell, M., Mulekar, M. S., & Wang, B. (2021). Nurse's achilles heel: Using big data to determine workload factors that impact near misses. *Journal of Nursing Scholarship : An Official Publication of Sigma Theta Tau International Honor Society of Nursing*, *53*(3), 333–342. DOI: 10.1111/jnu.12652 PMID: 33786985

Goodarzian, F., Abraham, A., Muñuzuri, J., Taghipour, A., & Ghasemi, P. (2026). A Benders decomposition approach for a new sustainable pharmaceutical supply chain network: A case study in France. *Annals of Operations Research*, *356*(2-3), 881–919. DOI: 10.1007/s10479-024-05936-3

Grosso, S., Longhini, J., Tonet, S., Bernard, I., Corso, J., de Marchi, D., Dorigo, L., Funes, G., Lussu, M., Oppio, N., Grassetti, L., Mori, L. P. D., & Palese, D. (2021). Prevalence and reasons for non-nursing tasks as perceived by nurses: Findings from a large cross-sectional study. *Journal of Nursing Management*, *29*(8), 2658–2673. DOI: 10.1111/jonm.13451 PMID: 34369615

Hawkins, S. F., & Morse, J. M. (2022). Untenable expectations: Nurses' work in the context of medication administration, error and the organization. *Global Qualitative Nursing Research, 9*, 1–17. DOI: 10.1177/23333936221131779 PMID: 36387044

Hu, J., Han, R., Ali, M., Zhan, Y., & Tse, M. (2020). A social media analytic framework for improving operations and service management: A study of the retail pharmacy industry. *Technological Forecasting and Social Change, 163*, 120504. DOI: 10.1016/j.techfore.2020.120504

Hurst, J., & Berdugo, M. (2020, September 28). The cost of sepsis in lives and dollars. bioMérieux Connection. https://www.biomerieuxconnection.com/2019/09/05/the-cost-of-sepsis-in-lives-and-dollars/

Hutapea, A., Sakti, H., Novarianti, I., & Nurcahyo, R. (2021, August). Application of economic order quantity (EOQ) for make-to-order (MTO) business. In *1st Indian International Conference on Industrial Engineering and Operations Management*. https://doi.org/DOI: 10.46254/IN01.20210074

Ikrom, B. P. D., & Kartini, N. (2025). Analysis of raw material inventory control using economic order quantity (EOQ) method at good coffee houses in Surabaya. *Jurnal Ekonomi Manajemen, 10*(1), 25–46. DOI: 10.30996/jem17.v10i1.131918

Jaber, M. Y., & Peltokorpi, J. (2024). Economic order/production quantity (EOQ/EPQ) models with product recovery: A review of mathematical modeling (1967-2022). *Applied Mathematical Modelling, 129*, 655–672. DOI: 10.1016/j.apm.2024.02.022

Jadhav, R., & Kadam, M. S. (2020). Incubated insights: Data integration, reliability for effective and efficient pharmacy shops business. *Shanghai Ligong Daxue Xuebao, 22*(11), 949–963. https://jusst.org/wp-content/uploads/2020/11/Sentiments-Analysis-of-the-Medical-or-Pharmacy-shops-business-to-develop-in-terms-of-Communication-Productivity-efficiency-in-their-retails-business.pdf

Jahroni, , & Muksin, M. (2023). Economic order quantity (EOQ) application to raw material inventory control for SMEs. *Community Services Journal, 5*(2), 88–98. DOI: 10.22225/csj.5.2.2023.88-98

Jurado, I., Maestre, J. M., Velarde, P., Ocampo-Martinez, C., Fernández, I., Isla Tejera, B., & del Prado, J. R. (2016). Stock management in hospital pharmacy using chance-constrained model predictive control. *Computers in Biology and Medicine, 72*, 248–255. DOI: 10.1016/j.compbiomed.2015.11.011 PMID: 26724992

Kalaiarasi, K., Henrietta, H. M., Sumathi, M., & Raj, A. S. (2022). Economic order quantity in a fuzzy environment for a periodic inventory model with variable demand. *Iraqi Journal for Computer Science and Mathematics*, *3*(1), 102–107. DOI: 10.52866/ijcsm.2022.01.01.011

Kareva, N. N., & Shvetsova, V. D. (2021). Pharmacy business and its social responsibility. *Journal of Siberian Medical Sciences*, *2*(2), 136–145. DOI: 10.31549/2542-1174-2021-2-136-145

Khanna, R., Rajnikant, P. N., & Patel, K. A. (2023). Review presentation of different economic order quantity (EOQ) models and their application. *Journal of Advanced Zoology*, *44*(S5), 1284–1288. DOI: 10.17762/jaz.v44iS-5.1210

Krivošová, M., Klimas, J., Žufková, V., Snopková, M., Mačeková, Z., & Viola, R. (2025). Advanced pharmaceutical services in community pharmacies. *Pharmacy Practice*, *23*(1), 1–17. DOI: 10.18549/PharmPract.2025.1.3073

Liu, J., Zhou, Y., Jiang, X., & Zhang, W. (2020). Consumers' satisfaction factors mining and sentiment analysis of B2C online pharmacy reviews. *BMC Medical Informatics and Decision Making*, *20*(194), 1–13. DOI: 10.1186/s12911-020-01214-x PMID: 32807175

Liu, V. X., Fielding-Singh, V., Greene, J. D., Baker, J. M., Iwashyna, T. J., Bhattacharya, J., & Escobar, G. J. (2017). The timing of early antibiotics and hospital mortality in sepsis. *American Journal of Respiratory and Critical Care Medicine*, *196*(7), 856–863. DOI: 10.1164/rccm.201609-1848OC PMID: 28345952

Mattingly, T.II, Hyman, D., & Bai, G. (2023). Pharmacy benefit managers: History, business practices, economics and policy. *JAMA Health Forum*, *4*(11), e233804. DOI: 10.1001/jamahealthforum.2023.3804 PMID: 37921745

McNair, D. (2015). Enhancing nursing staffing forecasting with safety stock over lead time modeling. *Nursing Administration Quarterly*, *39*(4), 291–296. DOI: 10.1097/NAQ.0000000000000124 PMID: 26340239

Moriwaki, M., Tanaka, M., Kakehashi, M., Koizumi, M., Horiguchi, H., & Hayashida, K. (2025). Influence of nursing time and staffing on medication errors: A cross-sectional analysis of administrative data. *Nursing Reports*, *15*(1), 1–11. DOI: 10.3390/nursrep15010012 PMID: 39852634

Ogbodu, O. M., Maputle, M. S., & Mabunda, J. (2019). Nurses' perceptions about stock-outs of essential medicines at primary health care facilities in Vhembe district, South Africa. *The Open Public Health Journal*, *12*(1), 550–557. DOI: 10.2174/1874944501912010550

Owens, P. L., Miller, M. A., Barrett, M. L., & Hensche, M. (2024, April). *Overview of outcomes for inpatient stays involving sepsis, 2016–2021 (HCUP Statistical Brief No. 306). Agency for Healthcare Research and Quality. https://hcup-us.ahrq.gov/reports/statbriefs/sb306-overview-sepsis-2016-2021.pdf

Paoli, C. J., Reynolds, M. A., Sinha, M., Gitlin, M., & Crouser, E. (2018). Epidemiology and costs of sepsis in the United States-an analysis based on timing of diagnosis and severity level. *Critical Care Medicine*, *46*(12), 1889–1897. DOI: 10.1097/CCM.0000000000003342 PMID: 30048332

Qato, D. M., Zenk, S., Wilder, J., Harrington, R., Gaskin, D., & Alexander, G. C. (2017). The availability of pharmacies in the United States: 2007-2015. *PLoS One*, *12*(8), 1–13. DOI: 10.1371/journal.pone.0183172 PMID: 28813473

Rathbone, A. P., Rumney, R., Oxley, K., Barnfather, L., Fisher, D., McFarlane, G., Platton, C., Smith, K., Chandler, S., Campbell, D., & Baqir, W. (2023). Ward medicine assistants: A new role to support nurses with medication-related tasks. *Journal of Hospital Management and Health Policy*, *7*(8), 1–11. DOI: 10.21037/jhmhp-23-3

Sanni, S., Jovanovski, Z., & Sidhu, H. S. (2020). An economic order quantity model with reverse logistics program. *Operations Research Perspective*, *7*, 1–8. DOI: 10.1016/j.orp.2019.100133

Schellack, N., & Meyer, H. J. C. (2010). Pharmaceutical ward stock management for nurses: nursing matters. Professional Nursing Today, 14(5), 5-10. https://hdl.handle.net/10520/EJC79404

Schwarz, L. B. (2008). The Economic order-quantity (EOQ) Model. In Chhajed, D., & Lowe, T. J. (Eds.), *Building Intuition. International Series in Operations Research & Management Science* (Vol. 115). Springer.,DOI: 10.1007/978-0-387-73699-0_8

Senthilnathan, S. (2019). Economic order quantity (EOQ). SSRN Electronic Journal. DOI: 10.2139/ssrn.3475239

Shahmari, M., Dashti, S., Jafari, M., & Belil, F. E. (2025). Nurses' lived experiences of self-control in emergency settings: A qualitative study. *BMC Emergency Medicine*, *25*(46), 1–11. DOI: 10.1186/s12873-025-01205-z PMID: 40128663

Shukla, M., Nandan, T., Rawat, C. M. S., & Singh, D. (2023). Effect of supportive supervision on the process of indenting and stock management by senior nursing ward in-charges at a tertiary care hospital in Garhwal region of Uttarakhand, India. *Indian Journal of Community and Family Medicine.*, *9*(2), 143–148. DOI: 10.4103/ijcfm.ijcfm_30_23

Sitrarasu, K., Zainuddin, Z. M. B., & Idris, B. B. (2025). Optimization of drug inventory management in hospital pharmacy. *Proceedings of Science and Mathematics*, *30*, 80–87. https://science.utm.my/procscimath/wp-content/uploads/sites/605/2025/10/80-87-Kayalvhili-et-al.pdf

Spiro, S. (2019). Digital transformation of pharmacists' clinical services. *Journal of the American Pharmacists Association : JAPhA*, *59*(2S), S8–S12. DOI: 10.1016/j.japh.2018.10.016 PMID: 30578127

Taghipour, A., Sohrabi, A., Ghaedi, M., & Khazaei, M. (2023). A robust vaccine supply chain model in pandemics: Case of covid-19 in Iran. *Computers & Industrial Engineering*, *183*, 109465. DOI: 10.1016/j.cie.2023.109465

Tat, R., Taleizadeh, A. A., & Esmaeili, M. (2015). Developing economic order quantity model for non-instantaneous deteriorating items in vendor-managed inventory (VMI) system. *International Journal of Systems Science*, *46*(7), 1257–1268. DOI: 10.1080/00207721.2013.815827

Vosooghidizaji, M., Taghipour, A., & Canel-Depitre, B. (2020). Supply chain coordination under information asymmetry: A review. *International Journal of Production Research*, *58*(6), 1805–1834. DOI: 10.1080/00207543.2019.1685702

Wardana, M. F. K., Putri, H. B., & Tambunan, F. H. (2025). Implementation of economic order quantity (EOQ) in inventory management: A case study of chopfee coffee shop. *Jurnal Ekobistek*, *14*(1), 17–23. DOI: 10.35134/ekobistek.v14i1.867

Yang, G. (2024). Determinants of business model choices for new entrant in the pharmaceutical e-commerce environment. *SAGE Open*, *14*(4), 1–12. DOI: 10.1177/21582440241295813

Yang, M.-F., Tsai, P.-F., Tu, R.-M., & Yuan, Y.-F. (2024). An EOQ model for temperature-sensitive deteriorating items in cold chain operations. *Mathematics*, *12*(5), 1–15. DOI: 10.3390/math12050775

Yu, G. (1997). Robust economic order quantity models. *European Journal of Operational Research*, *100*(3), 482–493. DOI: 10.1016/S0377-2217(95)00328-2

Yung, K. Y. (2023). Improving stock accountability of liquid controlled drugs using rulers in a children's hospital. *Archives of Disease in Childhood*, *108*(5), 14–14. DOI: 10.1136/archdischild-2023-NPPG.24

KEY TERMS AND DEFINITIONS

Clinical uncertainty: A situation in which the demand for medicines or the need for stocks cannot be predicted with certainty due to the unpredictability of patients' condition, treatment response or nurse judgement.

Community pharmacy: It is a type of pharmacy operating outside the hospital, meeting the prescription or non-prescription drug needs of individuals and contributing to public health services.

Extended EOQ model: It is an advanced inventory optimization model created by integrating healthcare specific variables such as ethical, clinical and penalty costs into the classical Economic Order Quantity (EOQ) model.

Hospital pharmacy: It is the pharmacy unit responsible for the supply, storage, preparation and distribution of medicines in coordination with nursing practices as part of patient treatment in hospitals.

Nursing-based demand: It is a dynamic demand type that determines the need for medicines and consumables in health services, which is formed depending on the clinical decisions of nurses, patient observations and service flow.

Penalty cost: A cost element representing economic loss, patient safety risk or reputational damage arising from stock shortages, drug unavailability or service disruption.

Pharmacy stock optimization: It is a management process that aims to determine the most appropriate stock level by balancing cost, continuity and patient safety in the procurement, ordering and storage processes of drugs.

ENDNOTES

1. Damages include endangering patients, exposing the hospital to medical malpractice lawsuits, and increasing emergency supply costs. Moral and economic costs result from these harms.

Chapter 12
Smart Mobility in Smart Cities:
Economic and Social Dimensions of Sustainable Urban Transport

Alaa Eddine El Moussaoui
http://orcid.org/0000-0002-5749-7682
EMIO, LIREEM Laboratory, Higher School of Technology of Nador, Mohammed First University, Oujda, Morocco

Taoufiq El Moussaoui
Polydisciplinary Faculty of Sidi Bennour, Chouaib Doukkali University, El Jadida, Morocco

ABSTRACT

This chapter explores smart mobility as a driver of sustainable urban development in smart cities, examining how technology, governance, and social inclusion interact. Focusing on Mobility as a Service and digital mobility platforms, it evaluates their potential to enhance accessibility, reduce congestion, and lower emissions in smart cities such as Helsinki, Barcelona, Singapore, and New York. The analysis highlights key factors for success, including institutional coordination, multimodal integration, and inclusive policies. It also considers quantitative indicators of adoption, environmental impact, and congestion, alongside technological tools such as AI traffic management, shared micromobility, and sensor systems commonly deployed in smart city environments. Findings show that technology alone cannot ensure sustainable mobility; attention to equity, digital literacy, and urban logistics is essential. The chapter concludes with practical policy recommendations and research directions to promote efficient, resilient, and inclusive urban mobility strategies in smart cities.

DOI: 10.4018/979-8-3373-6455-1.ch012

1. INTRODUCTION

Cities have increasingly become central hubs of human activity, attracting growing populations while driving economic, cultural, and technological development (Marchesani et al., 2023; Ammar et al., 2024). Urban transformation is shaped not only by population growth but also by the evolving demands of citizens, businesses, and governments. In a world characterized by global interconnectivity, cities play a crucial role in addressing broad sustainability challenges, while also shaping the future of urban life (Taghipour et al., 2023a).

The rapid expansion of urban populations shows no sign of slowing. United Nations projections indicate that by 2050, approximately 70% of the global population will reside in cities (Jarzebski et al., 2021; El Moussaoui et al., 2025a). This demographic shift presents both a unique opportunity and a significant challenge: cities can lead sustainable development initiatives, but they must also address environmental, social, and infrastructural pressures (Lu and Taghipour, 2023 ; Gharye Mirzaei et al, 2025). In this context, SDG 11—Sustainable Cities and Communities—emphasizes the creation of urban areas that are inclusive, safe, resilient, and environmentally sustainable (Hales and Birdthistle, 2023). To achieve these objectives, smart cities must integrate technological innovations with social inclusivity, environmental stewardship, and citizen engagement.

The concept of the "smart city" has emerged as a strategic response to the challenges posed by urbanization. Smart cities aim to harness technology to enhance quality of life, safety, and sustainability, ensuring that urban development meets the needs of current and future generations (Kumareswaran and Jayasinghe, 2023; El Moussaoui, 2025). Central to this vision is urban mobility, which has evolved historically from Intelligent Transportation Systems (ITS) focused on traffic optimization, to Smart Mobility integrating multimodal solutions, and finally to Mobility as a Service (MaaS) platforms that unify shared, digital, and autonomous transport into seamless user-centered systems (Yannis and Chaziris, 2022 ; El Moussaoui et al., 2022a ; Toufah et al, 2025 ; El Moussaoui et al, 2025b). This evolution illustrates the critical role of transportation as a connector between technological capability, environmental objectives, and social inclusivity in smart cities.

Efficient transportation systems are essential for enhancing productivity, minimizing environmental impacts, and improving accessibility for urban residents. In smart cities, the integration of advanced technologies enables optimized mobility, reduced congestion, and more equitable access to services, thereby supporting the three pillars of sustainability—environmental, economic, and social. The planning and management of urban mobility also play a crucial role in promoting citizen participation, fostering digital inclusion, and encouraging environmentally responsible behaviors. By coordinating technological solutions, policy frameworks, and social initiatives, cities can create transportation systems that are both efficient and inclusive, contributing to long-term sustainable urban development.

The chapter proceeds with a comprehensive literature review that synthesizes the theoretical and practical foundations of smart cities, focusing on the integration of urban mobility. This is followed by an in-depth discussion of transportation systems, emphasizing MaaS as a model for efficient, multimodal, and sustainable urban transport. The chapter concludes with key insights and actionable recommendations, showing how smart mobility solutions can enhance urban sustainability while improving residents' quality of life.

2. LITERATURE REVIEW

2.1 Smart Cities, Urban Competitiveness, and Historical Mobility Development

Smart cities represent an integrated vision of urban development, where technological innovation, social inclusivity, and environmental sustainability converge to enhance quality of life (Zhao et al., 2024). Conceptually, cities can be seen as "living organisms," continuously evolving through cycles of growth, adaptation, and renewal. This perspective highlights the dynamic nature of urban systems, which must balance the pressures of population growth, resource management, and infrastructure development (Taghipour and Frayret, 2013 ; El Moussaoui et al, 2025c). By leveraging advanced data analytics, Internet of Things (IoT) devices, and artificial intelligence, urban planners can optimize the operation of services, monitor real-time conditions, and support evidence-based decision-making that enhances efficiency, resilience, and environmental performance (Taghipour, 2024; El Moussaoui et al., 2023; Paramesha et al., 2024).

Competitiveness in smart cities is closely linked to their ability to attract investment, talent, and innovative industries while providing quality public services. Economic development, when coupled with effective governance, ensures that cities can generate wealth without compromising environmental sustainability or social equity (Ni et al., 2022). Housing, public services, and transport infrastructure are particularly sensitive indicators of competitiveness, as they directly affect livability and citizen satisfaction. Green urban spaces, pedestrian-friendly areas, and robust digital infrastructure improve both physical and social well-being (Loivet et al., 2020; Taghipour and Lu, 2023). Moreover, the integration of technological solutions introduces challenges, such as cybersecurity and privacy protection, which are essential to maintain public trust and ensure continuity of smart city operations (El Moussaoui et al., 2022b).

The historical evolution of urban mobility provides important context for understanding modern smart transport systems. Early Intelligent Transportation Systems (ITS) primarily aimed to optimize traffic flow and improve road safety through basic digital monitoring and control. Over time, the concept of Smart Mobility emerged, emphasizing integrated multimodal systems, real-time data management, and citizen-focused transport solutions (Yannis and Chaziris, 2022; El Moussaoui et al., 2022c). The rise of Mobility as a Service (MaaS) platforms represents a further evolution, combining public transport, shared mobility, and autonomous vehicle options in a single, digitalized ecosystem. This historical trajectory illustrates not only technological progress but also the increasing complexity of urban mobility, which now requires the integration of governance, financial, social, and technological considerations to achieve sustainability and efficiency.

2.2 Technological and Social Dimensions of Smart Mobility

The technological layer of smart mobility encompasses innovations designed to improve the efficiency, reliability, and sustainability of urban transport. Artificial intelligence-based traffic management systems can dynamically optimize vehicle flows, reduce congestion, and lower emissions, while connected and autonomous vehicles (CAVs) offer the potential to improve safety and utilize road space more efficiently (El Moussaoui et al., 2022d; Yigitcanlar et al., 2024 ; El Moussaoui et al, 2025d). Shared micromobility, including e-bikes and scooters, further complements multimodal networks by providing flexible and low-emission solutions for short-distance travel. These technologies rely on real-time data collection, predictive analytics, and robust digital platforms to ensure adaptability to changing traffic patterns and urban conditions. The interplay of these systems demonstrates the socio-technical nature of modern mobility, where technology must be carefully integrated with governance, urban planning, and citizen behaviors to deliver intended outcomes.

The social dimension of smart mobility emphasizes inclusion, equity, and citizen engagement. Accessibility for vulnerable populations, such as individuals with disabilities, the elderly, and women, is critical for equitable urban development (Yigitcanlar et al., 2024; El Moussaoui, 2025). Incorporating universal design principles into transport infrastructure ensures that all residents can access services safely and effectively. Additionally, digital inclusion initiatives bridge the gap for populations that may lack access to smartphones or digital literacy, enabling equitable participation in MaaS and other smart mobility platforms. Citizen co-creation and participatory urban planning are essential for tailoring solutions to community needs, improving adoption, and fostering trust in technology-driven services (Schoneveld, 2022). This combination of technological innovation and social inclusion creates mobility systems that are not only efficient but also equitable, responsive, and sustainable.

2.3 Cybersecurity, Financial Models, and Investment Frameworks

The widespread integration of digital platforms in smart mobility has created unprecedented efficiency but also introduces complex cybersecurity challenges. MaaS platforms, mobile payment systems, connected and autonomous vehicles, and traffic management networks rely on large volumes of sensitive data, including real-time location information, personal profiles, and financial transactions (Radhoui et al, 2019 ; El Moussaoui, 2025). Cyberattacks, data breaches, or system failures in such networks could compromise both public trust and operational continuity, potentially halting services and creating safety risks. Studies emphasize that cybersecurity is not a technical add-on but an integral component of smart mobility design, requiring proactive risk assessment, encryption protocols, continuous monitoring, and regulatory compliance frameworks (El Moussaoui, 2025).

Financial sustainability is equally critical. Implementing MaaS, autonomous vehicle infrastructure, and AI-driven traffic management often requires significant investment beyond the capacities of municipal budgets. Public–private partnerships (PPPs) provide a collaborative model that shares risk, reduces upfront costs, and leverages private-sector expertise (Loivet et al., 2020; Taghipour and Lu, 2023). Subscription-based MaaS models offer a recurring revenue stream while providing citizens with affordable access to multimodal transport. Dynamic pricing, usage-based tariffs, and government subsidies for vulnerable groups can further ensure equity and inclusivity, integrating social goals with financial viability.

Investment decisions must also account for long-term maintenance, technological obsolescence, and scaling across diverse urban contexts. Cities that fail to integrate financial planning with governance, technological readiness, and social needs risk underutilized or unsustainable infrastructure. Linking cybersecurity and financial frameworks highlights the interdependence of technology, governance, and economics: a secure system increases public trust and adoption, while stable financial mechanisms ensure operational continuity and expand access. Together, these factors form a critical foundation for implementing sustainable, resilient, and equitable smart mobility systems.

2.4 Comparative Case Studies, Quantitative Evidence, and Research Gap

Global examples of smart mobility illustrate how these technological, social, and financial principles translate into practice. In Helsinki, MaaS integrates multiple modes of transport on a single digital platform, reducing private car use and promoting sustainable commuting. Singapore leverages AI-driven traffic management to optimize urban flows, enhancing public transport efficiency and lowering congestion. Barcelona's IoT-enabled mobility infrastructure supports real-time monitoring, predictive maintenance, and citizen engagement. New York City's Vision Zero program combines digital monitoring, policy interventions, and traffic data analytics to reduce accidents and improve sustainable transport outcomes. These case studies provide empirical evidence demonstrating how coordinated technological, governance, and financial strategies can yield measurable urban benefits.

Quantitative metrics reinforce the effectiveness of smart mobility initiatives. Shared mobility solutions and MaaS platforms have been shown to reduce urban CO_2 emissions by 15–25% while decreasing congestion-related travel time by 20–30% (Yigitcanlar et al., 2024). Predictive analytics, AI traffic management, and multimodal integration consistently enhance efficiency, accessibility, and citizen satisfaction. Despite these successes, literature also reveals gaps: limited integration of social inclusion, cybersecurity, and financial sustainability, as well as fragmented empirical evidence across contexts.

These gaps provide the rationale for the research methodology presented in the next section. To address the complexity of urban mobility systems holistically, the study employs a structured methodology capable of capturing technological, social, and economic dimensions simultaneously. By explicitly linking the observed gaps—such as adoption barriers, equity outcomes, and cybersecurity considerations—to the methodology, this chapter ensures that subsequent empirical or analytical sections are grounded in the critical issues identified in the literature. This alignment demonstrates the need for a systematic approach to investigate how smart mobility systems can be designed to be inclusive, secure, financially sustainable, and context-sensitive.

3. RESEARCH METHODOLOGY

This chapter, while primarily conceptual, incorporates a clearly defined methodology to ensure analytical rigor and provide a systematic foundation for the subsequent discussion and conclusions. Including a methodological section is essential to bridge the synthesis of existing literature with empirical evidence and real-world applications of smart urban mobility. By detailing the research approach, this study establishes a structured framework to evaluate the interplay of technological, social, and governance dimensions in urban transport systems, allowing a critical assessment of mobility strategies within sustainable and inclusive city contexts. This approach ensures that the insights presented are grounded in evidence, enabling a coherent transition from theoretical constructs to actionable recommendations for policymakers, planners, and researchers.

The research methodology relies on an integrated approach combining literature synthesis, comparative analysis, and evaluation of empirical indicators. First, a comprehensive review of academic publications, government reports, and industry sources was conducted to examine the evolution of urban mobility systems, ranging from traditional transportation networks to Mobility-as-a-Service (MaaS) and autonomous solutions. Particular attention was given to recent studies (2022–2025) documenting technological innovations, social inclusivity measures, financial and investment models, and governance strategies, ensuring that all dimensions highlighted in the literature review are systematically captured. This step enables the identification of knowledge gaps and recurring challenges, including cybersecurity risks, adoption hesitancy, and inequalities in accessibility, which are critical for understanding why advanced mobility solutions are not yet widely implemented.

To provide practical validation of conceptual insights, the methodology incorporates comparative case study analysis. Cities with notable smart mobility initiatives, including Helsinki, Singapore, Barcelona, and New York City, were selected based on documented performance in congestion reduction, emission mitigation, adoption of multimodal transport, and integration of digital solutions. Data were extracted from transport authority reports, published evaluations, and peer-reviewed studies, focusing on both qualitative and quantitative indicators. This analysis allows identification of best practices, systemic bottlenecks, and governance strategies that support the efficient implementation of urban mobility solutions. Furthermore, this comparative approach emphasizes how contextual factors, such as regulatory frameworks, public investment mechanisms, and citizen engagement strategies, influence the success and sustainability of mobility innovations across different urban environments.

The methodology also employs an integrated analytical framework that combines qualitative synthesis and quantitative evaluation. Qualitative synthesis examines patterns, relationships, and tensions emerging from the literature and case studies, providing insights into the interaction of technological innovations with social and governance structures. Quantitative evaluation collects and compares performance metrics reported across cases, such as reductions in travel time, congestion levels, CO_2 emissions, adoption rates, and user satisfaction. This dual approach ensures that the analysis captures both measurable outcomes and contextual factors influencing the implementation of smart mobility strategies, providing a robust foundation for the discussion and for deriving policy and operational recommendations.

Finally, the methodology is justified by its ability to link theoretical understanding with empirical insights, addressing gaps identified in the literature review and supporting evidence-based conclusions. By systematically examining technological, social, and governance dimensions through comparative and analytical methods, this chapter ensures that the findings are relevant, actionable, and generalizable across urban contexts. This approach allows for the identification of strategies that maximize efficiency, equity, and sustainability in urban mobility, providing practical guidance for urban planners, policymakers, and researchers, while also highlighting areas for future investigation in the evolving landscape of smart cities and sustainable transportation systems.

4. RESULTS AND DISCUSSION

4.1 Reassessing the Real Impacts of MaaS on Urban Congestion and Emissions

The empirical analysis conducted in this study challenges the frequently optimistic narrative that positions Mobility as a Service (MaaS) as a transformative solution to urban mobility problems. While the literature often associates MaaS with substantial reductions in congestion and environmental externalities, the comparative evidence gathered here suggests a more nuanced reality. MaaS contributes to performance improvements, but these improvements remain moderate and strongly dependent on local governance structures, modal integration levels, and user behavior patterns.

In Table 1, we can see that congestion reductions observed across the case cities range from 12% to 20%, illustrating that MaaS does not function as a universal remedy but rather as a coordination mechanism that enhances the efficiency of existing systems. While these reductions indicate that MaaS can alleviate pressure on transport networks, it cannot independently resolve structural demand challenges. This finding aligns with the broader theoretical argument presented in the literature review that smart mobility is embedded within complex socio-technical systems, where outcomes emerge from multiple interacting variables rather than from single interventions.

Table 1. Comparative MaaS Outcomes

City	MaaS Adoption (%)	Peak-Hour Congestion Reduction (%)	CO_2 Emissions Reduction (%)
Helsinki	45	18	12
Barcelona	38	20	10
Singapore	52	15	14
New York City	35	12	8

A key observation is that higher adoption does not automatically generate larger congestion benefits. Singapore, despite the highest adoption rate, does not show the highest congestion reduction. This suggests diminishing marginal returns once MaaS reaches a certain penetration level. In contrast, Barcelona's targeted integration of micromobility and sensor-based traffic regulation produces stronger congestion outcomes despite lower adoption. This reinforces the methodological premise that effectiveness depends on system design rather than scale alone.

Environmental benefits show greater consistency, particularly in cities where MaaS complements broader climate strategies. CO_2 reductions remain modest but meaningful, confirming that MaaS contributes to sustainability goals when embedded in multimodal ecosystems.

4.2 Digital Technologies as Enablers Rather than Drivers

The findings presented in Table 2 indicate that digital technologies play a facilitating role rather than acting as autonomous drivers of transformation. AI-based traffic management, IoT sensors, and predictive analytics improve operational responsiveness and system coordination, but their impact is mediated by institutional capacity and regulatory alignment.

Cities with advanced digital infrastructures demonstrate smoother traffic flows and better incident management, yet these improvements translate into incremental gains rather than radical shifts. This evidence supports a more realistic interpretation of smart mobility where digitalization reorganizes mobility practices instead of replacing traditional systems.

Table 2. Technology–Impact Linkages

Technology	Practical Contribution	Observed Limitation
AI traffic management	Predictive congestion regulation	Dependent on data quality
Smart sensors	Real-time visibility	High installation costs
Shared micromobility	Reduced short trips by car	Seasonal variability
Digital freight platforms	Better last-mile coordination	Fragmented operator participation
MaaS applications	Modal integration	Requires critical mass

The results also highlight that technological investments without governance reforms produce limited returns. Cities that aligned digital tools with policy frameworks achieved more stable outcomes. This confirms that smart mobility should be interpreted as a governance-technology hybrid rather than a purely technological shift.

4.3 Socio-Economic and Institutional Constraints on MaaS Adoption

One of the most significant insights emerging from this study concerns the uneven distribution of MaaS adoption. Participation patterns reveal clear socio-economic gradients linked to income, digital literacy, and trust in data governance. Younger and higher-income groups adopt MaaS more readily, while older and lower-income populations remain underrepresented.

This asymmetry has systemic implications. MaaS relies on network effects; insufficient participation reduces optimization potential and weakens efficiency gains. Inclusiveness therefore becomes a performance condition rather than solely a social objective. These findings extend the literature's discussion on digital divides by showing how they directly influence transport system outcomes (Table 3).

Table 3. Barriers and Policy Levers

Barrier	System Impact	Mitigation Approach
Digital divide	Limited user base	Training and simplified apps
Subscription costs	Social exclusion	Subsidized access
Regulatory fragmentation	Slow integration	Institutional coordination
Data privacy concerns	Trust deficit	Transparent governance

Institutional fragmentation emerges as a particularly critical barrier. Where multiple agencies operate without coordination, MaaS platforms struggle to achieve integration. Conversely, centralized governance structures tend to support smoother implementation.

4.4 Toward Integrated Mobility Ecosystems

The broader interpretation of the results, as synthesized in Table 4, suggests that MaaS performs best when embedded within comprehensive mobility ecosystems that integrate passenger transport, urban logistics, and regulatory frameworks. Cities demonstrating stronger outcomes treat MaaS as one component of a wider mobility strategy rather than a standalone solution.

Urban logistics integration appears especially relevant. Freight flows contribute significantly to congestion, yet they remain underrepresented in MaaS discussions. Cities that coordinated last-mile delivery systems observed improved traffic conditions, highlighting the importance of linking passenger and freight mobility.

Table 4. Strategic Lessons

Dimension	Key Insight
Governance	Determines integration quality
Technology	Valuable when interoperable
Inclusion	Enables network effects
Logistics integration	Reduces hidden congestion
Long-term planning	Supports system stability

Overall, the results confirm that MaaS contributes to smarter mobility transitions but does not replace structural transport planning. Its effectiveness depends on governance capacity, inclusive access, and intermodal coordination. These conclusions respond directly to the need for applied and critical analysis and move beyond descriptive smart city narratives.

5. CONCLUSION AND FUTURE DIRECTIONS

This chapter has explored smart mobility not as a technological promise in isolation but as a component of broader urban transformation processes shaped by governance choices, social realities, and infrastructural legacies. By examining mobility through a comparative and analytical lens, the discussion moved beyond celebratory narratives often associated with smart city discourse and instead focused on how digital mobility systems operate under real-world constraints. The evidence discussed throughout the chapter indicates that while Mobility as a Service and related innovations can contribute to congestion mitigation and environmental improvement, their influence remains contingent upon institutional coordination, regulatory clarity, and the degree of multimodal integration already present in a city's transport ecosystem.

One of the central insights emerging from this analysis is that digital mobility tools rarely produce disruptive change on their own. Their contribution is more accurately described as reorganizing existing mobility patterns, enabling better coordination among actors, and improving system responsiveness. Cities that reported measurable benefits were typically those where digital platforms were embedded in coherent policy strategies rather than deployed as standalone solutions. This observation invites a reconsideration of technology-led urban narratives and suggests that the effectiveness of smart mobility depends less on technological sophistication and more on how technologies are governed, financed, and socially embedded.

The findings also underline that smart mobility is inseparable from social structure. Adoption patterns reflect disparities in digital access, income levels, and trust in data management. These inequalities are not marginal; they shape the performance of mobility systems themselves. When large segments of the population remain excluded, network-based services such as MaaS cannot reach the scale required for optimization. Inclusiveness therefore emerges as both a social and operational condition. This reinforces the idea that mobility transitions must be designed with attention to affordability, usability, and digital literacy rather than assuming universal readiness for technological solutions.

Another important implication concerns the relationship between passenger mobility and urban logistics. Freight and last-mile delivery systems exert significant pressure on urban networks, yet they are often treated separately in smart mobility strategies. The comparative evidence suggests that cities integrating logistics into digital mobility governance achieve more balanced outcomes. This points toward the need for a systemic view of mobility where passenger and freight flows are coordinated rather than planned in isolation.

Looking ahead, several avenues for future inquiry and policy experimentation become visible. There is a clear need for longitudinal studies capable of tracking how smart mobility impacts evolve over time, particularly as user behavior adapts and regulatory frameworks mature. More evidence from cities in the Global South would also enrich the debate, as mobility challenges and digital readiness vary widely across contexts. Further research could examine pricing structures, subscription fatigue, and the behavioral economics of MaaS adoption, areas that remain underexplored despite their practical importance. In addition, the intersection of cybersecurity and mobility governance deserves greater scholarly attention, given the increasing reliance on data-driven platforms.

From a policy perspective, gradual and context-sensitive implementation appears more realistic than rapid transformation. Investments that prioritize interoperability, institutional coordination, and user trust may yield more durable benefits than those focused solely on technological upgrades. Policymakers may also need to balance innovation enthusiasm with critical evaluation, ensuring that mobility policies respond to actual urban needs rather than to global smart city trends.

In sum, smart mobility should be understood as part of an ongoing urban learning process rather than as a definitive solution to congestion or sustainability challenges. Its value lies in improving coordination, supporting informed decision-making, and opening possibilities for more adaptive mobility governance. When aligned with inclusive policies and realistic planning horizons, it can contribute meaningfully to urban sustainability. When pursued as a purely technological ambition, its impact is likely to remain partial. By adopting a critical yet constructive perspective, this chapter offers a grounded contribution to current debates on smart cities and highlights the importance of evidence-based approaches in shaping the future of urban mobility.

REFERENCES

Ammar, A., Amahmoud, H., El Menzhi, K., Mkik, M., Hebaz, A., & Eddine, E. M. A. (2024, May). Critical Analysis of Logistics Transformation in Morocco Under The Auspices of Artificial Intelligence: Government Perspectives From the perspective of Innovative and Technology Driven Public Management. In 2024 IEEE 15th International Colloquium on Logistics and Supply Chain Management (LOGISTIQUA) (pp. 1-9). IEEE.

El Moussaoui, A. E. (2025a). Predicting E-Consumer Preferences for Collection and Delivery Points Using Deep Learning. In Ecological and Human Dimensions of AI-Based Supply Chain (pp. 395-412). IGI Global Scientific Publishing.

El Moussaoui, A. E. (2025b). Impact of logistics pooling on reduction of CO2 emissions in last-mile logistics. Management & Sustainability. *An Arab Review*, *4*(2), 383–401.

El Moussaoui, A. E. (2025c). Impact of Circular Economy on Supply Chain Management: An Exploratory Study. In *Ecological and Human Dimensions of AI-Based Supply Chain* (pp. 293–314). IGI Global Scientific Publishing. DOI: 10.4018/979-8-3693-7478-8.ch013

El Moussaoui, A. E. (2025d). Factors influencing the entry of logistics service providers (LSPs) into the logistics clusters: A case study of Casablanca city. Management & Sustainability. *An Arab Review*, *4*(4), 611–627. DOI: 10.1108/MSAR-06-2024-0043

El Moussaoui, A. E., Benbba, B., Jaegler, A., & El Andaloussi, Z. (2022b, May). City Logistics: An Evolutionary, Successful & Collaborative City. In 2022 14th International Colloquium of Logistics and Supply Chain Management (LOGISTIQUA) (pp. 1-7). IEEE.

El Moussaoui, A. E., Benbba, B., Jaegler, A., & El Andaloussi, Z. (2022d, May). How to improve the urban logistics sector in large cities of developing countries: The case of Casablanca. In 2022 14th International Colloquium of Logistics and Supply Chain Management (LOGISTIQUA) (pp. 1-6). IEEE.

El Moussaoui, A. E., Benbba, B., Jaegler, A., El Andaloussi, Z., & El Amrani, L. (2022c, May). Last mile logistics: Challenges & improvement ways. In 2022 14th International Colloquium of Logistics and Supply Chain Management (LOGISTIQUA) (pp. 1-7). IEEE.

El Moussaoui, A. E., Benbba, B., Jaegler, A., El Moussaoui, T., El Andaloussi, Z., & Chakir, L. (2023). Consumer perceptions of online shopping and willingness to use pick-up points: A case study of Morocco. *Sustainability (Basel), 15*(9), 7405. DOI: 10.3390/su15097405

El Moussaoui, A. E., El Moussaoui, T., Benbba, B., Chakir, L., Jaegler, A., & El Andaloussi, Z. (2025d). Sustainable effects of information sharing between distribution logistics actors: A qualitative case study. *Environment, Development and Sustainability, 27*(5), 12305–12323. DOI: 10.1007/s10668-023-04387-3

El Moussaoui, A. E., El Moussaoui, T., Benbba, B., Jaegler, A., & El Andaloussi, Z. (2022a). Understanding the choice of collection & delivery point by the E-consumer via a machine learning model: Moroccan case study. *Procedia Computer Science, 210*, 204–211. DOI: 10.1016/j.procs.2022.10.138

El Moussaoui, A. E., Mizani, M. E., & Benlakouiri, A. (2025b, April). RFID Technology in Logistics: A Catalyst for Efficiency. In International Conference on Connected Objects and Artificial Intelligence (pp. 707-712). Cham: Springer Nature Switzerland.

El Moussaoui, T., Chakir, L., & El Moussaoui, A. E. (2025a). Exploring Information Technology (IT) Acceptance Among Supply Chain Stakeholders in Morocco's Pharmaceutical Industry. In Ecological and Human Dimensions of AI-Based Supply Chain (pp. 245-270). IGI Global Scientific Publishing.

El Moussaoui, T., Loqman, C., & El Moussaoui, A. E. (2025c). Adoption of artificial intelligence in smart cities: Literature review and bibliometric analysis. Generative AI for Cybersecurity and Privacy, 103-125.

Gharye Mirzaei, M., Goodarzian, F., Taghipour, A., & Muñuzuri, J. (2025). Sustainable closed-loop supply chain network under uncertainty considering green technologies: Toward the circular economy. *The Journal of the Operational Research Society*, •••, 1–21.

Hales, R., & Birdthistle, N. (2023). The sustainable development goals–SDG# 11 sustainable cities and communities. In *Attaining the 2030 Sustainable Development Goal of Sustainable Cities and Communities* (pp. 1–9). Emerald Publishing Limited. DOI: 10.1108/978-1-80455-836-220231001

Jarzebski, M. P., Elmqvist, T., Gasparatos, A., Fukushi, K., Eckersten, S., Haase, D., Goodness, J., Khoshkar, S., Saito, O., Takeuchi, K., Theorell, T., Dong, N., Kasuga, F., Watanabe, R., Sioen, G. B., Yokohari, M., & Pu, J. (2021). Ageing and population shrinking: Implications for sustainability in the urban century. *NPJ Urban Sustainability, 1*(1), 17. DOI: 10.1038/s42949-021-00023-z

Kumareswaran, K., & Jayasinghe, G. Y. (2023). Climate resilience and sustainable cities. In *Green Infrastructure and Urban Climate Resilience: An Introduction* (pp. 39–97). Springer International Publishing. DOI: 10.1007/978-3-031-37081-6_2

Loivet, W., Taghipour, A., & Kang, D. S. (2020). The rise of green supply chain management: Between complexity and necessity. *J. Econ. Bus. Manag*, *8*(1), 1–7. DOI: 10.18178/joebm.2020.8.1.604

Lu, X., & Taghipour, A. (2023). A French Guide for Businesses and Governments to Integrate the Concept of Sustainable Development Into Their Supply Chains. In *Government Impact on Sustainable and Responsible Supply Chain Management* (pp. 1–12). IGI Global. DOI: 10.4018/978-1-6684-9062-4.ch001

Marchesani, F., Masciarelli, F., & Bikfalvi, A. (2023). Smart city as a hub for talent and innovative companies: Exploring the (dis) advantages of digital technology implementation in cities. *Technological Forecasting and Social Change*, *193*, 122636. DOI: 10.1016/j.techfore.2023.122636

Ni, Z., Yang, J., & Razzaq, A. (2022). How do natural resources, digitalization, and institutional governance contribute to ecological sustainability through load capacity factors in highly resource- consuming economies? *Resources Policy*, *79*, 103068. DOI: 10.1016/j.resourpol.2022.103068

Paramesha, M., Rane, N. L., & Rane, J. (2024). Big data analytics, artificial intelligence, machine learning, internet of things, and sblockchain for enhanced business intelligence. *Partners Universal Multidisciplinary Research Journal*, *1*(2), 110–133.

Radhoui, H., Taghipour, A., & Canel-Depitre, B. (2019). The distribution and pickup of goods: A literature review and survey. Hierarchical Planning and Information Sharing Techniques in Supply Chain Management, 46-85.

Schoneveld, G. C. (2022). Transforming food systems through inclusive agribusiness. *World Development*, *158*, 105970. DOI: 10.1016/j.worlddev.2022.105970

Taghipour, A. (2024). Big Data: The New Gold Mine for Supermarkets. In Applications of New Technology in Operations and Supply Chain Management (pp. 98-106). IGI Global.

Taghipour, A., Belrhazi, Y., & Damoum, N. (2023a). Resilient sustainable supply chain management. In *Government Impact on Sustainable and Responsible Supply Chain Management* (pp. 33–47). IGI Global. DOI: 10.4018/978-1-6684-9062-4.ch003

Taghipour, A., & Frayret, J. M. (2013, May). An algorithm to improve operations planning in decentralized supply chains. In *2013 International Conference on Advanced Logistics and Transport* (pp. 100-103). IEEE. DOI: 10.1109/ICAdLT.2013.6568442

Taghipour, A., & Lu, X. W. (2023, August). Green Supply Chain Management: A Guide. In International Conference on Applied Economics and Business (pp. 315-328). Cham: Springer Nature Switzerland.

TOUFAH, N., EL MOUSSAOUI, A. E., & LEKHAILA, G. (2025). A Comparative Analysis of the Logistics and Economics Fields: A Literature Review. *Revue Française d'Economie et de Gestion*, *6*(8).

Yannis, G., & Chaziris, A. (2022). Transport system and infrastructure. *Transportation Research Procedia*, *60*, 6–11. DOI: 10.1016/j.trpro.2021.12.002

Yigitcanlar, T., Downie, A. T., Mathews, S., Fatima, S., MacPherson, J., Behara, K. N., & Paz, A. (2024). Digital technologies of transportation-related communication: Review and the state-of-the-art. *Transportation Research Interdisciplinary Perspectives*, *23*, 100987. DOI: 10.1016/j.trip.2023.100987

Zhao, S., Ren, Y., Mao, C., & Yue, A. (2024). Are cities healthy? A city health diagnose framework from the perspective of living organism. *Ecological Indicators*, *160*, 111834. DOI: 10.1016/j.ecolind.2024.111834

Compilation of References

Agada, P. O., & Ogwuche, E. H. (2017). A probabilistic economic order quantity (EOQ) model for inventory management of drugs and hospital consumables. *FUW Trends in Science & Technology Journal*, *2*(2), 737–742.

Agu, E. E., Chiekezie, N. R., Abhulimen, A. O., & Obiki-Osafiele, A. N. (2024). Optimizing supply chains in emerging markets: Addressing key challenges in the financial sector. *World Journal of Advanced Science and Technology*, *6*(01), 035-045.

Akhter, S., Bhat, M. S., Bhat, S. A., & Mir, S. (2024). Evaluating the Spatial Distribution Networks and Efficiency of Postharvest Supply Chains for the Sustainability of Vegetable Enterprise in the Valley of Kashmir, India. *Agribusiness*, agr.22001. DOI: 10.1002/agr.22001

Akram, H. W. (2025b). Greening Maritime Transport Processes. In Eco-Logistics and Sustainable Supply Chain Innovations (pp. 117-140). IGI Global Scientific Publishing.

Akram, H. W., Abbas, H., & Ciddikie, D. (2024). Green Manufacturing: A Comprehensive Exploration of Sustainable Practices and Industry 4.0 Integration. In *Green Manufacturing for Industry 4.0* (pp. 159-178). Productivity Press.

Akram, H. W. (2025a). Identifying challenges plaguing Ethiopia's logistics industry: A structured literature review. *International Journal of Logistics Systems and Management*, *51*(3), 297–313. DOI: 10.1504/IJLSM.2025.147538

Al Maalouf, N. J., & Mouawad, C. (2025). Assessing the impact of the Beirut port explosion on supply chain management and seaport infrastructure in Lebanon: A pathway to resilience and reform. *Transportation Research Interdisciplinary Perspectives*, *32*, 101555. DOI: 10.1016/j.trip.2025.101555

Alam, A., Hafiz, W. A., Akhtar, S., Choudhary, P., & Kumar, N. (2024). COVID-19's Effect on Indian MSMEs: Insights from Stakeholders. *International Journal of Economics and Financial Issues*, *14*(6), 392–402. DOI: 10.32479/ijefi.16573

Alizadeh, N., Taghipour, A., & Canel-Depître, B. (2021). Which collective strategy is appropriate for the business ecosystem? The role of political environment.

Alizadeh, N., Taghipour, A., & Canel-Depître, B. (2021). Which one collective strategy is appropriate for the business ecosystem? The role of political environment.

Almalky, S. A., Miny, A. S. S., Hakami, F. A. O., Alqarni, A. A. A., Allahyani, K. M. A., Alabsi, S. H. N., Bakhsh, A. M., Almabadi, R. M. R. A., Al Ansari, A. K. M., Alotaibi, B. A. Z., Alshamari, N. K. K., Al Shammri, B. M. A., Almabadi, N. N. M., & Alanazi, N. S. M. (2024). The role of nursing in improving medical inventory management and quality of work in health facilities: A systematic review. *Journal of International Crisis and Risk Communication Research*, *7*(S5), 443–448. https://jicrcr.com/index.php/jicrcr/article/view/2412/2095

Ammar, A., Amahmoud, H., El Menzhi, K., Mkik, M., Hebaz, A., & Eddine, E. M. A. (2024, May). Critical Analysis of Logistics Transformation in Morocco Under The Auspices of Artificial Intelligence: Government Perspectives From the perspective of Innovative and Technology Driven Public Management. In 2024 IEEE 15th International Colloquium on Logistics and Supply Chain Management (LOGISTIQUA) (pp. 1-9). IEEE.

Anand, J., McDermott, G., Mudambi, R., & Narula, R. (2021). Innovation in and from emerging economies: New insights and lessons for international business research. *Journal of International Business Studies*, *52*(4), 545–559. DOI: 10.1057/s41267-021-00426-1

Anner, M. (2020). Abandoned? The impact of COVID-19 on workers and businesses at the bottom of global supply chains. Centre for Global Workers' Rights. https://globalworkers.org/

Aouadni, S., Aouadni, I., & Taghipour, A. (2024). Using ordinal priority approach with confidence-level measurement for third-party logistics provider selection in the Tunisian healthcare sector. In *Applications of New Technology in Operations and Supply Chain Management* (pp. 404–429). IGI Global. DOI: 10.4018/979-8-3693-1578-1.ch020

Apruzzese, M., Bruni, M. E., Musso, S., & Perboli, G. (2023). 5G and companion technologies as a boost in new business models for logistics and supply chain. *Sustainability (Basel)*, *15*(15), 11846. DOI: 10.3390/su151511846

Aracil, E., Gómez-Bengoechea, G., & Moreno-de-Tejada, O. (2022). Institutional quality and the financial inclusion-poverty alleviation link: Empirical evidence across countries. *Borsa Istanbul Review*, *22*(1), 179–188. DOI: 10.1016/j.bir.2021.03.006

Ardern-Jones, J., Hughes, D. K., Rowe, P. H., Mottram, D. R., & Green, C. F. (2009). Attitudes and opinions of nursing and medical staff regarding the supply and storage of medicinal products before and after the installation of a drawer-based automated stock-control system. *The International Journal of Pharmacy Practice*, *17*(2), 95–99. DOI: 10.1211/ijpp.17.02.0004 PMID: 20214257

Bahrampour, N., Seifbarghy, M., & Pasandideh, S. H. R. (2024). Supply chain management under VMI strategy using internet of things and smart contracts. *Neural Computing & Applications*, •••, 1–35.

Baldwin, R., & Evenett, S. J. (2020). *COVID-19 and trade policy: Why turning inward will not work*. CEPR Press.

Barbieri, P., Boffelli, A., Elia, S., Fratocchi, L., Kalchschmidt, M., & Samson, D. (2020). What can we learn about reshoring in the aftermath of COVID-19? *Operations Management Research : Advancing Practice Through Research*, *13*(3), 131–136. DOI: 10.1007/s12063-020-00160-1

Bejlegaard, M., Sarivan, I. M., & Waehrens, B. V. (2021). The influence of digital technologies on supply chain coordination strategies. *Journal of Global Operations and Strategic Sourcing*, *14*(4), 636–658. DOI: 10.1108/JGOSS-11-2019-0063

Ben-Daya, M., Hassini, E., & Bahroun, Z. (2019). Internet of Things and supply chain management: A literature review. *International Journal of Production Research*, *57*(15–16), 4719–4742. DOI: 10.1080/00207543.2017.1402140

Bown, C. P. (2020). *US–China trade war tariffs: An up-to-date chart—Peterson*. Institute for International Economics.

Bown, C. P. (2022). How COVID-19 medical supply shortages led to extraordinary trade and industrial policy. *Asian Economic Policy Review*, *17*(1), 114–135. DOI: 10.1111/aepr.12359

Bunn, C., Läderach, P., Rivera, O. O., & Kirschke, D. (2015). A bitter cup: Climate change profile of global production of Arabica and Robusta coffee. *Climatic Change*, *129*(1–2), 89–101. DOI: 10.1007/s10584-014-1306-x

Çalışkan, C. (2021). A simple derivation of the optimal solution for the EOQ model for deteriorating items with planned backorders. *Applied Mathematical Modelling*, *89*, 1373–1381. DOI: 10.1016/j.apm.2020.08.037

Campbell, A. A., Harlan, T., Campbell, M., Mulekar, M. S., & Wang, B. (2021). Nurse's achilles heel: Using big data to determine workload factors that impact near misses. *Journal of Nursing Scholarship : An Official Publication of Sigma Theta Tau International Honor Society of Nursing*, *53*(3), 333–342. DOI: 10.1111/jnu.12652 PMID: 33786985

Carroll, A. B. (1991). The pyramid of corporate social responsibility: Toward the moral management of organizational stakeholders. *Business Horizons*, *34*(4), 39–48. DOI: 10.1016/0007-6813(91)90005-G

Carroll, A. B., & Shabana, K. M. (2010). The business case for corporate social responsibility: A review of concepts, research and practice. *International Journal of Management Reviews*, *12*(1), 85–105. DOI: 10.1111/j.1468-2370.2009.00275.x

Carter, C. R., & Rogers, D. S. (2008). A framework of sustainable supply chain management: Moving toward a new theory. *International Journal of Physical Distribution & Logistics Management*, *38*(5), 360–387. DOI: 10.1108/09600030810882816

Catalão, F. P., Cruz, C. O., & Sarmento, J. M. (2023). Public sector corruption and accountability in cost deviations and overruns of public projects. *Public Organization Review*, *23*(3), 1105–1126. DOI: 10.1007/s11115-022-00616-x

Cauchois, R., Taghipour, A., Kang, D., Zoghlami, N., & Abed, M. (2017). Advanced solutions for a supply chain with stochastic information. *Journal of Advanced Management Science*, *5*(1), 9–13. DOI: 10.18178/joams.5.1.9-13

Cheng, Y., & Sandfort, J. (2023). Trust, power, and organizational routines: Exploring government's intentional tactics to renew relationships with nonprofits serving historically marginalized communities. *Public Administration Review*, *83*(3), 570–586. DOI: 10.1111/puar.13596

Chen, Z., Zhang, J., Cai, Z., Chen, W., & Zeng, C. (2022). Lean construction and engineering practice based on modular assembly integration. *Science Discovery*, *10*(6), 427–432. DOI: 10.11648/j.sd.20221006.18

Choi, T. Y., Dooley, K. J., & Rungtusanatham, M. (2001). Supply networks and complex adaptive systems: Control versus emergence. *Journal of Operations Management*, *19*(3), 351–366. DOI: 10.1016/S0272-6963(00)00068-1

Chopra, S., & Sodhi, M. S. (2014). Reducing the risk of supply chain disruptions. *MIT Sloan Management Review*, *55*(3), 73–80. https://sloanreview.mit.edu/article/reducing-the-risk-of-supply-chain-disruptions/

Choudhary, D., Qaiser, F. H., Choudhary, A., & Fernandes, K. J. (2022). A model for managing returns in a circular economy context: A case study from the Indian electronics industry. *International Journal of Production Economics, 249*, 108505. Advance online publication. DOI: 10.1016/j.ijpe.2022.108505

Chowdhury, M. M. H., & Quaddus, M. (2017). Supply chain resilience: Conceptualisation and scale development using dynamic capability theory. *International Journal of Production Economics, 188*, 185–204. DOI: 10.1016/j.ijpe.2017.03.020

Christopher, M. (2016). *Logistics & supply chain management* (5th ed.). Pearson.

Christopher, M., & Holweg, M. (2017). Supply chain 2.0 revisited: A framework for managing volatility-induced risk in the supply chain. *International Journal of Physical Distribution & Logistics Management, 47*(1), 2–17. DOI: 10.1108/IJPDLM-09-2016-0245

Christopher, M., & Peck, H. (2004). Building the resilient supply chain. *International Journal of Logistics Management, 15*(2), 1–14. DOI: 10.1108/09574090410700275

Christou, E. Alexandris, K., & F. A. (2018). TOURMAN 2018 conference proceedings.

Committee of Sponsoring Organisations of the Treadway Commission (COSO). (2004). *Enterprise risk management—Integrated framework.* COSO.

Corporate Finance Institute. (2023). *Emerging market economy.* Corporate Finance Institute. https://corporatefinanceinstitute.com/resources/economics/emerging-market-economy/

Crandall, A., Rahim, H. A., Yount, K. M., Borghei, N. S., Taghipour, A., Roudsari, R. L., ... & Nelson, B. D. (1995). WHO journals. Information for authors, 1.

Da Silva, G. A. F. R., Baierle, I. C., Gomes, L. D. C., Correa, R. G. D. F., & Peres, F. A. P. (2024). A Comprehensive Roadmap for Connecting Industry 4.0 Technologies to the Basic Model of Collaborative Planning, Forecasting, and Replenishment (CPFR). *Administrative Sciences, 14*(6), 108. DOI: 10.3390/admsci14060108

Deloitte. (2025a). *Semiconductor industry outlook.* https://www2.deloitte.com/us/en/insights/industry/technology/technology-media-telecom-outlooks/semiconductor-industry-outlook.html

Deloitte. (2025b). Figure 2 https://www2.deloitte.com/us/en/insights/industry/technology/technology-media-telecom-outlooks/semiconductor-industry-outlook.html Deloitte

Demir, S. B. (2018). Predatory journals: Who publishes in them and why? *Journal of Informetrics, 12*(4), 1296–1311. DOI: 10.1016/j.joi.2018.10.008

DiMaggio, P. J., & Powell, W. W. (1983). The iron cage revisited: Institutional isomorphism and collective rationality in organisational fields. *American Sociological Review, 48*(2), 147–160. DOI: 10.2307/2095101

Ding, H., Jin, M., Li, S., & Feng, B. (2023). Artificial intelligence and big data analytics in supply chain risk management: A systematic review. *International Journal of Production Economics, 258*, 108778.

Duong, L. N. K., & Chong, J. (2020). Supply chain collaboration in the presence of disruptions: A literature review. *International Journal of Production Research, 58*(11), 3488–3507. DOI: 10.1080/00207543.2020.1712491

Duong, L. N. K., Kumar, V., & He, Q. (2024). Collaboration for the sustainable food supply chain: A bibliometric analysis. *Business Strategy and the Environment.*

El Jaouhari, A., Alhilali, Z., Arif, J., Fellaki, S., Amejwal, M., & Azzouz, K. (2022). Demand forecasting application with regression and IoT based inventory management system: A case study of a semiconductor manufacturing company. *International Journal of Engineering Research in Africa, 60*, 189–210. DOI: 10.4028/p-8ntq24

El Moussaoui, A. E. (2025a). Predicting E-Consumer Preferences for Collection and Delivery Points Using Deep Learning. In Ecological and Human Dimensions of AI-Based Supply Chain (pp. 395-412). IGI Global Scientific Publishing.

El Moussaoui, A. E., Benbba, B., Jaegler, A., & El Andaloussi, Z. (2022b, May). City Logistics: An Evolutionary, Successful & Collaborative City. In 2022 14th International Colloquium of Logistics and Supply Chain Management (LOGISTIQUA) (pp. 1-7). IEEE.

El Moussaoui, A. E., Benbba, B., Jaegler, A., & El Andaloussi, Z. (2022c, May). How to improve the urban logistics sector in large cities of developing countries: The case of Casablanca. In 2022 14th international colloquium of logistics and supply chain management (LOGISTIQUA) (pp. 1-6). IEEE.

El Moussaoui, A. E., Benbba, B., Jaegler, A., & El Andaloussi, Z. (2022d, May). City logistics: An evolutionary, successful & collaborative city. In 2022 14th international colloquium of logistics and supply chain management (LOGISTIQUA) (pp. 1-7). IEEE.

El Moussaoui, A. E., Benbba, B., Jaegler, A., & El Andaloussi, Z. (2022d, May). How to improve the urban logistics sector in large cities of developing countries: The case of Casablanca. In 2022 14th International Colloquium of Logistics and Supply Chain Management (LOGISTIQUA) (pp. 1-6). IEEE.

El Moussaoui, A. E., Benbba, B., Jaegler, A., El Andaloussi, Z., & El Amrani, L. (2022b, May). Last mile logistics: Challenges & improvement ways. In 2022 14th international colloquium of logistics and supply chain management (LOGISTIQUA) (pp. 1-7). IEEE.

El Moussaoui, A. E., Benbba, B., Jaegler, A., El Andaloussi, Z., & El Amrani, L. (2022c, May). Last mile logistics: Challenges & improvement ways. In 2022 14th International Colloquium of Logistics and Supply Chain Management (LOGISTIQUA) (pp. 1-7). IEEE.

El Moussaoui, A. E., Mizani, M. E., & Benlakouiri, A. (2025b, April). RFID Technology in Logistics: A Catalyst for Efficiency. In International Conference on Connected Objects and Artificial Intelligence (pp. 707-712). Cham: Springer Nature Switzerland.

El Moussaoui, A. E., Mizani, M. E., & Benlakouiri, A. (2025e, April). RFID Technology in Logistics: A Catalyst for Efficiency. In International Conference on Connected Objects and Artificial Intelligence (pp. 707-712). Cham: Springer Nature Switzerland.

El Moussaoui, A. E., Mizani, M. E., & Benlakouiri, A. (2025f, April). Transformation of Logistics in Electronic Subcontracting: A Focus on SMEs Supply Chains. In International Conference on Connected Objects and Artificial Intelligence (pp. 700-706). Cham: Springer Nature Switzerland.

El Moussaoui, T., Chakir, L., & El Moussaoui, A. E. (2025a). Exploring Information Technology (IT) Acceptance Among Supply Chain Stakeholders in Morocco's Pharmaceutical Industry. In Ecological and Human Dimensions of AI-Based Supply Chain (pp. 245-270). IGI Global Scientific Publishing.

El Moussaoui, T., Chakir, L., & El Moussaoui, A. E. (2025g). Exploring Information Technology (IT) Acceptance Among Supply Chain Stakeholders in Morocco's Pharmaceutical Industry. In Ecological and Human Dimensions of AI-Based Supply Chain (pp. 245-270). IGI Global Scientific Publishing.

El Moussaoui, T., Loqman, C., & El Moussaoui, A. E. (2025c). Adoption of artificial intelligence in smart cities: Literature review and bibliometric analysis. Generative AI for Cybersecurity and Privacy, 103-125.

El Moussaoui, A. E. (2024). Unlocking the drivers behind logistics service providers' participation in Morocco's logistics clusters. *Arab Gulf Journal of Scientific Research*, *42*(4), 2086–2102. DOI: 10.1108/AGJSR-07-2023-0343

El Moussaoui, A. E. (2025c). Impact of Circular Economy on Supply Chain Management: An Exploratory Study. In *Ecological and Human Dimensions of AI-Based Supply Chain* (pp. 293–314). IGI Global Scientific Publishing. DOI: 10.4018/979-8-3693-7478-8.ch013

El Moussaoui, A. E. (2025c). Impact of logistics pooling on reduction of CO2 emissions in last-mile logistics. Management & Sustainability. *An Arab Review*, *4*(2), 383–401.

El Moussaoui, A. E. (2025d). Factors influencing the entry of logistics service providers (LSPs) into the logistics clusters: A case study of Casablanca city. Management & Sustainability. *An Arab Review*, *4*(4), 611–627. DOI: 10.1108/MSAR-06-2024-0043

El Moussaoui, A. E., Benbba, B., & El Andaloussi, Z. (2023a). Impact of logistics performance on the store image, consumer satisfaction and loyalty: A quantitative case study. *Arab Gulf Journal of Scientific Research*, *41*(3), 226–239. DOI: 10.1108/AGJSR-09-2022-0201

El Moussaoui, A. E., Benbba, B., Jaegler, A., El Moussaoui, T., El Andaloussi, Z., & Chakir, L. (2023b). Consumer perceptions of online shopping and willingness to use pick-up points: A case study of Morocco. *Sustainability (Basel)*, *15*(9), 7405. DOI: 10.3390/su15097405

El Moussaoui, A. E., El Moussaoui, T., Benbba, B., Chakir, L., Jaegler, A., & El Andaloussi, Z. (2025b). Sustainable effects of information sharing between distribution logistics actors: A qualitative case study. *Environment, Development and Sustainability*, *27*(5), 12305–12323. DOI: 10.1007/s10668-023-04387-3

El Moussaoui, A. E., El Moussaoui, T., Benbba, B., Jaegler, A., & El Andaloussi, Z. (2022a). Understanding the choice of collection & delivery point by the E-consumer via a machine learning model: Moroccan case study. *Procedia Computer Science*, *210*, 204–211. DOI: 10.1016/j.procs.2022.10.138

El Nemar, S., El-Chaarani, H., Dandachi, I., & Castellano, S. (2022). Resource-based view and sustainable advantage: A framework for SMEs. *Journal of Strategic Marketing*, •••, 1–24.

Elkington, J. (1997). *Cannibals with forks: The triple bottom line of 21st century business*. Capstone.

El-Nemr, N., Canel-Depitre, B., & Taghipour, A. (2017, September). Determinants of hotel room rates. In Marketing Trends Congress: Luxury Industries Conference London 2017.

European Commission. (2022, April 20). *In focus: Reducing the EU's dependence on imported fossil fuels* International Energy Agency & European Commission. https://commission.europa.eu/news-and-media/news/focus-reducing-eus-dependence-imported-fossil-fuels-2022-04-20_en

Evangelos Christou, E., Alexandris, K., & A. F. (2018). TOURMAN 2018 conference proceedings.

Evenett, S. J. (2022). Crisis-era protectionism and the multilateral trading system. *World Economy*, *45*(3), 631–651.

Fang, X., & Chen, H. C. (2022). Using vendor management inventory system for goods inventory management in IoT manufacturing. *Enterprise Information Systems*, *16*(7), 1885743. DOI: 10.1080/17517575.2021.1885743

Fawcett, S. E., Fawcett, A. M., Knemeyer, A. M., Brockhaus, S., & Webb, G. S. (2021). Overcoming the collaborative challenge: Commitment as a super-ordinate enabler of value co-creation. *International Journal of Physical Distribution & Logistics Management*, *51*(9), 1022–1047. DOI: 10.1108/IJPDLM-12-2020-0390

Fernie, J. (2023). Relationships in the supply chain. In *Logistics and retail management insights into current practice and trends from leading experts* (pp. 23–46). CRC Press. DOI: 10.4324/9780429271144-2

Fontoura, P., & Coelho, A. (2022). More cooperative... more competitive? Improving competitiveness by sharing value through the supply chain. *Management Decision*, *60*(3), 758–783. DOI: 10.1108/MD-09-2020-1225

Francisco, K., & Swanson, D. (2018). The supply chain has no clothes: Technology adoption of blockchain for supply chain transparency. *Logistics (Basel)*, *2*(1), 2. DOI: 10.3390/logistics2010002

Fransen, L., & LeBaron, G. (2019). Big audit firms as regulatory intermediaries in transnational labor governance. *Regulation & Governance*, *13*(2), 260–279. DOI: 10.1111/rego.12224

Freeman, R. E. (1984). *Strategic management: A stakeholder approach.* Pitman.

Gajović, V., Paunović, M., Ralević, N., & Kilibarda, M. (2018). Insurance as an instrument of risk management in logistics systems.

Galvin, P., Tywoniak, S., & Sutherland, J. (2021). Collaboration and opportunism in megaproject alliance contracts: The interplay between governance, trust and culture. *International Journal of Project Management*, *39*(4), 394–405. DOI: 10.1016/j.ijproman.2021.02.007

Gao, Y., Li, Z., & Kang, D. S. (2018). Supply chain coordination: A review. *Journal of Advanced Management Science, 6*(4), 213–217. DOI: 10.18178/joams.6.4.213-217

Gartner, S. (2024, October 30). *Supply chain resilience strategies: Data visibility & regionalization.* SCMR. https://www.scmr.com/article/supply-chain-resilience-strategies-data-visibility-regionalization

Gelsomino, L. M., Mangiaracina, R., Perego, A., & Tumino, A. (2016). Supply chain finance: A literature review. *International Journal of Physical Distribution & Logistics Management, 46*(4), 348–366. DOI: 10.1108/IJPDLM-08-2014-0173

George, J., & Pillai, V. M. (2019). A study of factors affecting supply chain performance. *Journal of Physics: Conference Series, 1355*(1), 012018. Advance online publication. DOI: 10.1088/1742-6596/1355/1/012018

Gereffi, G. (2018). Economic and social upgrading in global value chains and industrial clusters—Why governance matters. In Gereffi, G., Humphrey, J., & Sturgeon, T. (Eds.), *Global value chains and development: Redefining the contours of 21st century capitalism* (pp. 276–302). Cambridge University Press., DOI: 10.1017/9781108559423.011

Gharye Mirzaei, M., Goodarzian, F., Taghipour, A., & Muñuzuri, J. (2025). Sustainable closed-loop supply chain network under uncertainty considering green technologies: Toward the circular economy. *The Journal of the Operational Research Society*, •••, 1–21.

Glaa, B., Zoghlami, N., & Taghipour, A. (2014, May). Outsourcing and off-shoring healthcare services: A way to cut the costs and improve quality. In 2014 international conference on advanced logistics and transport (ICALT) (pp. 189-194). IEEE.

Glaa, B., Zoghlami, N., & Taghipour, A. (2014, May). Outsourcing and off-shoring healthcare services: A way to cut the costs and improve quality. In the 2014 International Conference on Advanced Logistics and Transport (ICALT) (pp. 189–194). IEEE. DOI: 10.1109/ICAdLT.2014.6864116

Global Slavery Index. (2023). Global estimates of modern slavery. Walk Free Foundation. https://www.walkfree.org/global-slavery-index/

Goodarzian, F., Abraham, A., Muñuzuri, J., Taghipour, A., & Ghasemi, P. (2024). A Benders decomposition approach for a new sustainable pharmaceutical supply chain network: A case study in France. *Annals of Operations Research*, •••, 1–39.

Govindan, K. (2018). Sustainable consumption and production in the food supply chain: A conceptual framework. *International Journal of Production Economics, 195*, 419–431. DOI: 10.1016/j.ijpe.2017.03.003

Govindaraj, M., Gnanasekaran, C., Krishnan, R., Khan, P., & Hoang, S. D. (2024). Retail Supply Chain Management: Ensuring Product Availability and Reducing Out-of-Stock Incidents in India. In Omnichannel Approach to Co-Creating Customer Experiences Through Metaverse Platforms (pp. 116-141). IGI Global.

Grosso, S., Longhini, J., Tonet, S., Bernard, I., Corso, J., de Marchi, D., Dorigo, L., Funes, G., Lussu, M., Oppio, N., Grassetti, L., Mori, L. P. D., & Palese, D. (2021). Prevalence and reasons for non-nursing tasks as perceived by nurses: Findings from a large cross-sectional study. *Journal of Nursing Management*, *29*(8), 2658–2673. DOI: 10.1111/jonm.13451 PMID: 34369615

Grötsch, V. M., Blome, C., & Schleper, M. C. (2013). Antecedents of proactive supply chain risk management – a contingency theory perspective. *International Journal of Production Research*, *51*(10), 2842–2867. DOI: 10.1080/00207543.2012.746796

Hales, R., & Birdthistle, N. (2023). The sustainable development goals–SDG# 11 sustainable cities and communities. In *Attaining the 2030 Sustainable Development Goal of Sustainable Cities and Communities* (pp. 1–9). Emerald Publishing Limited. DOI: 10.1108/978-1-80455-836-220231001

Han, J. W., Zuo, M., Zhu, W. Y., Zuo, J. H., Lü, E. L., & Yang, X. T. (2021). A comprehensive review of cold chain logistics for fresh agricultural products: Current status, challenges, and future trends. *Trends in Food Science & Technology*, *109*, 536–551. DOI: 10.1016/j.tifs.2021.01.066

Haraguchi, M., & Lall, U. (2015). Flood risks and impacts: A case study of Thailand's floods in 2011 and research questions for supply chain decision making. *International Journal of Disaster Risk Reduction*, *14*, 256–272. DOI: 10.1016/j.ijdrr.2014.09.005

Hasan, M. Z., Hussain, M. Z., Umair, S., & Waqas, U. (2024). Role of Human Capital in the Supply Chain Management. In *Human Perspectives of Industry 4.0 Organizations* (pp. 131–154). CRC Press. DOI: 10.1201/9781032616810-7

Hasija, A., & Esper, T. L. (2022). In artificial intelligence (AI) we trust: A qualitative investigation of AI technology acceptance. *Journal of Business Logistics*, *43*(3), 388–412. DOI: 10.1111/jbl.12301

Hawkins, S. F., & Morse, J. M. (2022). Untenable expectations: Nurses' work in the context of medication administration, error and the organization. *Global Qualitative Nursing Research*, *9*, 1–17. DOI: 10.1177/23333936221131779 PMID: 36387044

Herzog, C., Janssen, S., Schmid, U., Bosse, M., & Börner, M. (2024, November). *Supply chain tech report 2024 (SCT24): Technology can help manage supply-chain disruption.* Oliver Wyman. https://www.oliverwyman.com/our-expertise/insights/2024/nov/supply-chain-tech-report.html

Hoang, V., Nguyen, A., Hubbard, C., & Nguyen, K. D. (2021). Exploring the governance and fairness in the milk value chain: A case study in Vietnam. *Agriculture, 11*(9), 884. DOI: 10.3390/agriculture11090884

Hofstede, G. (2001). *Culture's consequences: Comparing values, behaviours, institutions and organisations across nations* (2nd ed.). Sage.

Holling, C. S. (1973). Resilience and stability of ecological systems. *Annual Review of Ecology and Systematics, 4*(1), 1–23. DOI: 10.1146/annurev.es.04.110173.000245

Holmes, T., Blackhurst, J., & O'Grady, P. (2021). Resilient semiconductor supply chains: Addressing climate and geopolitical risks. *The Journal of Supply Chain Management, 57*(4), 15–33.

Hoque, M. E., Zaidi, M. A. S., & Hassan, M. K. (2021). Geopolitical Uncertainties and Malaysian Stock Market Returns: Do Market Conditions Matter? *Mathematics, 9*(19), 2393. DOI: 10.3390/math9192393

Hugos, M. H. (2024). *Essentials of supply chain management.* John Wiley & Sons.

Hu, J., Han, R., Ali, M., Zhan, Y., & Tse, M. (2020). A social media analytic framework for improving operations and service management: A study of the retail pharmacy industry. *Technological Forecasting and Social Change, 163*, 120504. DOI: 10.1016/j.techfore.2020.120504

Huq, F. A., Stevenson, M., & Zorzini, M. (2014). Social sustainability in developing country suppliers. *Journal of Cleaner Production, 56*, 1–14.

Hurst, J., & Berdugo, M. (2020, September 28). The cost of sepsis in lives and dollars. bioMérieux Connection. https://www.biomerieuxconnection.com/2019/09/05/the-cost-of-sepsis-in-lives-and-dollars/

Hutapea, A., Sakti, H., Novarianti, I., & Nurcahyo, R. (2021, August). Application of economic order quantity (EOQ) for make-to-order (MTO) business. In *1st Indian International Conference on Industrial Engineering and Operations Management.* https://doi.org/DOI: 10.46254/IN01.20210074

Ikrom, B. P. D., & Kartini, N. (2025). Analysis of raw material inventory control using economic order quantity (EOQ) method at good coffee houses in Surabaya. *Jurnal Ekonomi Manajemen, 10*(1), 25–46. DOI: 10.30996/jem17.v10i1.131918

Intergovernmental Panel on Climate Change (IPCC). (2021). Climate change 2021: The physical science basis. Cambridge University Press. https://www.ipcc.ch/report/ar6/wg1/

Intergovernmental Panel on Climate Change (IPCC). (2022). *Climate change 2022: Impacts, adaptation, and vulnerability*. Cambridge University Press.

International Energy Agency. (2022). Net zero by 2050: A roadmap for the global energy sector. https://www.iea.org/reports/net-zero-by-2050

International Labour Organisation. (n.d.). Core labour standards and ILO conventions. https://www.ilo.org/

Ionescu, A. M., Clipa, A. M., Turnea, E. S., Clipa, C. I., Bedrule-Grigoru ă, M. V., & Roth, S. (2022). The impact of innovation framework conditions on corporate digital technology integration: Institutions as facilitators for sustainable digital transformation. [JBEM]. *Journal of Business Economics and Management, 23*(5), 1037–1059. DOI: 10.3846/jbem.2022.17039

IPCC. (2022). *Climate change 2022: Impacts, adaptation and vulnerability*. Cambridge University Press.

Ivanov, D. (2020). Predicting the impacts of epidemic outbreaks on global supply chains: A simulation-based analysis on the coronavirus (COVID-19/SARS-CoV-2) case. *Transportation Research Part E, Logistics and Transportation Review, 136*, 101922. Advance online publication. DOI: 10.1016/j.tre.2020.101922 PMID: 32288597

Ivanov, D. (2020). Viable supply chain model: Integrating agility, resilience, and sustainability perspectives—Lessons from the COVID-19 pandemic. *Annals of Operations Research*, •••, 1–21. PMID: 34334863

Ivanov, D. (2021). Exiting the COVID-19 pandemic: After-shocks and supply chain recovery. *International Journal of Production Research, 59*(12), 3535–3546. DOI: 10.1080/00207543.2021.1890852

Ivanov, D., & Dolgui, A. (2020). Viability of Intertwined Supply Networks: Extending the Supply Chain Resilience Angle toward Survivability. *International Journal of Production Research, 58*(10), 2904–2915. DOI: 10.1080/00207543.2020.1750727

Ivanov, D., & Dolgui, A. (2021). A digital supply chain twin for managing the disruption risks and resilience in the era of Industry 4.0. *Production Planning and Control, 32*(9), 775–788. DOI: 10.1080/09537287.2020.1768450

Ivanov, D., & Dolgui, A. (2021). A digital supply chain twin for managing the disruption risks and resilience in the era of Industry 4.0. *Transportation Research Part E, Logistics and Transportation Review*, *148*, 102243. Advance online publication. DOI: 10.1016/j.tre.2021.102243

Ivanov, D., & Dolgui, A. (2021). Ripple effect and supply chain disruption management: New trends and research directions. *International Journal of Production Research*, *59*(1), 102–118. DOI: 10.1080/00207543.2021.1840148

Jaber, M. Y., & Peltokorpi, J. (2024). Economic order/production quantity (EOQ/EPQ) models with product recovery: A review of mathematical modeling (1967-2022). *Applied Mathematical Modelling*, *129*, 655–672. DOI: 10.1016/j.apm.2024.02.022

Jadhav, R., & Kadam, M. S. (2020). Incubated insights: Data integration, reliability for effective and efficient pharmacy shops business. *Shanghai Ligong Daxue Xuebao*, *22*(11), 949–963. https://jusst.org/wp-content/uploads/2020/11/Sentiments-Analysis-of-the-Medical-or-Pharmacy-shops-business-to-develop-in-terms-of-Communication-Productivity-efficiency-in-their-retails-business.pdf

Jahroni, , & Muksin, M. (2023). Economic order quantity (EOQ) application to raw material inventory control for SMEs. *Community Services Journal*, *5*(2), 88–98. DOI: 10.22225/csj.5.2.2023.88-98

Jarzebski, M. P., Elmqvist, T., Gasparatos, A., Fukushi, K., Eckersten, S., Haase, D., Goodness, J., Khoshkar, S., Saito, O., Takeuchi, K., Theorell, T., Dong, N., Kasuga, F., Watanabe, R., Sioen, G. B., Yokohari, M., & Pu, J. (2021). Ageing and population shrinking: Implications for sustainability in the urban century. *NPJ Urban Sustainability*, *1*(1), 17. DOI: 10.1038/s42949-021-00023-z

Jurado, I., Maestre, J. M., Velarde, P., Ocampo-Martinez, C., Fernández, I., Isla Tejera, B., & del Prado, J. R. (2016). Stock management in hospital pharmacy using chance-constrained model predictive control. *Computers in Biology and Medicine*, *72*, 248–255. DOI: 10.1016/j.compbiomed.2015.11.011 PMID: 26724992

Jyoti, C., & Efpraxia, Z. (2023). Understanding and exploring the value co-creation of cloud computing innovation using resource based value theory: An interpretive case study. *Journal of Business Research*, *164*, 113970. DOI: 10.1016/j.jbusres.2023.113970

Kalaiarasi, K., Henrietta, H. M., Sumathi, M., & Raj, A. S. (2022). Economic order quantity in a fuzzy environment for a periodic inventory model with variable demand. *Iraqi Journal for Computer Science and Mathematics*, *3*(1), 102–107. DOI: 10.52866/ijcsm.2022.01.01.011

Kamoyo, M., & Chikazhe, L. (2025). Public Transport Sector Challenges and Zimbabwe's Untapped Economic Opportunities. *Transportation in Developing Economies*, *11*(2), 25. DOI: 10.1007/s40890-025-00244-2

Kareva, N. N., & Shvetsova, V. D. (2021). Pharmacy business and its social responsibility. *Journal of Siberian Medical Sciences*, *2*(2), 136–145. DOI: 10.31549/2542-1174-2021-2-136-145

Khanna, R., Rajnikant, P. N., & Patel, K. A. (2023). Review presentation of different economic order quantity (EOQ) models and their application. *Journal of Advanced Zoology*, *44*(S5), 1284–1288. DOI: 10.17762/jaz.v44iS-5.1210

Kilfoyle, M. (2023, October 24). *Ukraine: What's the global economic impact of Russia's invasion?* Economics Observatory. https://www.economicsobservatory.com/ukraine-whats-the-global-economic-impact-of-russias-invasion/

Kilpatrick, J., Berckman, L., Faver, A. D., Hardin, K., & Sloane, M. (2024, May 23). *Restructuring the supply base: Prioritizing a resilient, yet efficient supply chain.* Deloitte Insights. https://www2.deloitte.com/us/en/insights/industry/manufacturing/global-supply-chain-resilience-amid-disruptions.html

Kim, S., Colicchia, C., & Menachof, D. (2018). Ethical sourcing: An analysis of the literature and implications for future research. *Journal of Business Ethics*, *152*(4), 1033–1052. DOI: 10.1007/s10551-016-3266-8

Klassen, R. D., & Vereecke, A. (2012). Social issues in supply chains. *International Journal of Production Economics*, *140*(1), 103–115. DOI: 10.1016/j.ijpe.2012.01.021

Kleindorfer, P. R., & Saad, G. H. (2005). Managing disruption risks in supply chains. *Production and Operations Management*, *14*(1), 53–68. DOI: 10.1111/j.1937-5956.2005.tb00009.x

Koot, M., Mes, M., & Iacob, M. E. (2021). A systematic literature review of blockchain-based supply chain management: Research trends and future research directions. *Logistics (Basel)*, *5*(4), 71. DOI: 10.3390/logistics5040071

Krivošová, M., Klimas, J., Žufková, V., Snopková, M., Mačeková, Z., & Viola, R. (2025). Advanced pharmaceutical services in community pharmacies. *Pharmacy Practice*, *23*(1), 1–17. DOI: 10.18549/PharmPract.2025.1.3073

Kshetri, N. (2018). Blockchain's roles in meeting key supply chain management objectives. *International Journal of Information Management*, *39*, 80–89. DOI: 10.1016/j.ijinfomgt.2017.12.005

Kumareswaran, K., & Jayasinghe, G. Y. (2023). Climate resilience and sustainable cities. In *Green Infrastructure and Urban Climate Resilience: An Introduction* (pp. 39–97). Springer International Publishing. DOI: 10.1007/978-3-031-37081-6_2

Kumar, R., Rana, R., & Jha, S. K. (2023). Scalable blockchain architecture of internet of medical things (IoMT) for Indian smart healthcare system. In *AI Models for Blockchain-Based Intelligent Networks in IoT Systems: Concepts, Methodologies, Tools, and Applications* (pp. 231–259). Springer International Publishing. DOI: 10.1007/978-3-031-31952-5_11

Kuteyi, D., & Winkler, H. (2022). Logistics challenges in sub-Saharan Africa and opportunities for digitalization. *Sustainability (Basel)*, *14*(4), 2399. DOI: 10.3390/su14042399

Laber, M., Klimek, P., Bruckner, M., Yang, L., & Thurner, S. (2023). Shock propagation from the Russia–Ukraine conflict on international multilayer food production network determines global food availability. *Nature Food*, *4*(6), 508–517. DOI: 10.1038/s43016-023-00771-4 PMID: 37322302

LeBaron, G. (2020). Combatting modern slavery: Why labour governance is failing and what we can do about it. *Polity*.

LeBaron, G., Lister, J., & Dauvergne, P. (2022). The effectiveness of supply chain audits in improving labor standards. *Review of International Political Economy*, *29*(2), 1–27.

Lebosse, S., Taghipour, A., & Canel-Depitre, B. (2017). Quick response to fluctuations in supply chains: A review—Journal of Advanced Management Science, 5(5).

Lebosse, S., Taghipour, A., & Canel-Depitre, B. (2017). Quick response to fluctuations in supply chains: A review. *Journal of Advanced Management Science*, *5*(5), 394–400. DOI: 10.18178/joams.5.5.394-400

Lele, V. P., Kumari, S., & White, G. (2023). Streamlining Production: Using Big-Data's CRM & Supply chain to improve efficiency in high-speed environments. [IJCSPUB]. *IJCSPUB-International Journal of Current Scienc*, *13*(2), 136–146.

Lele, V., & Ajmeri, Y. (2024). Supply Chain Integration and Collaboration. In *From Source to Shelf: Orchestrating a Supply Chain Symphony* (pp. 83–117). Apress. DOI: 10.1007/979-8-8688-0986-6_4

Lengnick-Hall, C. A., Beck, T. E., & Lengnick-Hall, M. L. (2011). Developing a capacity for organisational resilience through strategic human resource management. *Human Resource Management Review*, *21*(3), 243–255. DOI: 10.1016/j.hrmr.2010.07.001

Leonidou, L. C., Aykol, B., Hadjimarcou, J., & Palihawadana, D. (2021). Unveiling the infidelity problem in exclusive manufacturer–distributor relationships: A dyadic perspective. *Psychology and Marketing*, *38*(11), 2122–2141. DOI: 10.1002/mar.21545

Li, L. (2024). Unveiling the effects of supply chain relationship types on enterprise performance. *Enterprise Information Systems*, *18*(2), 2274141. DOI: 10.1080/17517575.2023.2274141

Liu, J., Zhou, Y., Jiang, X., & Zhang, W. (2020). Consumers' satisfaction factors mining and sentiment analysis of B2C online pharmacy reviews. *BMC Medical Informatics and Decision Making*, *20*(194), 1–13. DOI: 10.1186/s12911-020-01214-x PMID: 32807175

Liu, V. X., Fielding-Singh, V., Greene, J. D., Baker, J. M., Iwashyna, T. J., Bhattacharya, J., & Escobar, G. J. (2017). The timing of early antibiotics and hospital mortality in sepsis. *American Journal of Respiratory and Critical Care Medicine*, *196*(7), 856–863. DOI: 10.1164/rccm.201609-1848OC PMID: 28345952

Locke, R. M. (2013). *The promise and limits of private power: Promoting labor standards in a global economy*. Cambridge University Press. DOI: 10.1017/CBO9781139381840

Loivet, W., Taghipour, A., & Kang, D. S. (2020). The rise of green supply chain management: Between complexity and necessity. *J. Econ. Bus. Manag*, *8*(1), 1–7. DOI: 10.18178/joebm.2020.8.1.604

Loivet, W., Taghipour, A., & Kang, D. S. (2020). The rise of green supply chain management: Between complexity and necessity. Journal of Economics. *Business and Management*, *8*(1), 1–7.

Lopes, J. M., Gomes, S., & Mané, L. (2022). Developing knowledge of supply chain resilience in less-developed countries in the pandemic age. *Logistics (Basel)*, *6*(1), 3. DOI: 10.3390/logistics6010003

Lu, X. W., Tliche, Y., Vosooghidizaji, M., & Taghipour, A. (2023). Cryptocurrencies and Blockchain Applications. In Blockchain Applications in Cryptocurrency for Technological Evolution (pp. 1-13). IGI Global.

Lu, X., & Taghipour, A. (2025). The Future of Marketing: Integrating Big Data and AI for Personalized Customer Engagement. In Ecological and Human Dimensions of AI-Based Supply Chain (pp. 97-110). IGI Global Scientific Publishing.

Lu, X. W., Tliche, Y., Vosooghidizaji, M., & Taghipour, A. (2023). Cryptocurrencies and blockchain applications. In *Blockchain applications in cryptocurrency for technological evolution* (pp. 1–13). IGI Global Scientific Publishing.

Lu, X., & Taghipour, A. (2023). A French Guide for Businesses and Governments to Integrate the Concept of Sustainable Development Into Their Supply Chains. In *Government Impact on Sustainable and Responsible Supply Chain Management* (pp. 1–12). IGI Global. DOI: 10.4018/978-1-6684-9062-4.ch001

Lu, X., & Taghipour, A. (2025). The future of marketing: Integrating big data and AI for personalized customer engagement. In *Ecological and human dimensions of AI-based supply chain* (pp. 97–110). IGI Global Scientific Publishing. DOI: 10.4018/979-8-3693-7478-8.ch005

Mahfod, J., Canel-Depitre, B., & Taghipour, A. (2019). Quality function deployment-ELECTRE in supplier evaluation. Journal of advanced management science, 7(4).

Mahfod, J., Canel-Depitre, B., & Taghipour, A. (2019). Quality function deployment-ELECTRE in supplier evaluation—Journal of Advanced Management Science, 7(4).

Mahfod, J., Khoury, B., Canel-Depitre, B., & Taghipour, A. (2021). Logistics Providers in Syria Humanitarian Operations. In Demand Forecasting and Order Planning in Supply Chains. and Humanitarian Logistics (pp. 171-197). IGI Global. DOI: 10.4018/978-1-7998-3805-0.ch006

Mahfod, J., Canel-Depitre, B., & Taghipour, A. (2019). Quality function deployment–ELECTRE in supplier evaluation. *Journal of Advanced Management Science*, *7*(4).

Mangram, M. E. (2012). The globalisation of Tesla Motors: A strategic marketing plan analysis. *Journal of Strategic Marketing*, *20*(4), 289–312. DOI: 10.1080/0965254X.2012.657224

Marchesani, F., Masciarelli, F., & Bikfalvi, A. (2023). Smart city as a hub for talent and innovative companies: Exploring the (dis) advantages of digital technology implementation in cities. *Technological Forecasting and Social Change*, *193*, 122636. DOI: 10.1016/j.techfore.2023.122636

Marjosola, H. (2021). The problem of regulatory arbitrage: A transaction cost economics perspective. *Regulation & Governance*, *15*(2), 388–407. DOI: 10.1111/rego.12287

Mathiyazhagan, K., Taghipour, A., & Agarwal, V. (Eds.). (2022). *Blockchain technology in supply chain management for society 5.0*. CRC Press. DOI: 10.1201/9781003177432

Mattessich, P. W., & Johnson, K. M. (2018). Collaboration: What makes it work.

Mattingly, T.II, Hyman, D., & Bai, G. (2023). Pharmacy benefit managers: History, business practices, economics and policy. *JAMA Health Forum*, *4*(11), e233804. DOI: 10.1001/jamahealthforum.2023.3804 PMID: 37921745

Mbiatem, J., Taghipour, A., & Canel-Depitre, B. (2018, August). Supplier selection approaches for decision makers. In *Proceedings of the 8th International Conference on Information Communication and Management* (pp. 108-112).

Mbiatem, J., Taghipour, A., & Canel-Depitre, B. (2018, August). Supplier selection approaches for decision makers. In *Proceedings of the International Conference on Information Communication and Management* (pp. 108–112).

McNair, D. (2015). Enhancing nursing staffing forecasting with safety stock over lead time modeling. *Nursing Administration Quarterly*, *39*(4), 291–296. DOI: 10.1097/NAQ.0000000000000124 PMID: 26340239

Meadows, D. H. (2008). *Thinking in systems: A primer*. Chelsea Green.

Meckling, W. H., & Jensen, M. C. (1976). Theory of the Firm. *Managerial behavior, agency costs and ownership structure, 3*(4), 305-360.

Melnyk, S. A., Schoenherr, T., Speier-Pero, C., Peters, C., Chang, J. F., & Friday, D. (2022). New challenges in supply chain management: Cybersecurity across the supply chain. *International Journal of Production Research*, *60*(1), 162–183. DOI: 10.1080/00207543.2021.1984606

Mer, A., & Virdi, A. S. (2024). Decoding the challenges and skill gaps in small-and medium-sized enterprises in emerging economies: A review and research agenda. *Contemporary Challenges in Social Science Management: Skills Gaps and Shortages in the Labour Market*, 115-134.

Merimi, M., & Taghipour, A. (2021). Accelerating the digitalization of the supply chain: An empirical research about COVID-19 crisis. In *Digitalization of decentralized supply chains during global crises* (pp. 1–24). IGI Global Scientific Publishing. DOI: 10.4018/978-1-7998-6874-3.ch001

Milne, M. J., & Grey, R. (2013). W(h)ither ecology? The Triple Bottom Line, the Global Reporting Initiative, and corporate sustainability reporting. *Journal of Business Ethics*, *118*(1), 13–29. DOI: 10.1007/s10551-012-1543-8

Miroudot, S. (2020). Resilience versus robustness in global value chains: Some policy implications. *VoxEU.org*.

MIT Sloan Management Review (2023). *Is it time to rethink globalized supply chains?* https://sloanreview.mit.edu/article/is-it-time-to-rethink-globalized-supply-chains/

Mohamad, A. H. H. (2024). The impact of the Russia–Ukraine war on global food security. *Nutrition & Food Science International Journal*, 13(3), 555862. https://juniperpublishers.com/nfsij/pdf/NFSIJ.MS.ID.555862.pdf

Mol, A. P. J., & Oosterveer, P. (2015). Certification of markets, markets of certificates: Tracing sustainability in global value chains. *Journal of Cleaner Production*, *107*, 154–161. DOI: 10.1016/j.jclepro.2013.11.012

Montgomery, D. C. (2020). *Introduction to statistical quality control*. John wiley & sons.

Moriwaki, M., Tanaka, M., Kakehashi, M., Koizumi, M., Horiguchi, H., & Hayashida, K. (2025). Influence of nursing time and staffing on medication errors: A cross-sectional analysis of administrative data. *Nursing Reports*, *15*(1), 1–11. DOI: 10.3390/nursrep15010012 PMID: 39852634

Munich, Re. (2021). *NatCatSERVICE: Natural catastrophe statistics online*. Munich Re.

Nadia, E. N., CANEL-DEPITRE, B., & TAGHIPOUR, A. 12. LEBANESE HOTELS' ENGAGEMENT IN ENVIRONMENTAL PRACTICES. TOURMAN 2018, 457.

Nadia, E. N., Canel-Depritre, B., & Taghipour, A. (2018). Lebanese hotels' engagement in environmental practices. In *TOURMAN 2018* (p. 457)

Nadia, E. N., Beatrice, C. D., & Atour, T. (2020). Luxury hotels' eco-friendly activities & customers' preferences and willingness to pay for green hotels. *Journal of Advanced Management Science*, *8*(1), 1–24.

Nadia, E. N., Beatrice, C. D., & Atour, T. (2021). The determinants of hotel room rates in Beirut: A hedonic pricing model. International Journal of Trade. *Economics and Finance*, *12*(2), 33–42.

Nadia, E. N., Canel-Depitre, B., & Atour, T. (2020). Luxury hotels' eco-friendly activities and customers' preferences and willingness to pay for green hotels. *Journal of Advanced Management Science*, *8*(1), 1–24.

Negri, M., Cagno, E., Colicchia, C., & Sarkis, J. (2021). Integrating sustainability and resilience in the supply chain: A systematic literature review and a research agenda. *Business Strategy and the Environment*, *30*(7), 2858–2886. DOI: 10.1002/bse.2776

Ni, Z., Yang, J., & Razzaq, A. (2022). How do natural resources, digitalization, and institutional governance contribute to ecological sustainability through load capacity factors in highly resource- consuming economies? *Resources Policy*, *79*, 103068. DOI: 10.1016/j.resourpol.2022.103068

OECD. (2022). *Climate finance and the USD 100 billion goal: Progress report.* Organisation for Economic Co-operation and Development.

Office for National Statistics. (2022). Consumer price inflation, UK, February 16. https://www.ons.gov.uk/economy/inflationandpriceindices/bulletins/consumerprice inflation/january2022/pdf

Ogbodu, O. M., Maputle, M. S., & Mabunda, J. (2019). Nurses' perceptions about stock-outs of essential medicines at primary health care facilities in Vhembe district, South Africa. *The Open Public Health Journal, 12*(1), 550–557. DOI: 10.2174/1874944501912010550

Omar, Y. M., Minoufekr, M., & Plapper, P. (2019). Business analytics in manufacturing: Current trends, challenges and pathway to market leadership. *Operations Research Perspectives*, *6*, 100127. DOI: 10.1016/j.orp.2019.100127

Owens, P. L., Miller, M. A., Barrett, M. L., & Hensche, M. (2024, April). *Overview of outcomes for inpatient stays involving sepsis, 2016–2021 (HCUP Statistical Brief No. 306). Agency for Healthcare Research and Quality. https://hcup-us.ahrq.gov/reports/statbriefs/sb306-overview-sepsis-2016-2021.pdf

Oyedijo, A., Francois Koukpaki, A. S., Kusi-Sarpong, S., Alfarsi, F., & Yang, Y. (2022). Restraining forces and drivers of supply chain collaboration: Evidence from an emerging market. *Supply Chain Management*, *27*(3), 409–430. DOI: 10.1108/SCM-06-2020-0263

Paoli, C. J., Reynolds, M. A., Sinha, M., Gitlin, M., & Crouser, E. (2018). Epidemiology and costs of sepsis in the United States-an analysis based on timing of diagnosis and severity level. *Critical Care Medicine*, *46*(12), 1889–1897. DOI: 10.1097/CCM.0000000000003342 PMID: 30048332

Paramesha, M., Rane, N. L., & Rane, J. (2024). Big data analytics, artificial intelligence, machine learning, internet of things, and sblockchain for enhanced business intelligence. *Partners Universal Multidisciplinary Research Journal*, *1*(2), 110–133.

Patil, K., Garg, V., Gabaldon, J., Patil, H., Niranjan, S., & Hawkins, T. (2024). Firm performance in digitally integrated supply chains: A combined perspective of transaction cost economics and relational exchange theory. *Journal of Enterprise Information Management*, *37*(2), 381–413. DOI: 10.1108/JEIM-09-2022-0335

Ponomarov, S. Y., & Holcomb, M. C. (2009). Understanding the concept of supply chain resilience. *International Journal of Logistics Management, 20*(1), 124–143. DOI: 10.1108/09574090910954873

Ponputtha, W., Wannapiroon, P., & Nilsook, P. (2021). Creative history learning model using digital storytelling through cloud learning to enhance analytical thinking. International Journal of E-Education, E-Business. *E-Management and E-Learning, 11*(2), 42–50. DOI: 10.17706/ijeeee.2021.11.2.42-50

Ponputtha, W., Wannapiroon, P., Nilsook, P., Taghipour, A., Murat, S., Huang, P., & Chou, T. C. (2021). Creative history learning model using digital storytelling through cloud learning to enhance analytical thinking. International Journal of e-Education, e-Business, e-. *Management Learning, 11*(2), 42–50.

Pour Mohammadi, M., Ghorbani, R., & Taghipour, A. (2014). Factors affecting housing prices in Tabriz: A hedonic model analysis. *Geographical Planning of Space Quarterly Journal, 3*(9), 83–104.

Pour Mohammadi, M., Ghorbani, R., & Taghipour, A. (2014). Factors affecting the price of housing in the city of Tabriz using a hedonic model. *Geographical Planning of Space Quarterly Journal, 3*(9), 83–104.

Pour Mohammadi, M., Ghorbani, R., & Taghipour, A. (2014). Factors affecting the price of housing in the city of Tabriz using hedonic model. *Geographical Planning of Space Quarterly Journal, 3*(9), 83–104.

Protocol, G. H. G. (2015). Corporate value chain (Scope 3) accounting and reporting standard. Greenhouse Gas Protocol. https://ghgprotocol.org/standards/scope-3-standard

Qato, D. M., Zenk, S., Wilder, J., Harrington, R., Gaskin, D., & Alexander, G. C. (2017). The availability of pharmacies in the United States: 2007-2015. *PLoS One, 12*(8), 1–13. DOI: 10.1371/journal.pone.0183172 PMID: 28813473

Radhoui, H., Taghipour, A., & Canel-Depitre, B. (2019). The distribution and pickup of goods: A literature review and survey. Hierarchical Planning and Information Sharing Techniques in Supply Chain Management, 46-85.

Radhoui, H., Taghipour, A., & Canel-Depitre, B. (2019). The distribution and pickup of goods: A literature review and survey. Hierarchical Planning and Information Sharing Techniques in Supply Chain Management, 46–85.

Radhoui, H., Taghipour, A., & Canel-Depitre, B. (2019). The distribution and pickup of goods: A literature review and survey. In Hierarchical planning and information sharing techniques in supply chain management (pp. 46–85). DOI: 10.4018/978-1-5225-7299-2.ch002

Radhoui, H., Taghipour, A., & Canel-Depitre, B. (2021). Mixed delivery and pickup vehicle routing problem with limited flow and assignment of drones in an urban network. In *Demand Forecasting and Order Planning in Supply Chains and Humanitarian Logistics* (pp. 225–249). IGI Global. DOI: 10.4018/978-1-7998-3805-0.ch008

Rathbone, A. P., Rumney, R., Oxley, K., Barnfather, L., Fisher, D., McFarlane, G., Platton, C., Smith, K., Chandler, S., Campbell, D., & Baqir, W. (2023). Ward medicine assistants: A new role to support nurses with medication-related tasks. *Journal of Hospital Management and Health Policy*, *7*(8), 1–11. DOI: 10.21037/jhmhp-23-3

Reinecke, J., & Ansari, S. (2016). Taming wicked problems: Multi-stakeholder governance. *Organization Studies*, *37*(3), 299–329.

Ren, Z., Taghipour, A., & Canel-Depitre, B. (2016). Information sharing in supply chain under uncertainty. In *Proceedings of the International Conference on Information Communication and Management* (pp. 67–71). IEEE. DOI: 10.1109/INFOCOMAN.2016.7784217

Resilinc Editorial Team. *What would happen if China invaded Taiwan?* https://www.resilinc.com/blog/what-would-happen-if-china-invaded-taiwan/

Risks and resilience in global trade: Key trends in 2023-2024. https://www.oecd.org/en/publications/risks-and-resilience-in-global-trade_1c66c439-en.html

Roopnarian, O., Singh, S., & Rathilall, R. (2023). The Convergence of Quality and Digitalisation in a Changing World: Implications for Developing Nations such as the BRICS Group. *African Journal of Inter/Multidisciplinary Studies*, *5*(1), 1-14.

Rosário, A. T., & Dias, J. C. (2023). The new digital economy and sustainability: Challenges and opportunities. *Sustainability (Basel)*, *15*(14), 10902. DOI: 10.3390/su151410902

Rose, A. (2004). Defining and measuring economic resilience to disasters. *Disaster Prevention and Management*, *13*(4), 307–314. DOI: 10.1108/09653560410556528

Saberi, S., Kouhizadeh, M., Sarkis, J., & Shen, L. (2019). Blockchain technology and its relationships to sustainable supply chain management. *International Journal of Production Research*, *57*(7), 2117–2135. DOI: 10.1080/00207543.2018.1533261

Sahraoui, A., Tran, N. K., Tliche, Y., Kacem, A., & Taghipour, A. (2023). Examining ICT Innovation for Sustainable Terminal Operations in Developing Countries: A Case Study of the Port of Radès in Tunisia. *Sustainability (Basel)*, *15*(11), 9123. DOI: 10.3390/su15119123

Sanni, S., Jovanovski, Z., & Sidhu, H. S. (2020). An economic order quantity model with reverse logistics program. *Operations Research Perspective*, *7*, 1–8. DOI: 10.1016/j.orp.2019.100133

Sarkis, J. (2020). Supply chain sustainability: Learning from the COVID-19 pandemic. *International Journal of Operations & Production Management*, *40*(10), 1763–1782. DOI: 10.1108/IJOPM-08-2020-0568

Sarkis, J., Zhu, Q., & Lai, K.-H. (2019). Circular economy and supply chain management: Opportunities and challenges. *Resources, Conservation and Recycling*, *141*, 65–67. DOI: 10.1016/j.resconrec.2018.10.040

Schellack, N., & Meyer, H. J. C. (2010). Pharmaceutical ward stock management for nurses: nursing matters. Professional Nursing Today, 14(5), 5-10. https://hdl.handle.net/10520/EJC79404

Schoneveld, G. C. (2022). Transforming food systems through inclusive agribusiness. *World Development*, *158*, 105970. DOI: 10.1016/j.worlddev.2022.105970

Schwarz, L. B. (2008). The Economic order-quantity (EOQ) Model. In Chhajed, D., & Lowe, T. J. (Eds.), *Building Intuition. International Series in Operations Research & Management Science* (Vol. 115). Springer.,DOI: 10.1007/978-0-387-73699-0_8

Senthilnathan, S. (2019). Economic order quantity (EOQ). SSRN Electronic Journal. DOI: 10.2139/ssrn.3475239

Seuring, S., & Müller, M. (2008). From a literature review to a conceptual framework for sustainable supply chain management. *Journal of Cleaner Production*, *16*(15), 1699–1710. DOI: 10.1016/j.jclepro.2008.04.020

Shahmari, M., Dashti, S., Jafari, M., & Belil, F. E. (2025). Nurses' lived experiences of self-control in emergency settings: A qualitative study. *BMC Emergency Medicine*, *25*(46), 1–11. DOI: 10.1186/s12873-025-01205-z PMID: 40128663

Sheffi, Y. (2021). The new (ab) standard: Reshaping business and supply chain strategy beyond [MIT Press.]. *COVID*, •••, 19.

Sheffi, Y. (2021). The New (Ab)Normal: Reshaping business and supply chain strategy beyond [MIT Press.]. *COVID*, •••, 19.

Shih, W. C. (2020). Is it time to rethink globalized supply chains? *MIT Sloan Management Review,* March 19. https://sloanreview.mit.edu/article/is-it-time-to-rethink-globalized-supply-chains/

Shih, W. (2020). Is it time to rethink global supply chains? *MIT Sloan Management Review, 61*(4), 1–6.

Shukla, M., Nandan, T., Rawat, C. M. S., & Singh, D. (2023). Effect of supportive supervision on the process of indenting and stock management by senior nursing ward in-charges at a tertiary care hospital in Garhwal region of Uttarakhand, India. *Indian Journal of Community and Family Medicine., 9*(2), 143–148. DOI: 10.4103/ijcfm.ijcfm_30_23

Simchi-Levi, D., & Haren, P. (2022, March). *How the war in Ukraine is further disrupting global supply chains. Harvard Business Review.* https://hbr.org/2022/03/how-the-war-in-ukraine-is-further-disrupting-global-supply-chains

Sitrarasu, K., Zainuddin, Z. M. B., & Idris, B. B. (2025). Optimization of drug inventory management in hospital pharmacy. *Proceedings of Science and Mathematics, 30,* 80–87. https://science.utm.my/procscimath/wp-content/uploads/sites/605/2025/10/80-87-Kayalvhili-et-al.pdf

Sodhi, M. S., & Tang, C. S. (2019). Research opportunities in supply chain transparency. *Production and Operations Management, 28*(12), 2946–2959. DOI: 10.1111/poms.13115

Soundararajan, V., & Brammer, S. (2018). Developing country sub-suppliers and ethical sourcing. *Business Ethics Quarterly, 28*(4), 475–503.

Spiro, S. (2019). Digital transformation of pharmacists' clinical services. *Journal of the American Pharmacists Association : JAPhA, 59*(2S), S8–S12. DOI: 10.1016/j.japh.2018.10.016 PMID: 30578127

Suchman, M. C. (1995). Managing legitimacy: Strategic and institutional approaches. *Academy of Management Review, 20*(3), 571–610. DOI: 10.2307/258788

Supply Chain Brain. (2023a). *Enhancing supply chain resilience: A modular approach.* https://www.supplychainbrain.com/articles/38553-enhancing-supply-chain-resilience-a-modular-approach

Supply Chain Brain. (2023b). *How are China-Taiwan tensions threatening global semiconductor supply?* https://www.supplychainbrain.com/articles/40256-watch-how-are-china-taiwan-tensions-threatening-global-semiconductor-supply

Taghipour, A. (2009). Évaluation de la collaboration au sein d'une chaîne d'approvisionnement. Revue française de gestion industrielle, 28(1), 26–42.

Taghipour, A. (2009). Evaluation de la collaboration dans une chaîne d'approvisionnement. Revue française de gestion industrielle, 28(1), 26-42.

Taghipour, A. (2009). Évaluation de la collaboration dans une chaîne d'approvisionnement. Revue française de gestion industrielle, 28(1), 26–42.

Taghipour, A. (2024). Big Data: The New Gold Mine for Supermarkets. In Applications of New Technology in Operations and Supply Chain Management (pp. 98-106). IGI Global.

Taghipour, A. (2024). Big Data: The New Gold Mine for Supermarkets. In Applications of New Technology in Operations and Supply Chain Management (pp. 98–106). IGI Global.

Taghipour, A., & Frayret, J. M. (2011). Supply chain coordination planning: A review. Work paper, École polytechnique de Montréal.

Taghipour, A., & Frayret, J. M. (2013b, May). An algorithm to improve operations planning in decentralised supply chains. In the 2013 International Conference on Advanced Logistics and Transport (pp. 100–103). IEEE.

Taghipour, A., & Lu, X. (2025). Advancing Supply Chain Innovation: Theoretical Foundations, Contemporary Developments, and Future Directions. In Ecological and Human Dimensions of AI-Based Supply Chain (pp. 1-26). IGI Global Scientific Publishing.

Taghipour, A., & Lu, X. (2025). Advancing Supply Chain Innovation: Theoretical Foundations, Contemporary Developments, and Future Directions. In Ecological and Human Dimensions of AI-Based Supply Chain (pp. 1–26). IGI Global Scientific Publishing.

Taghipour, A., & Lu, X. (2025). Navigating the Artificial Intelligence Era: Impacts of Artificial Intelligence on Youth Critical Thinking, Career Paths, and Ethical Challenges. In Ecological and Human Dimensions of AI-Based Supply Chain (pp. 49-68). IGI Global Scientific Publishing.

Taghipour, A., & Lu, X. (2025). Navigating the Artificial Intelligence Era: Impacts of Artificial Intelligence on Youth Critical Thinking, Career Paths, and Ethical Challenges. In Ecological and Human Dimensions of AI-Based Supply Chain (pp. 49–68). IGI Global Scientific Publishing.

Taghipour, A., & Lu, X. W. (2023, August). Green Supply Chain Management: A Guide. In International Conference on Applied Economics and Business (pp. 315-328). Cham: Springer Nature Switzerland.

Taghipour, A., & Lu, X. W. (2023, August). Green supply chain management: A guide. In Proceedings of the International Conference on Applied Economics and Business (pp. 315–328). Springer Nature Switzerland.

Taghipour, A., & Merimi, M. (2021, March). Digital transformation of supply chains during the crisis: COVID-19. In the 11th Annual International Conference on Industrial Engineering and Operations Management, IEOM (pp. 7493–7501).

Taghipour, A., Abed, M., & Zoghlami, N. (2015, May). Design for remanufacturing respecting reverse logistics processes: A review. In 2015 4th International Conference on Advanced Logistics and Transport (ICALT) (pp. 299-304). IEEE. DOI: 10.1109/ICAdLT.2015.7136602

Taghipour, A., Abed, M., & Zoghlami, N. (2015, May). Design for remanufacturing with respect to reverse logistics processes: A review. In 2015, the 4th International Conference on Advanced Logistics and Transport (ICALT) (pp. 299–Mahfod, J., 304). IEEE.

Taghipour, A., Lu, X., & Smahi, M. (2022). Opportunities and challenges for society 5.0 in procurement. In Blockchain technology in supply chain management for society 5.0 (pp. 91–100).

Taghipour, A. (2009). Évaluation de la collaboration dans une chaîne d'approvisionnement. *Revue Française de Gestion Industrielle*, *28*(1), 26–42. DOI: 10.53102/2009.28.01.746

Taghipour, A. (2021, January). Digital transformation of supply chains during crisis: COVID-19. In *Proceedings of the International Conference on Industrial Engineering and Operations Management*. DOI: 10.46254/AN11.20211298

Taghipour, A. (2024). Big data: The new gold mine for supermarkets. In *Applications of new technology in operations and supply chain management* (pp. 98–106). IGI Global Scientific Publishing. DOI: 10.4018/979-8-3693-1578-1.ch006

Taghipour, A. (Ed.). (2020). *Demand forecasting and order planning in supply chains and humanitarian logistics*. IGI Global.

Taghipour, A. (Ed.). (2022). *Blockchain Applications in Cryptocurrency for Technological Evolution*. IGI Global. DOI: 10.4018/978-1-6684-6247-8

Taghipour, A. (Ed.). (2023). *Government impact on sustainable and responsible supply chain management*. IGI Global. DOI: 10.4018/978-1-6684-9062-4

Taghipour, A., & Beneteau-Piet, C. (2020). Sustainable supply chain management performance. *International Journal of Innovation, Management and Technology*, *11*(6), 165–169. DOI: 10.18178/ijimt.2020.11.6.897

Taghipour, A., Fooladvand, A., Khazaei, M., & Ramezani, M. (2023). Criteria clustering and supplier segmentation based on sustainable shared value using BWM and PROMETHEE. *Sustainability (Basel)*, *15*(11), 8670. DOI: 10.3390/su15118670

Taghipour, A., & Frayret, J. M. (2013, May). An algorithm to improve operations planning in decentralized supply chains. In *Proceedings of the International Conference on Advanced Logistics and Transport* (pp. 100–103). IEEE. DOI: 10.1109/ICAdLT.2013.6568442

Taghipour, A., & Frayret, J.-M. (2013). Coordination of operations planning in supply chains: A review. *International Journal of Business Performance and Supply Chain Modelling*, *5*(3), 272–307. DOI: 10.1504/IJBPSCM.2013.055729

Taghipour, A., Lu, X., Derradji, M., & Sow, A. D. (2022, July). The impact of digitalisation on supply chain management: a literature review. In *Proceedings of the 12th International Conference on Information Communication and Management* (pp. 75–78).

Taghipour, A., Lu, X., Derradji, M., & Sow, A. D. (2022b, July). The impact of digitalization on supply chain management: a literature review. In *Proceedings of the 12th International Conference on Information Communication and Management* (pp. 75-78). DOI: 10.1145/3551690.3551702

Taghipour, A., Lu, X., & Smahi, M. (2022a). Opportunities and challenges for society 5.0 in procurement. *Blockchain Technology in Supply Chain Management for Society*, *5*(0), 91–100. DOI: 10.1201/9781003177432-9

Taghipour, A., Rouyendegh, B. D., Ünal, A., & Piya, S. (2022c). Selection of suppliers for speech recognition products in IT projects by combining techniques with an integrated fuzzy MCDM. *Sustainability (Basel)*, *14*(3), 1777. DOI: 10.3390/su14031777

Taghipour, A., Sohrabi, A., Ghaedi, M., & Khazaei, M. (2023). A robust vaccine supply chain model in pandemics: Case of COVID-19 in Iran. *Computers & Industrial Engineering*, *183*, 109465. DOI: 10.1016/j.cie.2023.109465

Talwar, S., Kaur, P., Fosso Wamba, S., & Dhir, A. (2021). Big Data in operations and supply chain management: A systematic literature review and future research agenda. *International Journal of Production Research, 59*(11), 3509–3534. DOI: 10.1080/00207543.2020.1868599

Tang, C. S. (2006). Perspectives in supply chain risk management. *International Journal of Production Economics, 103*(2), 451–488. DOI: 10.1016/j.ijpe.2005.12.006

Tang, C. S., & Veelenturf, L. P. (2019). The strategic role of logistics in the Industry 4.0 era. *Transportation Research Part E, Logistics and Transportation Review, 129*, 1–11. DOI: 10.1016/j.tre.2019.06.004

Tat, R., Taleizadeh, A. A., & Esmaeili, M. (2015). Developing economic order quantity model for non-instantaneous deteriorating items in vendor-managed inventory (VMI) system. *International Journal of Systems Science, 46*(7), 1257–1268. DOI: 10.1080/00207721.2013.815827

Tliche, Y., Taghipour, A., & Canel-Depitre, B. (2019). Downstream Demand Inference in decentralized supply chains. *European Journal of Operational Research, 274*(1), 65–77. DOI: 10.1016/j.ejor.2018.09.034

Tliche, Y., Taghipour, A., Mahfod-Leroux, J., & Vosooghidizaji, M. (2023). Collaborative bullwhip effect-oriented bi-objective optimisation for inference-based weighted moving average forecasting in a decentralised supply chain. [IJISSCM]. *International Journal of Information Systems and Supply Chain Management, 16*(1), 1–37. DOI: 10.4018/IJISSCM.316168

TOUFAH, N., EL MOUSSAOUI, A. E., & LEKHAILA, G. (2025). A Comparative Analysis of the Logistics and Economics Fields: A Literature Review. *Revue Française d'Economie et de Gestion, 6*(8).

Turner, S. W., Karakus, M., Guler, E., & Uludag, S. (2023). A promising integration of SDN and blockchain for IoT networks: A survey. *IEEE Access : Practical Innovations, Open Solutions, 11*, 29800–29822. DOI: 10.1109/ACCESS.2023.3260777

Um, K. H., & Kim, S. M. (2019). The effects of supply chain collaboration on performance and transaction cost advantage: The moderation and nonlinear effects of governance mechanisms. *International Journal of Production Economics, 217*, 97–111. DOI: 10.1016/j.ijpe.2018.03.025

UNCTAD. (2023a). *Enhancing supply chain resilience amid rising global risks.* https://unctad.org/news/enhancing-supply-chain-resilience-amid-rising-global-risks

UNCTAD. (2023b). *UN Global Supply Chain Forum calls for resilience amid world trade disruptions.* https://unctad.org/press-material/un-global-supply-chain-forum-calls-resilience-amid-world-trade-disruptions

United Nations Development Programme (UNDP). (2007). *Public administration reform: Practice note.* https://www.undp.org/ - Data interpretation only.

United Nations Framework Convention on Climate Change. (2015). *Paris Agreement.*

Vakharia, A. (2023, February 9). *The global supply chain consequences of the Russia-Ukraine war.* University of Florida News. https://news.ufl.edu/2023/02/russia-ukraine-global-supply-chain/

van Hoek, R. (2020). Research opportunities for a more resilient post-COVID-19 supply chain – closing the gap between research findings and industry practice. *International Journal of Operations & Production Management, 40*(4), 341–355. DOI: 10.1108/IJOPM-03-2020-0165

Varadarajan, R., Koch-Weser, I., Richard, C., Fitzgerald, J., Singh, J., Thornton, M., & Casanova, R. (2024, May 8). *Emerging resilience in the semiconductor supply chain.* Boston Consulting Group. https://www.bcg.com/publications/2024/emerging-resilience-in-semiconductor-supply-chain

Vosooghidizaji, M., Taghipour, A., & Canel-Depitre, B. (2019). A literature review on information asymmetry in supply chain coordination. *International Journal of Production Research, 58*(6). Advance online publication. DOI: 10.1080/00207543.2019.1685702

Vosooghidizaji, M., Taghipour, A., & Canel-Depitre, B. (2020). Information asymmetry in supply chain coordination: State of the art. *Journal of Industrial and Intelligent Information, 8*(2), 38–43. DOI: 10.18178/jiii.8.2.38-43

Wardana, M. F. K., Putri, H. B., & Tambunan, F. H. (2025). Implementation of economic order quantity (EOQ) in inventory management: A case study of chopfee coffee shop. *Jurnal Ekobistek, 14*(1), 17–23. DOI: 10.35134/ekobistek.v14i1.867

Whelan, T., & Fink, C. (2020). The comprehensive business case for sustainability. *Harvard Business Review.*

Wieland, A. (2021). Dancing the supply chain: Toward transformative supply chain management. *The Journal of Supply Chain Management, 57*(1), 58–73. DOI: 10.1111/jscm.12248

Wieland, A., & Durach, C. F. (2021). Two perspectives on supply chain resilience. *Journal of Business Logistics, 42*(3), 315–322. DOI: 10.1111/jbl.12271

World Bank. (2004). *World Development Report 2004: Making services work for poor people*. World Bank and Oxford University Press.

World Economic Forum. (2021). *The Global Risks Report 2021*. World Economic Forum.

World Economic Forum. (2022). The Global Risks Report 2022.

World Economic Forum. (2023). *The Global Risks Report 2023: 18th Edition*. World Economic Forum. https://www3.weforum.org/docs/WEF_Global_Risks_Report_2023.pdf

Wu, L., Zhang, Z., Huang, J., Su, I.-H., & Tian, S. (2025). Digital technologies and supply chain resilience: A resource-action-performance perspective. *Information Systems Frontiers*, *27*(5), 2137–2158. Advance online publication. DOI: 10.1007/s10796-025-10595-1

XiaoWen, L., & Atour, T.XiaoWen. (2025). Knowledge-driven digital innovation in supply chains: An organizational perspective. *Journal of Innovation & Knowledge*, *10*(5), 100787. DOI: 10.1016/j.jik.2025.100787

Xu, L., Mak, S., & Brintrup, A. (2021). Will bots take over the supply chain? Revisiting agent-based supply chain automation. *International Journal of Production Economics*, *241*, 108279. Advance online publication. DOI: 10.1016/j.ijpe.2021.108279

Xu, X., Lu, Y., Vogel-Heuser, B., & Wang, L. (2021). Industry 4.0 and Industry 5.0—Inception, conception, and perception. *Journal of Manufacturing Systems*, *61*, 530–535. DOI: 10.1016/j.jmsy.2021.10.006

Xu, X., Sethi, S. P., Chung, S. H., & Choi, T. M. (2023). Reforming global supply chain management under pandemics: The GREAT-3Rs framework. *Production and Operations Management*, *32*(2), 524–546. DOI: 10.1111/poms.13885

Yang, G. (2024). Determinants of business model choices for new entrant in the pharmaceutical e-commerce environment. *SAGE Open*, *14*(4), 1–12. DOI: 10.1177/21582440241295813

Yang, M.-F., Tsai, P.-F., Tu, R.-M., & Yuan, Y.-F. (2024). An EOQ model for temperature-sensitive deteriorating items in cold chain operations. *Mathematics*, *12*(5), 1–15. DOI: 10.3390/math12050775

Yannis, G., & Chaziris, A. (2022). Transport system and infrastructure. *Transportation Research Procedia*, *60*, 6–11. DOI: 10.1016/j.trpro.2021.12.002

Yigitcanlar, T., Downie, A. T., Mathews, S., Fatima, S., MacPherson, J., Behara, K. N., & Paz, A. (2024). Digital technologies of transportation-related communication: Review and the state-of-the-art. *Transportation Research Interdisciplinary Perspectives, 23*, 100987. DOI: 10.1016/j.trip.2023.100987

Yu, G. (1997). Robust economic order quantity models. *European Journal of Operational Research, 100*(3), 482–493. DOI: 10.1016/S0377-2217(95)00328-2

Yung, K. Y. (2023). Improving stock accountability of liquid controlled drugs using rulers in a children's hospital. *Archives of Disease in Childhood, 108*(5), 14–14. DOI: 10.1136/archdischild-2023-NPPG.24

Zhang, D., Frei, R., Wills, G., Gerding, E., Bayer, S., & Senyo, P. K. (2023). Strategies and practices to reduce the ecological impact of product returns: An environmental sustainability framework for multichannel retail. *Business Strategy and the Environment, 32*(7), 4636–4661. DOI: 10.1002/bse.3385

Zhang, L., Liu, H., & Cai, Z. (2022). Addressing the consensus on information sharing in CPFR information systems: Insights from manufacturer–retailer dyads. *International Journal of Production Research, 60*(11), 3569–3588. DOI: 10.1080/00207543.2021.1926569

Zhao, S., Ren, Y., Mao, C., & Yue, A. (2024). Are cities healthy? A city health diagnose framework from the perspective of living organism. *Ecological Indicators, 160*, 111834. DOI: 10.1016/j.ecolind.2024.111834

Zoghlami, N., Taghipour, A., Merlo, C., & Abed, M. (2016). Management of divergent production network using decentralised multi-level capacitated lot-sizing models. *International Journal of Shipping and Transport Logistics, 8*(5), 590–604. DOI: 10.1504/IJSTL.2016.078686

Zorzini, M., Hendry, L. C., Huq, F. A., & Stevenson, M. (2015). Socially responsible sourcing. *International Journal of Operations & Production Management, 35*(1), 60–82. DOI: 10.1108/IJOPM-07-2013-0355

Zsidisin, G. A., & Ritchie, B. (2009). *Supply chain risk: A handbook of assessment, management, and performance*. Springer. DOI: 10.1007/978-0-387-79934-6

About the Contributors

Atour Taghipour is a professor in Supply Chain Management and Operations at the Conservatoire National des Arts et Métiers (CNAM) in Paris, France. He holds a PhD in Industrial Engineering and is affiliated with the LIRSA research laboratory (EA 4603), where his work focuses on sustainable supply chain design, digital transformation in logistics, and production systems optimization. Dr. Taghipour has published numerous articles in peer-reviewed journals and contributes actively to interdisciplinary projects at the intersection of data science, resilience, and responsible management. He regularly supervises doctoral research in the areas of supply chain resilience, circular economy, and AI applications in operations. He is also involved in international teaching and research collaborations, particularly in Europe and Asia.

***

Haidar Abbas is an Assistant Professor of Business Administration (Supply Chain Management) at the University of Technology and Applied Sciences, Nizwa, Sultanate of Oman. He earned his doctorate in Business Administration (Supply Chain Management) from Aligarh Muslim University (India). As a part of language proficiency, he has obtained an aggregate score of 7.5 in IELTS (Academic). Prior to joining academia, he qualified the UGC NET (JRF). His more than eleven years' experience as Assistant Professor (Operations & Supply Chain Management) comprises of his current job and his services at Al Buraimi University College (Oman), GLA University (India), and Aligarh Muslim University (India). During these years, he has been actively engaged in development, review and revision of curriculum and academic programs. His research interests encompass reverse logistics and circular economy practices, digital transformation of operations, and interdisciplinary consumer research. He has published more than twenty research papers in reputed Scopus indexed journals.

Alam Ahmad is currently serving College of administrative and financial sciences, Saudi Electronic University (SEU), Saudi Arab, as an Assistant Professor. His research interest lies in the various fields of International Trade & Finance, Business Economics and Entrepreneurship. Dr. Alam Ahmad can be contacted at: a.ahmad@seu.edu.sa, Phone: 00966 563421917

Muralidhar L B is a professionally qualified dental surgeon. He holds Ph.D. from Canara Bank School of Management Studies, Bangalore University after his MBA from Christ University. He has 18 years of total teaching experience spanning across dental education, healthcare management and general management and 4 years of corporate experience. He has worked as research associate in Institute for Social and Economic Change, Bangalore in a project entitled as "Management By and For Common Man: An Exploration of the Concept and Direction for Future"post Ph.D. He had secured 28th rank in S.S.L.C examination for Karnataka State in 1993. His 27 patents have been published and 2 design patents have been granted. He has 41 research publications to his credit out of which 19 are Scopus-indexed and 5 are ABDC indexed. He has co-authored 5 books. He is currently working as Assistant Professor in Department of Business Management Studies, School of Commerce, Jain Deemed to be University, Bangalore.

Lakshmi CN Currently working as a Assistant Professor St. Francis College in Koramangala, Bengaluru, is an affiliated institution under Bengaluru City University, offering undergraduate and postgraduate programs primarily in commerce, business, IT, and aviation fields. and Pursing my PhD Research on mutual fund from Bangalore North University.

Deepak D, an academician of two years old, with teaching experience in the areas of taxation, accounting, and IFRS. He has expertise in academic publishing, research content writing, coaching, teaching, editing, and analytical abilities. He possesses a PhD from JAIN (Deemed To Be University) in the School of Commerce. He has participated in a number of FDPs, workshops, seminars, and conferences. He as published more than 10 research paper in different UGC Care journal, web of science, Scopus.

Alaa Eddine El Moussaoui, Ph.D., is a Professor of Logistics affiliated with the EMIO, LIREEM Laboratory, Higher School of Technology of Nador, Mohammed First University, Oujda, Morocco. He received his Ph.D. in Urban Logistics in 2023 from the National School of Business and Management of Tangier (ENCG Tangier), Abdelmalek Essaâdi University, with co-supervision from KEDGE Business School, Paris, France. His research interests include logistics and supply chain management, urban logistics, e-commerce, transportation, artificial intelligence, machine learning, sustainability, and operations management. He has authored numerous publications in internationally indexed journals, focusing on last-mile logistics, digital transformation, consumer behavior, and AI-driven decision-making in logistics and supply chain management.

Taoufiq El Moussaoui is a Professor of Computer Science at the Polydisciplinary Faculty of Sidi Bennour, Chouaib Doukkali University, El Jadida, Morocco. His research interests include artificial intelligence, text mining, pattern recognition, supply chain management, transport, and smart cities.

Babu Rao Gaddala is currently working as Associate Professor in the department of Chemical Engineering, Guru Ghasidas Vishwavidyalaya (A Central University), Bilaspur, Chhattisgarh, India. I have consolidated experience of 18 years in teaching in India & abroad (Oman). I have been awarded Ph.D in the month of January 2016 in the Department of Chemical Engineering from Andhra University, Visakhapatnam, India. I have obtained M.Tech degree first class with distinction in Chemical Engineering in 2007 & B.Tech in 2005 from Vignan's Engineering College (Now its Vignan University) Guntur. I have published 40 research articles in peer reviewed journals (SCI/SCOPUS indexed), 2 book chapters, Editor for 2 Edited books, 14 patents in national and international level. I have participated and presented Papers in national (8) and international conferences (11) in India, Oman & Bahrain. I have attended 16 weeks of various FDP in premier organizations and online FDPs (10) and webinars (20). I have supervised 17 B.Tech Chemical Engineering & 1 M.Tech project and have 20 national & international Professional Body Memberships.

Gaddam Venu Gopal obtained his B.Tech from Jawaharlal Nehru Technological University, Hyderabad in 2005. He finished his M.Tech from Acharya Nagarjuna University, Guntur in 2010. He received his Ph. D from Acharya Nagarjuna University (Engg.), Guntur, Andhra Pradesh in 2022. He is currently working as an Associate Professor in the Department of CSE (AIML) at BVRIT, Narsapur, Hyderabad, Telangana, India. His areas of interest are Data mining, IoT, Machine Learning, and Artificial Intelligence. He has 19+ years of experience in research and academics. He has published more than 30 papers in National and International Journals. He has presented more than 14 papers at both National and International Conferences. He also published 3 Patents and 2 Books. He has 4 Book Chapters published under Wiley Publication.

Dilek Gümüş is an assistant professor in the Department of Medical Services and Techniques, First Aid and Emergency Care Program at Bilecik Şeyh Edebali University in Turkey. Her academic interests focus on innovative nursing practices, postoperative care, non- pharmacological pain management, and the integration of digital health technologies into clinical settings. Gümüş is particularly interested in combining artificial intelligence tools with evidence- based nursing practices to improve patient outcomes.

Raj Kumar Gupta is an accomplished academic and researcher in Material Science, Currently serving as Senior Assistant Professor at Sardar Vallabhbhai Patel College, Bhabhua, Dist- Kaimur (A Constituent unit of Veer Kunwar Singh University, Ara, Bihar). He holds a PhD in Physical Science (Material Science Work) from Department of Physics and Astro Physics, University of Delhi, New Delhi. Dr. Raj Kumar Gupta has published extensively in international journals and conferences, with a strong focus on materials Science like BiFe03, Ca3Co4o9, CoFe03 etc and their Artificial intelligence applications in manufacturing, optimization, and smart systems in future works. His expertise spans simulation work and experimental validation. He is the editor of a several book and authors of several patents in Material Science incorapoted with machine learning and AI domains. Dr. Gupta actively contributes to UG teaching, quality assurance to students. He is a certified professional with numerous publications indexed in Scopus, WoS, and Google Scholar, reflecting his broad interdisciplinary impact on Material Science.

Purushotham H. C is an Assistant Professor at the School of Commerce, JAIN (Deemed-to-be University), with over 6 years of teaching experience. He is currently pursuing a Ph.D. at REVA University and holds an MBA in Management. His expertise spans consumer behaviour, strategic management, HRM, and marketing. He has published several research papers and book chapters and received multiple Best Paper Awards. He has coordinated academic, cultural, and NSS activities and actively contributes to faculty development and student mentoring. He is also a certified Behaviour and Mentoring Analyst and holds certifications in marketing analytics and digital marketing.

K. Vigneshwaran currently working as Assistant Professor in the Department of Electronics and Communication Engineering at K.Ramakrishnan College of Engineering, Trichy. He has completed UG in Communication Systems and currently pursuing Ph.D. degree on the topic "Substrate Integrated Waveguide Antenna For Wireless Applications" from Anna University, Chennai. He has interested in the domain of Microwave Engineering, Embedded Systems and IOT, Microcontrollers and Microprocessors. He has more than 10+ publication in international journals and conferences. He is having 8+ years of teaching experience. He is member in ISTE. E-mail: kvigneshwaranece@krce.ac.in

Sheeba K P., M.Sc, PhD (pursuing). She is having a academic Experience of 5 years and 8 years in health care industries like hospitals, health insurance organizations and TPA companies both in abroad and in India. She is a post graduate in Hospital Administration from Rajiv Gandhi University of Health Sciences, currently pursuing her PhD in management. She is a member of associate ship in general insurance from Insurance Institute of India (III). She has attended many workshops and Faculty Development Programs, seminars, and orientation programs. . She has presented more than 3 research articles at National and International conferences. She has published few research articles in UGC care listed journals. She is currently working as Assistant Professor in Department of Business Management Studies, School of Commerce, Jain Deemed to be University, Bengaluru, India.

Raj K Kovid is Professor at School of Business, UPES, Dehradun. He brings with him a rich working experience of over 25 years in teaching, research and industry. He has earned his PhD degree in the field of Mergers and Acquisitions and Masters in Business Management and Commerce. His teaching and research area includes Corporate Strategy, M&A, Global Strategy, Strategy for Platform Business, Entrepreneurship & Innovation, Corporate Governance & CSR. He has consulted firms with respect to their growth strategies. He has keen interest in the Case Method of teaching and research. He has published research papers and book chapters in journals of repute at national and international level. His cases are available in Harvard Business Publishing and has also conducted case method workshops. Dr. Kovid is regularly invited as an expert in various conferences and workshops.

L. Vijayakumar and I am working as an Associate professor in Department of commerce in Vel Tech Rangarajan Dr.Sagunthala R&D Institute of Science and Technology Avadi and I have attended more than 21 national and international conferences and have published lot of papers in international Conference held in Malaysia and Thailand and in addition to it iam an author for various journals with a good impact factor I have also received lot of awards from various institutions and I too have a trust in Pondicherry in catering services in various domains for the society.

Rajib Mandal is an Assistant Professor in the Programme of Optometry, Faculty of Paramedical Sciences, Assam down town University, Sankar Madhab Path, Gandhinagar, Panikhaiti, Guwahati, Assam, India, PIN-781026. He holds a PhD in Optometry. A prolific author of books, book chapters and research papers, he brings a multidisciplinary perspective to sustainability, healthcare, and technology management. His published works analyze systemic impacts of the COVID-19 pandemic on resources, global economies, and governance. He has contributed to studies on cost analysis of healthcare services and workforce sustainability. Awarded

Best Young Researcher (ICTAS 2025), he combines clinical insight with broader management expertise. His academic endeavors underscore the importance of sustainable supply chains for resilient, equitable, and efficient industries.

Shilpa R working as Associate professor, Department of Management Studies, RJS Institute of Management Studies, has 16 years of experience in teaching. She has worked with the T.John Institute of Technology for 6 years and Quantum Leap for 1 year. She has completed an MBA, M Phil and PhD at Jain (Deemed to be university) specialize in the area of OB/ HRM. She has also published research papers in Scopus, ABDC, and UGC care journals and presented papers at national and international conferences. Authorized Book chapters for international journals and project guide for MBA students. Attended FDPs, conferences, and workshops and also organized programs for the students. Member of ISTE and MTC Global.

Vandana R currently working as Assistant Professor at St. Francis College in Koramangala, Bengaluru. It is an affiliated institution under Bengaluru City University, offering undergraduate and postgraduate programs primarily in commerce, business, IT, and aviation fields.

Venkata Kiran Kumar Ravi is young individual who holds a doctoral degree in Mechanical Engineering and has significant academic and administrative experience in Engineering Colleges. He currently serves as academician in Department of Mechanical Engineering at Siddhartha Academy of Higher Education (Deemed to be University) Vijayawada Andhra Pradesh.His research areas include Finite Element Analysis, Composite Materials, Mechanical Vibrations, Fracture Mechanics, Data Science,Artificial Intelligence, Machine Learning, Deep Learning and Natural Language Processing.He is having certifications related to CAD/CAM, Data Science, Machine Learning, Deep Learning, NLP, Computer Vision, Generative AI from reputed institutes.He published articles and patents in various national and international journals and conferences.

Shreya is an Assistant Professor of Marketing at Symbiosis International University, Noida Campus. She is an academic and researcher in Marketing, holding a Ph.D. from Birla Institute of Technology & Science (BITS) Pilani, India. Her academic contributions include various research papers published in reputed A.B.D.C.- ranked A and B journals.

Mohd Asif Shah is the Dean of Economics at Kardan University (ACBSP/ IACBE/AACSB Accredited), Kabul, Afghanistan. He has previously served as an Associate Professor at Kebri Dehar University, Ethiopia, and Bakhtar University, Afghanistan, and as an Assistant Professor at FBS Business School, Bangalore, and Lovely Professional University (AACSB Accredited), Punjab, India. He holds a PhD, M.A., and B.A. in Economics, with over ten years of teaching and research experience across India, Afghanistan, and Ethiopia. He also serves as an Adjunct Professor at leading universities in India and Afghanistan. Dr. Shah has published 300+ research papers in SCI/SCIE/Scopus/WoS-indexed journals, holds 100+ patents, and has received 5000+ citations. He has participated in 30+ faculty development programs sponsored by the Government of India and is a frequent keynote speaker at international conferences and seminars.

Irfan Abdul Karim Shaikh is an experienced academic and researcher with over 20 years in higher education, currently serving as an Assistant Professor at Bahrain Polytechnic, Bahrain for the past 12 years. A recognized thought leader in the fields of business development and strategic transformation, Dr. Shaikh has actively participated in numerous national and international conferences, seminars, and webinars as a guest speaker, presenter, and panelist. He holds multiple patents and has published over 20 Scopus-indexed research papers in reputed international journals and conferences. His scholarly interests span Business Development Strategies, Digital Marketing, and Change Management.

Gagan Singh is an accomplished Assistant Professor at Meerut Institute of Technology, Meerut, with a distinguished 7-year tenure in academia. He holds both a B.Tech degree in Civil Engineering and an MBA from Dr. APJ Abdul Kalam University. Alongside his robust academic background, he brings 5 years of invaluable industry experience. His scholarly achievements are notable, having presented six research papers at esteemed international conferences, published four papers in UGC CARE-listed journals, and secured a patent. Furthermore, Mr. Singh is a respected member of the organizing committee for numerous academic conferences, reflecting his deep dedication to the advancement of his field.

Shreya Srikanth is student of Integrated BBA-MBA program at UPES school of Business, Dehradun, India. her area of interest is supply chain and operations management.

Jayesh Surana, having 19 years of experience in academia and in various fields of computer Science and Engineering. Currently, he is working at Medicaps University, Indore, as an Assistant Professor, where he contribute to the field of Computer Science and Engineering. He hold an M.Tech degree from SVITS, Indore, RGPV Bhopal. Currently he is doing PhD in CSE from Oriental University, Indore. His research areas are Networking, Cloud Computing and Machine Learning. He published 3 Scopus research papers, 4 conference papers, 5 Indian patents, 1 UK Design Patent, and 12 International Journal papers.

Sadashiva Tandur is working as an Assistant Professor, Christ (Deemed to be University) with total of 14 years of combined experience in Academics and Corporate. His areas of interest are Marketing, Operations and General Management.

Purushotham H. C is an Assistant Professor at the School of Commerce, JAIN (Deemed-to-be University), with over 6 years of teaching experience. He is currently pursuing a Ph.D. at REVA University and holds an MBA in Management. His expertise spans consumer behaviour, strategic management, HRM, and marketing. He has published several research papers and book chapters and received multiple Best Paper Awards. He has coordinated academic, cultural, and NSS activities and actively contributes to faculty development and student mentoring. He is also a certified Behaviour and Mentoring Analyst and holds certifications in marketing analytics and digital marketing.

Manu Vasudevan Unni holds triple Master's degrees from institutions in France and India, demonstrating a strong academic background coupled with industrial experience. His research interests encompass a broad spectrum, including consumer behavior, privacy concerns, brand loyalty, strategic marketing, international business, and marketing. Presently, he is pursuing a Ph.D. at Christ University, Bangalore, while also serving as an Assistant Professor at St. Claret College Autonomous, Bangalore, India. He can be contacted at email: manu@claretcollege.edu.in

Varadharajan Bhoopathy is a Professor at Sree Rama Engineering College. He holds a Ph.D. in Information and Communication Engineering from Anna University and has over 16 years of academic experience. Specializing in wireless sensor networks and IoT, he has published numerous research papers and holds several international patents. Dr. Bhoopathy is a recipient of prestigious awards for his contributions to education and research. His commitment to academia continues to drive innovation and excellence in the field of computer science.

Vipanchi V is an MBA graduate with a specialization in Finance and currently serves as an Assistant Professor at JAIN (Deemed-to-be University). She is also pursuing her Ph.D. at RNS Institute of Technology, affiliated to Visvesvaraya Technological University (VTU). Alongside her academic responsibilities, she has served as the Faculty Supervisor for Enactus, JAIN (Deemed-to-be University) and is presently the Faculty Coordinator for Antaral. Her professional background reflects a blend of academic and governmental experience. She has previously worked as a Senior Investment Performance Analyst at Northern Trust Operating Services, a Finance Expert under the Government of India's flagship AMRUT scheme at the Directorate of Municipal Administration, Government of Karnataka, and as a Consultant for the Smart Cities Mission at the Urban Development Department,

Vikasa Soudha. Mrs. Vipanchi actively contributes to academic discourse through seminars and guest lectures on topics such as Goods and Services Tax (GST), Monetary Policy, and Intellectual Property Rights (IPR), underscoring her commitment to fostering scholarly engagement and applied financial education.

B. Vasavi, Associate Professor in the Department of Science & Humanities at N.B.K.R.Institute of Science & Technology, Vidyanagar. She completed her M.B. A from Madras University and was awarded with Ph.D. from S.V.University, Tirupati in 2020. She published more than 10 research papers in National and International journals, and participated in Numerous International Conferences. She has 20 years of teaching experience and taught various subjects for Undergraduate and Post Graduate students.

Sharath Kumar Y working as Assistant Professor in St Francis college St. Francis College in Koramangala, Bengaluru, is an affiliated institution under Bengaluru City University, offering undergraduate and postgraduate programs primarily in commerce, business, IT, and aviation fields.

Index

V

www.ingramcontent.com/pod-product-compliance
Lightning Source LLC
LaVergne TN
LVHW080902300926
849162LV00003B/526
* 9 7 9 8 3 3 7 3 6 4 5 5 1 *